Twelve Classic Trout Streams in Michigan

A Handbook for Fly Anglers

Gerth E. Hendrickson

*Fully Revised
by Jim DuFresne*

Ann Arbor   ***The University of Michigan* Press**

Copyright © by the University of Michigan 1985, 1994, 2009
All rights reserved
Published in the United States of America by
The University of Michigan Press
Manufactured in the United States of America
⊗ Printed on acid-free paper

2012   2011   2010   2009   4   3   2   1

A CIP catalog record for this book is available from the British Library.

U.S. CIP data applied for.

ISBN-13: 978-0-472-03368-3
ISBN-10: 0-472-03368-9

Note: The information in this book is based on years of experience fishing
and studying these streams and is accurate and dependable to the best of the
author's knowledge. However, no book can anticipate all the problems and
hazards an angler may encounter on these streams. The author assumes no
responsibility for accidents or injury caused by failure to observe rules of safety.

To Jim

And afternoons on the river, evenings playing cards, and weekends at the cabin.

It never really mattered if we landed a trout or not.

j.d.

A young fly angler shows the concentration of a veteran as he follows his fly while fishing the Pere Marquette River.

Foreword

There is something about water that passes only once this way. Its journey stirs a longing in those of us mesmerized by the phenomenon to wander, to go along for the experience. We want to feel the power of a river, whether against our canoe paddle or the parabola in our favorite five-weight fly rod.

"Rivers are the earth's arteries," Verlen Kruger, world-renown canoeist whose adventures took him down the McKenzie, the Amazon and up and down the Mississippi, was fond of saying. To paraphrase *Trout Magic* author John Voelker (aka Robert Traver), trout do, indeed, live in beautiful places. Both men, native Michiganders, are now gone, but the truths they espoused live on. The author of *Twelve Classic Trout Streams in Michigan* is a man I never met, but I'm certain Gerth Hendrickson, who passed away a few years ago, enjoyed a long love affair with rivers, too.

Since it first appeared in 1985, Hendrickson's book has introduced legions of fly fishers to the state's most-treasured rivers. In this newest edition, author Jim Dufresne has made a good book better. Rivers have personalities. Over time those personalities change and they impact trout-fishing opportunities. Dufresne, author of more than twenty books, is a careful, consummate researcher and passionate fly angler. In this newest edition of Hendrickson's classic work, DuFresne has thoroughly documented those changes in access sites, flow rates, bottom structure and more. Jim's deft touch has improved the locator maps, making it easier than ever to find the best places to fish. He has woven interesting facts and local lore into and around the original chapters.

Modern trout anglers are lucky to have a wealth of Michigan rivers and streams to discover and to carry on the special sport first enjoyed by fly fishers more than 150 years ago. And they are lucky to have this book to help guide them to the best of all places to do it.

Tom Huggler
author of the *Fish Michigan* guidebook series

12 Classic Trout Streams in
Michigan

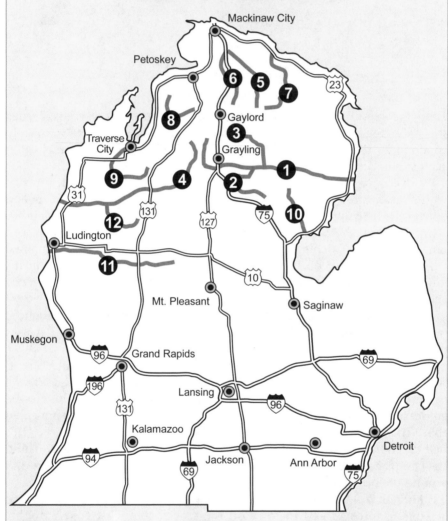

1	Au Sable Mainstream	**5**	Pigeon	**9**	Boardman
2	Au Sable South Branch	**6**	Sturgeon	**10**	Rifle
3	Au Sable North Branch	**7**	Black	**11**	Pere Marquette
4	Manistee	**8**	Jordan	**12**	Pine

Contents

Map Legend

There are 77 maps in *Twelve Classic Trout Streams in Michigan*; 19 river locator maps and 58 access maps. Locator maps will assist you in finding the various fishing sites along each river. Detailed access maps cover a particular stretch of a river and include riverbed symbols for gravel, sand, boulders, and clay and wading distances. Each fishing site is noted with a numbered fish icon on the access maps that can be used to cross reference it on the locator maps and in the text.

Roads and Trails

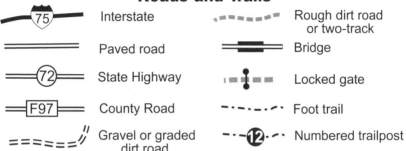

~75~	Interstate	●---●---●---	Rough dirt road or two-track
	Paved road		Bridge
~72~	State Highway		Locked gate
F97	County Road		Foot trail
	Gravel or graded dirt road	⑫	Numbered trailpost

Stream Symbols

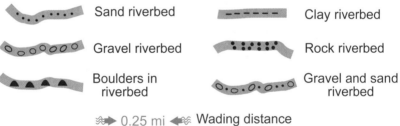

	Sand riverbed		Clay riverbed
	Gravel riverbed		Rock riverbed
	Boulders in riverbed		Gravel and sand riverbed

0.25 mi — Wading distance in river miles

Map Symbols

🐟8	Fishing access site	⌂	Trailhead
🚗	Parking area		Boat ramp
▲	Campground		DNR or park office
🛶	Canoe launch		Lodge or building

 Swamp, marsh or wetland

An angler fishes the most famous section of the Au Sable mainstream, a flies-only, catch-and-release stretch of the river known as the Holy Water.

Fly Fishing in Michigan
A Primer for a Great Sport in the Great Lakes State

The hatch occurred like clockwork on a warm afternoon in May. The nymphs of a mayfly species suddenly began ascending from the bottom of a cold and clear stream to the surface where they would struggle out of their skins and then, as duns, ride the current until their wings were dry enough to fly. At first there were only a few, then hundreds could be seen floating on the water and hovering over the stream.

Almost immediately the trout began to feed, forming rings with quiet slurps as they sucked in the floating duns. The rings would then float downstream before dissipating into the rippled surface of the current.

In the middle of all this was a fly angler, waders up to his chest, rod in one hand, an open fly box in the other. When the hatch began, a nervous excitement swept over him as he fumbled with flies, trying to determine the color and size of what was hatching. Now he was mesmerized by the event. Within casting distance of where he stood, a half-dozen trout were actively feeding, forming repeating rings in their corner of the stream.

The angler quickly tied a fly to his tippet, false cast twice, and then managed to drop it three feet in front of a rising trout. It showed no interest at first, but on the third attempt the fish rose and took the bait, a hook with nothing more than feathers and thread on it. He set the hook and the trout responded with a hard charge for the bottom of the stream. The fight between fish and angler, a time-honored tradition in Michigan streams everywhere, had commenced.

This is what this book is about: the sport, love, and heritage of fly fishing in Michigan. It was primarily written as a guide to help you get the most enjoyment possible from fishing some of the best trout streams east of the Rockies. Each of these 12 streams has a large population of stream-bred trout, ample public access, and water favorable to the wading fly angler. All are large enough and productive enough to accommodate much fishing pressure, yet all have stretches and access sites where you can sneak off to fish alone.

Equally important to many of us, these are streams of great natural beauty that provide aesthetic pleasure as well as the opportunity to catch trout. They have to be; trout will inhabit only cold, clean environments.

The northern part of Michigan's Lower Peninsula has more top-quality trout streams than any other comparable area east of the Rocky Mountains. The rivers described here are classic spring-fed streams with cold water that flows calmly and smoothly, with heavy and reliable hatches and depths that make wading possible. In their headwaters, these streams are narrow and brushy, favoring the bait or spin anglers over the fly fisher. But all soon broaden to provide a setting wide enough for easy fly casting. Five of the streams have sections with special rules limiting lures to flies only. Three —the Holy Water of the Au Sable, the South Branch of the Au Sable, and the Pere Marquette—feature no-kill fisheries.

These are young streams in geologic terms, having settled down in their present courses after the retreat of the glaciers some twelve thousand years ago. With the retreat of the ice, the earliest Indians moved into the area and used the rivers as a source of food and drink and as highways for canoe travel. Early European traders used the rivers for the same purpose and left the streams and woods much as they had found them.

It was the lumber barons and their armies of loggers that changed all this beginning in the 1840s. The riverbanks were stripped of their timber, much of it white pine, and log drives wrecked havoc on the riverbeds, degrading their capacity for food production and spawning for the fish. The original species, the grayling, was so easy to catch—anglers reputedly could catch two or three on a single cast—it was soon fished to extinction. Following the lumber boom, some attempts were made to farm the logged-out land, but the sandy soils and short growing season soon discouraged most farmers.

With many farmers bankrupted and discouraged, much of the land became tax-delinquent property during the 1930s and reverted to state ownership. Eventually state and national forests were created, the Civilian Conservation Corps arrived and planted millions of saplings, and river fisheries were rebuilt with the introduction of brook, rainbow, and brown trout. Nature repairs itself when given a chance and today these crystal-clear streams flow through some of the most attractive forests of the Midwest.

All of them have wild-bred trout. Several of the rivers have excellent runs of steelhead and lake-run browns in their lower reaches, but this guide is chiefly concerned with the resident trout fishery and with fly fishing in particular. Much of the lore of fly fishing in Michigan originated on these streams, while Trout Unlimited was founded on the banks of the Au Sable.

That's because these streams provide what many of us believe is the ultimate experience in fishing: the harmony of a perfect cast that places your fly just ahead of a feeding trout and the magic of watching the fish rise again to take a hook of feathers and yarn.

Bait, Lure, and Fly

Like most anglers, I caught my first trout on a worm, and I have fished many a trout stream with worms since then. But eventually I became captivated by fly fishing, although not because I consider it more sporting. Simply because it is more fun.

Thus this book is aimed at fly anglers, particularly those who have recently entered the sport and now are eager to explore Michigan's trout

Fishing for Grayling In Michigan

In the mid-1800s the grayling was the most common salmonid in Michigan's Lower Peninsula streams, with large schools of them thriving in the AuSable, Manistee, and Muskegon rivers. In the Upper Peninsula only the Otter River was known to contain grayling at the turn of the century. Ironically, it was also the last stream to contain the fish before the Michigan grayling was declared extinct in 1934.

To the earliest Michigan anglers, the grayling was everything they dreamed of in a sport fish. The brown trout had yet to reach America, rainbows were unknown, brookies were small trout that inhabited the hard-to-reach headwaters of streams. But the grayling was abundant and easy to catch. In his classic *Recollections of My Fifty Years of Hunting and Fishing*, William B. Mershon wrote:

Doubtless God could make a better fish than the Michigan Grayling but doubtless he never did...(No other fish) surpasses in beauty the peacock of its great dorsal fin and the rose pink of its canal fin. None have a more graceful shape . . . and adapted to glide through the water with great ease.

Articles in outdoor magazines brought hordes of anglers from all over the Midwest to fish for grayling in the 1880s. They quickly discovered that the grayling "lay like cordwood" in the Au Sable with the average fish being 10 to 12 inches in length. Using little more than hooks dressed with blue jay feathers or squirrel tail, anglers would attach three flies to their line and often catch three grayling on one cast. Stories of anglers landing a hundred pounds of grayling in a day were common. Commercial anglers also arrived, catching them by the tons and shipping them to the East Coast.

Such overfishing along with the heavy logging in the late 1800s finished off the grayling in most of the Lower Peninsula by the early 1900s. The logjams that scoured the streams on their way to the lumber mills all but destroyed grayling spawning areas. Cutting the trees down also caused serious silting problems, while the lack of the riverbank canopy and the shade those trees provided quickly made the streams too warm for the grayling. Thus that delicate balance of nature was tipped, and the grayling was never able to adapt quickly enough to survive.

A century after the height of Michigan's grayling craze, DNR biologists tried to bring the popular fish back. In 1987, 85,000 grayling yearlings were released in the AuSable, Manistee, and Cedar rivers along with 11 small lakes. To much fanfare and ceremonial speeches by dignitaries, the first fish, 40,000 seven-inch long yearlings, were released in the AuSable below the Mio Dam on April 20, 1987. Despite public enthusiasm for the program and a ban on catching grayling, the fishery never took hold and within a few years the re-introduction effort was discontinued. Occasionally an angler will claim to have caught a grayling in an unnamed lake but today the only reminder of the grayling in Michigan are faded photographs and a town in the middle of Crawford County.

An angler casts in the flies-only section of the South Branch of the Au Sable River in the Mason Tract.

streams. These 12 streams are the perfect places to begin. None of them are a lengthy drive Up North. All of them have wadable water and reliable hatches. Being Michigan's classic trout streams, most of them have outdoor shops nearby that will sell you the right flies for the day or put you in touch with guides who will lead you to where the biggest trout like to hide.

What I attempt to answer in this book are the basic questions for any trip to a trout stream to be successful. Where are the best access sites? How wide and deep is the river at them? Is it wide enough for fly casting or better suited for a spinning rod or bait? Is it shallow enough for easy wading or so deep it will overtop your waders? What are the bottom materials like? Will you stand on firm sand or gravel, slip on hard clay or muddy stones, or sink into soft sand or mud? How about the velocity of flow? Is it slow enough that you can wade easily upstream or so fast that you will be swept off your feet? All of these things are described or shown on the maps.

I also cover the regulations for each stream, including all that have special seasons, flies-only restrictions, or catch-and-release, no-kill stretches. I am glad to have some parts of trout streams restricted to fly-fishing, but I would not like to see all trout waters designated flies-only. The bait or spin anglers have as much right to their sport as the fly angler, and all have a common cause. It is the trout that bring them to the streams, and all want to preserve the trout streams and the trout fishery. The method of fishing should not alienate one group from the others.

Brooks, Browns, and Rainbows

The only trout native to Michigan streams was the **brook trout**; even the brookie was not originally found in most of the streams of the Lower Peninsula. It seems fairly well established that there were brook trout in the streams of the Upper Peninsula when Europeans first explored these waters, but only a few of the northernmost streams of the Lower Peninsula had trout at that time. Walter J. Hunsaker, president of the Michigan Fish Commission, wrote in 1919 (quoted in *Recollections of My Fifty Years of Hunting and Fishing In Michigan*, William B. Mershon 1923): "Except for the coast region from Traverse City on the Lake Michigan side to Rogers City on the Lake Huron side, practically all the brook trout that have inhabited the Lower Peninsula waters were artificially bred and artificially planted."

In a letter to William B. Mershon (Mershon 1923), Mr. Seymour Bower, superintendent of fisheries in Michigan, said:

As to the southern limit of native trout streams in Michigan, I think it is very well established that native trout had worked down as far south as the Boardman and its tributaries but no farther; and they inhabited most if not all of the streams flowing into Lake Michigan between the Boardman and the Straits. . . . Regarding the Lake Huron streams south of the straits, I think Bissel is not so certain as to how far down the trout had worked, but believe he concluded that Hammonds Bay or not far below was the dividing line.

From these accounts it appears that, of the streams described here, only the Pigeon, Sturgeon, Black, Jordan, and Boardman had native trout before any plantings. The remaining streams were the home of the grayling and had no trout until planted by man in the late 1800s. But brookie transplants quickly took hold because they loved the 57- to 60-degree water of spring-fed streams and colder headwaters of larger rivers found throughout the Lower Peninsula.

The first hatching and raising of brook trout in Michigan reportedly was by N. W. Clark of Clarkson, MI, in 1867 (Mershon 1923), and the first planting of brook trout was by A. N. Mershon,

Brook trout (Michigan DNR drawing)

the father of William B. Mershon. The brookies were planted in the Tobacco River in 1870. By 1874, brook trout were being planted in several streams, including the Pere Marquette, the Little Manistee, and the Manistee rivers.

Brook trout, the state fish of Michigan, doesn't grow nearly as large as rainbows or browns. An 8- to 10-inch brookie is average and a fish that exceeds 14 inches is a trophy. The largest brook trout are "coasters," lake-run fish that live in Lake Superior but return to tributaries to spawn in the fall. These fish often reach two to six pounds in weight. Brookies have a long, streamlined body with a large mouth that extends past the eye. Color variations include olive, blue-gray, or black above with a silvery white belly. The red spots on their sides, sometimes surrounded by bluish halos, are their most distinguishable feature.

Like all trout, brook trout require cool, clear, spring-fed streams and can often can be often be found under the cover of rocks, logs, and undercut banks. Larger brook trout often inhabit deep pools, such as secluded beaver ponds, moving to shallow water only to feed. Fly anglers, especially those just getting into the sport, love brookies because of the fish's lack of caution, hitting attractor

Rainbow trout (Michigan DNR drawing)

patterns and large flies with reckless abandon.

The first record of planting **rainbow trout** in Michigan was in the mid-1870s, when Mr. Clark with Daniel Fitzhugh of Bay City made a small planting of rainbows in the Au Sable. The first planting of rainbows by the Michigan Fish Commission was in the Paw Paw River in Van Buren County and the Boyne River in Charlevoix County in 1880. Most of the rainbows now caught in Michigan streams are **lake-run trout** or **steelhead trout**. There is evidence that the steelhead compete with the resident trout, and some of the streams that have heavy steelhead runs no longer support a first-class resident fishery. Many anglers believe that the fishing for resident browns on the Pere Marquette and the Rifle has declined, and the resident fishery on the Little Manistee has essentially disappeared.

Rainbows have radiating rows of black spots on tail, back, and sides. Resident rainbows have a pinkish horizontal band and pinkish gill cover with some black spots. The body of a steelhead is longer and sleeker than an inland rainbow, possesses a fainter pinkish horizontal band, and few if any black spots on the gill cover.

Brown trout, a close relative of the Atlantic salmon, were also brought to North American waters as exotics. In 1984, the West Michigan Chapter of Trout Unlimited celebrated the hundredth anniversary of the planting

of browns in the Pere Marquette River system, the first such planting of browns in the U.S. The first hatching of browns by the Michigan Fish Commission was put in the state's waters in 1889 (Mershon 1923). The

Brown trout (Michigan DNR drawing)

browns grew and thrived and are now the most abundant resident trout in most of the Lower Peninsula trout streams.

The back of a resident brown trout is usually brown or olive while its sides are light brownish to yellowish. A brown's major characteristics are large black, orange, or reddish spots on the body often with whitish to bluish halos. The fish has two dorsal fins including one adipose fin, an anal fin with 10 to 12 rays, and a square tail with few or no spots.

Brown trout have adapted extremely well in Michigan. They are the most wide-spread trout species in the state because the fish can live in water that is warmer and shallower than that preferred by brookies and rainbows. And unlike brookies, browns are wary and easily spooked by clumsy anglers splashing around in the stream. The diet of adult brown trout includes insects and their larvae, crustaceans, amphibians, small rodents such as mice, and other fish. Adults easily exceed 12 inches, and a trophy brown is anything over 20 inches.

Equipment

Rod: Fly rods are manufactured to an industry standard number system of 1 to 14 that specifies weight with weights 3 to 6 best suited for Michigan's trout streams. In particular a 5-weight, 8-foot rod is the overwhelming choice for Michigan anglers purchasing their first fly rod. Such a rod with a corresponding 5-weight line will cast dry flies sizes 12 to 22 and streamers up to size 4. It will easily handle a 12- to 18-inch trout but can also be used to toss sponge spiders for pan fish and even small plugs for bass. If you're stalking gin-clear creeks with small dry flies (sizes 18 to 24) and light tippets, a 4- or even 3-weight rod and line would produce a much more delicate presentation. But keep in mind that any wind at all will raise havoc with a novice caster or even an experienced one if the breeze is strong enough.

On Michigan trout streams you'll see rods in lengths from 6 to 9 feet.

Midland, MI: Home of Modern Fly Fishing

It was a trio of Midland anglers who ushered in the modern era of fly fishing. In 1945, Clare Harris, Paul Rottiers, and Leon Martuch Sr. used their training as chemical engineers to create a silicone-based fly floatant that helped flies float better and then formed Scientific Anglers to market the new product.

But they were still dissatisfied with the traditional lines that at the time were made with braided horsehair or silk and required hours of tedious hand-dressing and drying for only a few hours of fishing. While working on their kitchen stoves, Martuch and Harris boiled and brewed a special coating for braided-nylon line, and that led to a revolutionary product: a tapered, plastic-coated line that didn't require hours of maintenance. Called the Air Cel fly line, the new product was introduced in 1954 and immediately ushered in the era of modern fly fishing. Suddenly fly anglers spent their time casting, not drying.

In 1959, Scientific Anglers turned to 3M and used its microballoon technology to perfect its floating lines. By adding millions of micro-sized glass spheres to the fly-line coating, they created a less dense line that floated higher. The Midland company then developed sinking lines that sank at precise rates, specialty tapers for bass and salt-water fishing, and rods and reels that provided the perfect balance to its new lines.

In 1973, 3M acquired Scientific Anglers. Today 3M is a diversified $22 billion manufacturing company headquartered in St. Paul, MN, with 60,000 products, ranging from electronic graphics to Post-It notes.

Scientific Anglers has also grown. The 3M division now produces half of the fly lines used in the world. At the Midland plant they not only produce five hundred types of fly line for the Scientific Anglers brand, but also another thousand private-label lines that are sold by other companies. In 1995, 3M celebrated the fiftieth anniversary of Scientific Anglers by doubling the size of the Midland plant with a twelve-thousand-square-foot expansion.

Longer rods give you more casting power, make it easier to mend the line, and help keep your backcast high enough to avoid grass or low brush along the streams. Short rods, on the other hand, cast narrower loops, making them easier to handle on brushy streams – an important consideration if you like to stalk fish in the headwaters of rivers or small side streams.

There was a time when top-of-the-line rods were bamboo and everything else was fiberglass, but that all changed with the introduction of graphite in 1972. Virtually all rods today are made of graphite, which weighs 25 percent less than fiberglass and up to 45 percent less than bamboo. Thus a graphite rod can be longer but still lighter, allowing you to cast farther with less effort.

Line: Printed just above the grip of a rod will be the line weight for which it is balanced along with the rod's length and weight. As a rule you can use a line one size lighter or heavier than the recommended weight, but a balanced outfit, with the rod and line matched to each other, will produce the best casting results.

A fly line that is tapered along its length will cast more efficiently than a level line. Usually the forward section, or *front taper*, is thin at the tip but expands to a thicker section called the *belly*. The length and position of the belly determine the characteristics of a fly line or how far or delicately it will cast.

Walk into a well-stocked fly shop and the variety of lines on display, not to mention the prices, will leave you in a daze. Most novice fly anglers will match their 5-weight rod with either a double-taper or weight-forward, 5-weight, floating line. A double taper line features a long belly in the middle while both ends are tapered equally. Such a line does not cast as far as a weight-forward but is easier to mend. It is also more economical as you can reverse it when one end wears out.

In a weight-forward line the belly is short and located closer to the forward end. This allows the line to shoot out easily because it's pulling the thinner running line behind it. Beginners find weight-forward lines are easier to cast and are able to achieve greater distance with them than double-taper lines. But keep in mind that casting long distances isn't a priority when fishing Michigan trout streams, and in bushy conditions you'll soon realize that it's harder to roll cast a weight-forward line.

Leaders and Tippets: The leader is used to transmit energy from the fly line to deliver the fly. Three factors determine what length of leader to use, the water conditions, the type of fly line used, and the species of fish you're targeting. Sinking lines are almost always paired with short leaders of 3 to 5 feet in length so the line will quickly sink your fly and then keep it deep in the stream longer.

When fishing Michigan trout streams with dry or wet flies, the most common combination is a leader ranging in length from 7 to 12 feet tied to a floating line. If water conditions are high or murky making visibility poor, or if it's cloudy (trout are less spooky on overcast days), select a leader 7 to 8 feet in length. If low, clear, or still water is making trout line-shy, compensate with longer leaders of 9 to 12 feet. If wind is a problem or you're trying to cast a large, wind-resistant fly, a shorter leader will be more effective in turning over a fly in such conditions.

It's equally important for the proper energy transmission through the leader that the butt section—the heavier first half of the leader—be the correct size. If you tie on a leader with a small diameter butt, it will collapse when used with a large fly. Heavy butt leaders used on light lines will also collapse because the line cannot transmit enough energy to turn the leader over.

The rule of thumb is that the leader butt should be two-thirds the diameter of the tip of the fly line. For trout the leader butts are usually in the range of .019 to .023 of an inch. Thus, when fishing a typical Michigan trout stream with a 5-weight line, anglers often purchase a knotless 4X leader that is 7.5 feet long (butt .022) or, if they anticipate clear water and spooky fish, a 9-foot, 5X or 6X leader (butt .020).

At the end of the leader you tie on a tippet, a piece of nylon or fluorocarbon monofilament. The length of the tippet can be critical to the success of your fishing. Generally tippets are 20 percent of the overall length of a leader, usually 18 to 24 inches long. But if the water is slow and clear you might need to tie on a tippet 3 feet or longer, which will allow the fly to drift more naturally. In fast and rippled water or for night fishing, shorter tippets, 1 to 2 feet in length, might work as well and be easier to cast and handle.

Use small diameter tippets for small flies and vice versa for larger flies. The rule of thumb is to divide the size of a fly by 3 for the proper X rating of a tippet. A size-12 fly is normally fished with a 4X tippet, a size-18 fly with a 6X tippet, and so on. It is always best to tie on a tippet to a new leader even if the leader is the proper X rating for the fly. As you change flies or break one off in the trees, you'll know by the blood knot when it's time to add more tippet and in doing so will preserve the entire length of your leader.

Mayflies, Stoneflies, and Caddisflies

Reliable hatches of insects are what makes the fly fishing in Northern Michigan so enjoyable. You don't need a degree in entomology to quickly realize that when a species of mayflies is hatching it often turns into a feeding frenzy for trout. And that results in outstanding fishing.

The most important insect for fly anglers is the mayfly, of which biologists estimate there are more than 70 species hatching in Michigan. Life for a mayfly begins as a *nymph* living on the stream bottom before it swims to the surface and changes into a winged fly called a *dun* by splitting its nymphal skin. The dun sits on the water drying its wings and then flies away to nearby brush or trees in a process known as the hatch. This is when

Mayfly (drawing by Gina Mikel/www.scientificillustrator.com)

the insect is the most vulnerable and trout know it. So do anglers who try to match what is taking place in the form of nymphs, wet flies, and dry flies.

Eventually the dun molts again to emerge as a bright, mature insect called a *spinner* with glassy clear, upright wings and two or three long tails. At this stage males and females mate in the evening, eggs are deposited on the surface of the streams, and the insects die quickly, their spent wings falling on the water.

Stoneflies and caddisflies also follow a life-cycle pattern that begins in the water. The time of year and the life cycle of whatever is hatching will often determine what fly you should use. In May and June mayflies like blue-winged olives, Hendricksons and sulphurs will be hatching as well as several types of caddisflies. It's easy to tell them apart. Mayflies have upright wings and resemble a sailboat when floating on the water. Caddisflies have wings that resemble a tent, forming a 45-degree angle over their backs, and no tails. Stoneflies carry their wings folded flat over and parallel to their bodies.

Caddisfly (drawing by Gina Mikel/www.scientificillustrator.com)

Early in the season most of the mayflies and caddisflies will be in the range of sizes 10 to 16. Hendricksons appear dark gray, sulphurs a cream to yellow color, and caddisflies range from tan to black.

The height of the season for many fly anglers is the Hex hatch from late June to mid-July. During this period the giant Michigan mayfly, *Hexagenia limbata*, will hatch at night; normally wary trout throw caution to the wind and feast on the huge insects. This is the time to catch a trophy (see page 128). Late July through the dry days of August brings on the terrestrials. Land-

Stonefly (drawing by Gina Mikel/www.scientificillustrator.com)

dwelling insects such as grasshoppers and crickets peak in numbers and are often blown into the stream to the delight of trout. Anglers can do well at times with grasshopper imitations.

Matching the Hatch

If you're new to fly fishing, the best way to make sure you are carrying the proper flies is to find a fly shop with a knowledgeable staff near the rivers you plan to fish. You can purchase the right flies, pick up tips on where and how to fish them, and know you won't be wasting an afternoon casting something that is never going to attract trout. For this reason I have listed many of the established fly shops near the rivers I cover in the following chapters.

Other ways to find out what's working are to talk to anglers at the rivers you fish—you'll quickly discover fly anglers are very friendly people who are glad to share information—and to consult a Michigan emergence schedule chart, of which one is included in this book (see page 308).

Eventually you'll want to make streamside decisions on what fly to tie on. Observation is the key to making the right choice once you're at the river. This doesn't mean you need to learn the Latin names of insects or know their life cycles, though it helps. It means you need to be aware of what's taking place when you're on the water. To accomplish that, use a small aquarium net to catch insects on the water to study them. Also examine streamside foliage as insects are often resting there.

Once you see a pattern of insects the trout might be feeding on, the most important aspect to duplicate is the *size*, matching the natural size of the insect with the size of your fly. The second most important aspect of matching the hatch is *shape*. Basic shape is crucial to trout. If they are feeding on mayflies with upright wings, the folded, tent-shape wings of a caddis fly won't work.

Try to also match the *color*, though this is not as important as size and shape. If trout are appearing to be feeding on a white insect, they might pass up a gray or black fly. Finally the note the *action* of the insects. Are trout feeding on insects at a dead drift or on bugs that are skittering along the surface? You should offer your imitation in the same manner.

If you do not see insects on the surface or trout rising, there is a chance the fish are feeding subsurface. If that's the case, check the shallows for the signs of baitfish and then tie on a streamer to imitate a minnow. Turn over rocks on the stream bottom or use your aquarium net to search for nymphs and other bottom-dwelling insects and then use the size, shape, and color method to match them.

There will be times, however, when you will simply not see any insects. In these situations an attractor will often prompt a trout into a strike. Attractors are often large, bushy, colorful flies that don't imitate any insect in particular but are used to draw a fish's attention. The Royal Coachman and Adams are perhaps the most famous attractor flies in Michigan.

Michigan Flies and Hatch Chart

Thanks to its wealth of great trout streams, Michigan has also produced some of the best flytiers in America, and several important flies originated here. Probably the most famous Michigan fly is the Adams, designed by Len Halladay of Mayfield, Michigan (see page 234). This fly was first fished on the Boardman River, but is now used by fishermen throughout the United States. Other effective flies originating in Michigan include the Michigan Caddis, the Michigan Hopper, the Borcher's Special, the Skunk, and Robert's Yellow Drake. The Borcher's Special is similar to the Adams but has a dark brown body. The Skunk, tied wet or dry, is mostly black and white with white rubber legs. The wet Skunk usually is weighted and is hard to cast, but it can be very effective. Some of these flies are little known outside of Michigan, but they probably would take trout on most Midwestern and Eastern U.S. trout streams.

Every fisherman has a few favorites. My fly box always has a supply of Adams in sizes 12 to 16, and I use these whenever I am not sure what fly the fish are taking. Most fly fishermen also carry a supply of wet flies, nymphs, and streamers, although they may seldom use them when any surface activity is apparent. The Muddler Minnow, Maribou Muddler in various colors, Matuka streamers, and wet and dry Skunks are popular on

After fighting the current all afternoon, two anglers end their day on the Au Sable with the steep climb back to their car at Trout Unlimited Research Station access site.

How to Roll Cast

Fly fish long enough in Michigan and eventually you'll learn the roll cast. Our small streams and brushy banks, where you often find the biggest brook trout, are best fished with this specialty cast. Or not fished at all because in tight quarters you often don't have enough room for the backcast portion of a standard overhead cast.

The roll cast is best done with a double taper line and practiced on water to ensure a smooth lift. The tension from lawn grass is too unreliable to learn how to roll cast.

Figure 1: Roll casts depend on the back-cast forming a semi-elliptical loop called the "D" loop. Lift your rod tip up slowly; when your rod tip is behind you at the one o'clock position stop and wait a moment. This will let your line set in the water and help you load your rod.

Figure 1

"D" Loop

While lifting your rod, it is important that the line slide smoothly across the stream until it hangs by your side. To prevent tangling the line around the rod, tip your rod arm slightly away from your body to the two o'clock position.

Figure 2: Once the line has stopped sliding toward you, make a karate-chop, forward motion to roll the line out in front of you. Apply power with an accelerating snap of the forearm and hand and then quickly stop your rod tip with the tip pointed where you want the fly to land. Because the line is held by water tension, extra forward-and-down acceleration is needed as compared to an overhead cast when the line is totally in the air.

Figure 2

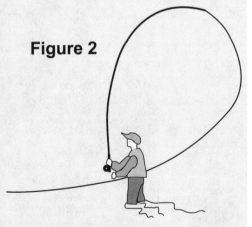

Stop the rod tip higher and the roll will remain in the air. Stop it lower and the line will be rolling closer or even on the water. A roll cast that is jerked forward without first pausing to allow the D loop to form will result in line piling in front of you.

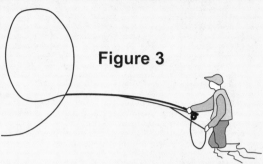

Figure 3: Let your fly line roll out in front of you. Your line should form a loop and then straighten out before laying on the water, with your leader and fly landing on the surface at the very end.

Figure 3

Another common use of the roll cast is to pick up line. This is especially useful when excessive slack or a sinking-tip line make the retrieval of a cast difficult. A quick roll cast will often straighten out a pile of slack or lift a sinking line to the surface, setting you up to begin a normal overhead cast.

most Michigan trout streams.

The Michigan Flies and Emergence Dates chart (page 308) includes the common names for the various insects found in Michigan streams as well as Latin names, along with when they emerge, the peak period for hatching, the various flies anglers use to imitate them, and the size of those flies. Many flies you see for sale in one state you won't see in another or even from one outdoor shop to the next in Michigan. Some flies will be in stock under the same name as the insect, light cahills, sulphur duns, or blue-winged olives for example. Other times they won't and you will have to ask what fly will work best for the hatch that is occurring. Sometimes buying flies can be almost as confusing as trying to decide which one to tie on at the river.

It's also very important to remember that the dates of emergence are approximate only and can vary substantially with weather conditions and the location and temperature of a stream. The Jordan River being further north and colder will experience hatches later than the Rifle River. The chart can serve as a rough guide, but again the best source of information the day you're going to fish is the local fly shop and other anglers already on the river.

A Word about Safe Wading

For each of the access sites described in this book I have provided information on wading conditions. These are the conditions you may expect during the regular trout season at normal late-spring and summer flows. In early spring, when the rivers are high, and after heavy rains in any season, the streams flow deeper and swifter, and wading conditions are quite different—more difficult and more dangerous. Wading conditions also change in places from year to year. The shallow water you waded easily last year may be scoured so deep that it overtops your waders. Or the deep hole you had to avoid may

There is no question the type of fly fishing this angler likes best.

be filled with sand. A thin veneer of gravel may be washed away, exposing the underlying slippery clay. Be especially watchful for such changes on your first trip of the season.

The twelve streams included in this book, like all first-class trout streams in the Midwest, have a large component of groundwater flow and consequently are relatively steady in discharge. Nevertheless, all streams fluctuate to some degree. The Pere Marquette, for example, has an average annual range in stage at Scottville of about 3.5 feet. The Manistee near Grayling rises only about 12 inches in an average year, but a rise of even six inches can change wading conditions drastically.

When you are about to wade into an unfamiliar stream, you should consider the four factors that chiefly influence safe wading, namely, depth of water, velocity of flow, character of streambed, and underwater snags and other hazards.

Obviously you want to avoid water that will top your waders, but the depth, coupled with the velocity, can also determine whether you can stand up in the stream. As a rule of thumb, you should not try to wade a stream if the depth in feet, multiplied by the velocity of flow in feet per second, is greater than 10. I'm not suggesting that you try to get an accurate measure of the velocity of flow before you enter the stream. But if the flow appears swift and the depth is greater than about two feet, it's best not to try it. Also, if you are having difficulty wading where the water is two feet deep, you will almost surely be swept off your feet if you step into water three feet deep.

The rule of ten cited above assumes a firm bed of sand or gravel and a strong fisherman. If the streambed is slippery clay or greasy rocks, the depth-times-velocity factor for safe wading is substantially smaller. Soft sand and mud also make wading difficult and sometimes dangerous. Soft sand is especially treacherous when approaching a deep hole from the upstream side. If you get too close the sand will give way beneath your feet, you will not be able to back out, and you will get a ducking.

Most Lower Peninsula streams are bottomed in sand and gravel, but there are areas of boulders and patches of hard slippery clay, as well as soft sand and mud. A few of the streams have small areas of bedrock or hard clay or marl resembling bedrock. The bedrock and hard clay can cause problems if you step from knee-deep water on the hard bottom to a hole that is over your head because of unconsolidated sand and gravel that sucks under like quicksand. The patches of clay are especially troublesome because they are often light in color and can be mistaken for sand. Felt soles are great on gravel but not much help on clay.

Underwater snags and trash can be hazardous to the wading anglers, especially at night. One way to avoid these hazards is to probe ahead with a wading staff or even a long stick you picked up in the woods. If you don't like to carry a staff you may be able to detect some of the hazards by probing ahead with one foot while keeping the other firmly planted on the bottom.

Wading at night is always difficult. The underwater snags, logjams, and boulders that are easily avoided in daylight may trip you up at night. The deep holes that overtop your waders are hard to see. If you like to be on the stream after dark, it is, no doubt, safer to fish with a companion than to go it alone. If you are fishing alone, arrive before dark and study the stretch you plan to fish to learn where to avoid the snags and holes.

It is almost always safer to wade upstream than down. It is easier to back away from danger with the current helping you than when the flow is pushing you into trouble. When wading an unfamiliar stream be especially watchful for a narrowing of the channel. This always means more difficult wading, for the narrowing channel means deeper water or faster flow, or both.

Another danger to the wading fisherman is a logjam or snag approached from the upstream side. A swift current may pin you against the log and you may not be able to back away. If a logjam or snag blocks your way it is safer to go around it than to try to climb over it or duck under it.

Avoid wading under bridges. The headwalls usually confine the stream to a narrow channel with consequent increase in depth and velocity. You will also encounter large boulders, broken concrete, or underwater pilings that could trip you up. Be on the lookout for a deep pool that commonly forms just below the bridge.

If you think, perhaps, that I dwell too much on the dangers that go with wading a trout stream, I can only say that I have experienced, or narrowly avoided, most of the disasters that can occur to the careless wader. Having eyes only for a rising trout on the South Branch of the Au Sable, I tripped over a large boulder, fell headfirst, and broke a prized fly rod. I was swept

An angler casts into the Holy Water of the Au Sable River at Keystone Landing. The famed Holy Water winds 8.7 miles from Burton's Landing to Wakeley Bridge.

off my feet trying to wade water too fast and deep on the Sturgeon, and I was pinned against a logjam on the Pigeon. Although warned of the danger, I had to swim for it in the Whirlpool on the Au Sable mainstream. In a small spring-fed creek in Southwestern Wisconsin I sank up to my hips in quicksand. I managed to pull myself out, but my boots are still buried in the creek. Trout fishing is too much fun to allow it to be spoiled by avoidable wading accidents.

On Not Getting Lost

Because most of the better trout streams are located in sparsely settled areas, special precautions should be taken to avoid getting lost. It is surprisingly easy to get lost on a trout stream. One cold September morning on the Escanaba River near Gwinn I managed to do it in just about five minutes. I was walking down the left bank looking for a good place to enter the river. When I came to a large, downed pine blocking my path it was easier to go around it on the landward side than to enter the river there, so I veered off to my left. When I rounded the pine I angled off to my right again, thinking to come back to the riverbank a few hundred feet downstream. But I walked and I walked—a hundred yards, two hundred yards, a quarter mile—and the river was not yet in sight. I reached in my pocket for the compass I always carry. I had left it in my other jacket. Dark clouds had blotted out the sun. The wind was blowing from the north, or was it the west? I knew the river had to be to the west, but which way was west? Resisting the impulse to run, I forced myself to sit down with my back against a tree and think things over. In a few minutes the clouds were blown away and the sun came out again. With the sun at my back I walked rapidly westward and soon saw the welcome gleam of the river ahead of me.

It is always a good idea to carry a compass or a compact GPS unit in your fishing vest, even when fishing a familiar stream. Both are a big help, but it may not always be enough. You might also want to carry a map of the area, with the best being the U.S. Geological Survey topographic maps, known simply as "topos." These maps come in a variety of scales, but the smallest scales available (1:24,000 or 1:63,360) are the most useful ones to anglers.

You can access and print out small sections of topos for free online from Maptech (800-627-7236; *www.maptech.com*) or order a digitized, interactive mapping program with all the quads for Michigan. Digital maps are more than just a topo on the screen of your computer. The base map that has been digitized is often the USGS quad, while the accompanying software, called a "map engine," makes the program interactive and allows you to customize a map for any outing. You can mark access roads to rivers or even fishing holes and add notes on water conditions and hatches for reference in the future. You can even plug in the coordinates from a GPS unit to make sure you find that hot spot again.

Another source of customized USGS quads is MyTopo (877-587-9004; *www.mytopo.com*). From the Montana-based web site you can create and order online a 1:24,000 scale map of the area you will be hiking in. The waterproof maps are 24 by 36 inches.

Also carry a good flashlight with fresh batteries (headlamps work the best for this), a supply of waterproof matches, a sandwich or candy bar, and your cell phone. If you do get lost, these things can add much to your comfort and peace of mind.

When fishing an unfamiliar stream in a wilderness area, it is a good idea to mark the spot where you enter the stream. Tie a white handkerchief or other marker to a bush overhanging the stream. When you are ready to leave the stream you will know just where to get out. Be sure to take your marker with you when you leave.

Can I Fish This Stream?

On a pleasant May morning in 1925, Gideon Gerhardt stepped into the Pine River to do a little trout fishing, but when he waded downstream to his favorite hole he discovered the river had been fenced off and posted with "No Trespassing" signs. The Ne-Bo-Shone Association, a private club of wealthy sportsmen that owned the land surrounding the Pine River, had erected the barrier across the stream to prevent access by wading anglers or canoes. The incident triggered the case of *Collins vs. Gerhardt*, which eventually made its way to the Michigan Supreme Court. In 1926, the state's highest court ruled in a landmark decision that the club may have owned the land but not the water and that the public had a common right to fish in any part of a navigable stream.

Early courts have defined navigable water, thus public waters, as any stream or river that has been used for the purposes of commerce, travel, or trade. One method to judge navigability was the "floating log test." Log drives had occurred on most Michigan rivers during the lumbering era at the turn of the century and were viewed as an act of commerce. Consequently, any lake or stream used for this purpose was considered navigable. Eventually whether a log could float down a stream or not became the yardstick in Michigan to determine whether the water was public or private.

A log, however, even one that floats, could hardly end the controversy of public versus private waters. Rest assured that all 12 trout streams covered in this book have long since been determined, usually in a court of law, to be navigable, public waters. All access sites covered in the following chapters are also public places where you can legally enter the river or stream. Once in the water you're free to fish and wade as far as you like.

But keep in mind that often you will wade past private property on one or both sides of the stream. Michigan law allows an angler to walk a route along a stream bank, even if the land is private and without written or oral consent, to avoid a natural or artificial hazard. That might be a dam, a deep hole, or a massive sweeper in the river or a fence. The law does not mean you can spread out on somebody's deck or dock to enjoy lunch or take a mid-day snooze while waiting for a hatch.

Until the courts come up with a more comprehensive definition of navigability than the floating log test, there will always be disputes between land owners and anglers as to whether secondary streams and small creeks are public waters. In this shady area of riparian rights, it's best to use common sense. Obviously if the land surrounding the small stream you want to fish is public, that is, state or national forest land, so is the water. If not it might be wise to ask at the local outdoor shop or even the property owners themselves. Most have few gripes with anglers who are non-intrusive and fish with a healthy respect for others' property.

Trout Stream Maps

For each of the streams I have included a set of maps. The small-scale location maps are based on county highway maps and show the channel of the stream and the major public roads leading to the stream. Numbered access sites are also shown on the location maps.

For each of the rivers, 6 to 15 access sites open to the public are mapped at a larger scale. I have not tried to cover every possible access but have included enough to give you several weeks of excellent fishing on each of these classic streams. The larger-scale site maps show the river channel in greater detail. These are based on USGS topographic maps and field research.

Not all roads shown are open to the public. Some newer roads and trails, especially those related to recent oil and gas development, are not shown.

Remember that the condition of the roads also can change. The road you once drove with ease may be blocked by deep potholes or downed timber the next time you try it. Also displayed on these maps is the character of the river's bottom materials, based on personal observation and years of fishing experience. The maps show only the predominate materials. An occasional boulder or small areas of bedrock, cemented sands, hard slippery clay, or soft sand and mud may occur at any site. The maps and text together should tell you what you need to know about the fishing conditions at each site.

Accommodations

Each of the rivers described here has at least one campground, if not several, where an angler can pitch a tent and spend the night almost within casting distance of the current. The campgrounds, either state forest or national forest, are rustic facilities with drinking water, vault toilets, fire rings, and picnic tables; these sites are well covered in the following chapters. Registration is onsite with no advance reservations accepted at any of them. Only the Rifle River passes through a state park, the Rifle River Recreation Area. There are no state parks on the other rivers, but many are only a short drive away and offer electrical hook-ups, showers, and even rental mini-cabins.

For the locations and facilities of all state forest and state park campgrounds, check the DNR web site (*www.michigan.gov/dnr*) and click "Recreation, Camping & Boating" on the homepage. For camping information in the Manistee National Forest (Pine and Pere Marquette rivers) and the Huron National Forest (Au Sable River), check the Huron-Manistee National Forests web site (*www.fs.fed.us/r9/hmnf*).

Dispersed camping is also permitted anywhere on state forest lands except where specifically prohibited or within a mile of a developed campground. Camping in an undeveloped area is free, but you need to obtain a Camp Registration Card (Form PR 4134) by calling or stopping in at any DNR regional or field office. Registration cards can also be obtained by emailing the State Forest Operations Section (*DNR-FMD-TREES@michigan.gov*) and requesting one be sent to you by mail. Primitive camping is also allowed anywhere in the Huron-Manistee National Forests except within 200 feet of water. You do not need a permit or even to register in advance with a ranger office or station.

Other accommodations listed in the book are motels, bed and breakfasts, and lodges. They have been highlighted because of either their close proximity to the rivers or their history of catering to fly anglers. Finally, the major tourist bureau for each river is provided; all of them have well-developed web sites with lengthy lists of accommodations in the area.

Michigan's Historic Fishing Lodges

Scattered across Michigan are numerous lodges where anglers have been gathering for years to fish for trout during the day and swap tales at night, usually in front of fieldstone fireplaces, sipping a single malt whiskey. Some of the lodges are open to the public, some are private clubs, some are summer residences. But they all have one thing in common; they sit on the banks of one of Michigan's classic trout streams. Here are but a few:

Camp Wa Wa Sum: Located on the Holy Water six miles east of Grayling is this historic 19th century lodge. Wa Wa Sum, Ojibwa for "plain view," was named by Chief David Shoppenagon because at the time the view from the high bank was unobstructed for miles due to extensive logging. Shoppenagon, an early Au Sable River guide, constructed the first building at the camp in 1880 and seven years later Rubin Babbit, Michigan's first wildlife officer, built the second. These buildings were constructed of red pine and tamarack logs and used as a fishing camp by a group of Toledo businessmen. Through the early 1930s, other cabins of various sizes were added and still stand today.

In 1980 the buildings and 251 acres of land were deeded to Michigan State University by descendants of two of the camp's six original owners. Kevin Gardiner, a descendant of Rubin Babbit, is the camp's present caretaker and the third generation of his family to perform these duties. Wa Wa Sum is now a Michigan State University research center that focuses on fisheries and forestry projects. But the massive log lodge and the beautiful Au Sable River that flows below are such a pleasant setting that Wa Wa Sum (517-355-3272; *www.canr.msu.edu/lmo/properties.htm#wawa*) is also used as a center for conferences and retreats, particularly by Trout Unlimited chapters.

Flint Rainbow Club: This stunning lodge with its wrap-around porch overlooking the Pere Marquette River is home to the Flint Rainbow Club that was founded in 1916 by a group of anglers, made wealthy in the early days of Oldsmobile and General Motors. After the first clubhouse burnt down in 1920, members purchased a building that served as an officers' barracks at Fort Custer near Battle Creek in World War I and had it disassembled and moved by railroad.

The lodge has 13 small bedrooms with old-fashioned sinks in each and a huge brick firehouse in the living room that heats the entire building when necessary. It is perched on the edge of the 50-foot bluff, overlooking a sharp bend in the river and a steel footbridge across it that allows members to reach other holes and runs. Located just a half mile west of M-37, the Flint Rainbow Club owns almost a mile of frontage on Pere Marquette's flies-only, catch-and-release section. The lodge is used by the 22 families, who are members of the club, and their guests.

Fuller's North Branch Outing Club: What began as the Douglas Hotel in 1916 is today the Fuller's North Branch Outing Club, a lodge on the North Branch of the Au Sable still dedicated to fly anglers. At its height, the North Branch Outing Club boasted such members as Henry and Edsel Ford, Harvey Firestone and the Dodge Brothers. In 1996 the Fuller family bought the historic but vacant lodge and opened it as an 12-room inn after two years of extensive renovation. Fuller's North Branch Outing Club (989-348-7951; *www. fullersnboc.com*; 6122 E. County Rd. 612) is a classic angler's inn. The lodge overlooks 400 feet of the North Branch, features a complete fly shop on the first floor, a comfortable lounge and dining area and a room to hang

and dry out your waders. Outside there are often as many Au Sable River boats in the parking lot as cars.

Barbless Hook: Perched above the Au Sable River at the east end of the Holy Water is George Griffith's cabin where on July 18, 1959, the Conservation Commission member and a group of concerned anglers founded Trout Unlimited. The name of the cabin is indicative of Griffith's philosophy and the proper name for TU's birthplace. A barb may hold a trout if the line goes slack, but a capable angler can keep a line tight until the fish is in the net. More importantly a barbless hook is easily removed from the trout so it can be released alive and unharmed.

The Michigan Council of Trout Unlimited ended up with the Barbless Hook after Griffith died in 1998. MCTU sold the cabin in 2005 but maintained an easement from the river and around the dock where a small memorial plaque dedicated to Griffith and the founding of TU has been placed.

Rayburn Lodge: This historic log mansion was built in 1923 on the banks of the Au Sable mainstream by a wildcatter, whose passion was gambling, not fishing. Another oilman, Don Rayburn, won the lodge in a poker game in 1947 and subsequently the area became known as the Rayburn Tract. Rayburn didn't fish either but eventually the lodge was sold, moved six miles down river and renovated, reopening as a bed and breakfast inn in 1996. Its new location on the Holy Water made it an immediate favorite among fly anglers. The sprawling Rayburn Lodge

(989-348-7482; *www.rayburnlodgebnb.com*; 1491 Richardson Rd.) has five bedrooms, a massive fireplace, a billiards room and common areas and porches where you can look down at the Au Sable in the evening and see what's hatching.

Barothy Lodge: In 1889, the Barothy family purchased a logging camp and 65 acres on the Pere Marquette River, intending to set it up as a medicinal herb and fruit farm. But after mineral springs were discovered on the property, they changed directions and turned their farm into a health spa, remodeling their farmhouse into a lodge with six bedrooms and a large dining area. Visitors arrived at the resort to relax, bathe in the river, and drink from the mineral springs. But what they quickly discovered was the great fishing for brown and rainbow trout in the Pere Marquette. Barothy Lodge went on to thrive as a fishing and hunting camp and soon other buildings were added, including Long House, which boasted 22 bedrooms and reputedly the first indoor toilet facilities north of Newaygo.

Today Barothy Lodge (231-898-2340, 877-898-2340; *www.barothylodge.com*; 7478 Barothy Rd.) is a 320-acre resort with 15 cabins that range in size from one to nine bedrooms and are scattered around a series of ponds in a wooded setting. Some have stone fireplaces, others hot tubs and many have outdoor decks where you can view the gently flowing Pere Marquette and watch driftboats pull in after a day of fishing. Dress code here is fishing vests and Gore-Tex waders. And while there are tennis courts, a swimming pool and basketball courts at the resort, clearly the most popular spot to hang out is the fish cleaning station.

Gates Au Sable Lodge: This 14-room, motel-style lodge is the ultimate retreat for fly anglers in Michigan. Located at Stephan Bridge of the Au Sable mainstream, the lodge was started in 1970 by Cal Sr. and Mary Gates and today is operated by their son Rusty Gates and his wife, Julie. Rooms feature picture windows overlooking the Holy Water, hooks for your waders outside and a place to hang your rod inside. Onsite is one of the best stocked fly shops in Northern Michigan while outside there is always a handful of Au Sable riverboats as the lodge is the hub of guide activity during the trout season.

But what many anglers love most is the resort's Hungry Fisherman Dining Room. This small restaurant features three tables, a view of the river, and a sign on a door that warns "Absolutely No Waders Allowed in the Dining Room!" The best dish to order is pan-fried trout and the best meal ends with a homemade apple dumpling for dessert. Afterwards wander down to the Au Sable where benches allow you to take in the river and watch an angler entice a rising trout with graceful casts. Even if you're a non-angler or not a guest at Gates Au Sable Lodge (989-348-8462; *www.gateslodge.com*; 471 Stephan Bridge Rd.) you can enjoy dinner in the restaurant with an advance reservation.

Fly Shops and Fishing Guides

Anglers entering the world of fly fishing are blessed in Michigan with not only a variety of streams to fish but also a large number of fly shops and fishing guides to assist them. A reputable shop, with a knowledgeable staff, is the best place to be outfitted with your first fly rod-reel-and-line combination, as your experience, budget, and the type of fishing you will be concentrating on will be carefully considered. Such fly shops, especially those near the rivers, are the best source of information on fishing conditions, hatches, and the best flies to purchase. For a list of fly shops in Michigan see page 311.

Scattered throughout the state are also a number of guides that specialize in fly fishing in various rivers. An afternoon with such a qualified angler is not only a way to learn the productive holes and runs of a river but also to get a hands-on, one-on-one lesson to improve your casting and ability to read the water.

Fishing guides are listed in chapters that cover the rivers but they are by no means an exclusive list for Michigan. The best source for professional guides is other anglers.

Rules, Regulations, and Fish You Should Not Eat

In the site descriptions and elsewhere in this book I have referred to "flies-only" and "special regulation" water in some reaches of the streams. You should understand that these rules and regulations can change from one year to next, and you should be aware of those currently in force. When you purchase your fishing license and trout stamp you will be provided with a *Michigan Inland Trout and Salmon Guide*, which summarizes all the rules and regulations for trout fishing in our state. You can also obtain the same guide through the DNR web site (*www.michigan.gov/dnr*) by clicking on Fishing and then Seasons & Regulations.

The DNR web site also has a Michigan Fish Consumption Advisory Guide that cautions you against eating certain fish in some waters and all fish in other waters. Fortunately, none of the trout in the rivers described here are included in these lists as of this writing. But keep in mind that migratory trout and salmon and other fish that enter these rivers from contaminated sources are included in this advisory.

Trout fishermen generally have the reputation of being good citizens on the streams, and they usually comply with both the spirit and letter of the rules. Many anglers now return most or all of their catch to the water. Limiting the kill of trout is helpful, but the future of trout fishing also requires the preservation of favorable trout habitat. You can help preserve the trout streams by supporting conservation organizations such as Trout Unlimited and the Federation of Fly Fishermen. Other steps you can take to maintain the trout fishery are described in the section "What Makes a Stream Fit for Trout—and How to Keep It That Way" (page 39).

An angler relaxes on a bench overlooking the Au Sable River at Camp Wa Wa Sum, a historic fishing lodge, now owned by Michigan State University.

What Makes a Stream Fit for Trout
And How to Keep It That Way

The thick deposits of permeable sand and gravel left by the Pleistocene glaciers are the key to the many outstanding trout streams in the northern part of Michigan's Lower Peninsula. These deposits absorb large quantities of rain and melting snow and feed them gradually to the streams to keep them flowing strong and cool during summer droughts. The water dissolves calcium and magnesium carbonate as it flows through the glacial materials and becomes hard and moderately alkaline; qualities favorable to trout habitat. Because the water entering the streams is cool it absorbs enough oxygen to satisfy the trout's requirements. The glacial deposits also supply the consolidated gravels on the streambed essential to spawning trout.

Under natural conditions these streams are nearly ideal trout waters, but most human interference, unless carefully controlled, will cause some deterioration in trout habitat.

What to Do about Pollution

Probably the greatest potential threat to Michigan trout streams is the discharge of industrial and municipal pollutants into the streams. The DNR has warned against eating certain fish in some of Michigan's lakes and streams because of chemical contaminants. The affected waters are listed under the Michigan Fish Consumption Advisory Guide available online at the DNR web site (*www.michigan.gov/dnr*).

None of the streams described here are included in these lists at the time of this writing, but this is no guarantee of future immunity. Furthermore, the advisory does apply to migratory fish that may enter some of these streams. For example, migratory trout and salmon that enter the Pere Marquette from Lake Michigan are included in the warning. The edibility of trout is not of major importance to those anglers who practice catch-and-release, but who wants to fish in a stream so polluted that the fish are not fit to eat?

The Surface Water Assessment Section of the Water Bureau for the Department of Environmental Quality (DEQ) monitors the quality of water in Michigan streams. In addition to sampling for chemical analysis, aquatic biologists check the streams for evidence of biologic degradation. These professionals cannot be everywhere at once, however, and the alert fisherman can help by reporting any signs of pollution in a favorite stream. An unusually rank growth of aquatic vegetation suggests an upstream source of nutrient discharge—possibly sewage wastes. Brown or gray slime on the riverbed is even stronger evidence of sewage pollution. Oil slicks on the water, detergent foam, unusual color, and chemical odor are other indicators of contamination. If you suspect that warm water is being discharged into the stream, check the water temperature above and below the point of discharge. Report any signs of pollution to the Pollution Emergency Alert System of the DEQ (800-292-4706).

Acid Rain

The effect of acid rain on the quality of water in lakes and streams has been the subject of concern in the past, especially in the Northeastern states and areas adjacent areas to Canada. Studies of snowmelt and early seasonal runoff in Northern Michigan have found a substantial reduction in pH (increased acidity) in some streams of the Upper Peninsula. Part of this increased acidity has been attributed to the flushing out of natural organic acids from the wetlands, but some of it probably comes from the release of inorganic acids derived from the atmosphere (acid rain). The pH values of Lower Peninsula streams were reduced only slightly because the large groundwater inflow to these streams keeps the water highly buffered.

The reduction of pH in some of Michigan's Upper Peninsula streams may be great enough to reduce the survival of trout fry. Further studies by the DNR will determine if increased acidity from atmospheric sources is becoming a serious threat to Michigan streams.

Sewage Disposal

Sewage effluent entering a trout stream has far-reaching effects beyond the obvious problems of odor and bacterial contamination. The BOD (biochemical oxygen demand) of the wastewater reduces the dissolved oxygen content of the stream. If the amount of wastewater is large in relation to the flow of the stream, the dissolved oxygen can go so low as to make the water unfit for trout. The rank growth of aquatic vegetation resulting from nutrients in the sewage wastes causes a wide fluctuation in the dissolved oxygen content of the stream, ranging from supersaturation in the daytime to well below saturation at night. This effect can extend downstream much farther than the initial decline in dissolved oxygen caused by the BOD of the effluent.

To combat this problem, Northern Michigan communities have substituted sewage lagoons as a means of disposing of municipal wastes instead of discharging sewage effluent directly into trout streams. In the 1970s both the towns of Grayling and Roscommon switched to sewage lagoon disposal. Before the change, the sewage effluent from Grayling had caused a decline in the nighttime dissolved oxygen content of the Au Sable that extended several miles downstream. The effluent had also caused a marked increase in coliform (sewage) bacteria below the outfall, and the nutrients stimulated an extremely dense growth of aquatic vegetation.

There is little doubt that the aesthetic quality of both the Au Sable's mainstream and the South Branch of the Au Sable is improved since the direct discharge of effluent stopped. The gray-brown slimes and the odor are

Trout Unlimited: From the Banks of the Au Sable

Trout Unlimited was born in 1959 on the banks of the famed Au Sable River when George Griffith invited 15 fly fishers to his summer cabin, The Barbless Hook. Griffith was a member of the Michigan Conservation Commission, the forerunner of today's Natural Resources Commission, and was concerned about the health of trout fisheries in Michigan along with promoting a radical new idea at the time: catch and release. You hook a trout and then you carefully return it to the river to live on.

Among those attending that first meeting were Dr. Casey Westell, who later laid the groundwork for TU's scientific approach to trout management; and Art Neumann, who ran a small fly shop in Saginaw and was an early proponent of catch and release. In September of 1959, Trout Unlimited was officially launched with 340 original members, of which almost two-thirds came from the Saginaw Valley area. Neumann was named first vice president and later wrote the Trout Unlimited philosophy:

Trout Unlimited believes that trout fishing isn't just fishing for trout.

It's fishing for sport rather than food where the true enjoyment of the sport lies in the challenge, the love and the battle of wits, not necessarily the full creel.

It's the feeling of satisfaction that comes from limiting your kill instead of killing your limit.

It's communing with nature where the chief reward is a refreshed body and a contented soul, where a license is a permit to use—not abuse, to enjoy—not destroy our trout waters.

It's subscribing to the proposition that what's good for trout is good for trout fisherman and that managing trout for the trout rather than for the fisherman is fundamental to the solution of our trout problems.

It's appreciating our trout, respecting fellow anglers and giving serious thought to tomorrow.

TU was still a fledgling conservation organization in 1961 when it achieved its first major victory, convincing conservation officials to replace Michigan's indiscriminate stocking of catchable-sized trout with stream improvement programs, fingerling planting, and protective fishing regulations. Word of the success in Michigan spread quickly, and trout anglers from Pennsylvania to California began to form TU chapters for the protection and preservation of coldwater fisheries in their region.

In 1963, Neumann became executive director of TU and moved the headquarters from Lansing to Saginaw, where it remained until the organization moved its headquarters to Denver in 1969. During that time Neumann was not only the spokesperson for TU but the heart and soul of the organization, working tirelessly to transform it from a group of anglers in Michigan to a conservation force recognized on a national level.

Today TU is based in Arlington, VA, and includes more than 140,000 members and 400 chapters nationwide, including 23 in Michigan.

gone, and the aquatic vegetation is not so rank.

Maintaining the Flow of the Streams

Because the favorable qualities of Michigan trout streams are largely dependent on groundwater inflow to the streams, any activity that reduces this flow is a threat to trout habitat. Drastic changes in land use in the watershed could reduce the amount of water percolating down to the water-bearing formations and consequently the groundwater inflow to the streams. The changes now going on—the construction of streets and roads and parking lots—may cause undesirable amounts of sediment to enter the streams, but they are not great enough to significantly reduce recharge to water-bearing formations.

Pumping of high-capacity wells near the rivers can reduce the flow of groundwater to the streams. This was the reason that Friends of the Cedar River Watershed challenged Shanty Creek Resort in court in 1998. The officials of the Bellaire ski and golf resort had announced their intentions to withdraw water at a rate of up to 2,600 gallons per minute (gpm) from the Blue Ribbon trout stream for irrigation and snow-making purposes. Eventually Shanty Creek agreed to withdraw only 300 gpm as well as control stormwater runoff and reduce the amount of chemical and pesticide use on the portion of the golf course near the river.

Effective water management also involves location and spacing of wells, regulations on the depth of the producing formations, and control of pumping. This is the work of professionals, but the trout fisherman can insist that management is planned and regulations enforced.

The diversion of water for agricultural use or for the production of bottled water could become a serious problem in future years. Such diversions could affect the flow of trout streams if the water is taken directly from them or from large-capacity wells near them. In 2003, a judge ordered the Nestle Ice Mountain water bottling plant to cease operations in Mecosta County, saying the 250 gpm it was pumping from wells was damaging the environment. Eventually Nestle reached a settlement with the environmental groups that brought the case to court, with the company agreeing to reduce pumping to 218 gpm. That sent Nestle searching to set up more bottling plants in Michigan, eyeing spring water from sites near trout steams in Osceola County and near the headwaters of the White River.

What to Do about Impoundments

Impoundments inevitably destroy that part of the stream that is flooded and may cause undesirable changes in streamflow, water temperature, and bottom sediments. Recent studies indicate that the removal of a dam has significant ecological benefits, including the return of a more naturalized flow, temperature regime, and sediment transport to the river system. Dam removals can also promote the rehabilitation of native species. This was the case of the Stronach Dam on the Pine River.

A Trout Unlimited member assists a new fly angler on the South Branch of the Au Sable during a weekend fishing clinic.

Located three miles upstream from the Manistee River, the Stronach became the only dam ever built on the Pine River when it was constructed in 1912. Because of its steep, sandy banks and logging operations that took place in the late 1800s, the Pine carries a high annual bedload of sand, which resulted in the reservoir gradually filling and the Stronach Dam being decommissioned in 1953. Negotiations with Consumers Energy led to a removal of the aging structure in stages that began in 1997 and was completed in 2003. The theory—and hope—was that a staged process of removal would allowed the Pine gradually to restore its channel in the areas upstream of the dam while causing the least amount of downstream environmental impact.

In an ongoing research effort that began in 1998, biologists from Michigan State University have studied the environmental impacts of Stronach Dam on the Pine River before and after its removal. Early indications are that the removal has resulted in the erosion of sand that covered 2.5 miles of upstream river habitat. This re-exposed gravel-cobble substrate is the original streambed that native trout prefer and should result in an increase of natural reproduction.

On the other hand, no existing impoundments should be removed without closely examining the results of such removal. The desirable effect of cooler water, for example, should be balanced against the possible undesirable result of added sediment load to the stream. An example of such a result was the great load of sand and silt carried down the Pigeon River upon failure of a dam in 1957. According to some observers, many spawning beds were smothered by the sediment, and recovery was slow. Another possible result of dam removal that may be considered undesirable by some anglers is the introduction of anadromous fish into waters now restricted to resident trout.

Because the potential damage is great, trout anglers should insist that no new impoundments are built. Reactivation of existing hydroelectric dams is also bad news. The regulation of streamflow for power production destroys the natural character of the river and may prove inconvenient or even disastrous to wading fishermen.

Saving the Bed and Banks

The character of the bed and banks of a trout stream affects its value as trout habitat and its attractiveness to anglers. Experiments have shown that an increase of sand sediment bedload in a trout stream can reduce the trout population to less than half its normal abundance (G. R. Alexander and E. A. Hansen, "Sand Sediment in a Michigan Trout Stream Part II," *North American Journal of Fisheries Management* 3 [1983]: 365–72). Discharge of sand and silt into streams by road building, ditch digging, and other earth-moving construction is a threat to trout streams that can easily be spotted by any angler. This kind of activity should be reported immediately, because the damage may occur very quickly. Call first on your local town and county officials, but also notify the nearest regional office of the DEQ.

Anglers end an afternoon of fishing in the Mason Tract with a half-mile hike back to their car. The 4,493-acre special management area protects 12 miles of the South Branch of the Au Sable.

Another result of human intrusion on the land, generally unwelcome to most anglers, is the urbanization of the stream banks. Clusters of riverside homes and cottages detract from the wilderness that many consider an essential ingredient of an attractive trout stream. Greenbelt zoning regulations now in force on the Au Sable and other Michigan streams require that a strip of natural vegetation be maintained along the river's edge. Minimum width of lots and setback restrictions for homes and waste disposal fields are also in effect. These regulations should help reduce the impact of further development on the streams. Trout fishermen, above all others, should welcome and comply with these rules.

Littering of bed and banks by stream users is still a problem, although the litter has been substantially reduced thanks to the Michigan's bottle deposit bill that was passed by voters in 1976 despite the beverage industry lobbying against it. The bottle bill requires a ten-cent deposit on all soft drinks, beer, and wine cooler containers, and anglers should support the effort by conservation groups to expand the current bill to cover bottled water, teas, and juices. Anglers can also help resolve the litter problem not only by refraining from discarding any material along the rivers themselves, but also by picking up and disposing of litter discarded by others. This is especially true of the bird nests of monofilament fishing line often seen along the banks and tangled up at the bottom of streams. Wading anglers are in the best position to remove and properly dispose of them.

Intense use of a stream by campers, paddlers, and anglers can also cause damage to the riverbed and riverbanks. Trampling of the banks on entering or leaving the stream can shove great quantities of sand into it and further expose the banks to erosion. Even more serious is the destruction of stream banks by off-road vehicles. The DNR has attacked these problems by moving the state forest campgrounds away from the stream banks, constructing boat ramps for launching canoes, building stairways down high sandy banks, and prohibiting motorized vehicles on streamside trails. However, none of these measures will help unless those of us who use the streams treat them as the valuable and fragile resource we know them to be.

Resident Trout versus Salmon and Steelhead

The introduction of salmon into classic trout waters is a controversial issue that has not been entirely resolved. Many trout anglers contend that the competition of the salmon damages the resident trout fishery and attracts crowds of careless fishermen who destroy trout habitat, trespass on private property, and generally make life miserable for the dedicated trout angler. Others argue that the salmon anglers should have equal rights with those who prefer trout, that the salmon fishery brings in millions of dollars of revenue to the state and local communities, and that the salmon and salmon fishers do no great damage to the trout fishery. The controversy is mainly about the chinook salmon, as the Atlantic salmon are not yet well established in streams of the Lower Peninsula, and many dedicated trout fishermen would welcome the chance to fish for Salmo salar. I confess to a bias in favor of the resident trout fishery and would like to see the salmon, at least the chinook salmon, confined to the lower reaches of the streams.

Trout anglers generally are less critical of the steelhead competing with the resident trout, for, after all, the steelhead is a trout, and many a dry-fly enthusiast is happy to fish for steelhead in season. However, it appears that the best steelhead streams generally do not have the best resident trout fishery, and it may prove desirable to manage some streams, such as the upper Au Sable and upper Manistee, for resident trout, and others, such as the Little Manistee, for steelhead.

Guard Your Trout Streams

In summary, what I am suggesting is that trout fishermen act as an advance guard to protect our trout streams. The people in state and local agencies designated to protect Michigan's water resources generally are doing the best they can, but a limited budget spreads their ranks very thin. Agencies such as the DNR are also subject to political pressure from all sides and must try to balance the legitimate needs of diverse interests. Trout anglers can train themselves to recognize potential threats to their favorite streams and report such threats to responsible government agencies. Even more important they can make their voices heard so that when politicians are debating controversial environmental issues the needs of the trout fishery are among those considered.

A spawned-out salmon lies in the Pere Marquette River. Many trout anglers contend that the competition from chinook salmon damages the resident trout fishery.

Other Allies

There are many organizations that are dedicated to preserving and improving the trout fishing resource in Michigan. Anglers should seriously consider joining such organizations both as a way to protect the fishery as well as for the fellowship of other anglers. Or as one angler once told me, you can learn a lot about fly fishing when you spend a day cleaning up a trout stream.

Trout Unlimited: Founded in Michigan, Trout Unlimited (TU) is now a national organization dedicated to conserving coldwater fisheries and seeks the support of all trout anglers—bait, fly, and spin. For membership or more information contact Trout Unlimited, P.O. Box 7400, Wooly Bugger, WV 22116 (800-834-2419; *www.tu.org*).

Michigan Council of Trout Unlimited: The Michigan Council of Trout Unlimited (MCTU) is the umbrella organization for 23 TU chapters in Michigan and their 7,000 members. MCTU's magazine, *Michigan Trout,* is an excellent resource for fly anglers. For more information check the MCTU web site (*www.mctu.org*).

Federation of Fly Fishers: Dating to 1965, the Federation of Fly Fishers (FFF) seeks the support of all fly anglers, whether they fish for trout or any other species. For membership or more information contact Federation of Fly Fishers, 215 East Lewis St., Livingston, MT 59047 (406-222-9369; *www. fedflyfishers.org*).

Anglers of the Au Sable: Founded in Grayling in 1987 to lobby for a catch-and-release fishery on the Au Sable, Anglers of the Au Sable is dedicated to the protection and preservation of the Au Sable and neighboring Manistee rivers. Affiliated with the Federation of Fly Fishers, Anglers of the Au Sable is a totally volunteer conservation group with no paid staff. For membership or more information contact Anglers of the Au Sable, 403 Black Bear Dr., Grayling, MI 49738 (989-348-8462; *www.ausableanglers.org*).

Michigan United Conservation Clubs: MUCC is the largest statewide conservation organization in the country with more than 120,000 members and 470 affiliated local conservation clubs. Although MUCC represents all anglers as well as hunters, among its conservation goals is to protect the state's trout waters from misuse and overdevelopment. Its magazine, *Michigan Out-of-Doors,* often features articles for fly anglers as well as a regular fly-of-the-month column. For membership or more information contact MUCC, P.O. Box 30235, Lansing, MI 48912-3785 (517-371-1041; *www.mucc.org*).

Trout Unlimited Chapters in Michigan

There are 23 Trout Unlimited chapters in Michigan, each dedicated to improving coldwater fisheries or adopted rivers through fundraisers and work parties in their region. Many also offer monthly meetings where much of the talk centers on fly fishing as well as fly-tying lessons and other classes and fishing trips. To join, check their website and attend a meeting.

Southeast Michigan

Ann Arbor
Ann Arbor Area Chapter
www.aaatu.org

Bloomfield Hills
Challenge Chapter
www.challengechapter.org

Detroit Area
Paul H. Young Chapter
www.paulyoungtu.org

Rochester
Clinton Valley Trout Chapter
www.clintonvalleytu.com

Lansing
Frank Perrin Chapter
www.lansing-tu.org

Rochester Hills
Vanguard Chapter
www.vanguardtu.org

Southwest Michigan

Grand Rapids
Schrems West Michigan
www.swmtu.org

Kalamazoo
Kalamazoo Valley Chapter
www.kvctu.org

Central Michigan

Midland
Leon P. Martuch Chapter
www.martuchtu.org

Saginaw
William B. Mershon Chapter
www.mershon-tu.org

Northern Michigan

Boyne City
Miller-VanWinkle Chapter
www.mvwtu.org

Gaylord
Headwaters Chapter
www.headwaterstu.org

Grayling
Mason/Griffin/Founders Chapter
www.masongriffithtu.org

Traverse City
Adams Chapter
www.tctrout.com

Upper Peninsula

Houghton
Copper Country Chapter
www.coppercountrytu.org

Marquette
Fred Waara Chapter
www.mctu.org/fredwaara.html

Newberry
Two Heart Chapter
www.mctu.org/twoheart.html

The following chapters have not yet developed websites, but contact information can be obtained through the Michigan Council of Trout Unlimited web site (*www.mctu.org*) by clicking on "Chapters."

Bay City
Arnold J. Copeland Chapter

Flint
Charles A Fellows Chapter

Cadillac
Pine River Area Chapter

Iron River
Iron County Chapter

Ironwood
Ottawa Chapter

Muskegon
Muskegon-White River Chapter

Federation of Fly Fishers Clubs in Michigan

The Federation of Fly Fishers was established in 1965 as a national organization of fly fishing clubs; by the end of that year 12 clubs had joined. Today there are more than three hundred including 11 in Michigan. These fishing clubs are a great source for classes, organized fishing trips, and companionship on the rivers. Like TU chapters, the best way to join is to attend a meeting.

Baldwin
Pere Marquette Watershed Council
www.peremarquette.org

Canton
Huron River Fly Fishing Club Inc.
www.huronflyfishing.com

Flushing
Greater Flint Muddler Minnows
www.greaterflintmuddlerminnows.com

Grand Rapids
Grand River Fly Tyers
www.grandriverflytyers.org

Grayling
Anglers of the AuSable
www.ausableanglers.org

Royal Oak
Michigan Fly Fishing Club
www.mffc.org

The following clubs have not yet developed websites, but contact information can be obtained through the Federation of Fly Fishers website (*www.fedflyfishers.org*) by clicking on "Councils and Clubs."

Charlotte
Frontier City Flycasters, Inc.

Howell
Wooly Bugger Fly Fishers, Inc.

Iron Mountain
Northwoods Fly Fishers

Okemos
Red Cedar Fly Fishers

Pentwater
West Michigan Hacklers

Michigan Angler: John D. Voelker

John D. Voelker is better known by his pen name, Robert Traver, than by his given name and best known for his legal thriller, *Anatomy of a Murder*, than as either a Michigan Supreme Court Justice or a passionate fly angler. But his love for trout is unquestionable, and his reflections on fishing, particularly in his collections of essays, *Trout Madness* and *Trout Magic*, rank with Ernest Hemingway's early short stories as among the finest fishing literature to emerge from Michigan.

The son of a barkeeper and the grandson of German immigrants, Voelker was born in Ishpeming, MI, in 1903 and honed his writing skills in Marquette at Northern State Normal School (now Northern Michigan University). Eventually Voelker headed south to Ann Arbor where he enrolled in the University of Michigan Law School. Voelker struggled at first but managed to earned a law degree in 1928 and along the way met Grace Taylor from Oak Park, IL. The two married and moved to Chicago where Voelker took an entry-level position with a large law firm.

But the barkeeper's son soon missed the woods and rugged beauty of the Upper Peninsula and the fighting spirit of a brook trout. After three years of living in a crowded city, he returned to Ishpeming where he was elected as prosecuting attorney of Marquette County in 1934 and filled that position off and on for twelve years before returning to private practice.

In 1952, Voelker agreed to defend Army Lt. Coleman Peterson, who was accused of murdering the owner of the Lumberjack Tavern in Big Bay, a small hamlet north of Marquette. The alleged motive was revenge for the rape of Peterson's wife; Voelker successfully defended his client who was declared not guilty by reason of temporary insanity.

The six-day trial left Voelker with a foundation of a novel and changed his life. Already a published author, Voelker soon began working on the courtroom drama and in 1956 St. Martin's Press accepted *Anatomy of a Murder* for publication. Ironically, Gov. G. Mennen Williams telephoned Voelker the same day, offering him a seat on the Michigan Supreme Court to fill the remainder of a vacant term.

Released in January 1958, *Anatomy of a Murder* was an instant hit. It was selected for the Book-of-the-Month Club and spent 65 weeks on the national bestseller lists, establishing the popular genre of legal thrillers. Later that year famed director Otto Preminger purchased the film rights and arrived in the Upper Peninsula to film it, with Jimmy Stewart, George C. Scott, and Lee Remick in tow. The 1959 movie was as successful as the book, earning an Academy Award nomination for best picture, while Stewart was nominated as best actor for playing the defense attorney.

Voelker was now at the height of his fame, but all he really wanted to do was fish at his beloved Upper Peninsula hideaway, Frenchman's Pond, and then write about fishing in the winter. Assured of a steady income and

John Voelker and Jimmy Stewart light up cigars on the set of Anatomy of a Murder, filmed in the Upper Peninsula in 1959. (Courtesy Archives of Michigan.)

willing publishers due to the success of the book and movie, he retired from the Michigan Supreme Court in 1959 and walked away from his legal career to do just that.

Voelker followed his national bestseller with *Trout Madness* in 1960, a series of short stories that led readers through a full trout season and introduced them to the remotely beautiful Upper Peninsula where Voelker loved to fish. Two more legal thrillers followed, but in 1974 Voelker returned to his roots and Frenchman's Pond with *Trout Magic*. In this series of short stories and essays Voelker writes about tall tales and fishing lore that range from a mysterious "dancing fly" to debunking fly anglers as the "world's greatest snobs."

But perhaps Voelker's most quotable line, at least among fly anglers, came from neither book nor legal thriller. Instead it appeared in *Anatomy of a Fisherman*, a large-format collection of photographs that was released in 1964. In his essay "Testament of a Fisherman," Voelker writes: "I fish because I love to; because I love the environs where trout are found, which are invariably beautiful, and I hate the environs where crowds of people are found, which are invariably ugly."

This is a man who clearly loved his trout. In 1991, Voelker died near his childhood home at the age of 88 but is still remembered in the Upper Peninsula as the person who traded fame for trout and bypassed Hollywood for the wild places where brookies live.

An angler cautiously wades across the Au Sable River in the Holy Water stretch at Trout Unlimited Research Station near Wakeley Bridge.

Mainstream of the Au Sable

Few places in this country are held in such high esteem that they are deemed "holy," but Michigan's Au Sable River is one of them. The 8.7 river miles of the mainstream from Burton's Landing to Wakeley Bridge, a special flies-only, no-kill stretch, is so revered by fly anglers it's called the Holy Water. Once you fish it, you'll understand why for more than a century anglers have stood in the cold, clean waters praising those above while casting a fly to the trout below.

The Au Sable is not only Michigan's most storied trout stream, it's often regarded as the best brown trout water in the Great Lakes region. And late at night, while anglers sip scotch around a campfire after a full day of fishing, it often becomes the finest trout stream east of the Rocky Mountains. Heady praise, but the fabled river lives up to it, combining healthy, stream-bred populations of trout with phenomenal insect hatches, a long history of fly fishing, and aesthetic beauty that is tough to match east or west of the Rocky Mountains. Little wonder why Trout Unlimited was founded on the banks of the Au Sable.

For the wading angler armed with a fly rod, it's hard to find better trout water than the mainstream from Burton's Landing to McMasters Bridge, a 19-mile stretch that is the focus of this chapter. This is particularly true of the Holy Water, where a moderate flow, firm gravel bottom, and relatively shallow depth make for easy wading, upstream or down. The river is also wide enough that you can cast a fly without hanging up on streamside vegetation while its hatches are so reliable you could set your watch to them.

The only drawback is that the quality fishing area is also one of the most popular places to canoe in Michigan. The number of boats can be so overwhelming from mid-June through August, particularly on the weekends, that it forces anglers to fish only in the morning or evening. Canoe traffic does drop off at every takeout the further downstream you head. Less than half of the canoes leaving the liveries in Grayling continue beyond Stephan Bridge, a four-hour paddle for most people. The few who continue beyond Wakeley Bridge are more serious paddlers who are planning to camp for the evening and generally are more respectful to anglers.

The Au Sable watershed is spread over eight counties in a 1,932-square-mile swath that stretches from its headwaters in southwest Otsego County to Lake Huron in Iosco County. More than 70 tributaries contribute to the Au Sable, with the significant ones being the East Branch, the South Branch, and the North Branch which all drain into the mainstream in Crawford County. This amazing river system is so cold and clear that it makes up 20 percent or 179 miles of the state's designated Blue Ribbon Trout Streams.

The mainstream is formed when Kolka and Bradford creeks, draining several lakes including Lake Tecon, merge three miles north of Frederic. The Au Sable begins as a small brook and for the next 12 miles flows southward through low cedar swamps and open tag-alder marsh, harboring mainly brook trout. In Grayling, the Au Sable swings eastward and just east of the town is joined by the East Branch to become a river of respectable size.

In the six river miles from the confluence of the East Branch to Burton's Landing, the bottom is predominately sand, and some parts are too deep to wade. Trout populations are low in this part of the river, and fishing pressure is light most of the season. The exception is during the Hex hatch, when giant Hexagenia limbata mayflies emerge from the abundance of silt found here attracting both large brown trout and anglers hoping to hook one.

In the Holy Water, from Burton's Landing to Wakeley Bridge, the river gradient is steeper, the flow a little faster at two to three miles per hour, and trout populations are much greater than in the upstream reaches. When no-kill regulations took effect fishing pressure declined somewhat on this section, but the Holy Water is still by far the most heavily fished stretch of the river. Despite the large numbers of anglers and paddlers, this section of the Au Sable continues to yield excellent fishing with good fly hatches throughout the season. In short, trout don't seem to mind the canoes but can still be easily fooled with a well-matched hatch.

The Au Sable from Wakeley Bridge downstream to McMasters Bridge is a nine-mile stretch of extremely variable character. It begins with fast water and gravel and clay bottom, then flows slowly through the "Stillwaters," where the bottom is mostly sand and banks are low. The South Branch enters the Au Sable in the upper part of the Stillwaters. Below the Stillwaters the river picks up speed again and flows in gravel riffles to McMasters Bridge. Fishing from boats is popular in this part of the river because of its depth and volume, although careful waders can fish some sections of it. Fishing pressure overall is relatively light compared with the flies-only reach.

Below McMasters Bridge, the Au Sable takes on a "big river" character, flowing alternately in deep sandy pools and shallow gravel riffles. Although some of the riffles can be waded, most of the fishing here is done by boat. The 79-mile Blue Ribbon designation that began on the mainstream at Country Road 612 ends at Luzerne Township Park in Oscoda County. Just downstream is Mio Dam, the first of six that slow the Au Sable with impounds. Finally, 115 miles from where the mainstream swings eastward in Grayling, the river reaches the end of its journey in Lake Huron.

Although best known as a brown-trout stream, the Au Sable also supports a substantial population of brook trout. They are especially eager to take a fly but are mostly small fish. An occasional resident rainbow can also be caught, particularly in the Stephan Bridge area.

Ironically Michigan's best known trout stream was not always a trout stream. Before 1890 grayling were the sport fish of the Au Sable system. Early

Rube Babbitt, a famed Grayling fishing guide, nets a trout in the Au Sable River in the early 1900s. (Courtesy Michigan Historic Trout Fishing Museum.)

lumbermen called the grayling "white trout" or "Crawford County trout," but in 1874 a local angler named I. W. Babbitt took several of the fish to Bay City for identification. Eventually the samples of the mysterious fish were sent out-of-state where biologists determined they were grayling. News of this prompted residents to change the name of their town from Crawford to Grayling to honor a fish that was so easy to catch in the Au Sable.

Extensive lumbering in the Au Sable watershed began in 1865 and peaked in 1890 when more than 330 million feet of logs were floated down the river that year to sawmills on Lake Huron. The last log drive held on the Au Sable was in 1910, but by then the grayling was already extinct, a victim of overfishing and the destruction of its habitat caused by the intense logging. The last Au Sable grayling was reportedly caught in 1908 by Dan Stephan just downstream from what today is Conners Flat Access Site.

The grayling may have died out, but the trout were on their way. The first to arrive in the Au Sable were rainbows, which were released in 1876. Nine years later I. W. Babbitt's son, Rube Babbit, took brook trout from the Jordan River and planted them in the East Branch of the Au Sable. The new species thrived, leading many anglers to blame the introduction of brook trout for the hurried demise of grayling. In 1891, seven years after the Pere Marquette became the first river to be planted with brown trout in North America, the Au Sable was also planted with browns from the U.S. Fish Commission Hatchery in Northville.

With fish to catch and a railroad arriving at the banks of the Au Sable

The Town of Grayling and the History of Fishing

Detroit may be Motor City and Battle Creek Cereal City but there can be little argument that Grayling is center of fly fishing in Michigan and possibly the Midwest. Not only does the Au Sable, the most famous trout stream east of the Rocky Mountains, flow through the heart of it, but Grayling has had a long and enduring history intertwined with anglers and guides devoted to catching a trout on nothing more than hooks dressed with feathers and fur.

If the hatch is off and the fishing is slow, you can spend an afternoon in Grayling taking in the sights and heritage that are fly fishing in Michigan and discovering the reason why Trout Unlimited was founded on the banks of the Au Sable. Here's where:

Crawford County Historical Museum (989-348-4461; *www. grayling-area.com/museum*; 97 Michigan Ave.) The historical complex surrounds the Grayling Depot, and in the depot itself is an intriguing first-floor exhibit of trout fishing in the Au Sable. Along with century-old bamboo rods and flies, there are displays on early Au Sable boat builders, guides, and the days when grayling, the fish, was king. Never seen a grayling? There is a mounted grayling in the museum that measures 18 inches in length. During trout season the museum is open Wednesday through Saturday from 10 a.m. to 4 p.m.

Devereaux Memorial Crawford Library (989-348-9214; 201 Plum St.) Fishing has one of the oldest and largest bibliographies in any field outside of politics, and the Grayling public library, rightfully so, features an outstanding collection of books about fly-fishing and fly-tying. The George Griffith and Marion Wright Memorial Collection was established in 2007, when Marion Wright, a Grayling resident and founder of the local Mason chapter of Trout Unlimited, died at the age of 90, and his heirs donated 22 of his fly-fishing books to the library. Most are rare first editions and signed by the authors. The following year Dr. Homer Smathers of West Bloomfield donated his collection of more than 500 fly fishing books, many signed first editions. Currently there are 400 books on display, including a copy of *Fishing with the Fly*, published in 1885, in which Charles F. Orvis gathered the wisdom of the finest anglers in nineteenth-century America. The library is open Monday through Thursday 9 a.m. to 7 p.m., Friday until 6 p.m., and Saturday until 2 p.m.

Grayling Fish Hatchery (989-348-7386; *www.hansonhills.org*; 4890 North Down River Rd.) In 1916, Rasmus Hanson, a leading lumberman in Grayling, organized the Grayling Fish Hatchery Club in an effort to save the grayling. They didn't succeed, but they went on to use the hatchery to stock the Au Sable with brown and brook trout. The state took over the hatchery in 1926 and operated it until the late 1960s. Eventually the hatchery became a Grayling public park in which its 11 ponds and raceways are still used to raise some 45,000 trout a year, ranging in size

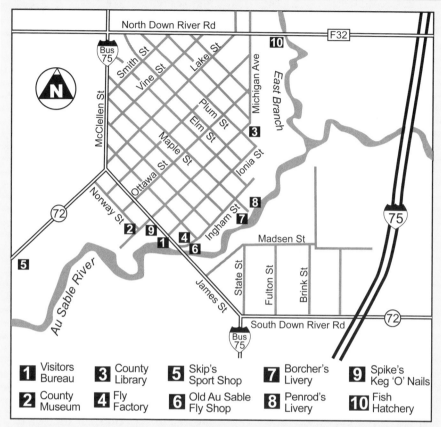

1	Visitors Bureau	**3**	County Library	**5**	Skip's Sport Shop	**7**	Borcher's Livery	**9**	Spike's Keg 'O' Nails
2	County Museum	**4**	Fly Factory	**6**	Old Au Sable Fly Shop	**8**	Penrod's Livery	**10**	Fish Hatchery

from fingerlings to fish more than 16 inches long. Needless to say, the hatchery is a great family attraction. Hours are noon to 6 p.m. Memorial Day through Labor Day.

Chief David Shoppenagon Historical Marker (200 Ingham St.) This marker on the doorstep of the Old Au Sable Fly Shop marks where David Shoppenagon, a Chippewa chief who moved to Grayling from the Saginaw Bay area, built his house on the banks of the Au Sable in 1876. The chief went on to become one of the most famous fishing guides in Grayling, hiring out to lumber buyers and other visitors in the late 1800s and early 1900s. The chief died on Christmas Day, 1911, and was believed to be 103 years old at the time.

The Fly Factory (989-348-5844; *www.troutbums.com*; 205 Ingham St.) This is Michigan's oldest fly shop, established in 1876, just 20 years after C.F. Orvis Company of Manchester, Vermont, was founded. Since then the shop has had five different locations but has never been more than 50 yards from the Au Sable River.

Grayling Canoe Liveries: There are half a dozen canoe liveries in

The Town of Grayling and the History of Fishing

the area that service the Au Sable River, but two have been anchored to the banks of this storied stream for more than 60 years. Almost side-by-side in the heart of Grayling are Borchers Canoeing and Bed and Breakfast (989-348-4921; *www.canoeborchers.com*; 101 Maple St.) and Penrod's Au Sable River Resort (989-348-2910; *www.penrodscanoe.com*; 100 Maple St.). Borchers was founded in 1932 by Ernie Borcher, a famous Au Sable fly tyer who created the Borchers Special pattern, a fly that is still a popular choice during the brown drake hatch. In 1939, the Penrod family established a resort across the street by building 14 log cabins that overlook the Au Sable. Today both resorts offer accommodations, canoe rentals and vehicle drop-off service for anglers.

Spike's Keg 'O' Nails (989-348-7113; 301 N. James St.) Okay, so maybe this longtime Grayling tavern has nothing directly to do with fly fishing, but the fact remains that a lot of anglers stop by to enjoy a juicy burger and a cold beer after a day on the Au Sable. Harold "Spike" MacNeven opened the tavern the day after prohibition ended on May 29, 1933, and among the restaurant's patrons was his friend, boxer Jack Dempsey. During the 1950s members of the Detroit Red Wings would stop for a bite to eat on their way north to Sault Ste. Marie for training camp.

in 1873, Grayling prospered as an angler's paradise and soon was home to a lengthy list of legendary guides, boat builders and fly tiers. Babbitt, who arrived as surveyor for the railroads, opened a fishing camp on the Au Sable where his son, Rube, hired out as a guide. He often worked with David Shoppenagon, a Chippewa chief who arrived in the early 1870s from the Saginaw River Valley. In 1876 Shoppenagon built a home on the banks of the Au Sable, where today the I-75 Business Loop crosses, and then went on to become a canoe and paddle maker as well as one of Grayling's best-known river guides in the late 1800s and early 1900s.

Many others contributed to Grayling's rich history in fly fishing. Arthur E. Wakeley perfected the Au Sable riverboat in the late 1800s by making it 24-feet long so the angler at the front had more room to cast. Noted fly tiers include guide Ernie Borcher and Clarence Roberts, a conservation officer assigned to Grayling in the 1940s. Their patterns, particularly Borcher's Special and Robert's Yellow Drake, are still sold in shops today and used on the river. In 1959, George Griffin, a member of the Michigan Conservation Commission, pitched the idea of a national organization, based on Ducks Unlimited, to a dozen other anglers at his cottage on the banks of the Au Sable. From that night on the concept and chapters of Trout Unlimited spread rapidly across the country.

By the 1960s, the Holy Water was already flies-only when extensive research showed that, despite the special regulation, this reach held few large trout. To correct that, a 12-inch minimum size was placed on the

Grayling lumberman Rasmus Hanson poses with a stringer of trout taken from the Au Sable River in the 1920s. (Courtesy Michigan Historic Trout Fishing Museum.)

section in 1973. Six years later it was changed in favor of a "slotted-size limit," where anglers could only keep trout between eight and 12 inches and over 16 inches. By the 1980s, a movement was under way to designate the Holy Water as a year-round, flies-only, no-kill fishery. It was a controversial proposal at the time that heatedly divided anglers as well as locals, but it finally was passed and put into effect in 1989.

Other than the Holy Water, upstream from Burton's Landing and downstream from Wakeley Bridge, the mainstream is open during the regular trout season from the last Saturday in April through September. Fishing is open to all tackle, and the daily harvest is five fish, with no more than three of them being 15 inches or larger. The minimum size is ten inches for brookies and 12 inches for rainbows and browns.

The Au Sable is excellent trout habitat because it features the most stable flow of any stream in the country. The sand and gravel deposited by the last glacial retreat allow precipitation to soak into the soil. This results in numerous springs feeding the mainstream a constant flow of cold, clear, and clean water not subject to large changes in stage or velocity. In an average year, river levels range only a foot higher at high water than at normal low flow. An unusually great snowmelt or heavy rains can bring this up a bit, but overall the Au Sable is a remarkably steady stream.

In turn, trout thrive in cool summer water temperatures and in the upper river find ample gravel beds for spawning. Water temperatures sometimes go higher than 75 degrees F in the sandy area below Grayling, but the water rarely gets that warm in the flies-only, no-kill section. Brook trout, the least tolerant of warm water, seem to thrive in this section of the river as well as browns. According to DNR population studies at Stephan Bridge, the Holy Water stretch shows a long-term average of more than a hundred pounds of trout per acre or double that of most trout streams elsewhere in the state.

Then there are those prolific and diverse fly hatches, the Au Sable's best-known feature. Hatches begin occurring in late March when the days begin to warm and the snows begin to melt after the long Northern Michigan winter. Black stoneflies are usually the first to appear, followed with much anticipation among fly anglers by the Hendricksons. In rapid succession, little black caddis and mahogany and sulphur mayflies also appear in May through early June.

In June and July there are exceptional hatches of brown drakes, Isonychia (white-gloved howdies), the tiny but prolific tricos, and, in the sandy, silty areas found outside of the Holy Water, the Hex hatch.

Accommodations

Accommodations for the Au Sable begin in Grayling and are scattered east along the legendary river. They range from motels and bed and breakfasts in town to historic fishing lodges and rustic campgrounds overlooking the Holy Water. The closer you are to the river, the more likely you'll need reservations for any weekends from opening day in April through June. An extensive list of area accommodations is available from the Grayling Visitors Bureau (800-937-8837; *www.grayling-mi.org*).

Within Grayling, motels line the I-75 Business Loop and include national chains as well as *Fay's Motel* (989-348-7031, 800-257-3010; *www.faysmotel.com*; 78 N. I-75 Business Loop) with rooms and cottages featuring kitchenettes. Nearby is *River Country Motor Lodge* (989-348-8619, 800-733-7396; *www.rivercountrymotorlodge.net*; 257 N. I-75 Business Loop) with rooms that feature microwaves and mini-refrigerators.

Overlooking the Au Sable within town are a pair of longtime resorts that double as canoe liveries. *Penrod's* (989-348-2910, 888-467-4837; *www.penrodscanoe.com*; 100 Maple St.) has 14 classic log cabins with all but one lining the river. Across the street, *Borchers Bed and Breakfast* (989-348-4921, 800-762-8756; *www.canoeborchers.com*; 101 Maple St.) features six rooms and a wrap-around porch overlooking the Au Sable.

There are also a number of lodges lining the Au Sable downstream. The best known is *Gates Au Sable Lodge* (989-348-8462; *www.gateslodge.com*; 471 Stephan Bridge Rd.) with a 16-room motel and small restaurant on the banks at Stephan Bridge in the middle of the Holy Water. Also in the quality fishing area is *Rayburn Lodge* (989-348-7482; *www.rayburnlodgebnb.com*; 1491 Richardson Rd.). This magnificent log lodge offers five rooms on the north bank opposite Louie's Landing Access Site. On the north bank of the river at Wakeley Bridge is *Jim's Cabin Rentals* (989-348-3203; 1706 Wakeley Bridge Rd.) with a pair of cozy cabins and a canoe livery while at

The Au Sable Riverboat

Construction of a railroad to Grayling in 1873, and the subsequent "discovery" of grayling as an easy-to-catch sportfish, led to the development of a world-renowned, recreational fishery on the Au Sable River. The fishing attracted anglers from Cleveland, Cincinnati, Indianapolis and Chicago as well as from overseas and the sudden demand resulted in river guides refining the Au Sable riverboat to float their clients.

The long, narrow boats first began appearing in the mid-1870s but it's debatable who was responsible for the unusual design. One theory holds that it was the result of Native Americans, such as guide Chief David Shoppenagon, making modifications to their dugout canoes to accommodate clients. Others believed logging companies developed the flat-bottom craft in order to move tools and other equipment to camps along the Au Sable.

What isn't debated is that the boat is unique to the Grayling area, a stable craft designed to accommodate the fickle currents, abrupt curves and sand-gravel bottom of the Au Sable. Most riverboats were 24 feet long and usually built out of white pine or cedar planks. Although they were only two-and-a-half feet wide, they weighed 300 to 400 pounds and lacked a keel so they could be pushed through the river by a guide with a long pole from the stern. The shallow draft and low walls allowed the boat to ride high in the water. An old chair with the legs cut off was placed at the bow so an angler could see trout rising and easily cast toward the rings. Under the chair was a live well for his fish.

One of Grayling's best known boat builders was Arthur Wakeley, whose father arrived in 1879 and claimed a homestead at what is today Wakeley Bridge. Wakeley played a key role in the design of the riverboat by making it longer. He used a blacksmith's forge to make his own tools and fittings for his boats, including copper nose covers to protect the bow from hidden boulders, logs and sand bars.

The Au Sable riverboat is still a common sight on the river today. You can also see one of Wakeley's boats, built in 1918, in the Crawford County Historical Museum. Or you can even buy one. The Old Au Sable Boat Company (989-348-0120; *www.ausableboats.com*) builds 24-foot-long riverboats ranging in price from $5,995 to $8,495.

McMasters Bridge is **Wyandotte Lodge** (989-348-8354; *wyandottelodging. com*; 1320 S. McMasters Bridge Rd.) with rooms and cabins.

Campgrounds: There are five rustic state forest campgrounds on the river between Grayling and McMasters Bridge. Two of the most popular ones are on the flies-only, no-kill section of the river. Burton's Landing is three miles east of Grayling via M-72 (South Down River Road) and has 12 sites just off the river. Keystone's Landing four miles east of Grayling via M-72 is a gem. The campground has 18 wooded sites situated on a bluff above the

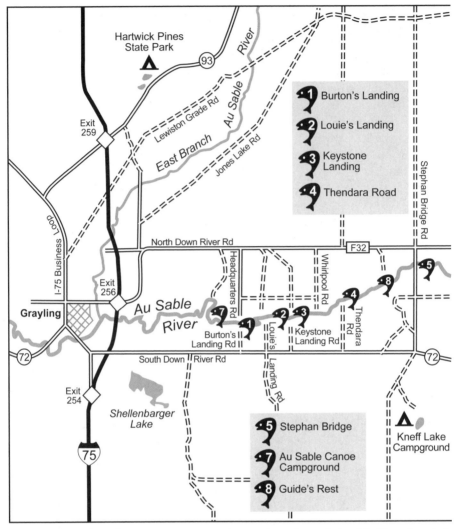

Au Sable. In the afternoon you can sit on the edge of the bluff and watch trout rise to a hatch.

The other three campgrounds are reached by North Down River Road (County Road F-32). Au Sable River Canoe Campground is 4.1 miles from the I-75 Business Loop in Grayling and has eight sites accessible by vehicles and additional walk-in sites for canoers. White Pine Canoe Campground is east of Wakeley Bridge (see access description below for directions) and has walk-in sites, drinking water, and vault toilets outside of the flies-only, no-kill section of the river. Also on the north banks between Wakeley Bridge and McMasters Bridge is Rainbow Bend Campground (see access description below for directions) with seven drive-in sites.

The nearest state park and one of the nicest in the Lower Peninsula is Hartwick Pines (989-348-7068) off M-93, three miles north of Grayling. The state park has a hundred-site campground with hook-ups for trailers.

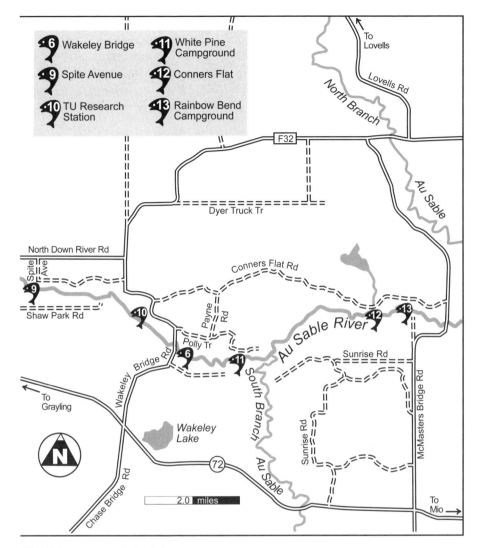

6 Wakeley Bridge	11 White Pine Campground
9 Spite Avenue	12 Conners Flat
10 TU Research Station	13 Rainbow Bend Campground

To Lovells

Lovells Rd

North Branch

Au Sable

F32

Dyer Truck Tr

North Down River Rd

Spite Ave

9

Shaw Park Rd

10

Conners Flat Rd

12 13

Payne Rd

Au Sable River

Polly Tr

6 11

Sunrise Rd

Wakeley Bridge Rd

South Branch

Sunrise Rd

McMasters Bridge Rd

To Grayling

N

Wakeley Lake

Chase Bridge Rd

72

Au Sable

Au Sable

2.0 miles

To Mio →

Fly Shops and Guides

As might be expected, there is no shortage of places to purchase a handful of flies or anything else for the Au Sable. Most shops in the area also maintain a hatch board that is updated daily. In Grayling, at the I-75 Business Loop Au Sable River Bridge and across the road from each other, are *The Fly Factory* (989-348-5844; *www.troutbums.com*; 205 Ingham St.) and *Old Au Sable Fly Shop* (989-348-3330; *www.oldausable.com*; 200 Ingham St.). The Fly Factory is Michigan's oldest fly shop, dating back to 1876 and only 20 years younger than C. F. Orvis of Manchester, Vermont. Just west of town is *Skip's Sport Shop* (989-348-7111; 5765 W. M-72) catering to everybody from fly anglers to deer hunters. At Stephan Bridge, *Gates Au Sable Lodge* (989-348-8462; *www.gateslodge.com*) has one of the best fly shops in the area.

Gates, the Fly Factory, and the Old Au Sable Fly Shop all arrange guided fly trips on the Au Sable, either by wading or in an Au Sable riverboat. *Jim's Cabin Rentals* (989-348-3203) also offers guide service, as does *Old Au Sable Boat Company* (989-348-0120; *www.ausableboats.com*) in the traditional riverboats. Other fly fishing guides working the Au Sable include Bob Ankney of *Up North Anglers* (989-745-1908; *upnorthanglers.com*) and Dave Wyss of *Guilt-Trip Charters* (989-348-3203; *www.guilttrip.com*).

Maps of the Au Sable

Straddling I-75, Grayling is the staging area for anglers fishing the famed Holy Water of the upper Au Sable. Two roads, South Down River Road and North Down River Road, extend east from the town and lead to all the access sites described in this chapter. Thus the 13 sites have been divided between South Down River Road for those on the south bank and North Down River Road for those on the north bank.

The main road for anglers is South Down River Road, which departs from the I-75 Business Loop on the south side of Grayling as M-72 and provides access to six sites, including the popular ones at Keystone Landing and Stephan Bridge. North of downtown Grayling and just before Elmwood Cemetery, North Down River Road (also labeled County Road F-32) departs east from the I-75 Business Loop, crosses the East Branch of the Au Sable, and then crosses I-75 on an overpass. North Down River Road then swings north before resuming east to provide access to the other seven access sites.

Several of the north bank access sites, Trout Unlimited Research Station, White Pine Canoe Campground, Conners Flat, and Rainbow Bend Campground, are just as easily and probably more quickly reached from South Down River Road.

South Down River Road

Burton's Landing

GPS N 44° 39.774'
W 84° 38.805'

The flies-only, no-kill section of the Au Sable, the Holy Water, begins at Burton's Landing. The state forest campground is reached from South Down River Road that departs from the I-75 Business Loop in Grayling to the east as M-72. Within three miles turn north (left) on Burton's Landing Road. The posted entrance to this 12-site campground is reached in 0.4 mile, and nearby is a pair of canoe launches. The popularity of this place among paddlers is clearly evident; the second launch site is capable of holding 50 vehicles.

Fly anglers also love Burton's Landing as it marks the start of the Au Sable's special regulations, and the campground provides easy access to the river. On the weekends in mid-May and June this campground can get filled at times but in general is not as popular with anglers as Keystone Landing,

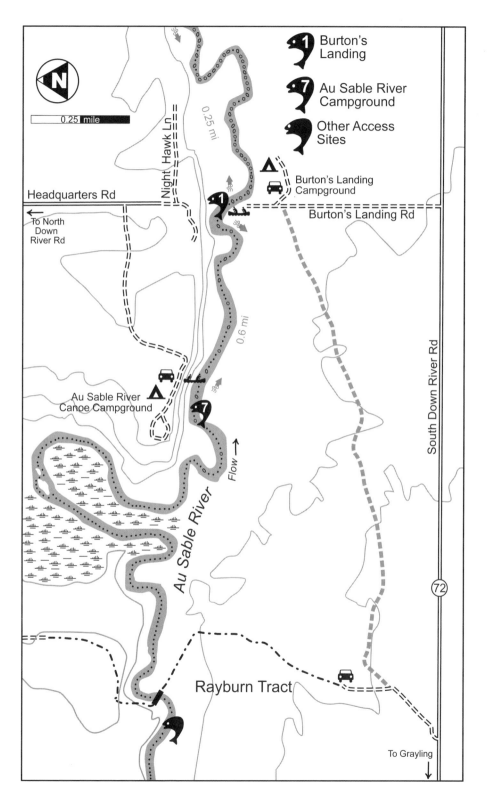

Burton's
Landing

Au Sable River
Campground

Other Access
Sites

0.25 mile

Headquarters Rd

Night Hawk Ln

0.25 mi

0.6 mi

Burton's Landing
Campground

Burton's Landing Rd

← To North
Down
River Rd

Au Sable River
Canoe Campground

Au Sable River

Flow →

South Down River Rd

Rayburn Tract

72

To Grayling

A fly angler casts towards shore while his guide uses a pole to control their Au Sable riverboat near Keystone Landing in the Holy Water.

the next state forest campground downstream.

The river is 80 to 90 feet wide here and two to four feet deep, with some deeper holes. Bottom is mostly gravel going downstream from the landing where you will encounter classic riffle-pool waters and an abundance of log jams, drowned logs along the banks and deep pools, all of them holding trout. Upstream standard trout regulations apply, and the bottom is considerably more sandy. Velocity is moderate. Wading is easy at normal flows, and there is plenty of room for fly casting. The riverbank on the south side is generally less than five feet high. On the north side the bank is generally higher and sandier. Coniferous trees, brush, and some hardwoods line the banks.

The north bank upstream from the landing all the way to the canoe camp is state land, and the south bank is state land from the landing downstream a quarter of a mile. The rest of the river frontage is all private land. It's a 0.8-mile wade to Louie's Landing, the next public access site on the flies only, no-kill waters, a section that most anglers need an entire afternoon to fish.

 **Louie's Landing**

GPS N 44° 39.925'
W 84° 38.252'

Map: page 68

This road ending provides access to the water only and does not have facilities to launch a canoe or even much space to park a vehicle. From Burton's Landing, continue east on South Down River Road (M-72) for half a mile and then turn north (left) on Louie's Landing Road. The gravel road ends in a half mile at the river, where along the shoulders there is parking for four or maybe five vehicles.

Private property surrounds both sides of the Au Sable here, upstream and down. To fish this part of the river without trespassing on private property, most anglers wade upstream, either at the start or the finish of their outing. Upstream wading is not too difficult, as the velocity of flow is moderate, and the river is usually only two to three feet deep. There are a few deep holes and some of them will overtop your waders, but these can easily be avoided. Bottom is mostly gravel, with some sand. Trout cover in the form of drowned logs, submerged stumps, and fallen trees is abundant and the highest concentration of brook trout in the Upper Au Sable is found in these waters between Louie's Landing and Thendara Road.

The river is 90 to 100 feet wide, and the banks on the south side are five to ten feet high. On the north side they are more than 20 feet high in places, low and swampy in others. Pine, spruce, and cedar trees line the lower banks; upland pine and aspen top the higher banks. Just upstream from the access site is a private foot bridge across the river.

3 Keystone Landing

GPS N 44° 39.882'
     W 84° 37.632'

Map: page 68

Prior to 1975, this was a public access site called Highbanks, where camping was permitted. Strong friendships were forged among the camping anglers in those early years and no doubt led to Keystone Landing becoming an official state forest campground. The campground is reached from South Down River Road (M-72), a half mile east of Burton's Landing or four miles from the I-75 Business Loop in Grayling.

Turn north (left) on Keystone Landing Road to reach the campground entrance in half a mile. Keystone Landing has 18 rustic sites set well back from the river and day-use parking in the campground as well as limited parking at the canoe launch.

This is superb water, with good fly hatches, especially the early hatches of May: Hendrickson, blue-winged olive and black caddis. This leads to an excellent trout population—all stream-bred trout with brookies more abundant here than other parts of the river. Add the special quality fishing regulations and it's easy to understand the popularity of this reach.

The river is about 100 feet wide and two to four feet deep, with some deeper holes. One of these deeper holes is called the "Whirlpool," located, appropriately enough, at the south end of Whirlpool Road, 0.7 mile downstream from Keystone Landing. If you approach too close to this hole from the upstream side the shifting sands will undermine your footing and you will get a dunking. Many anglers have had to swim for it in the Whirlpool.

The river bottom is mostly gravel with some sand. Stream velocity is moderate, and wading is fairly easy if you keep an eye out for the occasional

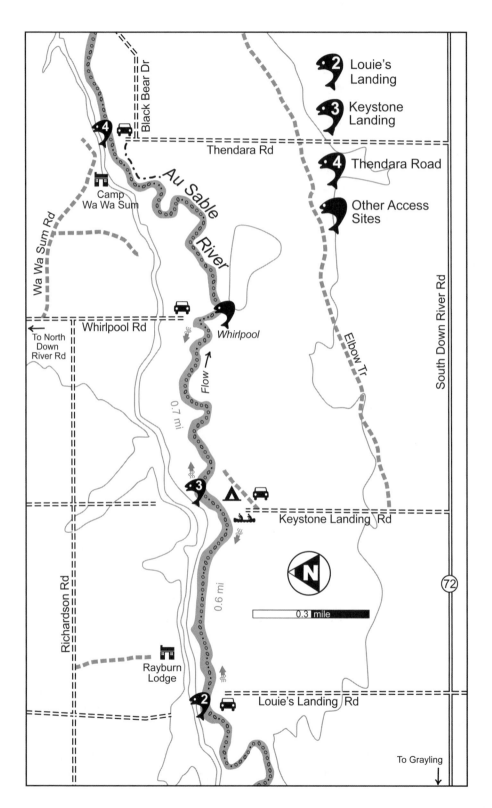

Louie's Landing
2

Keystone Landing
3

Thendara Road
4

Other Access Sites

Black Bear Dr

4

Camp Wa Wa Sum

Wa Wa Sum Rd

Au Sable River

Thendara Rd

South Down River Rd

Elbow Tr

Whirlpool Rd

To North Down River Rd

Whirlpool

Flow

0.7 mi

Richardson Rd

3

Keystone Landing Rd

N

0.3 mile

0.6 mi

Rayburn Lodge

2

Louie's Landing Rd

72

To Grayling

deep holes. However, the night fisherman should watch out for boulders and some log rafts anchored in the stream to serve as trout cover. Other cover is provided by drowned logs and snags along both banks.

Keystone Landing picked up its original name from the predominately high south bank. The north bank is generally low, and, in places, swampy. Except for the grassy areas fronting some of the streamside cabins, the banks are lined with cedar, pine, aspen, oak, and some brush. Two stairways at the campground allow easy access to the river.

This is one of the most heavily fished areas of the river, yet it continues to yield good fishing, year after year. Fishing early and late during the summer allows you to avoid most of the canoe traffic, which can be especially heavy on weekends. But keep in mind that in May and early June most of the good hatches are in the afternoon and you will have no choice but to simply endure the canoes that float through.

The south bank from Keystone Landing downstream to the Whirlpool is all state land. The north bank is all private.

4 Thendara Road

GPS N 44° 40.174'
W 84° 36.402'

This is another road end on the south side that allows anglers to access the Au Sable's flies only, no-kill waters. Continue east on South Down River Road (M-72), a mile past Keystone Landing or five miles from the I-75 Business Loop in Grayling, and then turn north (left) on Thendara Road. You reach the road end in 0.8 mile where there is parking along the shoulders for 10 vehicles.

Upstream, the river is 90 to 100 feet wide and two to four feet deep, with some holes six feet deep. Bottom is gravel and sand. A path leads 200 yards upstream, allowing you to avoid a few deeper hole before entering river. Good trout cover is provided by logjams, snags, and stumps, and by the depth of water itself. Not that far upstream is the impressive log lodge of Camp Wa Wa Sum, a historic fishing camp on the north bank. Once above it you will see few cabins or homes on the river in an area known to harbor large brown trout.

Downstream, the river is 100 to 120 feet wide and one to three feet deep, with a few holes that will cause problems. With the shallower depth, wading is easier downstream than up, but more cabins and homes line the river here, and trout cover is not nearly as plentiful. Bottom is sand and gravel. A little more than half a mile downstream from Thendara Road is a deep hole on the outside of a sharp bend that usually holds some large trout.

There is a high sandy bank on the north side of the river opposite the end of the road and some high banks on both sides of the river upstream. Downstream, the banks are generally low and swampy.

5 *Stephan Bridge*

GPS N 44° 40.737'
W 84° 34.403'

In the love and passion that the Au Sable invokes, Stephan Bridge is the heart of it. Located in the middle of the Holy Water, the public access site near the bridge is not only a cornerstone for fly anglers, it is also a popular take-out landing for rented canoes. It should be no surprise that located at the bridge is Gates Au Sable Lodge, one of Michigan's classic fly fishing lodges (see page 34).

The bridge is reached by turning north on Stephan Bridge Road from South Down River Road (M-72), 1.4 miles east of Thendara Road or 6.4 miles from the I-75 Business Loop in Grayling. Within 1.5 miles, or just south of Gates Au Sable Lodge, turn east (right) on a dirt road posted with a DNR canoe launch sign to quickly reach the access site.

This large access site is on the south bank of the river a few hundred feet downstream of the bridge. On summer weekends it is often overrun by canoers, kayakers, and tubers putting in their various crafts. It's best to park away from the river to avoid the cars and trailers whipping through to haul boats back to the liveries. The site is equipped with outdoor toilets.

If you can avoid the weekend rush of paddlers, or the aluminum hatch as locals call them, this reach of the Au Sable is beautiful water. The river is 100 to 120 feet wide here and two to three feet deep, composed of long, swift, shallow riffles with an occasional deeper hole both upstream and down. Bottom is mostly gravel with some sand and the velocity is moderate. Wading is easy, and there is plenty of room to cast a fly. Banks are mostly low on both sides of the river and are wooded with cedar, spruce, and pine. Drowned logs and snags give trout cover, generally better along the north bank than the south.

Stephan Bridge has some of the highest percentages of resident rainbows among all trout in the upper Au Sable. DNR surveys in the past have shown that as much as 25 to 35 percent of the trout population are rainbows with the rest browns and a few brookies. The excellent fly hatches, particularly Hendrickson and sulphurs in May, good trout populations, and easy wading make this reach a favorite of the fly anglers. Although it is usually heavily fished, other anglers can be avoided by wading upstream or down away from the landing and Gates Au Sable Lodge.

Downstream the Au Sable steadily increases until its volume is almost doubled by the time it flows under Wakeley Bridge at the east end of the Holy Water reach. It is possible to fish downstream to the Spite Avenue access site, a wade of roughly a mile. Except for the public access site, the riverbanks on both sides are all private land.

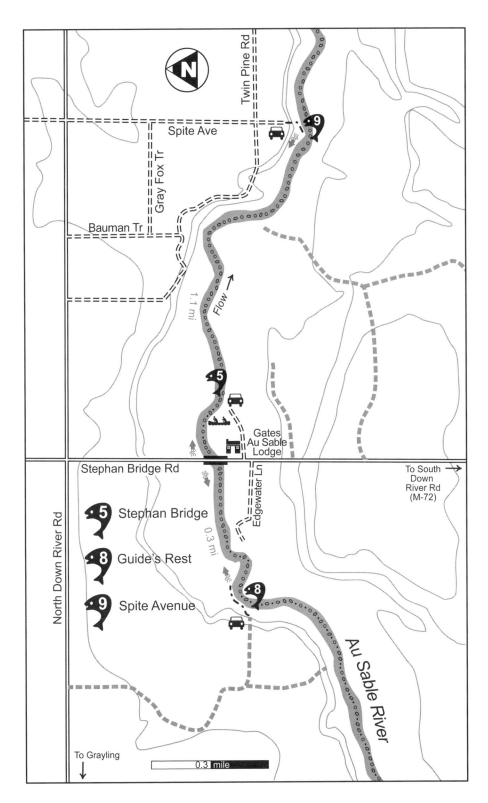

N

Twin Pine Rd

Spite Ave

Gray Fox Tr

Bauman Tr

1.1 mi

Flow →

Gates
Au Sable
Lodge

Stephan Bridge Rd

To South
Down
River Rd
(M-72)

North Down River Rd

Edgewater Ln

0.3 mi

5 Stephan Bridge

8 Guide's Rest

9 Spite Avenue

Au Sable River

To Grayling

0.3 mile

6 Wakeley Bridge

GPS N 44° 39.537'
W 84° 30.317'

Map: page 75

Just downstream from Wakeley Bridge, this public access site is less popular with wading anglers than other sites upstream. The fast current and slippery clay bottom in places make wading extremely difficult. Cleated soles and a wading staff help, but caution still has to be used.

Wakeley Bridge Road is 9.2 miles from the I-75 Business Loop via South Down River Road (M-72), or 2.8 miles east of Stephan Bridge Road. Turn north (left) for the bridge and within two miles, or 150 yards before crossing the river, turn east (right) on Heritage Road, which is posted with a DNR canoe launch sign. Heritage Road leads to both the canoe launch and a separate parking area. The launch is the site that Thomas Wakeley, the father of famed boat builder Arthur Wakeley, selected for his homestead in 1879.

From the parking area, a path leads a hundred yards north to the river. The Au Sable is relatively narrow here—60 to 90 feet wide—and two to four feet deep, with some holes that might flood your waders. Bottom is mostly gravel and hard, slippery clay. The banks are low, forested with hardwood, conifer, and some brush. Trout cover is sparse. Downstream the bottom gets sandier as you approach the Stillwaters stretch of the Au Sable. Except for the public access site, this is all private property.

Downstream from Wakeley Bridge the river is under standard regulations and open to bait, spinning lures, or flies. Upstream from the bridge special regulations of flies-only, no-kill are in effect.

North Down River Road

7 Au Sable River Canoe Campground

GPS N 44° 39.928'
W 84° 39.288'

Map: page 65

This state forest campground is more popular with canoeists than fly anglers as it lies outside the flies-only, no-kill stretch of the Au Sable. From the I-75 Business Loop head north of downtown Grayling and just before Elmwood Cemetery turn east (right) on North Down River Road (County Road F-32). Follow North Down River Road as it crosses I-75 on an overpass and then swings north before resuming east. Within 4.1 miles from the I-75 Business Loop turn south (right) on Headquarters Road, a paved road with a directional sign for the state forest campground. Headquarters Road ends at the entrance of the campground, 1.2 miles from North Down River Road.

Au Sable River Canoe Campground has eight sites accessible by vehicles but additional walk-in sites for canoers. A long stairway leads down to the water while trails skirt the bluff above the river.

The Au Sable is about 80 to 90 feet wide here and three to six feet deep.

The bottom is sand, with scattered patches of gravel. Silt and muck deposits, sometimes called "loonsilt," are common along the banks. The riverbanks are alternately low and swampy and high and sandy near the campground. The low banks are lined with brush and swamp conifers, the high banks with upland pine and aspen. The river can be waded with caution at normal stages. The river flow is slow to moderate, so you can wade upstream without too much trouble, as long as you keep to the shallower parts. There is plenty of room to cast a fly without hanging up on streamside vegetation.

Just two miles upstream the Au Sable flows through the vast Shellenbarger Marsh, or, as locals refer to it, "the Swamp," a reach of the river that is usually too warm to hold trout. The mainstream begins to cool when it reaches the campground, but still the fishing is only mediocre. The exception is when the Hexagenia limbata hatch occurs in late June and then this part of the river yields some very large trout.

8 Guide's Rest

GPS N 44° 40.556'
W 84° 35.403'

Map: page 71

Trout Unlimited owns two tracts on the flies only, no-kill stretch of the Au Sable that serve as popular access sites for anglers. Best known is Guide's Rest, reached from the I-75 Business Loop (McClellen Street) in Grayling by heading east on North Down River Road (County Road F-32) for 6.8 miles. Turn south (right) onto a two-track that can be very sandy at times and is marked along North Down River Road by a large "Welcome to Guide's Rest" memorial sign. Veer left at the fork in the two-track to reach a parking area 0.7 mile from North Down River Road.

There is easily space for half a dozen vehicles in the parking area and a foot path to the Au Sable. The walk in is only 100 yards and ends near a memorial to Jim Wakeley and a picnic table, the perfect place to relax while waiting for the next hatch. The Au Sable is 70 to 80 feet wide here and two to three feet deep. The bottom is gravel with an occasional boulder breaking up the current. There is a lot of submerged roots and sunkened logs to provide trout and make this stretch a great place to cast for trout. Some anglers fish down to Stephan Bridge, a wade of half a mile.

9 Spite Avenue

GPS N 44° 40.623'
W 84° 33.725'

Map: page 71

This access site on the north side of the river is the result of volunteer work by Trout Unlimited members who built a mammoth stairway to the river in 1986 and then reinforced the banks. From the I-75 Business Loop (McClellen Street) in Grayling head east on North Down River Road (County Road F-32). Within 8.3 miles, or 0.8 mile east of the intersection with Stephan Bridge Road, turn south (right) on Spite Avenue. Within half a mile, where Spite

Avenue swings sharply east to become Twin Pine Road, is a posted parking area capable of holding half a dozen vehicles.

The stairway leading to the water is so long there's a bench halfway down, no doubt for anglers climbing up after a long day on the river. The Au Sable at the bottom of the stairs is 50 to 60 feet wide and two to three feet deep, ideal for both casting and wading. The bottom is a mix of gravel and sand and there is ample trout cover. This is flies-only, no-kill water and upstream and downstream the river flows past private property and cabins.

•10 Trout Unlimited Research Station
GPS N 44° 40.166'
W 84° 31.053'

This spot on the flies-only, no-kill stretch of the Holy Water is another parcel owned by Trout Unlimited and maintained as a public access. Most fly anglers prefer it over the nearby Wakeley Bridge launch.

The TU Research Station is reached from Wakeley Bridge Road, which departs south from North Down River Road ten miles east of the I-75 Business Loop. You can also pick it up from South Down River Road (M-72) 9.2 miles from I-75 Business Loop in Grayling. From Wakeley Bridge, head north a mile and then turn west (left) on a two-track marked with a small, easy-to-miss post that says "T.U. Access." If you reach Conners Flat Road, you've gone too far. The two-track is rough but can be followed by most vehicles and within a quarter mile reaches a parking area for four to five vehicles.

From the parking area a 200-yard trail provides access to the water, passing a plaque dedicated to Art Neumann, one of the original founders of Trout Unlimited, and a picnic table at the beginning. You then steeply descend to the river at the end. The river is 60 to 80 feet wide here and two to four feet deep. A slow to moderate current swirls past lots of submerged logs and other cover for trout, and a grassy islet that splits the river into two channels. Just upstream you wade past Thunderbird Lodge, while Wakeley Bridge lies more than a mile downstream.

This is not only a productive place to cast a fly but also a beautiful spot whether you're an angler or not. Near the parking area a short trail posted "River Overlook" climbs to a bench on a high bluff where you can take in the Au Sable below and anybody fishing this reach.

•11 White Pine Canoe Campground
GPS N 44° 39.413'
W 84° 28.508'

You technically can't drive to White Pine because the state forest campground is designed for canoers. But you can park nearby and walk to it where you'll no doubt encounter a lot more paddlers during the summer than anglers. White Pine is downstream of the Au Sable's flies-only, no-kill regulations and attracts anglers using bait or spinning lures.

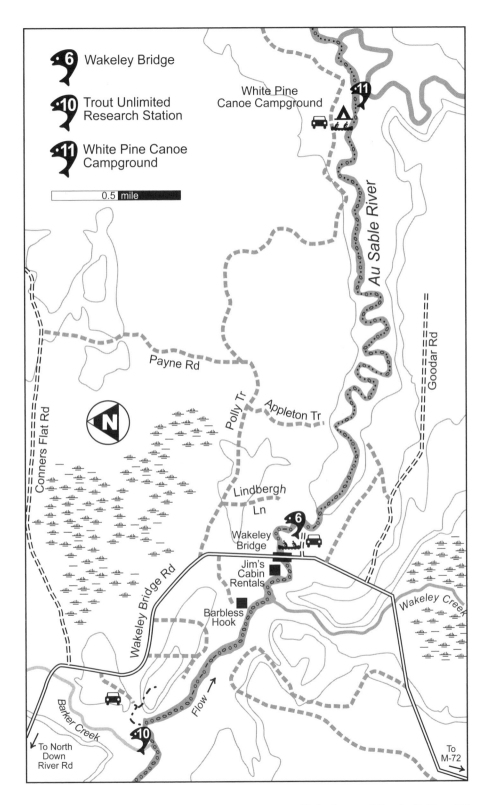

6 Wakeley Bridge

10 Trout Unlimited Research Station

11 White Pine Canoe Campground

0.5 mile

White Pine Canoe Campground

11

Au Sable River

Payne Rd

Polly Tr

Appleton Tr

Conners Flat Rd

Goodar Rd

N

Lindbergh Ln

Wakeley Bridge

6

Jim's Cabin Rentals

Barbless Hook

Wakeley Bridge Rd

Wakeley Creek

Flow

Barker Creek

10

To North Down River Rd

To M-72

The easiest way to reach White Pine is from Wakeley Bridge Road. Just 0.3 mile north of Wakeley Bridge, turn east (right) on Polly Trail, a two-track that is signposted. Ignore Lindbergh Lane and Appleton Trail, private roads that head south to riverside cabins, and continue east on Polly Trail. Within 0.8 miles you arrive at an intersection where Payne Road swings sharply north, while Polly Trail veers off to the east (right). Continue on Polly Trail as it winds east then south before reaching a large yellow gate in 1.2 miles from Payne Road.

The locked gate is a service entrance for the campground, and there is parking for two or three vehicles near it. White Pine is an open grassy area bordering the Au Sable with vault toilets, picnic tables, and drinking water. It's a short walk through the campground to the river, where you can access the water via stairways and footpaths along the banks.

This is the beginning of the stretch of the Au Sable known as the Stillwaters, which extends four miles downstream to Conners Flat. Here the river becomes wide, 120 to 150 feet, and flat with a flow that is slow to moderate. The bottom is sand, soft mud, and some gravel and boulders. Much of the river here is too deep for easy wading, and caution must be used at all times but particularly for anglers fishing at night. The left bank (north) is five to eight feet high at the campground, forested with scattered pine and oak and some brush. The south bank is generally lower. Trout cover is sparse in this part of the river, but the sand and soft mud along the bottom here and all through the Stillwaters produce excellent Hexagenia limbata hatches in late June or early July.

12 Conners Flat

GPS N 44° 40.288'
W 84° 26.294'

This public access site is on the east edge of the Au Sable's Stillwaters. From M-72 (South Down River Road), 6.2 miles east of Wakeley Bridge Road, turn north (left) on McMasters Bridge Road (F-97) and then west (left) on Conners Flat Road 0.4 mile after crossing the Au Sable. Follow the winding dirt road for 2.2 miles to an intersection posted with a "Conners Flat" access sign. This dirt road heads south for 0.2 mile to the access site, a beautiful spot overlooking a bend in the river. From the parking area a stairway descends to a rough boat launch on the river.

Located 2.2 miles downstream from the confluence of the South Branch and the mainstream, this is the beginning of what is often referred to as the Au Sable's "big water." The river is 100 to 120 feet wide here. You can wade with caution along the banks in places, but mid-channel will cause problems during normal and even low water levels. The bottom is sand, gravel, and silt, with a few boulders. The flow is slow to moderate. The north bank at the access site is three to four feet high, sparsely forested with oak, maple, and popple. The south bank is low and swampy, with a dense cover of cedar and popple. Trout cover is somewhat sparse but this is another prime area for the

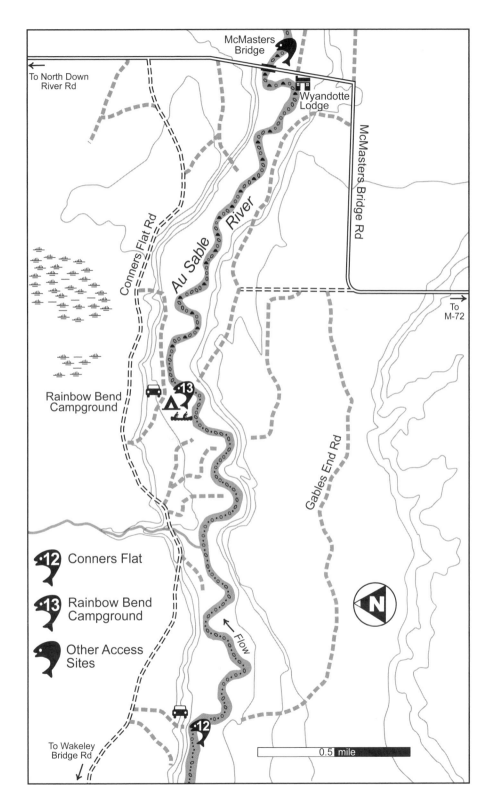

McMasters
Bridge

To North Down
River Rd

Wyandotte
Lodge

McMasters Bridge Rd

Conners Flat Rd

Au Sable River

To
M-72

Rainbow Bend
Campground

Gables End Rd

13

Flow

N

12 Conners Flat

13 Rainbow Bend
Campground

Other Access
Sites

12

To Wakeley
Bridge Rd

0.5 mile

Fly-Fishing Classes and Schools

One of the best ways to extend your knowledge of flies and the insects they represent is to enroll in a fly-tying class. Many Trout Unlimited chapters host such classes during the winter as do many outdoor stores like Cabela's (*www.cabelas.com*), Bass Pro Shops (*www.basspro.com*), and Hank's Fly Fishing (*www.hanksflyfishing.com*). You don't jump into fly tying to save money. You won't. At even $2 a fly, you still have to tie an awful lot of them just to pay for the vice. But even if you don't invest in the equipment and materials to practice on your own, a beginner's class will teach you about the flies best suited to Michigan trout streams, when to use them during the hatches, and how to fish them.

And who knows, you might even tie a fly well enough in class to use later on the river. Then you'll discover what fly tiers have always known: few things are as satisfying as fooling a trout with a fly that you tied.

Throughout northern Michigan, a number of fly-fishing schools are staged every summer and are usually a weekend of classroom lectures, casting lessons outside and an afternoon on a local trout stream with the instructors. Here are a few of the schools that can improve the techniques and knowledge of anybody new to the sport of fly fishing.

Federation of Fly Fishers: The FFF Great Lakes Council (*www.fffglc. org*) stages a fly-fishing school and conclave in mid- to late June at R. A. MacMullen Conference Center adjacent to North Higgins Lake State Park near Roscommon. Workshops are designed for beginning, intermediate or advanced anglers, while the outings are staged on the Au Sable and Manistee rivers. The school includes lodging, meals, and instructors.

Michigan Council of Trout Unlimited: The Michigan Council fly-fishing school (*www.mctu.org*) is held at Ranch Rudolf (231-947-9529) on the Boardman River south of Traverse City. Staged in early June during Michigan's Free Fishing Days, the school also offers three levels of instruction with outings to nearby Boardman and Manistee rivers.

Orvis Fly Fishing Schools: These two-day schools are held through the trout season at the Homestead Resort near Glen Arbor. The Orvis schools use an onsite trout pond and personal videotaping to teach and perfect your fly casting. They feature Orvis equipment, a four-to-one student-to-instructor ratio and outings to the Boardman River. For more information contact Orvis Streamside Shop (231-933-9300; *www. streamsideorvis.com*).

Fly Girls: Founded in 1996 to provide fly fishing opportunities for women, Fly Girls (*www.flygirls.ws*) stages a women's fly-fishing school in early June at Fullers North Outing Club on the North Branch of the Au Sable River. The three-day school includes lodging, meals and a two-to-one student-to-instructor ratio.

Schmidt Outfitters: This Wellston outfitter offers a variety of fly fishing schools including introduction to fly fishing, an advanced casting course, and a school designed for children. Only minutes from the Manistee River, Schmidt Outfitters (231-848-4191; *www.schmidtoutfitters.com*) features a dedicated classroom, casting pond, and lodging facilities.

Hawkins Outfitters: Based in the Traverse City area, Hawkins Outfitters (231-228-7135; *www.hawkinsflyfishing.com*) offers two-day advanced schools for fly anglers with the first day devoted to casting lessons and on-the-river fishing and the second day being a guided float trip on the Manistee or Pere Marquette river.

Pine Ridge Lodge: The Lewiston resort (989-786-4789; *www.bbonline.com/mi/pineridge*) stages three-day schools designed to introduce anglers to fly fishing and utilizes the North Branch and Main Stream of the Au Sable River. The school includes meals, lodging, and equipment.

Bob Linsenman's Au Sable Angler: This Mio fly shop (989-826-8500; *www.ausableangler.com*) offers a series of one-day classes on fishing with streamers for intermediate anglers. The day is split into classroom work, casting on a pond, and an afternoon float trip on the Au Sable.

Hex hatch, when fishing pressure will be heavy. Use extreme caution if you arrive for a bit of night fishing for big browns in water this deep.

●13 Rainbow Bend Campground

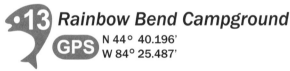

GPS N 44° 40.196'
W 84° 25.487'

Map: page 77

This state forest campground is also located downstream from the confluence of the South Branch and mainstream of the Au Sable or 0.7 mile downstream of Conners Flat. From McMasters Bridge it is reached by heading north for 0.4 mile and then west (left) on Conners Flat Road. Follow this dirt road for 1.5 miles to the posted entrance to the campground, a dirt road that heads southeast (left) for a third of a mile.

The campground is divided into Lower Rainbow Bend, a camping area for canoers, and Upper Rainbow Bend which features seven rustic sites that are accessible to car campers. From a day-use parking area a trail extends 150 yards to a canoe launch where you can access the river. The Au Sable is 80 to 90 feet wide here and deep enough at mid-channel to flood your waders. The bottom is gravel, sand, and boulders, and the footing is not too secure. in places. Still you can wade with caution at normal low flows as long as you stay clear of the swifter, deeper mid-channel.

The north bank at the campground is five to ten feet high, with an open forest of oak and maple. The south bank is low and swampy, covered with cedar and popple. Trout cover is sparse. Like Conners Flat, fishing pressure can be heavy during the Hex hatch but is generally lighter the rest of the season than areas west of Wakeley Bridge. This is not easy water to fish, but there are some good trout to be caught here.

Casting for big browns in the South Branch of the Au Sable River near the Highbanks Access Site in the Mason Tract.

South Branch of the Au Sable

The South Branch was once the personal wilderness of the wealthy and the well-connected. Now this tributary of the Au Sable River is the most extensive stretch of prime trout stream in the public domain. How lucky are we? For almost 12 miles, from Chase Bridge to Smith Bridge, the South Branch flows through the Mason Tract, land that was donated to the state of Michigan to preserve the remote and undeveloped nature of this special river.

Count your blessings and then step into your waders. The South Branch has a reputation for big browns and is renowned for its brown drake and Hexagenia hatches. Fly anglers from throughout the Midwest arrive in June for that middle-of-the-night opportunity to hook a 20-inch-plus brown trout feeding on giant mayflies.

The river is designated a Blue Ribbon Trout Stream for 19 miles, from near Roscommon to its confluence with the mainstream of the Au Sable. But it is the waters downstream from Chase Bridge, all designated a quality fishing area, that are rich in trout and prized the most by fly anglers. The first 4.5 miles is a flies-only, no-kill fishery. The catch-and-release regulations went into effect in 1983, six years earlier than on the Holy Water of the mainstream.

The next 12 miles, from the Lower Highbanks access site to the mainstream, is also flies-only with a daily possession of two fish with a ten-inch minimum size for brookies and 15 inches for browns. Both areas are open to fishing year-round but downstream from Lower Highbanks you can only keep browns and brookies during the regular trout season, from the last Saturday in April to September 30.

The South Branch begins in Roscommon County as the outlet for Lake St. Helen and flows north as a warm water stream, too warm to support a trout fishery. Within 15 miles the South Branch swings west and reaches the town of Roscommon where the cold-water tributaries of Robinson Creek and Beaver Creek begin to cool its temperatures significantly. It resumes a northerly flow from Roscommon and within 3.5 miles reaches Steckert Bridge, the beginning of good trout-holding water and reliable hatches. An influx of groundwater also begins to flow into the South Branch, and by the time it reaches Chase Bridge, six miles downstream from Roscommon, it is a first-class trout fishery with water temperatures cool enough to keep browns hanging around throughout the summer.

This is also the start of the Mason Tract, the focus of this chapter.

Like other rivers in this region of the Lower Peninsula, the grayling had disappeared from the South Branch by the early 1900s and the white pine was already gone from its banks. The river, planted with trout since the 1880s, caught the eye of Orlando Barnes. In 1909 Barnes began purchasing land on both sides of the river and then formed the South Branch Ranch, a working sheep ranch and something of an exclusive fishing club. The club reportedly had only six other members but owned all of the riverfront between Chase Bridge and Smith Bridge with the exception of a single 40-acre tract called Forest Rest. At what is today the Downey's Place access site, members built a log clubhouse and named it Wolfville Lodge after a wolf was shot nearby.

Within ten years the club dissolved but Charles Downey, probably the most passionate angler of the group, purchased all the forties fronting the river and built an impressive house at Downey's Place. Among the anglers who traveled north to fish with Downey was his nephew, William C. Durant, who had already created General Motors in 1908. Durant loved the South Branch so much that he purchased the riverfront property from Downey's widow in 1929. That year he began building his private castle on the banks of the South Branch, a $500,000 home that boasted 42 rooms, seven fireplaces, and its own source of electric power. It was wired for a ticker tape so he could keep tabs on Wall Street, while nearby an airstrip was built so a plane could deliver his mail. In 1930, the Durants spent the holidays in the unfinished home overlooking the South Branch. Less than two months later it was destroyed by a fire, and today only the foundation and bits of rubble are visible.

After Durant's death in 1947, his widow sold the land to industrialists D. B. Lee and George Mason, and within a few years Mason acquired the entire tract. An avid fly angler, Mason was also a dedicated conservationist who served as president of Ducks Unlimited. It was on the banks of the South Branch one evening that Mason suggested to his long-time friend, George Griffith, that there should be an organization for trout as there is for ducks.

Mason never saw the establishment of Trout Unlimited. He was only 63 when he died in 1954 of acute pancreatitis and pneumonia in Detroit. But by then he had managed the two accomplishments for which he'll long be remembered; he created American Motors Corporation just months before his death, and he re-wrote his will to bequeath to the state 1,500 acres surrounding 14 miles of the South Branch. The gift was contingent that the area be used as a permanent game preserve and never be developed, that no part shall ever be sold by the state, and that no camping be allowed in the area for 25 years.

The state accepted the gift. From that 1,500-acre seed, the Mason Tract has been gradually enlarged into a 4,493-acre special management area designed to protect the quality fishing waters of the South Branch. Other than Canoe Harbor, a longtime campground that was originally located outside the tract, camping is still not allowed. Neither has there been any development. The only structure in the tract is Mason Chapel, built in 1960 with funds provided by the Mason family to provide anglers with a place of reverence and reflection.

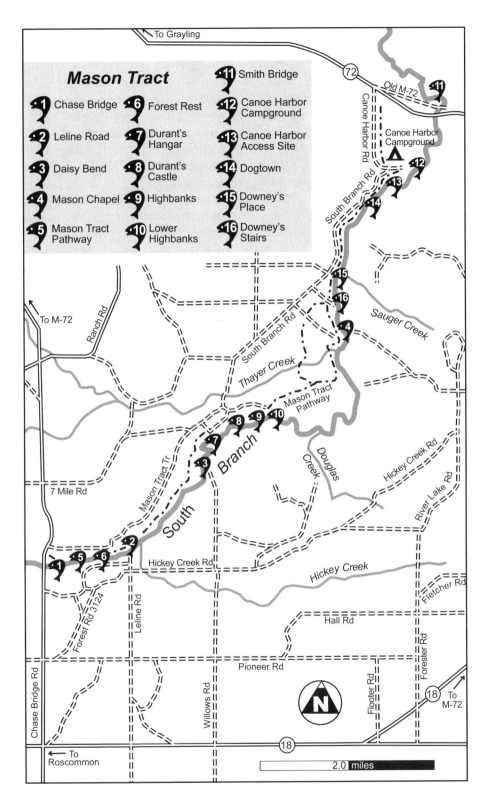

Mason Tract

1 Chase Bridge
2 Leline Road
3 Daisy Bend
4 Mason Chapel
5 Mason Tract Pathway
6 Forest Rest
7 Durant's Hangar
8 Durant's Castle
9 Highbanks
10 Lower Highbanks
11 Smith Bridge
12 Canoe Harbor Campground
13 Canoe Harbor Access Site
14 Dogtown
15 Downey's Place
16 Downey's Stairs

To Grayling

72

Old M-72

Canoe Harbor Rd

Canoe Harbor Campground

South Branch Rd

Sauger Creek

South Branch Rd

To M-72

Ranch Rd

Thayer Creek

Mason Tract Pathway

Mason Tract Tr

South Branch

Douglas Creek

Hickey Creek Rd

River Lake Rd

7 Mile Rd

Hickey Creek Rd

Hickey Creek

Fletcher Rd

Forest Rd 3124

Leline Rd

Hall Rd

Chase Bridge Rd

Willows Rd

Pioneer Rd

Flooter Rd

Forester Rd

18

To M-72

N

18

← To Roscommon

2.0 miles

We should all pause to pray; the South Branch is classic fly water. Thanks to the Mason Tract, anglers have almost unlimited access along the best stretches of it, far more places to cast a fly than what is described in this chapter. The river is not always an easy one to fish, however. The flow of the South Branch is much more variable than that of either the mainstream or the North Branch, and consequently wading and fishing conditions change greatly from day to day. In particular, early in the trout season and after heavy rains, the South Branch flows fast, high, and murky, and the rounded cobbles and boulders are slippery. At such times the deeper holes are harder to spot than when the water is clearer at normal flows.

Trout populations generally are lower on the South Branch than on the mainstream or North Branch, but anglers who know the river do well here. Fishing pressure can be heavy on the South Branch during the drake and Hexagenia hatches. But the abundance of access sites spreads anglers out, and most of the summer you'll find fishing pressure is light to moderate. There is also the Mason Tract Pathway, an 11.5-mile network of trails, most of which is a 9.5-mile, one-way hike from a trailhead near Smith Bridge to Chase Bridge. The trail winds its way along the western bluffs and highbanks that the South Branch flows beneath and allows the adventurous to hike to remote stretches of the river. In general, the farther you walk from the access roads, the better your chances of fishing alone on the river.

As a canoe trail, the South Branch is almost as popular as the mainstream with several liveries in Roscommon supplying rental canoes and drop-off service. The vast majority of canoers put in at Chase Bridge and pull out at Smith Bridge, a four-hour paddle. Their numbers restrict daytime fishing during the summer, particularly on weekends, but you'll encounter few canoes on the river in early morning or late evening.

In the final stretch of the South Branch, the five river miles from Smith Bridge to the mouth on the mainstream, there is little public access and most anglers fish it from a boat. You can launch a canoe at Smith Bridge, float downstream to the mouth, and then continue in the mainstream to Conners Flat Public Access Site or Rainbow Bend Campground. For the most part this reach of the South Branch features a slow current, a sandy bottom, and depths that are too deep to wade.

Like all the streams in this part of Michigan, the water is hard and high in calcium and magnesium, and slightly alkaline. The supply of nutrients is more than adequate to support the variety of insects trout feed on while the sand and muck along the banks are the reason for the excellent brown drake and Hexagenia hatches. These hatches occur almost simultaneously from early June into July. The hex hatch occurs well after dark, usually from 10 p.m. to 4 a.m., but drakes often appear earlier in the evening, around 8 p.m., and in the first hour of daylight the next morning.

Other common mayfly and caddis hatches often occur a few days earlier on the South Branch than the mainstream of the Au Sable because of the warmer water temperatures.

Accommodations

Accommodations and other services are split between Grayling and Roscommon. Roscommon is closer but Grayling has a far greater choice. See accommodations in the Mainstream of the Au Sable River chapter (page 60) or contact the Grayling Visitors Bureau (800-937-8837; *www.grayling-mi.org*). On the northwest side of Roscommon is the ***Tee Pee Motel*** (989-275-5203, 866-503-4095; *www.tee-pee.com*; 333 W Federal Hwy.) with rooms, 14 modern campsites featuring water, sewer and electric hook-ups and a log cabin that sleeps four to six. The motel also has a restaurant onsite.

Campgrounds: There are no campgrounds in the heart of the Mason Tract nor is dispersed camping allowed. On the north end of the tract is Canoe Harbor Campground, a large state forest facility with 39 drive-in rustic sites along with walk-in sites for paddlers and hikers, vault toilets and drinking water. None of the drive-in sites are directly on the river.

Fly Shops and Guides

For flies or a last-minute purchase of equipment, it's best to drive to Grayling as Roscommon offers little. Grayling-based guides will also float the South Branch and a list of them is available in the Mainstream of the Au Sable chapter. You can arrange a fish-and-float trip in Roscommon through ***Hiawatha Canoe Livery*** (989-275-5213, 888-515-5213; *www. canoehiawatha.com*; 1113 Lake St.).

Maps of the South Branch

Most anglers reach the South Branch by departing I-75 at either Roscommon, exit 239, and following M-18 east or Grayling at exit 254 and heading east on M-72. For this reason the descriptions of the 16 access sites have been divided up into three groups based on the easiest way to reach them.

The East Bank covers the first four sites that are on the east side of the river and accessed by heading 2.5 miles east on M-18 to Chase Bridge Road. Mason Tract Trail covers the next six access sites, all located on the west side of the river along this narrow, rutted two-track. From M-18, Mason Tract Trail is reached by heading north on Chase Bridge Road. You will cross the bridge in two miles, and a quarter mile beyond there the Mason Tract Trail is posted where it heads east into the woods.

The final six sites are covered in Canoe Harbor and South Branch Roads and are described from M-72 beginning with Smith Bridge and moving upstream to finish at Downey's Stairs. From I-75 Business Loop in Grayling, the north end of Chase Bridge Road is 9.2 miles east on M-72, and Canoe Harbor Road is 12.6 miles.

The following directions along with GPS coordinates and maps have been carefully researched to help you find the access site where you want to fish. But keep in mind that the Mason Tract on both sides of the river is a maze of dirt roads, two-tracks, and trails, the majority of which are not signposted. If you fish this river long enough you will eventually spend an afternoon fruitlessly wandering around on two-tracks. It's part of the South Branch experience. Still a car equipped with a GPS unit or a compass will assist you greatly in not getting lost in the woods.

The East Bank

1 Chase Bridge
GPS N 44° 32.415'
W 84° 33.020'

Chase Bridge is the upper limit of the flies-only no-kill, quality fishing waters of the South Branch and a major launch area for paddlers. From Roscommon head northeast on M-18 and in 2.5 miles out of town turn north (left) on Chase Bridge Road. The bridge and launch site is two miles north of M-18. There is a parking lot southeast of the bridge with a vault toilet and Charlie's Well, a memorial to Charlie Egeler, an angler who loved the South Branch.

Chase Bridge has long been associated with trout fishing. James Oliver Curwood, author of *The Grizzly King*, a book published in 1916 and turned into a major film in 1988 titled *The Bear*, once lived on the hill south of this bridge. Curwood's primary home was in Owosso but he wrote many of his stories at his South Branch lodge, including *Green Timber*. On the north bank, just west of the bridge, is the Bay City Fishing and Hunting Club that was established in 1912.

At the bridge the South Branch is 70 to 80 feet wide and two to three feet deep, with some deeper holes. Bottom is mostly gravel, with some sand and muck near the banks. The velocity is moderate, and wading is fairly easy at normal flows. Upstream the river is open to all tackle during trout season and has a daily possession of five fish with no more than three at 15 inches or longer. Minimum size for browns and brookies is eight inches.

Downstream of the bridge, the river enters the Mason Tract with its flies-only, no-kill regulations. The banks are lower than upstream and swampy, lined with cedar, willow, and brush. Logs, snags, and overhanging brush provide cover for large browns. During the summer, however, canoers launching their crafts can be intense in the morning, but in the afternoon it is often quieter than stretches further downstream in the Mason Tract.

2 Leline Road
GPS N 44° 32.452'
W 84° 31.797'

The end of Leline Road provides walk-in access on the south bank of the river a mile downstream from Chase Bridge and near a private residence called Forest Rest. The easiest way to reach the site from Chase Bridge Road is to turn east on Pioneer Road a mile south of Chase Bridge. Within a mile turn north (left) on Leline Road, and in another mile you come to

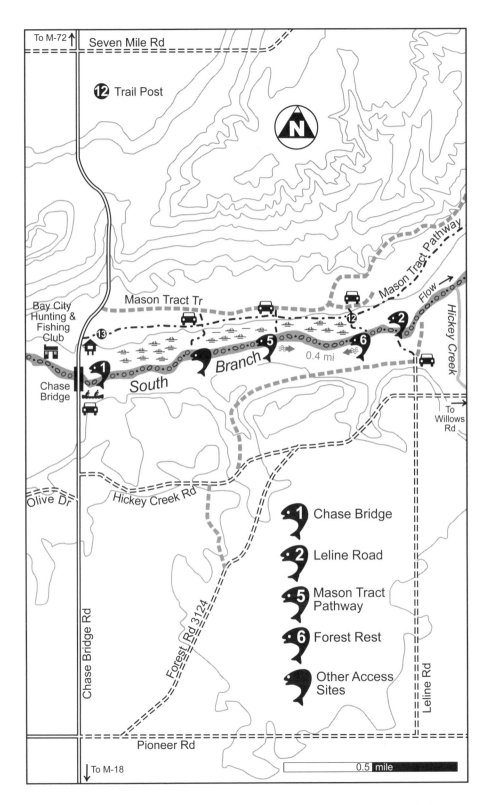

To M-72 ↑
Seven Mile Rd

⑫ Trail Post

Ⓝ

Mason Tract Tr

Bay City
Hunting &
Fishing
Club

⑬

Mason Tract Pathway

⑫

❷

Flow →

Hickey Creek

❺

South

Branch

0.4 mi

❻

Chase
Bridge

❶

To
Willows
Rd

Olive Dr

Hickey Creek Rd

Chase Bridge Rd

Forest Rd 3124

Leline Rd

❶ Chase Bridge

❷ Leline Road

❺ Mason Tract
Pathway

❻ Forest Rest

Other Access
Sites

Pioneer Rd

↓ To M-18

0.5 mile

the intersection with Hickey Creek Road. Continue north on the two-track and in 200 yards you come to a parking area at the edge of a bluff. A pair of two-tracks descend the bluff to the river. The one to the east (right) leads to Forest Rest. The one to the west (left) provides access to the river. Carefully check this two-track if you're thinking of driving in closer. This road can be extremely rutted and sandy. It's far safer to walk in as the South Branch is only a hundred yards away.

The river is 70 to 100 feet wide here and two to three feet deep with some deeper holes. Bottom is mostly gravel although the trail ends at a marshy stretch along the south bank with a bit of mud and silt. The trail to the river leads to where a grassy islet divides the South Bank into a pair of channels. Downstream the banks are low and covered with hardwood, conifer, and much brush. Velocity is moderate, making wading fairly easy at normal flows. The river is also wide enough for easy fly casting and trout cover, especially around the islet, is ample. Fishing pressure usually is light even though this is part of the flies-only, no-kill water.

3 Daisy Bend

GPS N 44° 33.331'
W 84° 30.672'

Map: page 93

This beautiful spot offers some excellent trout waters to fish but is not nearly as popular as most of the access points along the west bank. The easiest way to reach Daisy Bend is from M-18 by turning north on Willows Road two miles east of Chase Bridge Road. Follow Willows Road north for three miles and the two-track will end at a cul-de-sac parking area marked by a "Quality Fishing Area" sign. Keep in mind that Willows Road between Pioneer Road and Hickey Creek Road is extremely rutted and sandy. If you're worried about your vehicle getting stuck, then enter from Chase Bridge Road, where 0.3 mile south of the river you head east on Hickey Creek Road. Within 2.1 miles you'll come to an intersection with Willows Road. Turn north (left) and follow the two-track a mile to its end.

From the parking area a short trail leads to the South Branch where anglers' trails head in both directions along the riverbank. The easiest path to follow is downstream, but upstream brings you to a sweeping curve where the river is 60 to 80 feet wide, two to three feet deep and well shaded by cedars leaning over the banks. The current is moderate over a bottom of predominately gravel, so the wading is easy. There is room to cast and lots of coverage for trout to hide in. Caddis hatches are excellent in this reach.

4 Mason Chapel

GPS N 44° 34.710'
W 84° 28.594'

Map: page 99

This is another beautiful spot along the South Branch but not an ideal one for wading anglers. The water is deep here so you must wade cautiously. The

As impressive as the mansion was, Durant's Castle was just as mysterious in its demise. Built on the banks of the South Branch, William Durant's vision was a personal castle in a wilderness retreat overlooking one of the finest trout streams in northern Michigan. The man who founded GM in 1908 began the project in late 1929 and oversaw the construction of the French château home that included, among other things, a music room, library, barber shop, gymnasium, two-story tower entrance, even an eight-car garage and a stable. Durant and his wife stayed in the home over Christmas, 1930, even though the interior wasn't quite finished. On Feb. 5, 1931, the unoccupied palace burned to the ground.

Since then the cause of the mysterious fire has always been ripe material for local opinion and theories. Some believe that the fire was a result of the combustion from painters' rags left behind; others contend a rare electrical storm in the middle of winter was the cause. One popular theory was the fire was sabotage by members of the fledgling UAW, which Durant had refused to acknowledge as a union.

What is known is that the stock market crash of 1929 and the Great Depression strained Durant's finances. At some point he decided to deviate from the expensive fireproof steel and cement construction used on the lower floors and opted for cheaper wooden rafters and gables in the roof. In the end, this may have been why the greatest fishing lodge ever built in Michigan was destroyed by fire.

chapel and dock on the river make it a favorite place for paddlers to pull out for a break.

The easiest way to reach the chapel is from Chase Bridge Road where 0.3 mile south of the river you would turn east on Hickey Creek Road. Follow the two-track through the intersections with Leline Road and Willows Road and veer left at the Forester Road intersection. Hickey Creek Road will come to a stop sign at a T-intersection, 5.7 miles from Chase Bridge Road. Turn north (left) on this dirt road, which on many maps is labeled River Lake Road. Within a mile you arrive at a crossroads that is posted as Forest Road 4210 to the east. Turn west (left) on it and in 0.8 mile you arrive to where Forest Road 4208 is posted and veers off to the left. Head right, and in 0.9 mile you arrive at the parking lot for Mason Chapel.

The parking area is large enough to hold five or six vehicles, and from it a trail climbs a hill and then swings left to arrive at the chapel. Also known as Fisherman's Chapel, this small shrine was built in 1960 in honor of George Mason. The stone chapel with its slate roof is 50 feet above the river in a serene setting and includes this inscription: "Here may the fisherman receive the same inspiration which led George W. Mason, a true sportsman, to bequeath to the public this land and this sanctuary beside his beloved river." No doubt many anglers do.

From the chapel a stairway descends the bank to a dock on the South Branch while an angler's trail heads upstream along the river. The South Branch is 50 to 70 feet wide here and two to four feet deep with wide, winding bends that create deep pools. Wade cautiously here. The bottom is mostly gravel with scattered boulders, and the banks are heavily wooded.

Mason Tract Trail

5 Mason Tract Pathway

GPS N 44° 32.612'
W 84° 32.265'

Map: page 87

This access site is right along the Mason Tract Pathway and the walk is a short one to a very productive stretch of the South Branch. Head north a quarter mile from Chase Bridge and turn east (right) on the Mason Tract Trail, which is signposted. Within half a mile there is a small parking lot to the south (right) of the dirt road, overlooking the Mason Tract Pathway. There is space for three or maybe four vehicles.

A foot path crosses the pathway and within 100 yards reaches the South Branch. The river widens here to 80 to 90 feet and is two to three feet deep, making it easy to wade and even easier to cast a fly into. There is also good trout cover in the form of sweepers and submerged logs.

6 Forest Rest

GPS N 44° 32.639'
W 84° 32.001'

Map: page 87

This site is located almost on the opposite bank from the Leline Road access site and a river mile downstream from Chase Bridge. Turn east on Mason Tract Trail, 0.2 mile north of Chase Bridge, and within 0.6 mile you come to a clearcut on your left—a reminder of how narrow the preserve is—and a rutted two-track veering off to the right. Continue on the rutted two-track for another 200 yards and look for a trail to the right. This two-track once looped back to Mason Tract Trail but logging operations have obliterated part of it.

The foot path to the river quickly crosses the Mason Tract Pathway at post no. 12, marking where part of Forest Rest, a private 40-tract, was located on the river in 1910. Within 200 feet you descend a stairway to the South Branch. The river is 70 to 80 feet wide and two to three feet deep with a gravel bottom. Wading and casting are easy here.

It would also be easy to begin at the access site just upstream and fish down to Forest Rest, a wade of 0.6 mile, using the stairs as a landmark to indicate where to get out and return via the Mason Tract Pathway, or to turn around.

An angler releases a brown trout in the South Branch of the Au Sable in the Mason Tract. Almost 12 miles of the South Branch flows through the special preserve.

Durant's Hangar

GPS N 44° 33.736'
W 84° 30.748'

This is the first of several popular access points reached from a two-track near the east end of Mason Tract Trail. The site picks up its name from the hangar and airstrip that William Durant maintained in the 1930s. From Chase Bridge Road, head east on Mason Tract Trail, passing the two-track to Forest Rest. Continue east on Mason Tract Trail as it passes through more clearcuts. Within 2.6 miles from Chase Bridge Road or 0.3 mile after passing a junction with a two-track from the west, turn south (right) on a two-track. Naturally, nothing is posted. Within 200 yards you arrive at a large sandy parking area capable of holding a dozen vehicles, though you sincerely hope there aren't that many there, and marked by a "Quality Fishing Area" sign.

From the parking area a trail leads into the brush and quickly crosses the Mason Tract Pathway. You then descend a bluff into a swampy area before reaching the river. The South Branch is 60 to 70 feet wide and two to four feet deep with a moderate to fast flow. The bottom is a mix of gravel, sand, and clay that results in some excellent brown drake and Hex hatches.

Durant's Castle

GPS N 44° 33.913'
W 84° 30.406'

During much of the summer, Durant's Castle is a more popular access site for canoers, with its large dock and picnic area, than for anglers. The easiest way to reach the Castle is to follow the directions given above for Durant's Hangar but pass up the two-track to the large, sandy parking area. Instead, continue along on Mason Tract Trail for another 0.3 mile, or 2.9 miles from Chase Bridge Road, and then turn southeast (right) on a two-track. This two-track is sometimes referred to as the east entrance to Durant's Castle; within 200 yards it swings right. A parking area will soon appear on the left along with a bright yellow gate blocking the start of the trail and a "Quality Fishing Area" sign.

The trail leads 250 yards to the river, first passing through a picnic area with a vault toilet and a display on Durant's Castle. You can still see parts of the stone foundation and fireplace from the mansion that William Durant built. The 42-room castle may have been a wooded retreat for the founder of GM, but what amused locals the most was a ticker tape that kept the millionaire in contact with the New York stock market. The house didn't last long, as fire destroyed it in 1931 before it was completely finished.

The trail also crosses Mason Tract Pathway, marked by post no. 10, and then descends to a large deck on the South Branch. The deck doubles as a dock for canoers and a handicapped-accessible fishing platform. You'll find the river is 60 to 80 feet wide and three to five feet deep at normal flows,

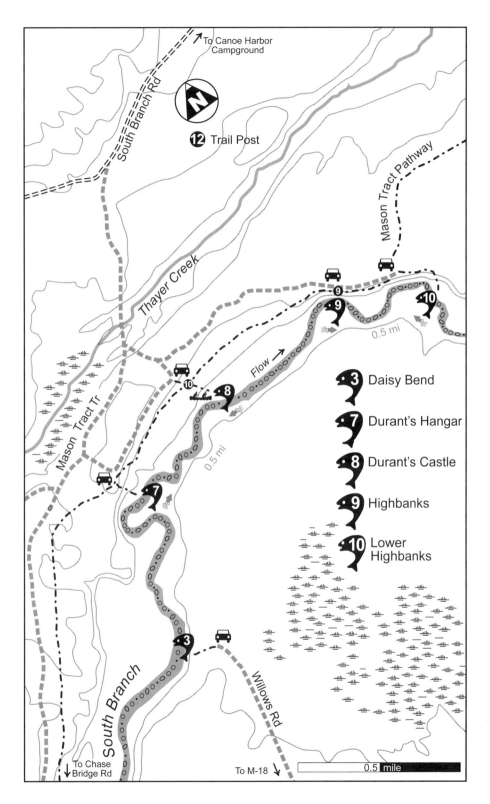

To Canoe Harbor
Campground

South Branch Rd

12 Trail Post

Mason Tract Pathway

Thayer Creek

0.5 mi

Flow

Mason Tract Tr

0.5 mi

3 Daisy Bend

7 Durant's Hangar

8 Durant's Castle

9 Highbanks

10 Lower
Highbanks

South Branch

Willows Rd

To Chase
Bridge Rd

To M-18

0.5 mile

with some deeper holes. Bottom is gravel, sand, clay, and boulders. The flow is fast and wading is not easy, even at normal flows. At high flows, wading is impossible. There is plenty of room to cast a fly. The west bank where the deck is located is high and sandy, with hardwood, pine, and some brush. The right bank is lower and brushier. Fishing pressure usually is very light.

Highbanks

GPS N 44° 33.982'
W 84° 29.798'

Map: page 93

Located in the heart of the Mason Tract, this site is one of the most beautiful and best stretches for wading anglers. You reach it from the same two-track entrance described above for Durant's Castle, reached 2.9 miles along the Mason Tract Trail from Chase Bridge Road. Follow the two-track for 200 yards, then turn left at a sign marking the Mason Tract. Within 0.6 mile you'll arrive at a large parking area capable of holding a dozen cars and a "Quality Fishing Area" sign.

A foot trail quickly leads to post no. 9 of the Mason Tract Pathway on the edge of the bluff known as the Highbanks. Also located here are a bench overlooking the river and a long stairway that descends 76 steps to the water below. The river is 80 to 100 feet wide and two to three feet deep over a predominately gravel and rocky bottom. The current is moderate so the wading is easy, and there's ample room to cast. Best of all, the sweepers, submerged logs, and overhanging cedars provide plenty of cover for trout.

Lower Highbanks

GPS N 44° 33.977'
W 84° 29.544'

Map: page 93

What used to be the site of a canoe landing is now another good stretch of the river for anglers. From the Highbanks parking area (see description for the Highbanks site) continue east along the two-track until it ends in 0.3 mile, where there is a small parking area posted with a "No Wheeled Vehicles" sign. The Mason Tract Pathway cuts through the parking area, while the trail to the access site departs from the right side of the parking area and skirts the high river bluff. Stay close to the edge of the bluff, and within 300 yards from the parking area you'll descend to a low spot and arrive at a small stairway to the river.

Lower Highbanks marks a change in regulations on the South Branch. Downstream it is flies-only, but you are allowed a daily possession of two fish with a ten-inch minimum length for brook trout and 15 inches for browns. Upstream the river is flies-only, no-kill water. The South Branch is 70 to 80 feet wide and two to three feet deep. Like the Highbanks, the current is moderate over a firm gravel bottom for easy wading, while the river is loaded with submerged logs and other cover for trout. A common outing is to begin at the Highbanks and fish to the Lower Highbanks, a wade of half a mile.

Canoe Harbor and South Branch Roads

11 Smith Bridge

GPS N 44° 36.880'
W 84° 27.335'

Map: page 96

Located 2.2 river miles from the Au Sable mainstream, this access is the main take-out for paddlers floating the South Branch, and during the summer it can get busy. It's best to park your vehicle well away from the canoe landing area in that season. The public launch is at the east end of Old M-72, reached from Grayling by heading east on M-72 for 9.2 miles. Old M-72 is 200 yards southeast of Canoe Harbor Road and veers off M-72 to the northeast (left) as a gravel road. Within a mile you cross the one-lane steel bridge and then swing right into a huge parking lot where spanning the river just to the south is the current bridge that M-72 uses to cross the South Branch.

At the launch site the South Branch is 80 to 90 feet wide and two to four feet deep, with some deeper holes. Bottom is gravel and boulders with a little sand and muck. Velocity is moderate to fast, but at normal flows wading is fairly easy. Wading under the bridges is difficult even at normal flows. Trout cover is fair upstream, better downstream and by wading downstream, even just a few hundred feet, you can easily escape the commotion of the canoers. The banks are alternately high and low, forested with conifer and hardwood, mostly pine and birch, and some brush at streamside.

The site is surrounded by private property with cabins perched above the water. This reach lies in the flies-only segment of the river where the daily possession is two fish. Despite the intense use by canoeists and anglers, this area still holds many large brown trout.

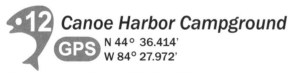

12 Canoe Harbor Campground

GPS N 44° 36.414'
W 84° 27.972'

Map: page 96

The original Canoe Harbor Campground was located right on the river southeast of its present site. But heavy streamside erosion by its users forced the DNR to move the popular drive-in campground farther away from the river in 1975. Today the original site is still maintained as a walk-in camping area for hikers and canoeists. The campground is reached from M-72, where Canoe Harbor Road is well posted 9.2 miles east of Grayling. Head south on Canoe Harbor Road for 0.8 mile to the campground entrance to the east (left).

This rustic campground is large with 39 drive-in sites well scattered along a single loop in a forested area of pines and hardwoods. None are close to the river. To reach the South Branch, follow the loop to a small parking area on its east side. A gated service drive leads 300 yards to the walk-in camping area near the river. If the campground is busy and finding parking is a challenge, you have to ask yourself, do I really want to fish here? You'll find much better places elsewhere in the Mason Tract.

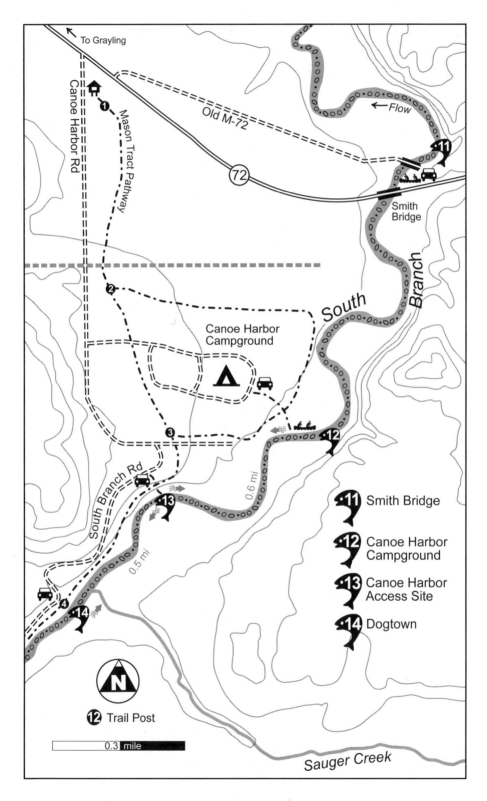

To Grayling

Canoe Harbor Rd

Mason Tract Pathway

Old M-72

72

← Flow

South Branch

Smith Bridge

Canoe Harbor Campground

South Branch Rd

0.6 mi

0.5 mi

11 Smith Bridge

12 Canoe Harbor Campground

13 Canoe Harbor Access Site

14 Dogtown

N

12 Trail Post

0.3 mile

Sauger Creek

The river is 70 to 90 feet wide at the campground and two to four feet deep, with some deeper holes. Bottom is mostly gravel, with some sand and muck. Velocity is moderate to fast. The river can be waded with caution at normal flows but is unwadable at high water in early spring and after heavy rains. Thanks to a fierce storm in the late 1990s, fish cover is plentiful.

Although the activity makes this spot less popular with anglers, if you arrive early or late in the trout season, especially in early morning or late evening, you can still enjoy your own stretch of the river here.

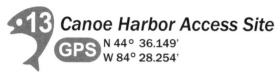

13 *Canoe Harbor Access Site*

GPS N 44° 36.149'
W 84° 28.254'

This is often a better alternative than Canoe Harbor Campground for anglers, even if they are camped there. From M-72, head south on Canoe Harbor Road and continue on South Branch Road. Within 1.3 miles of M-72, or half a mile south of the campground, is a small parking area on the east (left).

The Mason Tract Pathway skirts the parking area from north to south while the trail to the river departs due east. Follow the trail as it sharply descends a hill and then reaches the river in a hundred yards from where you left your vehicle. The South Branch is 80 to 90 feet wide and two to four feet deep with a bottom of gravel and sand. The wading is manageable in normal water levels and the trout coverage is excellent here.

14 *Dogtown*

GPS N 44° 35.995'
W 84° 28.380'

Dogtown is one of most popular angler sites on the South Branch. It picks up its name from when market hunters camped here in the 1800s. The professional hunters would use rifles, traps and dogs to hunt wild game that was shipped to restaurants in Chicago and on the East Coast.

From M-72, Dogtown is reached by heading south on Canoe Harbor Road and passing the entrance to the campground. Just beyond the campground Canoe Harbor Road swings sharply east while you continue south (right) on South Branch Road. Within half a mile, or 1.6 miles from M-72, Dogtown is reached where South Branch Road descends a steep hill and swings sharply to the right at the bottom. The parking area is on the east (left) side of the road at the bend and is capable of holding nine or ten vehicles.

From your vehicle follow a trail that quickly reaches the Mason Tract Pathway. Head right on the pathway briefly and then left on the first trail heading for the river. The walk to the water is short, less than 80 yards. You'll find the South Branch 80 to 90 feet wide and two to four feet deep at normal flows. There are some deeper holes and some patches of sand and muck, but the bottom is mostly gravel and the wading is fairly easy. Velocity is usually moderate to fast. There is plenty of room to cast a fly, and there is ample trout cover for big browns to hide in. The riverbanks on both sides are alternately high and low, forested with hardwoods, conifers, and much brush. This is part of the Mason Tract and is flies-only water with a daily possession of two fish. Fishing pressure is moderate to heavy.

•15 Downey's Place

GPS N 44° 35.284'
W 84° 28.942'

Several access points are clustered together in an area that was the site of Downey's Place, a home built in the early 1900s by Charles Downey, who at one point owned most of the river from Smith Bridge to Chase Bridge. From M-72, head south on Canoe Harbor Road and continue on South Branch Road. Within 2.6 miles from M-72, or a mile beyond Dogtown, is an intersection with a dirt road coming in from the northwest (right). Opposite this intersection is a large parking area posted with a "Downey's" sign.

A trail heads southeast and in 200 yards arrives in an open, grassy area marked in the middle by post No. 5 of the Mason Tract Pathway. Nearby a pair of stone stairways, left over from Downey's Place, lead down to the river, while just downstream in the water are the rocky remains of an old bridge.

The South Branch is 70 to 90 feet wide here and two to four feet deep at normal flows, with some deeper holes. Bottom is mostly gravel and boulders with nice stretches of riffles but also some muck and sand along the banks. Flow is moderate to fast with the wading easy during normal flows, but difficult when the river is high. In the immediate area, the west bank is high and remains fairly open, with grass, hardwood, pine, and some brush. The east bank is low and brushy.

You are out of the no-kill water but still are restricted to flies only. This is a popular reach of river, and it is heavily fished during the major hatches.

•16 Downey's Stairs

GPS N 44° 35.087'
W 84° 28.957'

This site is the result of a massive stairway built by the Paul Young Chapter of Trout Unlimited in 1976 to prevent the sandy high banks from eroding into the river. From M-72, head south on Canoe Harbor Road and continue on South Branch Road. Within 2.9 miles from M-72, turn southeast (left) on a two-track. Follow it 0.3 mile to a cul-de-sac parking area at the end that is capable of holding a dozen vehicles.

Passing through the parking area is the Mason Tract Pathway. Head south on the trail, and you will quickly come to the stairways that descend to the river. At the bottom is a log bench where no doubt many anglers have sat waiting for a hatch to occur. The South Branch is 70 to 80 feet wide and two to four feet deep with a bottom of sand and gravel and brush along the banks. The casting is easy and the trout cover, in the form of cedar sweepers and submerged logs, is plentiful. Downey's Stairs is in the flies-only stretch of the South Branch but out of the no-kill water.

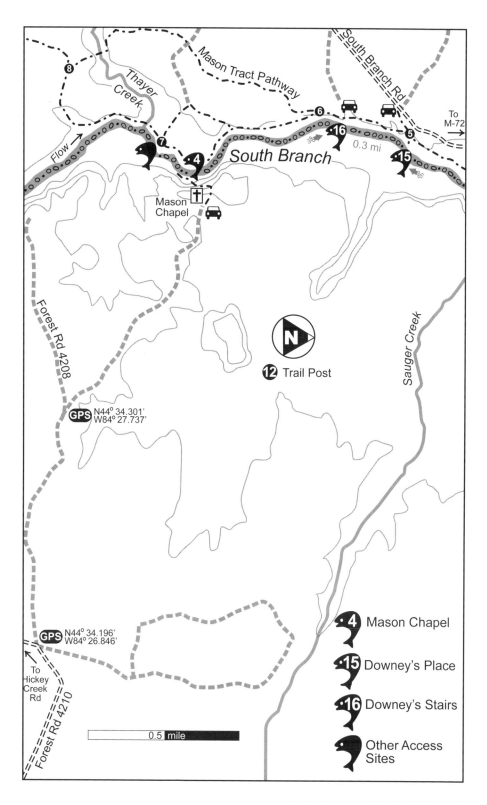

Thayer Creek

8

Mason Tract Pathway

South Branch Rd

To M-72

Flow

7

4

South Branch

6

16

0.3 mi

5

15

Mason Chapel

Forest Rd 4208

N

Sauger Creek

12 Trail Post

GPS N44° 34.301'
W84° 27.737'

GPS N44° 34.196'
W84° 26.846'

To Hickey Creek Rd

Forest Rd 4210

0.5 mile

4 Mason Chapel

15 Downey's Place

16 Downey's Stairs

Other Access Sites

Michigan Angler: Everett F. Kircher

Everett F. Kircher is known as a visionary who took a ridge with a modest 500-foot vertical drop and turned it into Boyne Mountain Ski Resort and eventually into Boyne USA, the largest privately-held, four-season resort company in North America. Along the way he transformed the Northern Michigan economy by blending golf with skiing at his resorts, improved the snow gun and in 1970 introduced the world's first quad chairlift at Boyne Mountain.

Impressive accomplishments. But it was fly fishing, not skiing, that was Kircher's passion. It's the reason he states in the opening sentence of his autobiography, *Everett Kircher: Michigan's Resort Pioneer*; "I'd rather be known as a great fly fisherman."

Kircher was introduced to fishing during a family vacation to Blooming Rose, MO, in 1928. An uncle took the then 12-year-old to the Old Piney River, they caught a mess of fish and right then Kircher knew he had found his passion. From that moment on there was almost never a year in his life that Kircher didn't throw a line into the water somewhere.

Although Kircher fished with bait, plugs and lures, it was fly fishing that captivated him the most. He thought casting a fly to where a trout was lurking and then teasing that fish into striking was the most challenging way to fish. And Kircher thrived on challenges whether it was business or fishing.

After Boyne Mountain opened in 1948, Kircher built his home along the banks of the nearby Boyne River and fished it almost nightly during the season for browns, rainbows and brookies. He also traveled the country to fish. It's one reason he purchased Big Sky Resort in Montana in 1976. He loved the trout-rich country where it was located. At the doorstep of the ski resort were the Gallatin and Madison rivers, world-class trout streams, while nearby was the equally-famous Yellowstone River.

He became particularly enamored with fishing for Atlantic salmon on a fly and chased the species throughout the world from Iceland and Russia to Labrador and New Brunswick in Canada. But it was in Norway where Kirchner experienced his greatest moment as an angler when he hooked a salmon in the Alta River that he had to battled for an hour and half. When his guide finally netted the salmon both were shocked at how large it was. The fish weighed 47 pounds and set a new world record at the time for the largest Atlantic salmon ever caught with a fly rod. Today a replica of the trophy is mounted and on display at Boyne Mountain's Everett Restaurant.

Even after suffering from a stroke, Kirchner continued to fish late in life. He had a path cleared along his beloved Boyne River at his home so he could fish his favorite holes from a golf cart. He could no longer ski or even handle the current wading in a trout stream but he could still drop a

Everett F. Kircher is best known as the founder of Boyne Mountain Ski Resort but his first passion in life was fly fishing. (Courtesy Boyne USA, Inc.)

fly with deadly precision.

"The greatest thing on earth is fly fishing," Kircher said in an interview in 2000. "I put more pride in my fly fishing than I do skiing. I'm 83 years old and I'm still fly fishing. I quit skiing six years ago."

The quality fishing area of the North Branch, which includes flies-only regulations, begins above Twin Bridges and continues downstream 21 river miles to the mouth.

North Branch of the Au Sable

Steeped with history, filled with brookies and browns, blessed with an abundance of hatches, the North Branch is a top-quality trout stream that lacks only the legendary reputation of the Au Sable's mainstream. Many fly anglers prefer it over the Holy Water. It's not nearly as heavily fished, and its limited access, shallow water, and numerous sweepers result in little to no canoe traffic above Kelloggs Bridge.

In short, you have a good chance of fishing alone here for a much more relaxing and rewarding day on the water.

The North Branch begins as an overflow from Otsego Lake in southern Otsego County and flows generally southeastward to the Crawford County line. Here it turns south to the village of Lovells and then south and southeast to enter the mainstream a mile below McMasters Bridge or 36 miles from its headwaters. Much of the river frontage north of Lovells is state land, and there is ample public access here. Downstream (south) from Lovells there is relatively little public land, and you'll find access much more limited.

Because the North Branch drains several lakes in the headwaters, its upper portions are too warm in summer for ideal trout water. But by the time the river turns south toward Crawford County, an influx of groundwater has cooled it into a Blue Ribbon Trout Stream that supports some of the finest brookie fishing in the Au Sable River system. Browns are also plentiful from the Crawford County line all the way to the mainstream, but most wading anglers concentrate on the five-mile stretch upstream from Lovells where the state owns much of the frontage and access sites are numerous between Twin Bridges and Lovells Bridge.

The flies-only water of the North Branch begins at the Sheep Ranch Public Access Site above Twin Bridges and continues downstream about 21 river miles to the mouth. Much of the river in Otsego County and all the river in Crawford County are wide enough for fly casting, but sections downstream from Kelloggs Bridge are often too deep to wade. The North Branch in the Lovells area has been dubbed "old man's fishing." Other than an occasional deep hole, the river here is mostly only knee deep and the wading is easy, hence its popularity.

The width of the North Branch is much more variable than that of the mainstream or South Branch. From its confluence with Chub Creek in southern Otsego County all the way to the mouth it varies in width from about 40 to more than 150 feet. The changes in width can be quite abrupt and should be a warning to wading fishermen. When the stream narrows, the depth or velocity—or both—must increase, and wading will be more difficult and at times impossible.

The National Guard Artillery Range borders the upper North Branch on the south in Otsego County and on the west in Crawford County. For obvious reasons, you should avoid crossing over into the military reservation.

Although the North Branch can be canoed from the Pipe Springs Public Access Site near the Crawford County line to the mouth, most canoeists pass up the trip. There are logjams and structures to avoid, and gravel riffles and sandy shoals to pull through at low water. Canoe liveries are reluctant to use the North Branch—their canoes would take a beating when used by inexperienced paddlers—and to most anglers that's good news. On summer weekends you do not experience the "aluminum hatch" as you would on the mainstream or South Branch.

Like other branches of the Au Sable, the North Branch was first the focus of lumbermen with large-scale logging taking place in the mid-1800s. A pair of dams were built in 1870 with Dam Two constructed 10 miles north of Lovells and Dam Four downriver from the village. Ten years later the Jackson, Lansing, and Saginaw Railroad was extended from Grayling to a spot on the river that would eventually become Lovells. Trains carried lumber out and anglers in as word of the phenomenal fishing, first grayling then brook trout, spread across the Midwest and to the East Coast. In 1898, with Lovells hovering around a thousand, Thomas E. Douglas arrived to build a sawmill and general store. But the Canadian-born entrepreneur was so impressed by the trout-filled North Branch that in 1916 he expanded his store into a hotel called the Douglas House and founded the North Branch Outing Club. The membership fee for the exclusive sportsman's club was $25, a steep price in those days, but the club boasted 53 members its first year and later the likes of Henry and Edsel Ford, John and Horace Dodge and Thomas Edison as well.

According to the historical accounts of William B. Mershon, a Saginaw lumberman and conservationist, the North Branch was considered even better than the mainstream for brook trout in the late 1800s. The North Branch is still a top-notch brookie stream today, although it probably pales compared to the early 1900s when the size limit was only eight inches and a daily creel was 50 trout. There are fewer browns than brookies in the upper North Branch, but the browns run to larger size. Populations of brook trout in the North Branch above Kelloggs Bridge vary widely. The highest concentrations are found between Twin Bridges and Lovells and are generally higher than those of the Holy Water.

The flow of the North Branch is remarkably stable, more so than either the mainstream or certainly the South Branch. Wading conditions do not change as drastically on the North Branch as anglers experience on the South Branch. The summer water temperatures on the upper North Branch occasionally go as high as 80 degrees F, higher than on the Holy Water of the Au Sable and much higher than the optimum for brook trout. It is probable that the trout protect themselves from the high temperatures by seeking out the colder areas where large amounts of groundwater enter the stream. Schools of brook trout can often be seen in springs areas in late summer.

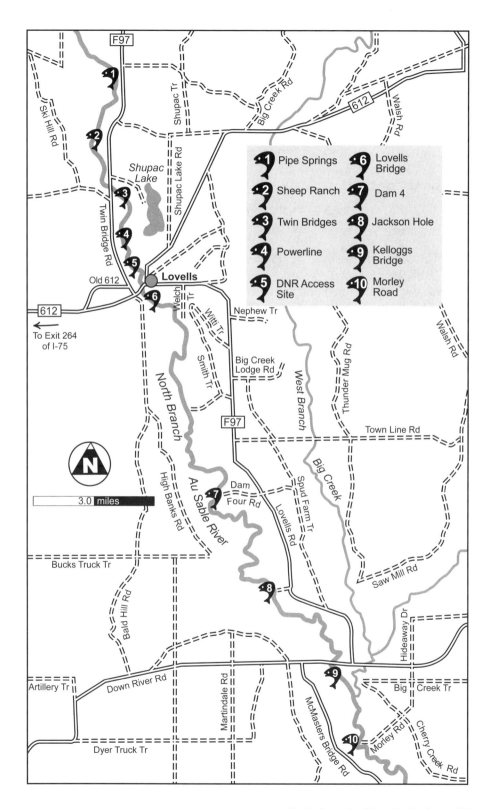

1	Pipe Springs	**6**	Lovells Bridge
2	Sheep Ranch	**7**	Dam 4
3	Twin Bridges	**8**	Jackson Hole
4	Powerline	**9**	Kelloggs Bridge
5	DNR Access Site	**10**	Morley Road

F97

Shupac Tr

Big Creek Rd

612

Walsh Rd

Ski Hill Rd

Shupac Lake Rd

Shupac Lake

Twin Bridge Rd

Old 612

Lovells

612

Welch Tr

Witt Tr

Nephew Tr

To Exit 264
of I-75

Smith Tr

Big Creek Lodge Rd

West Branch

Thunder Mug Rd

Walsh Rd

F97

Town Line Rd

N

3.0 miles

High Banks Rd

Au Sable River

Dam Four Rd

Lovells Rd

Spud Farm Tr

Big Creek

Saw Mill Rd

North Branch

Bucks Truck Tr

Bald Hill Rd

Hideaway Dr

Artillery Tr

Down River Rd

Martindale Rd

McMasters Bridge Rd

Big Creek Tr

Morley Rd

Cherry Creek Rd

Dyer Truck Tr

Because of the warmer water, fly hatches occur earlier on the North Branch than on the mainstream or South Branch. Overall the North Branch has strong fly hatches, particularly Hendricksons in April and May and sulphur duns, little black caddis, and brown drakes from May to early June. The Hex hatch usually only takes place near the lower portions of the river, but tricos, the tiny white-winged blacks fished in sizes 22 to 28, occur throughout much of the North Branch in July and August. When there is no obvious hatch, North Branch trout respond well to attractor patterns.

Accommodations

Although the wide variety of motels in Gaylord and Grayling are within easy driving distance from the North Branch, Lovells offers its own riverside accommodations.

The most interesting is **Fuller's North Branch Outing Club** (989-348-7951; *www.fullersnboc.com*) located at the Lovell's Bridge at 6122 E. County Rd. 612. The bed and breakfast was built as a hotel in 1916 and from the beginning was the home of the North Branch Outing Club, a popular sportsmen's club. Fuller's has 12 rooms overlooking four hundred feet of the North Branch, a comfortable lounge downstairs, a sleeping porch upstairs, and a place to hang your waders. Nearby at 8374 Twin Bridge Road are **Bud's Cabins** (989-348-8400; *www.budscabins.com*), four log cabins on the North Branch. Each cabin sleeps four and has a kitchenette. At night anglers gather to swap fish stories at the Riverside Tavern, where there is an outdoor deck overlooking the North Branch and anybody fishing this stretch of prime trout stream.

Campgrounds: Camping is permitted at the access sites Pipe Spring and Sheep Ranch, although there are no facilities at them. Just minutes from the Twin Bridges access site is Shupac State Forest Campground on Campground Trail. The rustic campground has 30 sites, vault toilets, and a boat launch on the shores of Shupac Lake, a designated trout lake.

Fly Shops and Guides

Along with guestrooms and a lounge, Fuller's contains a well-stocked fly shop and can arrange guides for a full day in an Au Sable riverboat or a half day of wading in the North Branch.

Also in Lovells is **Hartman's Fly Shop** (989-348-9679, 877-363-4702; 6794 E. County Rd. 612). This long-time shop dates back to 1947 when Vern and Edith Hartman moved to Lovells from Flint after vacationing on the river for several years. Their original shop consisted of one showcase of trout flies in their living room, but eventually they expanded to a building adjoining their home. Traditionally the shop would close after deer season, and during the winter the couple would tie 12,000 flies to be ready for the trout opener. Hartman's also will arrange guide service in a drift boat, in an Au Sable riverboat, or for wading.

The North Branch Outing Club

Lovells was already a booming lumber town when Thomas E. Douglas arrived in 1898 and built a sawmill and a general store. Realizing that logging was on the wane and fascinated by the abundance of trout fishing in the North Branch, Thomas decided to promote fishing and in 1916 expanded his store into a hotel he called the Douglas House. The lodge features 20 guest rooms, lavish common spaces, and was illuminated in the evening by electricity generated in his mill. It reputedly had a huge ice box with 45 drawers to hold the catch of the day.

Anglers arrived from around the Midwest, the East Coast, and even aboard, at first by train and sometimes by private railroad cars. Right from the beginning the Douglas House was home to the North Branch Outing Club. Douglas founded the sportsman's club, and it quickly turned into a social gathering of America's elite with members and their guests such as Henry and Edsel Ford, Thomas Edison, Harvey Firestone, the Dodge brothers, Ernest Hemingway, and royalty from Europe. Hotel guests enjoyed what was considered at the time to be world-class fly fishing on the North Branch and then in the evening were treated to homecooked meals by Douglas's wife and later his daughter, Margaret.

Margaret Thomas ran the hotel until 1971 and continued to live there until 1991. In 1996 the Fuller family bought the historic lodge and turned it into Fuller's North Branch Outing Club. "It took two years to restore it until we were comfortable having guests," said Todd Fuller.

The inn is still a classic, well deserving of its placement on the National Register of Historic Places in 2001. The lodge features 12 rooms, including the Douglas Suite, a room with a private bath and a porch overlooking the river, where the Douglas family lived. Downstairs the common areas are eight thousand square feet of maple floors accented by sugar pine moldings and windows of the original hand-blown glass. One room is filled with wall hooks and benches so anglers can remove their waders and set aside their rods after a long day of fishing. In the adjoining sitting area, among the comfortable sofas and chairs, is a television, the only one in the inn. But there are no phones in the rooms. "It's a step back in time, a getaway from the buzz," said Fuller.

It's living history on one of Michigan's most famous trout streams.

Maps of the North Branch

Ten access sites are covered on the North Branch, five upstream from Lovells, one at the Lovells Bridge where County Road 612 crosses the river and four downstream. This makes Lovells the logical headquarters for the North Branch no matter where you plan to fish and it can be easily reached from I-75 by departing at exit 264 and heading east on County Rd. 612 for 12 miles. It's important to remember that the roads, two-tracks, and trails in the military reservation south and west of the river are not open to the public.

Pipe Springs Public Access

GPS N 44° 50.969'
W 84° 29.167'

Pipe Springs Public Access Site is reached from Twin Bridge Road (County Road F97) a half mile south of the Crawford/Otsego County line or 3.3 miles north of the Lovells Bridge on County Road 612. After crossing the North Branch on Twin Bridges, continue heading north for another 1.7 miles and then look for an inconspicuous two-track road leading off to the west (left). The GPS coordinates mark the start of this rough dirt road which leads 70 yards through the woods then ends as a loop in a grassy open area along the river. Camping is allowed here, and there is enough space for a dozen tents and trailers. There are no designated camping spaces, but it is wise to camp some distance from the water to protect the shoreline and to keep out of the way of anglers accessing the river via a stairway and a primitive boardwalk that extends over the mud along the banks.

Also referred to as the Black Hole, the site picked up its name from a pair of pipes on the east bank of the river where the springs gurgled up through the ground. The width of the North Branch varies considerably along this segment. Downstream from the access site it is 70 to 90 feet wide and two to three feet deep with some deeper holes. Upstream it is 50 to 70 feet wide and two to four feet deep with some holes that will flood your waders. Bottom is gravel and sand with some muck. The stream velocity is slow to moderate in the wider areas and moderate to fast where the stream narrows. Wading downstream is fairly easy if you watch out for the deeper holes. Upstream, wading is more difficult, and there is some water that cannot be waded. The stream is wide and open enough for easy casting of a fly rod. Trout cover, some of it man-made, is adequate. There is a good population of large brown trout in this part of the North Branch.

There are no special regulations for this water, and a few spin and bait anglers will mix in here with fly fishers, particularly on opening weekend and in May. Early season fly hatches are good on this water, sometimes better than on the mainstream. Fishing pressure is usually moderate.

Sheep Ranch

GPS N 44° 50.045'
W 84° 29.497'

Heading south towards Lovells the next public access site is the Sheep Ranch, a half mile north of Twin Bridges or 2.2 miles north of County Road 612. The site is actually reached from a two-track that is marked along Twin Bridge Road by a "Sheep Ranch Access Site" sign. The two-track is a loop, and in the middle of it is the best footpath to the river marked with a "Fishing Access Site" sign.

The name of the access site dates back to World War II when sheep were

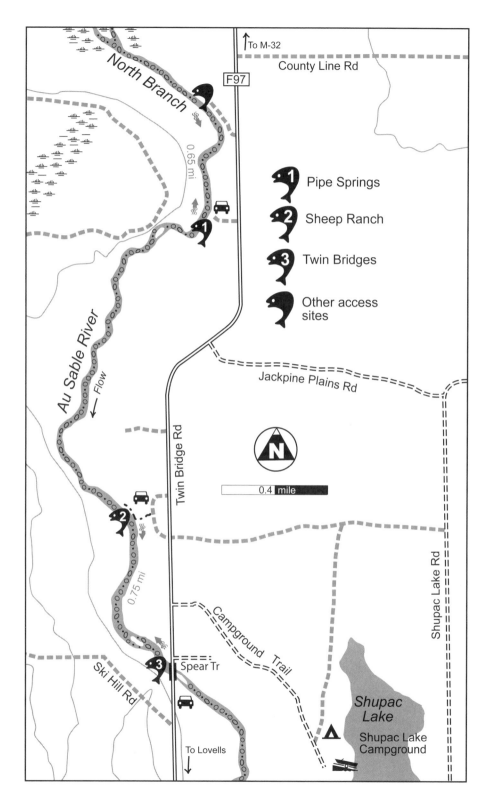

To M-32

County Line Rd

F97

North Branch

0.65 mi

Au Sable River

Flow

1 Pipe Springs

2 Sheep Ranch

3 Twin Bridges

Other access sites

Jackpine Plains Rd

N

0.4 mile

Twin Bridge Rd

0.75 mi

Shupac Lake Rd

Campground Trail

Spear Tr

Ski Hill Rd

Shupac Lake

Shupac Lake Campground

To Lovells

raised here to support the war effort. Today most of the area is still an open grassland area with scrub jack pine and poplar closing in. There is ample parking for vehicles, and along the main trail it's a five-minute walk to the river.

A "Quality Fishing Area" sign at streamside marks the exact boundary between the standard-regulation water upstream and the flies-only, special-regulation water downstream. The riverbanks, both sides, are state land at the access site and upstream. Downstream from the access site, both banks are private.

Other than a 30-foot-wide chute just below the "Quality Fishing Area" sign, the river ranges from 50 feet wide to 100 feet wide downstream from the narrow channel of fast water. The depth is two to three feet deep with a few deeper holes, and the bottom is gravel with some sand, muck, and boulders. Velocity of flow is slow to moderate, making wading easy, and there is more than enough room to cast a fly. The banks are low and brushy. Fish cover is very good.

This is a pleasant reach to fish, and you may often have the river to yourself here. Fly anglers usually stick to the flies-only water, leaving the river upstream to the bait and spin fishermen. It is possible to fish downstream to the Twin Bridges Access Site, a wade of 0.75 mile.

3 Twin Bridges
GPS N 44° 49.678'
W 84° 29.435'   Map: page 109

Twin Bridges is 1.8 miles north of the intersection of Twin Bridge Road with County Road 612. Parking is tight along the road, but the east shoulder has enough room for two or three vehicles above and below the bridge. You'll find a wider shoulder and better parking about a quarter mile north of the bridge.

This is all private land, except for the road right-of-way, and there are several homes and cabins on the river. On both sides of the bridge there are stairs leading down to the water, after which you will have to stick to the channel, fishing upstream or down.

The North Branch is 100 to 125 feet wide here and one to three feet deep, with a few deeper holes. Bottom is gravel, sand, and some muck. Velocity is slow to moderate and wading is easy. Upstream from the bridge the river is loaded with sweepers and other trout cover along with a small grassy island. Downstream a large brushy island begins at the bridge and splits the North Branch into a pair of channels.

Overall you'll find the river is wide and open for easy fly fishing. The banks are four feet high and either brushy or are lined with hardwoods and a few conifers. This is a popular access for anglers so expect moderate fishing pressure, especially on the weekends.

Michigan Historic Trout Fishing Museum

In an effort to save a one-room schoolhouse facing demolition in 1990, local residents created the Lovells Township Historical Society, staged fundraisers, and moved the beloved building behind the township hall. The school was renovated into the Lovells Historic Museum.

Ten years later the Society was at it again, collecting donations and recruiting volunteers to build a log cabin next to the schoolhouse. In 2002, the one-room cabin opened as the Michigan Historic Trout Fishing Museum, the only museum in the state dedicated to the history of trout fishing, particularly fly fishing. "That's what our intent is, to keep its focus on fly fishing in Lovells," said Society member Glen Eberly.

If the fishing is slow or you need a mid-day break from the water, the Lovell's Trout Fishing Museum is an interesting place to step out of your waders. Located on Twin Bridge Road and open Saturday and Sunday from 9 a.m. until 4 p.m. during the summer, the museum is filled with rods, reels, the fly collection of noted fly tier Bob Smock, and a lot of historical photos

Opening day at the Michigan Historic Trout Fishing Museum.

and articles from Lovells' golden era of fly fishing. Permanent exhibits cover the North Branch Outing Club and the days when grayling was king. Seasonal ones range from vintage bamboo fly rods to the founding of Trout Unlimited on the banks of the Au Sable River.

The best time to visit the museum is the last Saturday in April when the Lovells Township Historical Society stages its annual Historical Trout Opener Festival with speakers, fly tying demonstrations, and casting competitions. During that often chilly weekend, a cup of the Society's steaming bean soup is reason enough to leave the North Branch.

4 Powerline

GPS N 44° 48.932'
W 84° 29.409'

This access is 0.9 mile from County Road 612 along Twin Bridge Road or just south of Loeffler Road, and indeed it has a powerline running through the middle of it and over the river. There is a parking area for four or five vehicles on the east side of the road that is posted with a "Fishing Access" sign. A trail departs Twin Bridge Road and follows the powerline east, reaching the river within a hundred yards.

The North Branch is 150 feet wide and two to three feet deep. It's broken up by numerous small grassy islands, sunken logs, and other excellent cover for trout. The bottom is predominately gravel and along with a moderate current makes for easy wading and fishing.

5 DNR Access Site

GPS N 44° 48.472'
W 84° 28.186'

Just a half mile from the Lovells Bridge and County Road 612 is an unmarked two-track that leads a hundred yards to this public access site. The two-track ends at a small cul-de-sac where there is parking for possibly five or six cars and a "Fishing Access Site" sign letting you know you're in the right place. A trail descends a low bluff and winds through the woods a hundred yards before arriving at the river.

The river is not as wide here as at the Powerline but still open enough for easy casting. The bottom is predominately gravel and the depth is two to three feet and even shallower upstream. Small grassy and marshy islands break up the channel downstream as well as man-made structure.

From the Powerline through this access and to Lovells Bridge is some of the best water of the North Branch for fly anglers. The excellent trout cover gives rise to larger fish than further upstream and the gravel river bottom supports reliable hatches of mayflies and caddisflies including Hendrickson, march brown, mahogany, and sulphur duns.

Though private land surrounds the access sites, the wading is easy and you could easily fish from one site to the next. Beginning here it's a 0.75-mile wade upstream to the Powerline and than a half mile walk on Twin Bridge Road to return to your vehicle. Downstream it's only a 0.6-mile wade to Lovells Bridge, where along the way you can step out for a beer and a bite to eat at the Riverside Tavern. It's also a half mile walk from the bridge back to the DNR access site.

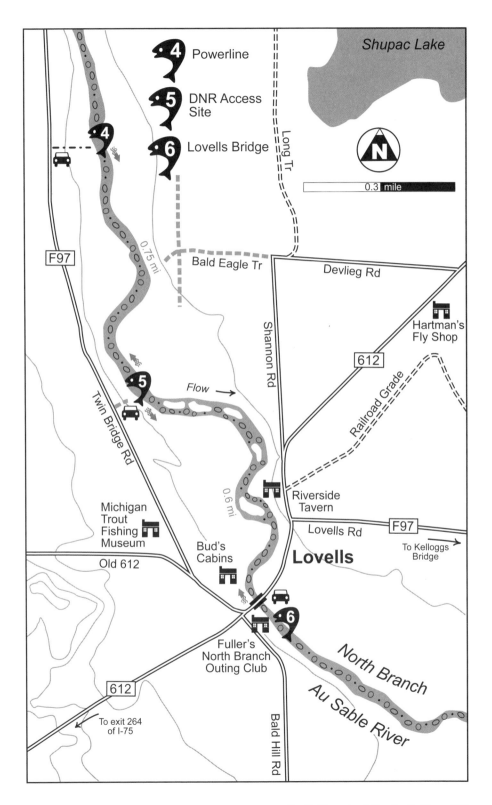

Powerline

DNR Access Site

Lovells Bridge

Shupac Lake

0.3 mile

Long Tr

Bald Eagle Tr

Devlieg Rd

F97

0.75 mi

Shannon Rd

Hartman's Fly Shop

612

Railroad Grade

Flow →

Twin Bridge Rd

0.6 mi

Riverside Tavern

F97

Lovells Rd

To Kelloggs Bridge

Michigan Trout Fishing Museum

Old 612

Bud's Cabins

Lovells

612

To exit 264 of I-75

Fuller's North Branch Outing Club

Bald Hill Rd

North Branch

Au Sable River

6 Lovells Bridge

GPS N 44° 48.249'
W 84° 28.895'

Map: page 113

Lovells Bridge is where County Road 612 crosses the North Branch. Adjacent to the bridge is Fuller's North Branch Outing Club, a bed and breakfast, with a fly shop. There is room to park three or four cars east of the bridge on the shoulder of County Road 612.

The river is 60 to 100 feet wide here and two to three feet deep, with some deeper holes. Bottom is mostly gravel, with some sand and muck. The velocity is moderate and wading is fairly easy. The right bank is high and steep, the left bank lower and brushy. The land is all private except for the road right-of-way. Trout cover is somewhat sparse the farther downstream of the bridge you wade. Being right in Lovells and flowing past Fuller's, the fishing pressure is usually heavier than the access sites further upstream.

7 Dam Four

GPS N 44° 45.360'
W 84° 26.488'

From Lovells County Road F97 (Lovells Road) first heads east and then swings south toward the rest of the access sites. The first is Dam Four, reached four miles south of Lovells or 3.5 miles north of County Road F32 (North Down River Road). Dam Four Road, a well-graded dirt road, is posted along County Road F97 and leads 0.75 mile west to the river where there are parking along the shoulders and a large staircase for access to the water.

Dam Four was the site of one of Henry Ford's many lodges in Michigan, and the caretaker's house still stands as a private residence. Upstream from the stairway are a few of the old pilings remaining from the original dam loggers built to help float timber.

The river is a hundred feet wide with depths that range from knee-deep to holes that will float your hat. Although the river is wide, it is broken up by a series of grassy islands, the largest right in front of the stairway. This is an excellent stretch for fly anglers. The bottom is a mixture of gravel and sand, and the water for the most part has a pool-and-riffle character to it. The road end is surrounded by private property but a trail does follow the riverbank a short way upstream.

8 Jackson Hole

GPS N 44° 43.871'
W 84° 26.294'

From Dam Four, head south on County Road F97 (Lovells Road) for 1.6 miles to reach the access road to Jackson Hole. There are two roads here, both labeled Jackson Hole Trail. But the first is a two-track posted with a DNR

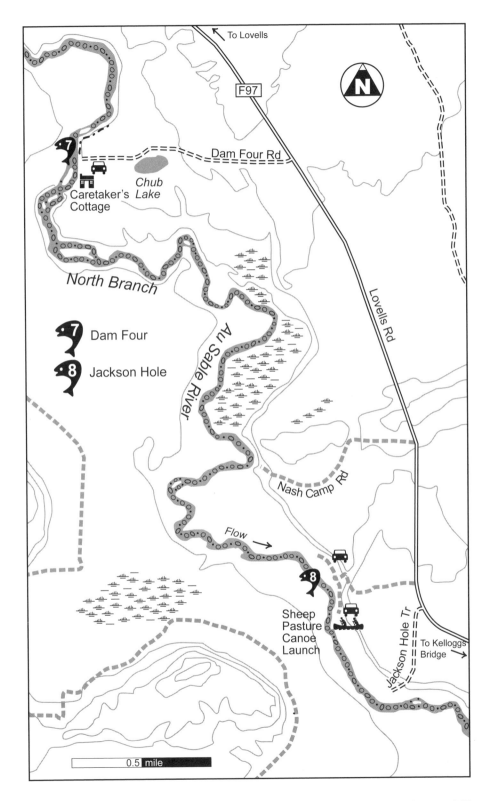

To Lovells

F97

N

Dam Four Rd

7

Chub Lake

Caretaker's Cottage

North Branch

Au Sable River

Lovells Rd

7 Dam Four

8 Jackson Hole

Nash Camp Rd

Flow

8

Sheep Pasture Canoe Launch

Jackson Hole Tr

To Kelloggs Bridge

0.5 mile

boat access sign and heads west to the river and a developed canoe launch. The second is a well-graded dirt road that leads to cottages. If coming from Grayling, the access road is the second Jackson Hole Trail, 1.9 miles from County Road F32 (North Down River Road).

This public access site, also referred to as Sheep Pasture, provides the most extensive access to the lower North Branch. There is a large acreage of state land here with more than half a mile of public frontage on both banks. At one time camping was allowed here but is now prohibited.

Within a third of a mile the two-track access road splits with the right-hand fork heading north a short way to a small parking area, capable of holding five or six vehicles, and a trail to the water. Here the river is more than a hundred feet wide with a depth of two to three feet, making it much easier to wade than stretches downstream. The bottom is a mix of gravel and sand with some marl along the shoreline, making it one of the better places along the North Branch to wait for the Hex hatch.

The left-hand fork skirts the river to the south before ending at the Sheep Pasture Canoe Launch, where you'll find vault toilets, a parking area, and lots of "No Camping" signs. This stretch of the river is only 40 feet wide and waist-deep or deeper with some holes that need to be avoided. The constricted North Branch flows fast here, and the wading could be challenging at times if not impossible during periods of high water.

Overall the trout fishing can be very good at Jackson Hole. This segment of the North Branch has good trout cover, structure, and undercut banks that hold large browns and reliable hatches. Just be careful where you step when wading.

 9 Kelloggs Bridge

GPS N 44° 42.986'
W 84° 25.170'

Kelloggs Bridge is on County Road F32 about 18 miles east of Grayling or less than half a mile west from the intersection of North Down River Road and Lovells Road. There is room to park six or seven vehicles in a parking area posted by the Headwaters Land Conservancy on the south side of the road just east of the bridge. All the land around the bridge is privately owned so anglers need to be respectful and stay in the river.

The river is 60 to 100 feet wide and two to four feet deep, but there are many holes and deep runs that will cause you problems. Equally important the flow is fast and wading is not easy. At high water, wading is very often impossible.

The best fishing is upstream where there are riffles, small islands, sweepers, and sunken logs that hide large browns. The river bottom is mostly gravel, with some sand and muck. Low banks forested with pine, hardwood and some brush line the river here and, if the water levels are normal or low, the casting is easy.

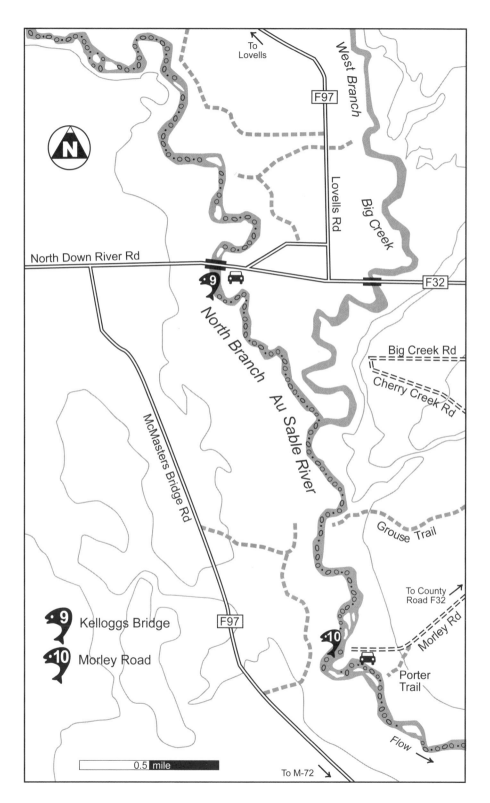

To
Lovells

West Branch

F97

Lovells Rd

Big Creek

North Down River Rd

9

F32

North Branch Au Sable River

Big Creek Rd

Cherry Creek Rd

McMasters Bridge Rd

Grouse Trail

To County
Road F32

Morley Rd

10

Porter
Trail

9 Kelloggs Bridge

10 Morley Road

F97

Flow

0.5 mile

To M-72

Anglers examine an Au Sable riverboat during the Historical Trout Opener Festival held on the first weekend of trout season in Lovells.

 ## Morley Road

GPS N 44° 41.850'
W 84° 24.673'

Map: page 117

The West Branch of Big Creek enters the North Branch almost a mile downstream from Kelloggs Bridge and changes it significantly. At times the North Branch is almost two hundred feet wide after the confluence with Big Creek. The final access site is downstream even further and reached from Lovells Road (County Road F97) by turning east (left) on County Road F32

Fishing the Trico Hatch

Tricorythodes, or Tricos as many anglers call them, is the genus of tiny mayflies of which there are 18 species in North America. The most common one in Michigan is Tricorythodes stygiatus, a gnat-sized mayfly that hatches from July through September usually with two to three hours of sunrise, which for some anglers is a much more civilized time to be fishing than in the middle of the night.

Tricos are small, but the emerging nymphs and duns are easy prey for trout. At such times anglers tie on a tiny, white-winged black, a small dry fly fished in sizes 18 to 28, which can be extremely effective when the hatch is on. In early July, Trico hatches can be matched with size-18 and size-20 hooks, but as the season progresses each generation of Tricos that comes off the water gets smaller. By the middle of August the hatch is best matched by size-28 flies.

With such small offerings, leaders should taper down to 5X for a size-18 fly and to a gossamer-like 7X or even 8X for a size-28 fly. Leader lengths can range from nine feet to 15 feet, depending on your casting proficiency, wind, and the type of water being fished. The shorter the leader, of course, the easier it is to make an accurate cast. The longer the leader the less chance of scarring the fish.

While the entire Trico hatch, from emerging nymph to egg-laying adult, can be fished, it's the spinner fall that triggers a massive feeding spree among trout. With clouds of spinners in the air, even large trout will feed on them, often delicately sipping them as the tiny mayflies land on the surface of the stream to lay their eggs. Rivers with strong Trico hatches include the Au Sable mainstream, the North Branch of the Au Sable, the Black, the Manistee, the Boardman and the Pere Marquette.

Fishing the Trico hatch can be surprisingly good, but keep in mind that you're casting an incredibly small fly on very fine tippet. That can be frustrating at times for beginner fly anglers. And if you're an older angler and a trout breaks off your size-28 fly, better have the reading glasses handy to tie on another.

and then south on Morley Road within a mile. Follow Morley Road for 1.8 miles and it will end at a "Quality Fishing Area" sign on the North Branch. Parking is tight here, but there is room for three or four vehicles along the shoulder on the south side of the road.

The river is 150 feet wide here and two to four feet deep, making it open enough for easy casting and wadable during normal water levels. But the velocity is swifter, and there are numerous holes and deep runs, particularly upstream from Morley Road, so extreme caution in wading must be used no matter what the water conditions are like. There are cabins on both sides of the road, so if the water is running high there is little opportunity to cast from the bank.

An angler departs the Manistee River after an afternoon of fishing at the Yellow Trees Access Site, a canoe launch downriver of M-72.

Manistee River

Paralleling the Au Sable in location, if not in reputation, is the Manistee River. From their headwaters the two rivers flow south, and, at one point in Crawford County, are less than three miles apart, so close that the Chippewa and Ottawa Indians used the rivers to paddle and portage from Lake Huron to Lake Michigan. At M-72 the two rivers each go their separate ways. The Au Sable heads 120 miles east to Lake Huron, first passing through a stretch that fly anglers regard as the Holy Water.

The Manistee heads west. From its beginning in the southeast corner of Antrim County, it gathers size and velocity until it discharges into Manistee Lake and then Lake Michigan as the third-longest river in the state. Its 216-mile journey is surpassed by only the Grand River (262 miles) and the Muskegon (227 miles). Along the way the Manistee and its tributaries drain 1,780 square miles in 11 counties.

Aesthetically, the Manistee is one of our most attractive rivers, maybe even more so than the Au Sable. Its waters flow cool and clean, and its banks are forested with pine, cedar, spruce, poplar, maple, and oak. In the fall, the brilliant warm colors of the hardwoods are pleasingly contrasted with the deep greens of the conifers. The Manistee has never had the cabin development or the intensive fishing pressure of the Au Sable, and the upper reaches, particularly the Deward Tract, have a much more wilderness-like atmosphere than the Holy Water.

While the Au Sable is renowned, even revered, among fly anglers, the Manistee is also considered a classic trout stream. The river consists primarily of sand and silt bottom that has been blessed with fallen logs, undercut banks, beautiful pools, riffled tailwaters, and sharp bends all holding trout. It has its own flies-only section, while 36 miles of it, from Deward to the confluence with its North Branch near Sharon, is designated as a Blue Ribbon Trout Stream. This is the section that is best suited for wading anglers and is covered in this chapter.

Manistee's winding nature—its Indian name, *Manistiqweita*, means "crooked river"—is partly responsible for its natural appearance. Loggers and the destructive path they left behind came late to the Manistee. The river was so crooked and choked with logjams that early timber cruisers reported long stretches of open water were rare. Logging company crews clearing the river for log drives from Lake Michigan did not reach Sherman until 1870, and the interior portion of the watershed was not logged until well after that.

By then a railroad had reached Deward, the main center of lumbering activity on the upper Manistee and home of one of the largest sawmills in the country. The rail line connected Deward to East Jordan, where the timber was then loaded on barges and shipped to Chicago or points east. That spared the upper Manistee from the scouring of annual log drives that ruined so many other trout streams in Michigan. No doubt it's also why good catches of grayling were still being reported on the Manistee at the turn of the century and long after the fish had disappeared from most of the Au Sable.

The Manistee was also one of the last of the great rivers in Michigan to remain free flowing. The Tippy Dam was not completed until in 1918, and the Hodenpyl Dam didn't come online until 1925. The upper Manistee escaped such hydropower projects altogether.

The Manistee begins at an elevation of 1,250 feet in the sandy glacial hills of Antrim County near the border with Otsego County, and six miles southeast of Alba. A handful of spring-fed tributaries merge to form its headwaters; from there the Manistee descends quickly, four feet per mile in its upper half, gathering an influx of groundwater along the way. Within only two miles the Manistee crosses Mancelona Road as a 20-foot wide trout stream already attracting the attention of bait and spin anglers along with fly fishers skilled in casting in tight, bushy settings.

Downstream from Mancelona Road, the Manistee enters the Deward Tract, the ghosttown site of Deward and now a special, non-motorized area that includes both banks of the river. Walk-in access ranges from a few hundred yards to a half-mile hike before you reach the Manistee, now ranging 30 to 50 feet in width and two to four feet in depth. Wading is easy and backcasts are possible. Best of all, this is brook trout country. The ten miles of water in the Deward Tract has gravel beds for spawning, plenty of cover, strong hatches, and natural reproduction that sustains the healthiest population of brookies found anywhere in the Manistee. Add the fact that few canoes are seen this far upstream and the Deward Tract becomes an excellent place for anglers new to the sport of fly fishing. You have room to a cast a fly to brookies that always seem eager to take it.

The Deward Tract ends at Cameron Bridge, and for the next ten miles downstream the Manistee is almost all sand bottom, with few patches of gravel. The banks are alternately coniferous swamp and pine upland, and the river is two to four feet deep, easily wadable if you keep an eye out for deeper holes and runs. A mile before the river reaches M-72, the bottom becomes more gravelly, and gravel bottom predominates from here to about two river miles below the state highway.

Manistee River Bridge on M-72 also marks a change in regulations on the Manistee. Upstream the river is open to all tackle from the last Saturday in April to Sept. 30 with a daily possession of five fish with no more than three of them 15 inches or larger. Minimum size for brook trout is ten inches, browns 12 inches.

From M-72 to CCC Bridge is the Manistee's flies-only stretch with tackle limited to artificial flies. The river is open year round, but you can keep fish

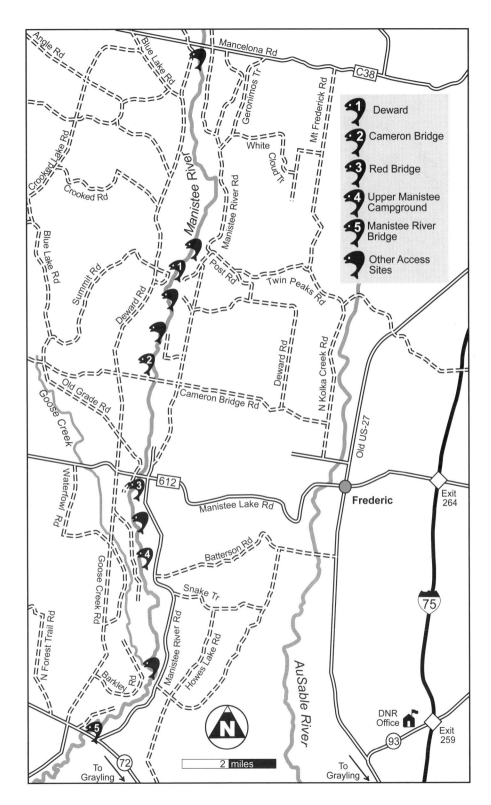

Angle Rd
Mancelona Rd
C38
Blue Lake Rd
Geronimos Tr
Mt Frederick Rd

1 Deward
2 Cameron Bridge
3 Red Bridge
4 Upper Manistee Campground
5 Manistee River Bridge
Other Access Sites

Crooked Lake Rd
White Cloud Tr
Crooked Rd

Manistee River

Blue Lake Rd
Summit Rd
Deward Rd
Manistee River Rd
Post Rd
Twin Peaks Rd

1

Deward Rd
N Kolka Creek Rd

2

Old Grade Rd
Cameron Bridge Rd

Goose Creek

Old US-27

612
Manistee Lake Rd
Frederic
Exit 264

Waterfowl Rd
3

Batterson Rd

Goose Creek Rd
4

Snake Tr

75

N Forest Trail Rd
Manistee River Rd
Howes Lake Rd

Barkley Rd

DNR Office
Exit 259
93

5
To Grayling
72
N
2 miles

AuSable River

To Grayling

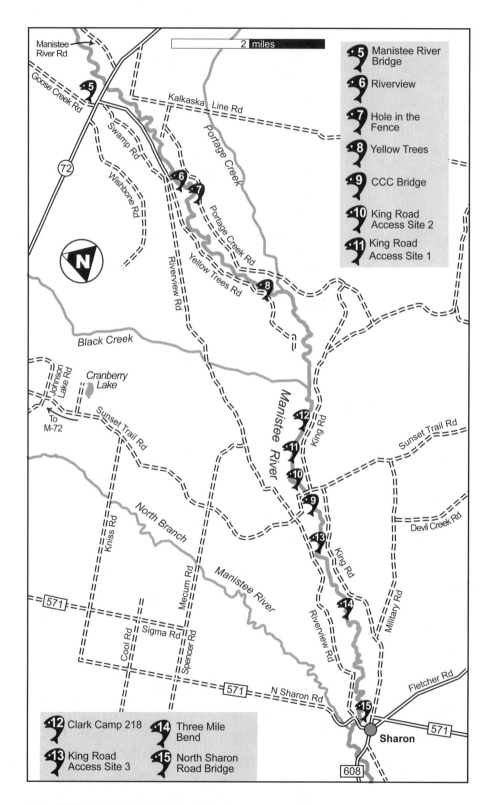

2 miles

5 Manistee River Bridge

6 Riverview

7 Hole in the Fence

8 Yellow Trees

9 CCC Bridge

10 King Road Access Site 2

11 King Road Access Site 1

Manistee River Rd

Goose Creek Rd

Kalkaska Line Rd

Portage Creek

Swamp Rd

72

Wishbone Rd

Portage Creek Rd

N

Riverview Rd

Yellow Trees Rd

Black Creek

Johnson Lake Rd

Cranberry Lake

To M-72

Sunset Trail Rd

Manistee River

King Rd

Sunset Trail Rd

North Branch

Kriss Rd

Devil Creek Rd

Mecum Rd

Manistee River

King Rd

571

Cool Rd

Sigma Rd

Spencer Rd

Riverview Rd

Military Rd

571

N Sharon Rd

Fletcher Rd

Sharon

571

608

12 Clark Camp 218

13 King Road Access Site 3

14 Three Mile Bend

15 North Sharon Road Bridge

only during the trout season from the last Saturday in April to Sept. 30. The daily limit is two fish, and the minimum size is ten inches for brookies and 15 inches for browns and rainbows. Downstream from CCC Bridge to US-131, the regulations revert to what they were upstream from M-72, including the river being open to all tackle.

The 17-mile flies-only stretch of the Manistee can be waded at the access sites described in this chapter as long as you keep an eye on the water level and use caution. Even at normal water levels you'll find the river more difficult to wade due to a swifter current and more numerous pools and runs that need to be avoided. Then there is that sandy bottom, where depth and consistency can change unexpectedly and quickly, much more so than gravel. But it's easy to cast in a river that's often 80 feet wide or more, and in general there is better cover here for trout and thus the trout are bigger. The number of brookies greatly diminishes but browns are numerous and rainbows begin appearing in noticeable numbers around CCC Bridge.

The North Branch empties into the Manistee at Sharon and the river changes character again at that point, becoming significantly deeper, faster, and unwadable in most places. Below Tippy Dam the Manistee is open to Lake Michigan and is renowned for its strong runs of steelhead and salmon. In fact, the Manistee is better known to steelheaders, who line the banks below Tippy Dam every spring, than fly anglers who arrive mid-summer armed with dry flies and nymphs. Despite being a Blue Ribbon Trout Stream with strong hatches, easy access, and even a flies-only stretch, the Manistee receives considerably less fishing pressure than its more famous twin to the east. No doubt the Au Sable's legendary reputation keeps a fair number of fly anglers from focusing on the Upper Manistee.

Although early French explorers called the Au Sable "the river of sands," the upper Manistee is far sandier than the Au Sable. The sandy streambed with limited gravel for spawning accounts for the lower trout productivity on the Manistee. Still, the Manistee is considered ideal trout water. Thanks to the deep glacial sands where it begins, the Manistee is remarkably stable, providing a steady flow of cold water year round with little fluctuation in depth or temperature. The Manistee is more stable than even the Au Sable, and its summer water temperatures are cooler as well.

The colder temperatures account for the later hatches on the Manistee. Even though it flows at the same latitude as the Au Sable, the Manistee often experiences hatches four to 10 days later. The Manistee can not produce the biomass of aquatic insects like the Au Sable due to its lack of gravel. But its sand and silt bottom is ideal for burrowing mayflies of which the Hexagenia limbata is the largest and best known. Many anglers believe the Manistee rivals the South Branch of the Au Sable for the best Hex hatches in the state.

Other hatches to focus on are Hendrickson and little black caddis beginning in early May, followed by sulphur dun mayfly in late May to early June and brown drakes in June. When the Hex hatch occurs from late June to early July, gray drakes will often be hatching during the day. In mid-summer many anglers will turn to terrestrials such as grasshopper and ant patterns or elk hair caddis flies in sizes 10 through 14 to entice trout.

Canoeing activity can be heavy on the Manistee at times, but not to the extent of the Au Sable mainstream. The most traffic will be seen between Cameron Bridge and M-72. Canoes and the driftboats of fishing guides will also be encountered between M-72 and Sharon but not nearly as many.

Accommodations

Like the Au Sable, Grayling serves as the main base for anglers fishing the Manistee, especially the sections upstream from M-72. For accommodations see the Mainstream of the Au Sable chapter (page 60) or contact the Grayling Visitors Bureau (800-937-8837; *www.grayling-mi.org*).

The only resort directly on the upper portions of the Manistee is *Whispering Pines Resort* (989-348-2044; *www.whisperingresort.com*; 11763 W. 612) located just off CR 612 at Red Bridge, five miles west of Old US-27 in Frederic. The resort offers four cabins overlooking the river. Originally built in the late 1940s, the cabins feature cast-iron gas log fireplaces, fully equipped kitchens, and cable TV.

Kalkaska is a convenient base for fishing the Sharon area and other sites downstream from M-72. Among the better motels in town is *All-Seasons Resort* (231-258-0000; 800-806-1580; *www.kalkaskaallseasons.com*; 760 S. Cedar St.), right along US-131. The Kalkaska Chamber of Commerce (231-258-9103; *www.kalkaskami.com*; 353 S. Cedar St.) can also provide a list of lodging in the area.

Campgrounds: There are four state forest campgrounds on the upper river and one privately owned campground. Three of the state forest campgrounds are covered as access sites; exact directions to them are provided below. The Upper Manistee River Campground, eight miles southwest of Frederic via CR 612 and Goose Creek Road, has 30 drive-in sites on two loops and 10 walk-in sites for canoers. The Manistee River Bridge Campground, eight miles west of Grayling on M-72, has 23 spaces. CCC Bridge Campground, ten miles southeast of Kalkaska via M-72 and Sunset Trail Road, has 39 sites. All three have canoe launches and are very popular with paddlers during the height of the summer. On weekends they can be full.

Also on the Manistee is Goose Creek Trail Camp, a state forest campground designed primarily for equestrians following the Shore-to-Shore Trail. The campground has 12 rustic sites and is located on Manistee River Road, half a mile south of CR 612. Whispering Pines Resort also has a small camping area with water and electric hook-ups for trailers and recreational vehicles.

Fly Shops and Guides

Grayling has several fly shops as well as fishing guides that work the Manistee. A list of them is available in the Mainstream of the Au Sable chapter. Many

On a chilly opening day of trout season, a fly angler hooks his first brookie of the year on the Manistee River just downstream from Red Bridge.

The Hex Hatch

The best-known hatch in Michigan, one that enjoys legendary status among fly anglers, is the Hex hatch. Still occasionally referred to as the Michigan Caddis, the Hexagenia Limbata is actually the world's largest mayfly, with adults often two to three inches in length. Life for a Hex begins as a nymph burrowed in silt at the bottom of the stream for more than a year before swimming to the surface in a fast, agile, wiggling motion.

Once on the surface the Hex can sometimes take up to two minutes to escape its nymphal shuck and get airborne as a dun. The mayfly then flies into nearby brush or trees to dry its wings. A day or two later the spinner fall occurs: the adult insects soar into the air and mate after sundown, and then females dip to the surface of riffled water and ride the current as they release up to eight thousand eggs each. All this commotion takes place in the safety of darkness, usually from 10 p.m. to 4 a.m. When combined with the insect's large size and its prolific numbers, it's easy to understand why even the wariest brown trout throws caution to the wind, comes out of hiding to surface feed when the Hex hatch is on.

Known to many as simply "the event," Hex hatches take place over the course of two to three weeks from late June into early July with warm, windless, and dark nights being the ideal times to be on the river. The first hatches of the season are the best, with trout rising to Hexes with reckless abandon. Later, having already gorged themselves on the huge chunks of protein for a few nights, the fish react sporadically and are more selective.

Predicting the Hex hatch is nothing short of a crapshoot. You may be blessed with the right conditions at the right time of the year on a river that's known for its Hexes but still spend the entire night waiting fruitlessly for something to happen. Fish often enough, and eventually you will witness the massive insects appearing as emerging duns or falling spinners, and all around you will be the noisy slurps of trophy trout feeding. You cast blindly into the darkness, hoping you don't get hung up in the brush on the other side of the river. When a 22-inch brown hits that fly you know it instinctively, even if you can't see it. The entire event may last only 20 to 40 minutes. Cast fast and furiously.

The most common strategy for the Hex hatch is to arrive early to scout your spot before dark. Look for a place where there is good cover along the bank: submerged logs, snags, tree stumps, and roots. Wade out and practice casting to such cover to get a feel of the distance you'll need that night. Then head back to shore and pick out a comfortable spot to sit and wait for the hatch. Stream etiquette dictates that other anglers who come along should respect your claim and move upstream or down a respectable distance from you. And there will be other anglers. On some of the better-known rivers, fishing the Hex hatch is rarely a solitary pursuit.

In the middle of the night anglers can be almost shoulder to shoulder.

Once the hatch starts most anglers, standing in the river in the middle of the night, listen for rising trout. A splashy sound heard after dark is often a young trout. Older and thus larger trout sip the insects off the surface with a deliberate sucking or slurping sound. If you can identify or even sense where a slurp is coming from, try to count between its rises. If a trout is rising every sixth count, cast above the direction of the sound on a five count. And then hold on.

Two of Michigan's best Hex rivers are the Manistee, particularly from Yellow Trees Landing down to the CCC Bridge, and the South Branch in the Mason Tract. Because the insect prefers marl-laden or silty areas, the Holy Water of the Au Sable mainstream is a poor choice. But further downstream from Wakeley Bridge to Mio Pond is excellent, with the best area being from Conner's Flats downstream.

Because the Hex is a huge insect and the trout that feed on it are often large, the imitation needs a sturdy hook to handle those trophy fish and consequently must have plenty of buoyancy. Almost every fly shop in Michigan sells a giant Michigan mayfly pattern. If not, then the Roberts Brown Drake, in sizes six to eight, is considered one of the best all-around flies during the Hex hatch with some anglers going even larger to size-four and size-two hooks. Other patterns used during the hatch include Hex Wulff, Madsen's Hex Spinner, even the Muddler Minnow.

You can also fish the nymph stage, and a size-eight Clark Lynn nymph is an effective pattern. But fishing to individual trout that you hear in the middle of the night is what the Hex hatch is all about. Blindly dropping a fly a foot above a 20-inch brown actively feeding is the reason you're standing among clouds of insects in a cold river at 1 a.m.

Traverse City–based guides float the upper Manistee in driftboats and Au Sable riverboats. A list of these guides is in the Boardman River chapter.

In Kalkaska, you'll find a selection of flies and advice on what's hatching at *Jack's Sport Shop* (231-258-8892; *www.jackssport.net;* 212 Cedar St.). Also based in Kalkaska is longtime guide Charlie Weaver of *Jack Pine Savage Guide Service* (989-348-3299; email: *charliew@freeway.net*), who uses an Au Sable riverboat for trips on the upper Manistee. Flies and guide service are available in Wellston on the lower Manistee at *Schmidt Outfitters* (231-848-4191; www.schmidtoutfitters.com; 918 Seaman Rd.).

Any canoe livery in Grayling will arrange a fish-and-float trip for anglers on the Manistee but two liveries are located right on the river. *Shel-Haven Canoe Rental* (989-348-2158; *www.shelhaven.com*) is located across from the Manistee River Bridge Campground on M-72 and *Long's Canoe Livery* (989-348-7224, 231-258-3452; *www.longscanoelivery.com*) is three miles north of M-72 on Manistee River Road.

Maps of the Manistee

The 15 access sites covered in this chapter have been divided between Upstream of M-72 and Downstream of M-72. Most of the sites are reached via graded dirt roads and two-tracks with M-72 from Grayling and County Road 612 from Frederic serving as the main accesses to the secondary roads. The directions for sites one through four begin at Frederic, reached by departing from I-75 at exit 264, and then heading west on CR 612. The directions for the rest of the sites begin on M-72, reached by departing I-75 at exit 254 and following the I-75 Business Loop through Grayling.

Although not as challenging as navigating unmarked two-tracks through the Mason Tract, finding some of the access sites along the Manistee can still test your map and GPS skills. Also be aware that if the weather has been wet your vehicle might not make it down every two-track: you should not hesitate to turn around if you're unsure about road conditions. A good map to the region is the *Grayling Area Recreation Map*, available at the Grayling Visitors Center, which is located on the banks of the Au Sable along the I-75 Business Loop.

Upstream of M-72

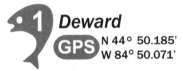

1 Deward

GPS N 44° 50.185'
W 84° 50.071'

The Four Corners of Michigan is where Antrim, Crawford, Kalkaska, and Otsego Counties meet. Spilling out into all four of them is the Deward Tract, a long, narrow, 4,720-acre preserve split in half by the Upper Manistee. With the exception of one private holding, the Deward Tract places ten miles of the river in public domain, ensuring that the area will always remain pristine, undeveloped and accessible to anglers.

The easiest way to reach the Deward Tract is from Frederic. At Old US-27 in town, head west on County Road 612 for 0.7 mile and then turn north (right) on Kolka Creek Road. Within 1.3 miles turn west (left) on Cameron Bridge Road and follow it for 3.2 miles to Manistee River Road. Posted at this intersection is a large, wooden sign that announces "Deward Tract." Turn north (right) onto Manistee River Road and you have entered the Deward Tract.

The tract is a restricted, nonmotorized area bordered by Manistee River Road to the east and Deward Road to the west. From these two roads a handful of two-tracks head toward the Manistee but stop well short of it, usually ending with a small parking area and a locked gate. A foot trail leads to the river. Some access sites in the Deward Tract are difficult to find or involve a hike of 0.3 mile or more. Camping is permitted in the tract, but you must keep within 50 feet of a road open to motorized vehicles. In other words, you cannot camp on or near the stream banks.

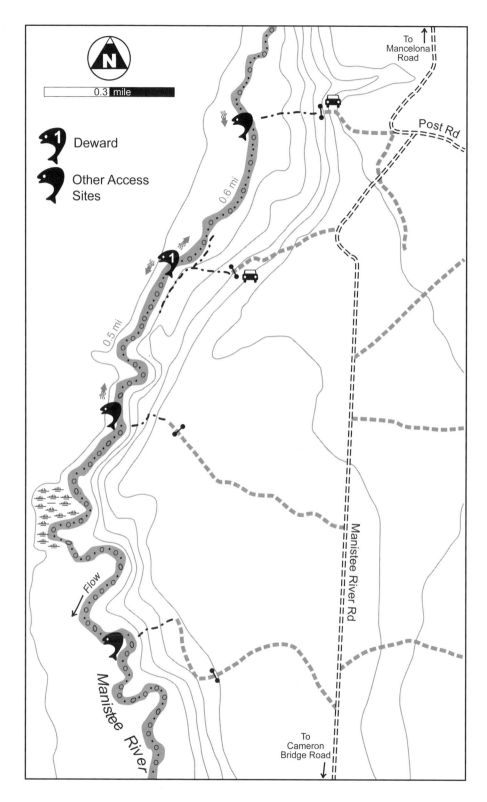

N

0.3 mile

1 Deward

Other Access Sites

0.6 mi

0.5 mi

To
Mancelona
Road

Post Rd

Manistee River Rd

Flow

Manistee River

To
Cameron
Bridge Road

The Deward Tract

One of the last great stands of white pine in the Lower Peninsula gave rise to the bustling mill town of Deward, which in turn resulted in a nonmotorized area where today anglers hike to the Manistee River for what the DNR calls a "quality fishing experience." From axes and railroads to fly rods and foot trails, we have gone full circle in the Deward Tract.

The tract takes its name from the town of Deward, a major logging center that was established in 1900 by lumberman David E. Ward, who owned the heart of the last remaining stands of virgin white pine in northern Michigan. At its height in the early 1900s, Deward had a population of 800 and was home to one of the largest sawmills in the United States, capable of milling 200,000 feet of white pine in 20 hours, or so boasted the *Frederic Times* newspaper in 1903. The mill and the loggers were so efficient that within a decade the pine was gone and all that remained was a sea of stumps. The mill was dismantled and moved in 1912, and within 20 years Deward was a ghost town without a single resident left.

Eventually the land reverted to the state, and in 1958 a 42.5-acre area along the west bank of the Manistee River was dedicated as a Pine Stump Preserve to protect a field of giant stumps from white pine cut around 1900. Other protection wasn't needed until the late 1970s, when riders of off-road vehicles (ORVs) turned the tract into their private playground, often riding through the Manistee River. In 1980, the state designated 4,720 acres as a special, nonmotorized management area and in 2003 even banned snowmobilers from the tract.

Located where the corners of Antrim, Crawford, Kalkaska, and Otsego Counties meet, the Deward Tract is seven miles long, 1.5 miles wide, and split down the middle by ten miles of the Manistee River. Today the only remains of the town are old foundations and railroad grades. What has returned is the wildlife—mink, beavers, and otters are quite common along the river corridor, and turkeys, coyotes, and even bear can be found in the woods—and the trees, from scattered oak and pine to cedar, balsam fir, and densely planted red pine plantations.

But what the Deward Tract represents to many is a quality trout stream and quiet sanctuary to escape the relentless push of progress. You do have to hike in, but the walk is short, and once on the water you'll be free of the deadlines, demands and duties of life in the city. For many anglers that's a quality fishing experience whether they land a trout or not.

This site is perhaps the easiest to locate. From Cameron Bridge Road, follow Manistee River Road for 2.6 miles and then look for a two-track to the west (left) posted with an "Open Road" sign as well as a sign with a binocular icon designating it as a wildlife viewing area. Follow the two-track for 0.3 mile; it will end at a locked gate and a small parking area. A trail leads 300 yards to the Manistee, passing a pair of old bridge abutments and

An angler casts towards rising brook trout on the upper Manistee River.

foundations left over from Deward's heyday as a logging town. At the river there is fencing along the bank and a stairway to the water to prevent further erosion. Anglers' trails head both upstream and downstream for a hundred yards or so.

Here the Manistee is 30 to 40 feet wide and less than three feet deep. The bottom is mostly sand with scattered patches of gravel, but gravel becomes more abundant downstream. Banks upstream are low, mucky, and somewhat open; downstream, the banks are high and sandy. This is a pleasant place to fish, and an abundance of trout cover in the form of stumps, sunken logs, and undercut banks hides wild brookies and a few browns. The open grassland on the east bank upstream makes fly fishing relatively easy for such a narrow stream. About a mile downstream the river deepens; at this point some holes and runs may top your waders. There is also a sand trap here that must be avoided; fortunately it is well marked.

Another access site in the Deward Tract is just north of this one. From Manistee River Road, head north for 0.3 mile to an intersection in a large clearing. This is the former site of the town of Deward. Post Road is posted and heads east (right) as a well graded dirt road. Manistee River Road jogs west (left) but quickly resumes north (right) again; here a two-track continues west toward the river. Within two hundred yards the two-track enters the forest and ends at a red gate and a small parking area. From here a trail continues almost a quarter mile west before reaching the Manistee.

2 Cameron Bridge
GPS N 44° 47.990'
W 84° 50.464'

Cameron Bridge is a starting point for many paddlers on the Upper Manistee River; most of them will pull out at M-72, a four- to five-hour float. From Frederic, head west on County Road 612 for 0.7 mile and then turn north (right) on Kolka Creek Road. Within 1.3 miles turn west (left) on Cameron Bridge Road and follow it 3.7 miles to the bridge. There is room to park three or four cars west of the bridge.

The Manistee is 40 to 50 feet wide here. Upstream, it is one to three feet deep, with some deeper holes. At the bridge and downstream, it can be more than four feet deep at mid-channel. Bottom is sand and gravel upstream, mostly sand downstream. Velocity is moderate. There is a high, sandy bank on the east side of the river downstream from the bridge. Otherwise the banks are low, sandy, or mucky, forested with conifer and hardwood. There are some brushy banks, especially upstream from the bridge. Except for the road right-of-way, the banks are private property, upstream and down.

The river can be waded most places upstream from the bridge. Downstream it is wadable, but caution needs to be used at mid-channel. The river is open and wide enough for fly fishing. Although considered one of the best spots on the Manistee for resident trout, the river here is not usually heavily fished. In late June there can be good Hex hatches on this stretch.

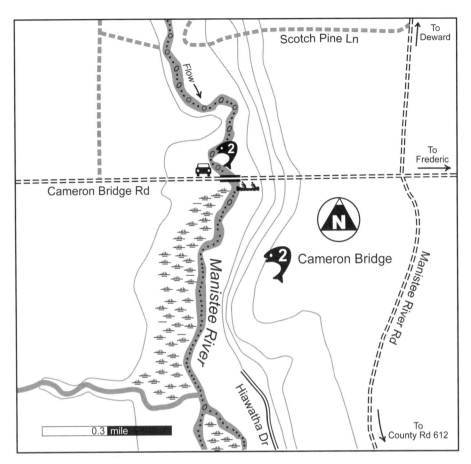

3 *Red Bridge*

GPS N 44° 46.270'
W 84° 50.456'

Map: page 137

The largest and busiest canoe launch on the Upper Manistee is located at Red Bridge, where County Road 612 crosses the river. The bridge is 5.3 miles west of Old US-27 in Frederic via CR 612. From Grayling head west on M-72 for six miles and then north on Manistee River Road. You'll reach CR 612 in 4.4 miles, where the bridge is just to the west. On the east side of the bridge are a large canoe launch on the south side of the road and steps to the water on both sides. There is ample parking along the shoulders.

The Manistee is 60 to 80 feet wide and generally more than three feet deep at mid-channel. It can be waded with caution in places, but there are holes that will flood your waders. Velocity of flow is moderate. The bottom is sand, soft and shifting in places, and the footing for wading is not always the best. The banks at the bridge and downstream are high and sandy, with pine forest and some grassland. Upstream, the banks are coniferous swamp.

The river here is wide enough for easy fly casting. Fishing pressure is usually moderate but in June this is one of the most popular places for night fishing during the Hex hatch.

4 Upper Manistee River Campground

GPS N 44° 44.959'
W 84° 50.286'

This large and attractive state forest campground is spread out in a stand of mature red pine, oak, and maple and includes 30 drive-in sites and a group camping area for canoers. Needless to say, the campground includes a considerable amount of frontage on the west bank of the Manistee.

From Red Bridge on County Road 612 head west and in 0.6 mile turn south (left) on Goose Creek Road. Follow the dirt road for a mile and then turn east (left) on Upper Manistee Campground Road, marked by a DNR campground sign. This winding road leads east and then south to reach the entrance of the campground in 0.9 mile. You can also pick up Goose Creek Road from M-72 just west of the Manistee River Bridge. It's a 4.5-mile drive north on Goose Creek Road to reach Upper Manistee Campground Road.

Perhaps the best place to park is just south of the campground entrance where there is a large day-use parking area off the Upper Manistee Campground Road. A trail heads east from the parking lot, skirts the group canoe campsites, and in 100 yards reaches the river. Here you'll find another footpath that follows the west bank upstream for more than half a mile, passing six stairways, two small landing docks, and plenty of places to fish the river along the way. The trail makes it easy to fish upstream and then return on foot to your vehicle.

The Manistee is 40 to 50 feet wide here and one to four feet deep. However, there are some deeper holes, and at least one of these is over your head. The bottom is almost entirely sand, soft and shifting in places. The river divides into more than one channel in places where it swirls pass small grassy islets. Banks are alternately high and sandy and low and mucky, forested with conifer. The river is wide enough for easy fly casting and shallow enough to wade if you watch out for the deeper holes and shifting sands.

Fishing pressure is usually light here because during the summer the area can be busy with canoes and campers. But by fishing in the morning and evening you can avoid most of the river users and land browns, brookies, and even an occasional rainbow. This is also a good area for brown drake and Hex hatches in June, while in August the grassy banks make hopper fishing productive. Another mid-summer hatch on this stretch is tricorythodes, the gnat-size mayflies whose imitations are tied on hooks ranging from No. 20 to No. 28. The tricos appear a couple of hours after sunrise, before most canoers are on the water, making it an ideal hatch for this reach of the Manistee.

There are two access sites between County Road 612 and M-72 on the east bank of the Manistee that are reached from Manistee River Road. Goose Creek Trail Camp, a state forest campground designed primarily for equestrians on the Shore-to-Shore Trail, is half a mile south of CR 612. Long's Canoe Livery

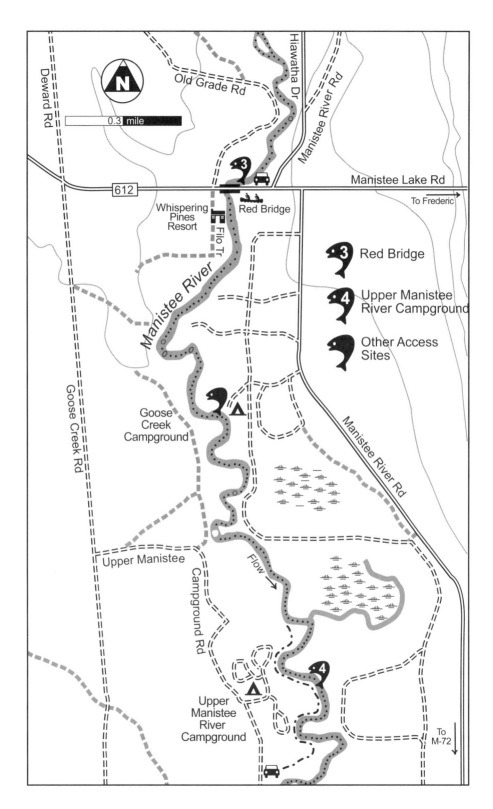

N

0.3 mile

Deward Rd

Old Grade Rd

Hiawatha Dr

Manistee River Rd

612

Manistee Lake Rd

To Frederic

Whispering
Pines
Resort

Filo Tr

Red Bridge

Manistee River

Goose
Creek
Campground

Goose Creek Rd

Upper Manistee

Campground Rd

Flow

Upper
Manistee
River
Campground

Manistee River Rd

To
M-72

3 Red Bridge

4 Upper Manistee
River Campground

Other Access
Sites

(989-348-7224, 231-258-3452; *www.longscanoelivery.com*) is three miles north of M-72 on Manistee River Road, which for a small fee allows anglers to park and access the Manistee.

5 *Manistee River Bridge*

GPS N 44° 41.554'
W 84° 50.831'

Manistee River Bridge is where M-72 crosses the trout stream. You'll find the conditions upstream from the bridge as different as night and day from those downstream. Upstream or down, this is a very busy access point along the river, thanks to the Shel-Haven Canoe Livery on the east side of the bridge and the state forest campground on the west side.

The bridge is eight miles west of Grayling on M-72. The entrance of the Manistee Bridge Campground is just west of the bridge and on the north side of the busy state. The state forest campground has 23 sites scattered along four loops and a small parking area for noncampers. A fence runs along the high banks of the campground, and many sites are within view of the river below, while Loop 1 and Loop 3 have stairways leading down to the water, placing you on the river directly across from the canoe livery docks.

Upstream from the bridge the Manistee is 80 to 90 feet wide and two to four feet deep with some deeper holes. The bottom is gravel and the river is wide enough here for easy casting as well as easy wading. Banks are high and sandy, forested with pine and some oak. On the south side of M-72, directly across from Shel-Haven, is a canoe launch with additional parking and angler access to the river. Downstream from M-72 the flies-only, quality fishing area of the Manistee begins. But be forewarned: during normal water levels the river below the bridge is three to six feet deep and often too deep and fast to be waded safely.

This can be a busy place during the summer and often the campground is filled on weekends as many paddlers end their day here. During the week, early in the morning and early in the season you can arrive to find a quiet setting and some good fishing for both browns and brookies.

Downstream of M-72

6 *Riverview*

GPS N 44° 40.177'
W 84° 52.649'

A better place to step into Manistee River's flies-only section than the Manistee River Bridge is Riverview Access Site, reached by driving west on M-72. Within 0.3 mile of Manistee River Bridge, turn south (left) on Riverview Road and follow the paved road. In two miles the pavement ends, and Riverview Road swings southwest for CCC Bridge while Yellow Trees Road continues south, immediately passing the posted Riverview Access Site.

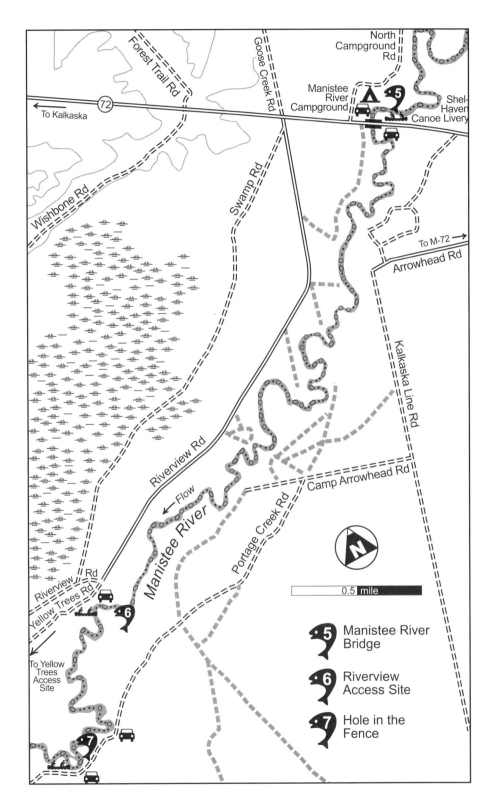

Forest Trail Rd

Goose Creek Rd

North
Campground
Rd

72

To Kalkaska

Manistee
River
Campground

Shel-
Haven
Canoe Livery

Wishbone Rd

Swamp Rd

To M-72 →

Arrowhead Rd

Kalkaska Line Rd

Riverview Rd

←Flow

Manistee River

Camp Arrowhead Rd

Portage Creek Rd

N

0.5 mile

Riverview Rd

Yellow Trees Rd

6

To Yellow
Trees
Access
Site

7

5 Manistee River
Bridge

6 Riverview
Access Site

7 Hole in the
Fence

The site has a parking lot for a dozen cars and a canoe ramp with steps that lead down to the water. Other than the channels that encircle a small islet right in front of the canoe landing, the river is 70 to 80 feet wide. Depth ranges from two to five feet along a bottom that is mostly sand with intermittent patches of gravel. You are now in the quality fishing area of the Manistee River, which is flies-only with a daily limit of two fish. Also keep in mind that shoreline both upstream and downstream from the access site is private property.

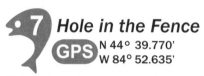

7 Hole in the Fence

GPS N 44° 39.770'
W 84° 52.635'

Map: page 139

This is the best access on the east side of the Manistee between M-72 and the King Road area upstream from CCC Bridge. Only 1.2 river miles downstream from Riverview, Hole in the Fence is actually a pair of sites a short distance from each other, allowing anglers to start at one and pull out at the other.

From the I-75 Business Loop in Grayling head west 6.2 miles on M-72 and then veer left onto Arrowhead Road. Follow the paved road for a mile, where it swings south (left) and becomes Kalkaska Line Road. Follow the graded dirt road for 0.7 mile and turn west (right) on a graded dirt road that on some maps is labeled as Camp Arrowhead Road. Within 0.4 mile veer left onto Portage Creek Road and follow this road for 1.2 miles.

The first site is a high bank close to the road with a log fence skirting its edge and marked by a "Quality Fishing Area" sign. There is a parking lot on the east side of Portage Creek Road. A massive stairway leads down to the river. The site overlooks a wide bend where the Manistee is 40 to 50 feet wide and two to three feet deep with a bottom of predominately sand. The casting is easy and so is the wading in normal water levels. The opposite bank is low and swampy, and along both sides of the river there is cover for trout in the form of sunken logs, submerged roots, and sweepers.

Continue another 0.2 mile south along Portage Creek Road to reach the second site, this one posted with a "Hole in the Fence" sign. On the east side of the road is a large parking area, and on the west side a canoe ramp leads down the bank to the water. What looks like the west bank is actually an island that forces the Manistee into a tight bend. The river here is 60 to 70 feet wide with the same depth and sandy bottom as the first access site. From one site to the next would be a 0.4-mile wade.

8 Yellow Trees Landing

GPS N 44° 41.554'
W 84° 50.831'

Back on the west side of the Manistee and 3.7 miles south of the Riverview Access is Yellow Trees Landing, one of the Manistee River's best destinations for fly fishers. This is due partly to the poorly marked, dirt roads leading to

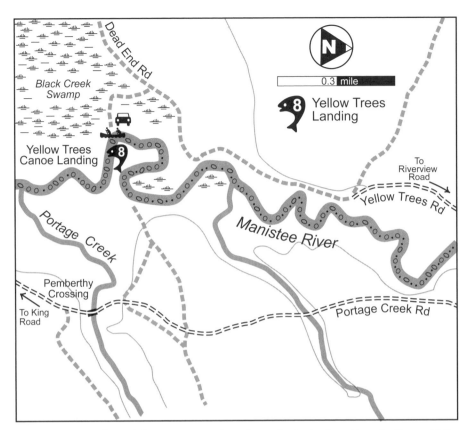

the access site (less fishing pressure) and partly to its location in the middle of the river's flies-only stretch.

To reach the canoe landing from M-72, turn south on paved Riverview Road for 2.1 miles to where the pavement ends at a V junction in the road. To the right of Riverview Road is the dirt road that heads for CCC Bridge. To the left is Yellow Trees Road, a rougher dirt road that immediately passes the Riverview Access Site and then continues south.

Within 2.4 miles you come to another unmarked split where a two-track heads west (right). Stay to the left to continue south on Yellow Trees Road; in 0.6 mile you will come to the end of the road, a spot where three two-tracks merge. One very rough two-track heads south but is blocked by a log barrier. To the west (right) are two more, the first posted as "Mixed Traffic" that extends northwest. Follow the second one that heads into a pine plantation. Within a half mile you bump along to an intersection marked by a yellow "Canoe Landing" sign. Turn east (left) here to reach Yellow Trees Landing within a quarter mile. If the weather has been wet you may have trouble with the mud holes in the two-tracks toward the end; otherwise most vehicles can reach this isolated spot.

Yellow Trees is a beautiful spot where the river is 80 to 90 feet wide and flows through a wide bend and around a small islet just downstream. The two-track ends at a small turnaround with parking, along with a stairway that leads down to a canoe launch. Once you're in the water there's not a cabin or cottage in sight.

The river ranges from two to six feet in depth over a bottom of a mix of gravel and sand, though you will encounter patches of mud where the current slows. Best wading is upstream where the Manistee is wider and the current slower. In either direction there is good trout cover. Anglers with a good sense of timing can experience outstanding hatches of gray drakes, brown drakes, and hexagenia mayflies. Just 0.3 mile downstream, Portage Creek empties into the Manistee from Lake Margrethe. Known as a good brook trout stream, Portage Creek can also be reached on the east side of the Manistee via Portage Creek Road and Arrowhead Road from M-72.

9 CCC Bridge

GPS N 44° 36.929'
W 84° 59.513'

Split on both sides of the bridge, CCC Bridge State Forest Campground is popular with canoeists and a busy one during the summer. The bridge marks one end of the flies-only, quality fishing area of the Manistee. Downstream from the bridge, the river is open to all tackle and has a daily possession of five fish of which no more than three can be 15 inches or larger. Brook trout must be at least ten inches long, brown trout 12 inches.

The most direct route to CCC Bridge is to head west on M-72. Within 6.7 miles from Manistee River Bridge, or 14.7 miles from Grayling, turn south (left) on Sunset Trail Road. Follow this dirt road for 8.4 miles to CCC Bridge. As you head south there will be several dirt roads and two-tracks leading off both west and east, but Sunset Trail will clearly be the main road at each intersection. Just before reaching the bridge, you pass Riverview Road which extends east to M-72 near Manistee River Bridge. On a map this dirt road appears to be a shorter route, but keep in mind that Riverview Road is extremely rutted and sandy halfway between M-72 and CCC Bridge; only four-wheel-drive vehicles should attempt it.

To get to the CCC Bridge from Sharon, head east from County Road 571 on Military Road. Within 1.8 miles you reach a Y intersection where you will follow the northeast fork (left) to continue on King Road. This graded dirt road reaches Sunset Trail Road just south of CCC Bridge in 3.4 miles.

The state forest campground has seven sites east of the bridge overlooking the flies-only stretch of the river, and 32 sites along with a canoe launch west of the bridge. There is a stairway to the river next to site No. 18 on the west side, and a second set of steps just upstream from the bridge on the south bank of the river in its flies-only section.

At CCC Bridge the Manistee is a big river, 100 to 120 feet wide and three to six feet deep at mid-channel. Bottom is sand with a few patches of gravel. Velocity of the current is moderate and parts of the river here can be waded with care at normal flows if you are careful to avoid the holes. At high flows the river is too deep to wade. In general the wading is easier upstream in the

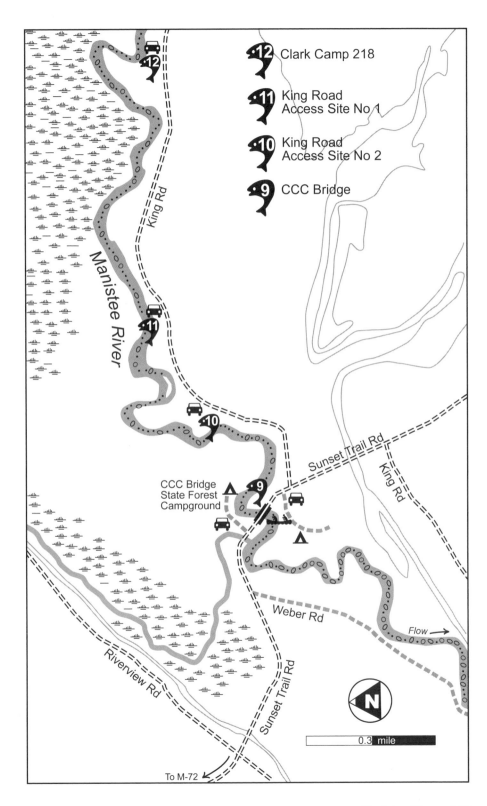

12 Clark Camp 218

11 King Road
Access Site No 1

10 King Road
Access Site No 2

9 CCC Bridge

Manistee River

King Rd

CCC Bridge
State Forest
Campground

Sunset Trail Rd

King Rd

Weber Rd

Flow →

Riverview Rd

Sunset Trail Rd

To M-72

N

0.3 mile

flies-only water, where there is still plenty of room to cast a fly. The banks at the campground are high and sandy, with an open stand of pine and hardwood. Upstream and down are low, brushy banks.

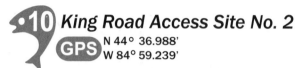

10 King Road Access Site No. 2

GPS N 44° 36.988'
W 84° 59.239'

Map: page 143

For almost three miles east of CCC Bridge, King Road is a beautiful dirt road that hugs the flies-only section of the Manistee River and passes two-tracks with names like River Bend Drive and Catch & Release Avenue. You just know the fly fishing is good here and it is. Scattered along King Road are seven access points, some just unmarked pullovers where you are so close to the water you can practically cast from your car. Two are private access sites open to fly anglers only.

The first public access, a DNR site posted with a "Quality Fishing Area" sign, is reached 0.3 mile east of CCC Bridge and Sunset Trail Road. From the small parking area a stairway extends down a low, forested bank to a stretch of the Manistee that is 50 to 60 feet wide and three to six feet deep. It's certainly wadable during normal fishing conditions, but you must keep an eye out for the deeper holes. The bottom is predominately sand with an occasional patch of gravel. An afternoon can be spent wading from CCC Bridge to this site.

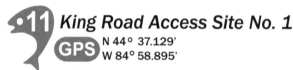

11 King Road Access Site No. 1

GPS N 44° 37.129'
W 84° 58.895'

Map: page 143

Continuing east along the Manistee River, you pass a private access for fly anglers and then arrive at another state access site, 0.7 mile from CCC Bridge. The south bank is higher and more heavily forested than the previous access site while the north bank is lined by tag alder and other low bushes. The river is 70 to 80 feet wide here and three to six deep with a sandy bottom. From the parking lot, you can plop down on the edge of the low bluff overlooking the water and wait for the hatch to begin, easily scanning a hundred yards upstream or downstream.

12 Clark Camp

GPS N 44° 37.112'
W 84° 58.260'

Map: page 143

In another half mile east, or 1.1 miles from CCC Bridge, you reach Clark Camp 218, a private fishing retreat. The camp has set up another "fly fishers only" access point that is well marked along King Road and open to any fly angler. The access site is actually 20 yards off King Road with parking for two, maybe three vehicles. A stairway leads down a low, open bank to where

Celebrating Trout and Fly Fishing

There are a number of special events in Michigan devoted to either fishing for trout or the sport of fly fishing. Some are little more than a county festival with rides and cotton candy. Others are for serious anglers. Here are but a few:

National Trout Festival (*www.nationaltroutfestival.com*): Held on opening weekend of trout season since 1933, this festival is a celebration not so much of trout fishing as it is the arrival of spring in northern Michigan. Sure there are carnival rides and corn dog stands, but in the morning and the evening everybody is out fishing because Kalkaska rivals Grayling as the heart of Michigan trout country.

Historical Trout Opener (*www.lowellmuseum.org*): Also staged during the trout opener is this delightful festival in tiny Lovells that borders the North Branch of the Au Sable River. Events take place behind the township hall at the Michigan Trout Fishing Historical Museum and Lone Pine School House and usually include fly tying demonstrations, casting workshops and spicy chili or bean soup for all those anglers chilled from a morning standing in the North Branch.

Midwest Fly Fishing Expo (*www.mffc.org*): The state's premier fly fishing event is held at Macomb Community College Sports & Expo Center at 12 Mile and Hays Roads in Warren in early March. The hall is filled with booths selling everything from guided trips and Sage rods to all the material you'd ever need to tie a fly. The two-day event is filled with seminars and casting workshops featuring such renowned fishers as Gary Borger.

Invitational Fly Tying Expo (*www.fffglc.org*): Held in the first week of December at the Ingham County Fairgrounds in Mason, this event features more than 100 fly tyers who sit at their benches and demonstrate what every wanna-be fly tyer needs to know. Want to get into fly tying? Attend this expo and bring your wallet.

Kalkaska, home of the National Trout Festival, honors the fish with a brook trout statue and fountain downtown.

the Manistee River, 30 to 40 feet wide, flows through a bend. The bottom is a mix of sand and gravel with soft muck banks where the current slows in the bend. The depth is three to four feet and you'll find the current swifter than at the previous access points on King Road. But overall this stretch is wadable, if you're conscious of the deeper holes, with good coverage for trout and more than enough room to cast.

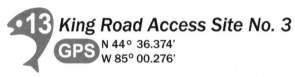

13 King Road Access Site No. 3
GPS N 44° 36.374'
W 85° 00.276'

Flies-only regulations end at CCC Bridge, and farther downstream the Manistee River is under general trout regulations and open to all tackle. Downstream from the bridge the water is deep and brook trout more scarce. But it can be cautiously waded at normal water levels, and it's possible to hook resident rainbows along with large browns.

To reach the access sites to the west, head south of CCC Bridge on Sunset Trail Road for 0.3 mile and then turn west (right) on King Road. Within a mile you'll reach a DNR access site with a large parking area for a dozen vehicles and a stairway leading down to the river.

At this site the Manistee River is 90 to 100 feet wide with a depth of one to four feet, making for easy wading over a bottom of sand and gravel. You'll find deeper holes upstream, while downstream the Manistee splits into a pair of channels that flow around a bushy islet before rejoining within 100 yards. Undercut banks and logjams provide considerable trout cover here. The current in the channels can be swift at times, and you're likely to encounter more paddlers and tubers during summer weekends than what is seen upstream from CCC Bridge.

14 Three Mile Bend
GPS N 44° 35.844'
W 85° 01.653'

Three Mile Bend is an access site and canoe launch halfway along the Manistee between CCC Bridge and Sharon. From Sharon head east on Military Road for 1.8 miles to the Y intersection with King Road. Veer northeast (left) on King Road to reach the site in 1.2 miles. From CCC Bridge head south on Sunset Trail Road for 0.3 mile and then turn west (right) on King Road. Within 2.6 miles the site will appear on the north side of the road.

The site has parking for a dozen vehicles, a vault toilet, and stairs down to the canoe landing. Right in front of the landing an island separates the Manistee into a pair of channels. Upstream or downstream of the island the Manistee is 100 to 120 feet wide and two to four feet deep, with some holes downstream more than six feet deep. Bottom is sand with a few gravel patches. The velocity is slow to moderate, and much of the river can be waded at normal flows.

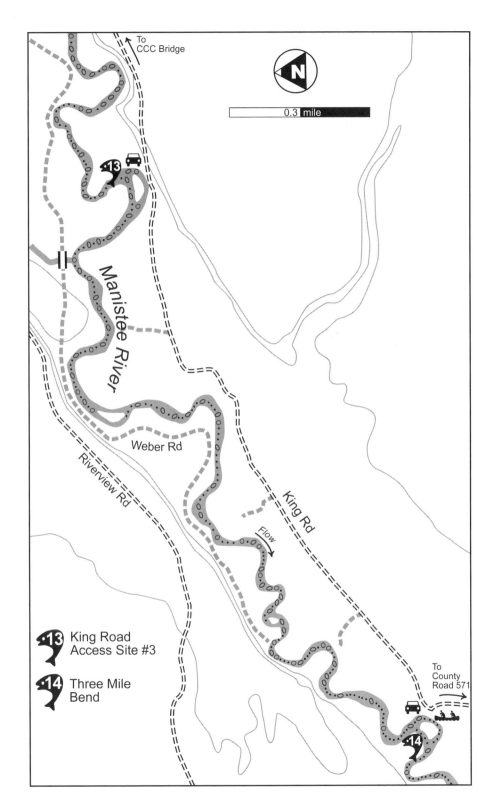

To
CCC Bridge

N

0.3 mile

Manistee River

Weber Rd

Riverview Rd

King Rd

Flow

13 King Road
Access Site #3

14 Three Mile
Bend

To
County
Road 571

A fly angler talks to canoeists on the Manistee River. The Manistee is a popular river to paddle during the summer but does not draw as large a number of canoers as the Au Sable, Pere Marquette, or the Pine.

Drowned logs and snags along the banks provide good trout cover, while upstream you'll find pools and riffles to fish. At the inside curve of the bends and along the banks are stretches of mud and marl that make this reach a good one during the Hex hatch. The south bank is five to eight feet high, forested with hardwood and some large white pines. The north bank is lower, with coniferous swamp and some brush. Fishing pressure here is very light.

 ## 15 *North Sharon Road Bridge*
GPS N 44° 35.326'
W 85° 04.650'

North Sharon Bridge is generally considered the last access site that wading anglers can fish along the Manistee. To reach the bridge from M-72, turn south on County Road 571 (also labeled Sigma Road), 17.6 miles west of Grayling. At one point CR 571 swings west for a mile and then resumes its southerly direction on North Sharon Road, where it is well posted. Within two miles the paved county road becomes a well-graded dirt road; in ten miles from M-72 it arrives at North Sharon Bridge.

There is room to park on both sides of North Sharon Road southwest of the bridge. Just upstream from the bridge Big Cannon Creek empties into the Manistee. Just downstream the North Branch merges. Almost all wading is done upstream where the river is 100 to 130 feet wide. You encounter

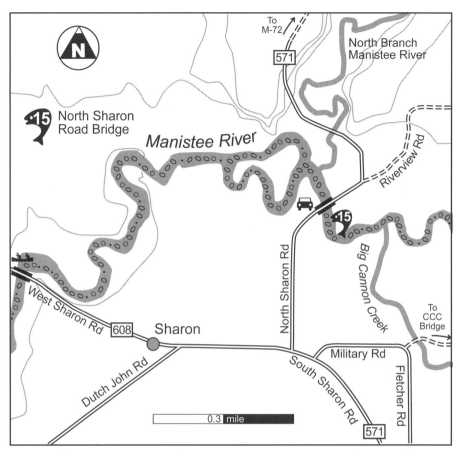

gravel riffles less than three feet deep that alternate with deep pools, some more than six feet deep. Parts of the river here can be cautiously waded at normal flows, but keep in mind the velocity is fast, the rocks are slippery, and wading is never easy.

The bottom is mostly gravel and cobbles with some sand. The banks are alternately high and sandy and low and mucky, forested with hardwood and some pine. There is some brush along the river's edge. Cover is sparse in this part of the river and fishing pressure is usually light.

A fly angler studies his fly box during a hatch on the Pigeon River downstream from the Pigeon Bridge State Forest Campground.

Pigeon River

The poor Pigeon. We've been hard on this legendary trout stream that flows through the heart of Pigeon River Country State Forest.

The stream picks up its name from the passenger pigeon, a species that numbered in the billions and at one point constituted 25 to 40 percent of the total bird population of the United States. Flights of the passenger pigeon migrating over the Pigeon River were said to be a mile wide and take several hours to pass overhead. Then the onslaught came. Between logging that destroyed their nesting grounds and market hunting, passenger pigeon numbers were plummeting by 1860, and in 1914 the last known bird died in captivity at the Cincinnati Zoological Garden.

Logging continued until 1910 and was followed by uncontrolled forest fires and failed attempts to farm the barren land. In 1919, tax-reverted lands, often failed farms, were designated as a state forest. The second-growth forests healed the land so well from the earlier ravages that the 105,000-acre Pigeon River Country State Forest became known as the "Big Wild," home of a reintroduced elk herd and three Blue Ribbon Trout Streams. But ecological disaster struck again when in 1957 the earthen dam of the Lansing Club Pond on the Pigeon River washed out during heavy rains, releasing heavy sediments down the river.

Amazingly, the dam, now owned and managed by Song of the Morning Ranch, failed once more in 1984 and again 24 years later in 2008. Both times sediment and huge volumes of water were flushed down the Pigeon River, causing large-scale fish kills. In 1984, DNR biologists estimated 53 percent of the trout were killed in the first few miles downstream from the dam and more than 33,000 overall. In 2008, the water flow of the Pigeon went from a normal 60 cubic feet per second to 185 cfs to six cfs after the dam malfunction was discovered and the gates closed. The extreme fluctuations of water were as damaging to the trout as the silt that was washed down. No doubt, Song of the Morning Ranch will find itself in court, as it did in the mid-1980s, battling the state and conservation groups for years to come.

The poor Pigeon. Cut-and run-logging practices, the trampling of the oil industry drilling for natural gas in the 1970s, and three dam failures in less than 50 years have had their effect on the river. Yet, through it all the Pigeon has rebounded and no doubt will again, which is the reason that 21 miles of it, from near Old Vanderbilt Road Bridge to M-68, has been designated a Blue Ribbon Trout Stream.

In 1982, the Pigeon was also designated a Wild and Scenic River by the Michigan Natural Resources Commission. Few streams in the Lower

Crowned by Gaylord at 1,350 feet in elevation, the central plateau of the Lower Peninsula is a moraine left behind during the last ice age, whose crest forms a significant divide. To the south drain the Au Sable River system and the state's best-known trout waters. From the northern slope rise three Blue Ribbon Trout Streams: the Pigeon, the Sturgeon, and the Black, which flow north before merging together and emptying into Lake Huron as the Black River.

These three rivers roughly parallel each other in close proximity and at one point the Black River is less than two miles from the Pigeon. In the beginning they flow through an area that is blessed with large tracts of state land, crisscrossed with two-tracks and trails, and dotted with campgrounds. In other words, a paradise for a trout angler: ample access, plenty of places to pitch a tent, a choice of rivers to fish but with very little driving between them. You could spend a summer in Pigeon River Country State Forest and not have enough time to fish every stretch of water that looks appealing. Thus the question for most anglers new to the area is: which river to fish?

The Black is renowned as Michigan's premiere wild brook trout fishery. The river has the distinction of having the highest reproduction rate of brookies in the state and has been managed to stay that way, to the point of removing brown trout.

The Sturgeon has the coldest water and the fastest flow by far. Heavy rains at times make wading nearly impossible in many stretches. It is inhabited primarily with brown trout and rainbows that are the offspring of lake-run steelhead. Once outside the state forest, very little of the Sturgeon flows through public lands and below Trowbridge Road the river so closely parallels I-75 that it's difficult at times to escape the sounds and sights of summer traffic. But for the opportunity to hook and land a trophy brown trout on its late summer run from Burt Lake to cooler water, this is the river of choice.

The Pigeon flows north between the two, through large tracts of state land, making it possibly the most scenic and wilderness-like trout stream. It holds all three species, brook, brown, and resident rainbow trout, and it has the qualities of being the healthiest trout fishery of the three. But the Pigeon has yet to reach its potential due primarily to the Song of the Morning Dam, which has failed three times in the past 50 years. To survive and reproduce, trout need water that is cold, clean, and clear. The impoundment offers none of those as the sun warms its water, and then irregular fluctuations send it downstream with an increase of silt.

Hopefully someday the dam and the issues surrounding it will be resolved either in court or by a cooperative effort of all parties involved. Then the Pigeon can return to being one of Michigan's legendary trout streams in an area blessed with them.

Which river to fish? The Pigeon River Country State Forest offers three Blue Ribbon Trout Streams and numerous places to pitch a tent or park a trailer.

Peninsula are more deserving of such protection. More than a third of the Pigeon flows through state land, most of it in the Pigeon River Country State Forest, and vast stretches of its banks still remain undeveloped, providing the cushion it needs to maintain its superb water quality.

Access is good, both by vehicle and on foot for the adventurous. Public campgrounds along it are plentiful. The trout will come back.

Wedged between the Sturgeon River to the west and the Black River to the east, the Pigeon River rises from a cedar swamp northeast of Gaylord and flows northward 43 river miles before emptying into Mullett Lake near Indian River. The Pigeon's size does not change drastically due to the lack of large tributaries. The largest is the Little Pigeon River that flows into the mainstream three miles below Red Bridge. Up to that point the Pigeon is fed by a handful of small streams and springs that seep gently but steadily into it.

A tiny brook in its headwaters, the Pigeon is more than 60 feet wide in places in the lower river and a hundred feet wide at its mouth. Forest cover is mostly coniferous swamp in the headwaters, but hardwoods are more plentiful in the lower reaches. Above Pigeon Bridge Campground most of the river frontage is private property. From Pigeon Bridge downstream to McIntosh Landing most is state land, but there are some private holdings. Downstream from McIntosh Landing most land is again private.

Fly anglers begin concentrating on the Pigeon at the Old Vanderbilt Road Bridge. Upstream the river is not easy to fish because the channel is narrow, and overhanging branches make casting difficult. But at the bridge and downstream the river is wider and more open, fly casting is easier, and there is an excellent population of brook trout eager to take your fly.

Between Pigeon Bridge Campground and Pine Grove Campground there are ten miles of river virtually unequalled in the state for unspoiled scenic beauty. The river is wide enough for fly fishing, and most of it is wadable at normal flows. There is easy access to the river at several points as well as places to access it on foot, increasing your chances of having a stream all to yourself.

Downstream from Pine Grove Campground the Pigeon is wider and deeper, making wading more challenging and impossible at high flows. Slippery boulders and bedrock in places are an additional hazard that wading anglers need to be conscious of. Trout populations generally decline the further you go downstream, but the fish may run larger. Brown trout predominate over brook trout in this part of the river, and rainbows begin to appear. Most anglers and biologists feel the river downstream from Pine Grove and certainly from Red Bridge was relatively unaffected by the 2008 dam failure.

Like the Au Sable, the Pigeon River has a large component of groundwater inflow that keeps a good flow during summer droughts and cools the water. Unlike the Au Sable, however, the Pigeon receives a large amount of surface runoff from the steep morainal hills with less permeable soils just north of

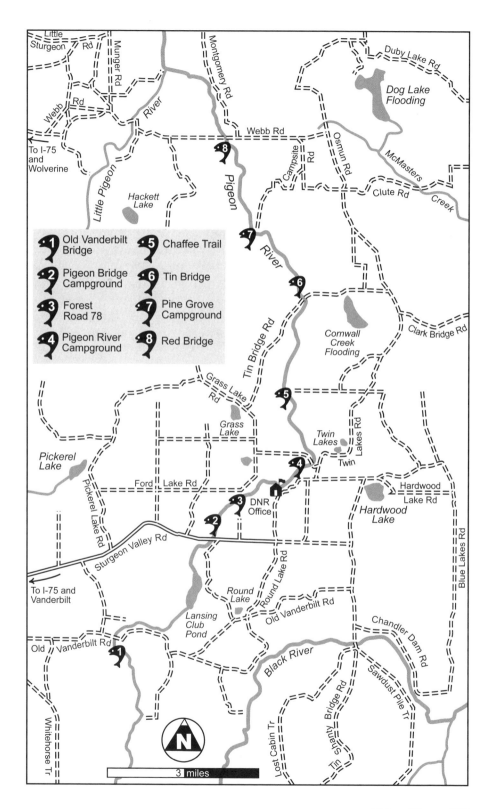

Gaylord. For this reason the Pigeon rises faster and higher than the Au Sable after heavy spring rains and snowmelt. The average annual range in stage on the Pigeon near Vanderbilt is 3.3 feet, whereas the Au Sable rarely rises more than one foot.

Summer water temperatures on the Pigeon run a little higher than the optimum for trout. The maximum summer temperatures generally increase downstream, where groundwater inflow is not so great. Like all the trout streams in the northern part of the Lower Peninsula, the water is hard and slightly alkaline, not likely to be affected by acid rains.

Hatches are good on the Pigeon and generally occur a week to 10 days later than on the Au Sable and Manistee rivers upon which most hatch charts, including the one in this book, are based. Hendrickson, blue-winged olive, sulphur, and caddis hatches are common, while brown drake and Hexagenia limbata are limited to a handful of areas with silt beds such as below Tin Bridge.

Anglers on the Pigeon are rarely bothered by canoes. The river from Pigeon Bridge to Tin Bridge is not for inexperienced paddlers due to logjams, sweepers, and tight bends. Such obstruction and the many portages required to get around them discourage all but a relatively few experienced canoers.

Accommodations

Gaylord and to a lesser degree Wolverine and Indian River have a variety of lodging. For accommodations in Indian River or Wolverine, see the Sturgeon River chapter or contact the Indian River Tourist Bureau (231-238-9325; *www.irtourism.com*).

The Gaylord Area Convention & Tourism Bureau (800-345-8621; *www.gaylordmichigan.net*) lists 17 accommodations, ranging from such national chains as Holiday Inn Express (989-732-2200; 1201 W. Main St.)—right downtown and close to I-75—to the more upscale Marsh Ridge Resort (989-732-5552, 800-743-7529; *www.marshridgelodging.com*; 4815 Old US-27 South) just south of the city, which includes an onsite restaurant and bar.

Campgrounds: There are eight rustic campgrounds in the Pigeon River Country State Forest, including four on the Pigeon River. Three of them are also access sites described in this chapter. The Pigeon Bridge Campground, ten miles east of Vanderbilt on Sturgeon Valley Road, has ten sites, none of them directly on the river but all only a short walk away. The Pigeon River Campground, reached via Sturgeon Valley Road and Twin Lakes Road, is the largest on the river with 19 sites, seven of them overlooking the trout stream. More remote and secluded is Pine Grove Campground, 12 miles east of Wolverine and reached from Campsite Road south of Webb Road. Pine Grove has six sites in a very pleasant forested setting.

Also near the Pigeon is Elk Hill Trail Camp, reached from Sturgeon Valley Road by heading north on Twin Lakes Road and Osmun Road. This ten-site campground is on the northern spur of the Shore-to-Shore Horse Trail and is designed for equestrians and their horses but is open to anybody.

Fly Shops and Guides

Pick up your flies before leaving Gaylord. The best places for flies and advice are the **Alphorn Shop** (989-732-5616; 137 W. Main St.) or **Jay's Sporting Goods** (989-705-1339; *www.jayssportinggoods.com*; 150 Dale Rd.).

Maps of the Pigeon

Paralleling the Pigeon from five to ten miles to the west is I-75, making Gaylord (exit 282), Vanderbilt (exit 290), and Wolverine (exit 301) the best places to stage a trip into the Pigeon River Country State Forest. The easiest and most direct way to reach the first five access sites—Old Vanderbilt Bridge, Pigeon Bridge Campground, Pigeon River Campground, Forest Road 78, and Chaffee Trail—is to head east from Vanderbilt on Sturgeon Valley Road. The paved road reaches Pigeon Bridge Campground in ten miles and Twin Lakes Road in 11.3 miles. Head north (left) on Twin Lakes Road to reach Pigeon River Campground, Chaffee Trail, and even Tin Bridge.

Tin Bridge, Pine Grove Campground, and Red Bridge are easier to reach from Wolverine. Depart exit 301 and head east on Afton Road until it swings north in a mile. Continue east on Webb Road and you'll arrive at Red Bridge in 7.3 miles from I-75 and pass Campsite Road to Pine Grove Campground in 8.8 miles. Webb Road ends at Osmun Road, where you can head south to reach Tin Bridge or Chaffee Trail.

The dirt roads and two-tracks in the Pigeon River Country State Forest are not always well posted and can be confusing at times. It's best to stop at the state forest headquarters, an impressive log lodge on Twin Lakes Road a mile north of Sturgeon Valley Road, to pick up a map of the area. You can also contact Pigeon River Country State Forest (989-983-4101) in advance and request one. The headquarters, which includes interesting displays, is open only two to three days a week, usually on Wednesday and Thursday from 8 a.m. to 4 p.m., but has an information area outside for off hours.

Old Vanderbilt Bridge

GPS N 45° 07.688'
W 84° 30.396'

Map: page 159

Upstream from Song of the Morning Pond (also labeled Lansing Club Pond on many maps), the most popular and, for all practical purposes, the only access point for fly anglers is the Old Vanderbilt Bridge. From the Pigeon Bridge Campground, head west on Sturgeon Valley Road for three miles and then south on Dudd Road. Within a mile the pavement ends along Dudd Road, and in 1.5 miles you reach the posted intersection of Old Vanderbilt Road, a well-graded dirt road. Head east and the bridge is reached in 0.3 mile. There is limited parking along the shoulders of the road.

The Pigeon is 35 feet wide at the bridge, but the banks are brushy and fly casting can be challenging in places. The riverbed is mostly gravel, channel depth is less than three feet, and wading is fairly easy at normal flows. Banks are generally low and forested with mixed hardwoods and conifers. Never having been scarred by the repeated dam failures at Song of the Morning Ranch, this stretch holds good numbers of brook trout and a few browns that hide among stumps, submerged logs, and the overhanging brush along the banks. Fishing pressure is light; the river frontage is all private land.

 2 *Pigeon Bridge Campground*

GPS N 45° 09.398'
W 84° 27.918'

Map: page 161

This rustic campground is a longtime favorite among trout anglers who arrive at the state forest for a few days of fishing. Its location makes it the ideal base to fish much of the upper river, while departing from the campground is the Shingle Mill Pathway, providing adventurous anglers even more access. It is also easy to reach. From Vanderbilt head east on the paved Sturgeon Valley Road, and within ten miles you will cross the Pigeon River and come to the campground on its east bank.

The state forest facility has ten sites and from site No. 8 a path leads down to the river. Heading downstream you'll find a well-marked Shingle Mill Pathway veering off into the woods to the right and an angler's trail hugging the bank to the left. The Pigeon is a beautiful river here, flowing crystal clear between banks forested with mixed hardwoods and conifers. The channel is about 40 feet wide and generally less than four feet deep, with a few deeper holes. There is considerable trout cover and at times you will have to go to the banks to get by some of the deeper holes. Bottom is chiefly gravel, with some sand and muck. Velocity is moderate at normal flows. Wading is easy, except during periods of high runoff, and fly casting is much easier here than in upstream reaches.

Fishing pressure can be heavy at times near the campground, but it's easy to escape other anglers. At the back of the campground is the posted trailhead for the Shingle Mill Pathway, a trail system composed of five loops. The first two, the 0.75-Mile Loop and the 1.25-Mile Loop, are short and can provide anglers additional access to the river. Head left for post No. 4 from the trailhead to reach the river quickly. The 0.75-Mile Loop continues downstream where at post No. 4 it merges into 1.25-Mile Loop. Together the west side of these loops parallels the river for a half mile where it would be easy to bushwhack to the water. Eventually the 1.25-Mile Loop climbs a ridge to post No. 3, where the 6-Mile Loop continues downstream but remains high above the water, making access from the trail more challenging. You can also pick up the pathway where it's marked on the west side of Pigeon Bridge and head downstream, but cutting east to the river is more difficult. If you fish upstream from the Pigeon Bridge, stay in the river channel. The riverbanks upstream are private land.

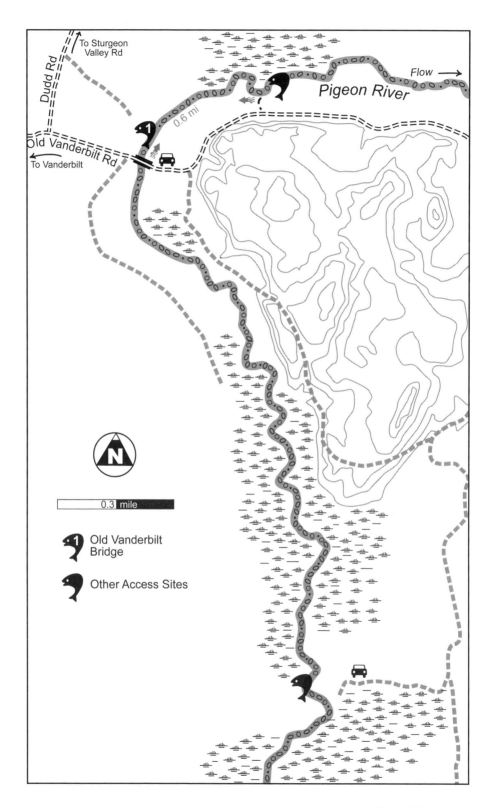

To Sturgeon Valley Rd

Dudd Rd

To Vanderbilt

Old Vanderbilt Rd

0.6 mi

Pigeon River

Flow →

N

0.3 mile

Old Vanderbilt Bridge

Other Access Sites

3 Forest Road 78
GPS N 45° 09.987'
W 84° 27.497'

For those with a sense of adventure and high clearance on their vehicle Forest Road 78 provides a rough route to another access point. The two-track is 0.4 mile east of Pigeon Bridge Campground on Sturgeon Valley Road and is posted. Turn north (left) and follow the two-track 0.7 mile as it skirts a power line and forces you to carefully negotiate some deep ruts along the way. FR 78 crosses the Shingle Mill Pathway and then ends at a dirt barrier. You have to walk the final 100 yards. The Pigeon River is 30 to 40 feet wide and one to three feet deep. The river is tight at the road end but 200 yards upstream it flows through an open meadow where the casting is easier.

Before the 2008 dam failure, this stretch held good populations of both brookies and browns and an increasing number of rainbows. Considerable log structure provides cover while the bottom is gravel with enough sand and silt to produce good Hex hatches in late June.

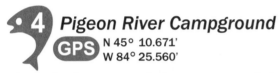

4 Pigeon River Campground
GPS N 45° 10.671'
W 84° 25.560'

This is the largest state forest campground along the Pigeon River and the most popular. On weekends in July and August it's often full. This puts a lot of commotion near the water, and anglers who are staying here should be prepared to wade a ways before locating a quiet stretch of water.

To reach the campground from Pigeon Bridge, head east on Sturgeon Valley Road 1.3 miles to where the pavement ends at an intersection. Turn north (left) on Twin Lakes Road, pass the impressive log lodge that serves as the Pigeon River Country State Forest Headquarters, and in 1.8 miles you'll curve east and reach the posted entrance to the Pigeon River Campground. Just beyond it is the posted intersection with Hardwood Lake Road continuing to the east while Twin Lake Road turns north (left) again.

Of the campground's 19 sites, seven of them are directly on the river, while at the south end is a small parking area for anglers. A second parking area is located right at the bridge where Pigeon Bridge Road (also labeled Ford Lake Road on some maps) crosses the Pigeon River at the north end of the campground. Either upstream or downstream you'll find the river 35 to 40 feet wide and one to three feet deep in normal conditions. The bottom is gravel and the wading is easy. Brookies and more so brown trout inhabit this reach along with a few rainbows.

The Shingle Mill Pathway actually passes through the campground and then uses the bridge to the Pigeon to the west side. Upstream the trail parallels the river all the way to the state forest headquarters, but most of the time it is high on a ridge, making access to the water not impossible but much more challenging. Downstream it quickly swings west away from the river.

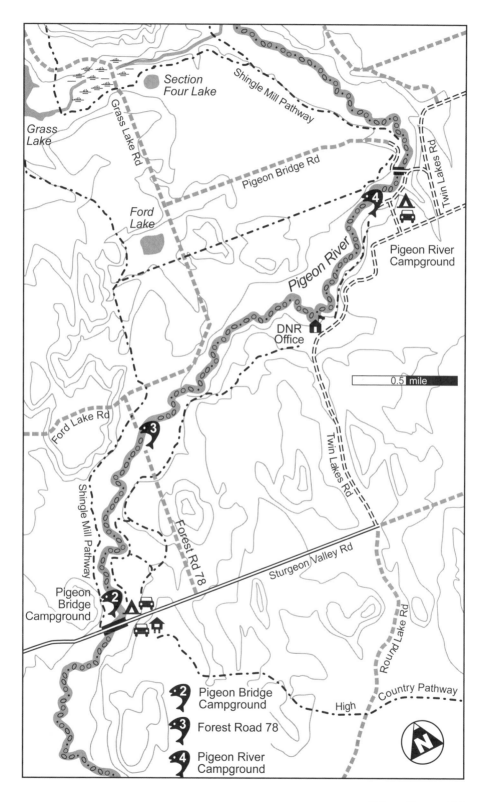

Section Four Lake

Grass Lake

Grass Lake Rd

Shingle Mill Pathway

Pigeon Bridge Rd

Ford Lake

Pigeon River

Twin Lakes Rd

4

Pigeon River Campground

DNR Office

0.5 mile

Ford Lake Rd

3

Shingle Mill Pathway

Twin Lakes Rd

Forest Rd 78

Sturgeon Valley Rd

Round Lake Rd

Pigeon Bridge Campground

2

Country Pathway

High

2 Pigeon Bridge Campground

3 Forest Road 78

4 Pigeon River Campground

N

5 Chaffee Trail

GPS N 45° 11.940'
W 84° 25.438'

If you find the number of campers and anglers too overwhelming at the state forest campgrounds along the Pigeon River, then pack your boots and rod and seek out this remote and lonely spot. But be forewarned; this stretch of the river is not easy to reach.

From the Pigeon River Campground continue north on Twin Lakes Road for two miles, passing Twin Lakes and then Lost Lake along the way. Within 0.75 mile north of Lost Lake, turn west (left) on an unmarked two-track. On most maps, including those from the state forest headquarters, the road is labeled Chaffee Trail. You'll know you're on the correct two-track if Hemlock Lake pops into view within 0.3 mile. This small trout lake is open to artificial lures or flies only from the last Saturday in April to Sept. 30.

A quarter mile past the lake you reach a well-posted intersection with Forest Road 51. This two-track is also posted as a segment of the Shore-to-Shore Horse Trail and to the south leads to Elk Hill Trail Camp. Chaffee Trail continues west and within 0.35 mile arrives where the two-track becomes rough and fallen trees are often blocking any further travel by vehicle. At this point it's best to complete the journey on foot or by mountain bike. In the next half mile you pass Forest Road 52 to the south and then Forest Road 48 to the north. Both are posted. From FR 48 it's another 300 yards to where Chaffee Trail ends on a bluff, 200 yards from the river. Look for a path, but if one isn't visible then simply descend the steep hill and cross the low ground through a mix of hardwood and conifer to the stream. If bushwhacking it, a marker to guide you back to the road can be helpful.

The river here is a bit deeper and the flow is faster than at the upstream sites, and wading is not so easy. At high flows the river is unwadable. Upstream, the river at mid-channel is generally more than three feet deep, and it may overtop your waders in places. Downstream, it is generally shallower, but there are some deep holes. The Pigeon is only 35 feet wide here but still wide enough for careful fly casting. Logs and snags in the river provide good trout cover, and, needless to say, fishing pressure is very light.

6 Tin Bridge

GPS N 45° 13.473'
W 84° 25.719'

Once the site of a state forest campground on the west bank, Tin Bridge is an easy-to-reach access site in the middle of the Pigeon River Country State Forest. From Pigeon River Campground, head north on Twin Lakes Road and continue on it as it becomes Osmun Road at the Cheboygan County Line. Within 4.2 miles of the campground, turn west (left) on Tin Bridge Road. Follow the graded dirt road and in 1.5 miles you pass a two-track posted "Cornwall Flooding Dayuse Access" to the south. In another 0.7 mile you'll

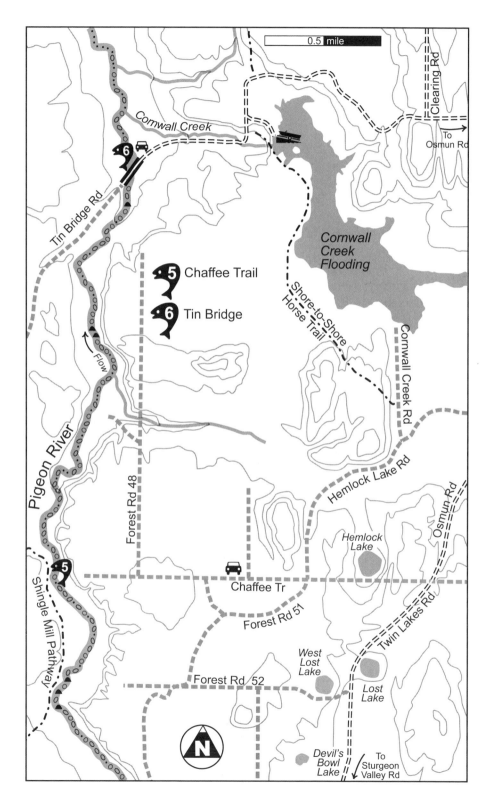

0.5 mile

Clearing Rd

Cornwall Creek

To
Osmun Rd

6

Tin Bridge Rd

Cornwall
Creek
Flooding

5 Chaffee Trail

6 Tin Bridge

Shore-to-Shore
Horse Trail

Flow

Cornwall Creek Rd

Pigeon River

Hemlock Lake Rd

Osmun Rd

Forest Rd 48

Hemlock
Lake

5

Shingle Mill Pathway

Chaffee Tr

Forest Rd 51

Twin Lakes Rd

West
Lost
Lake

Lost
Lake

Forest Rd 52

N

Devil's
Bowl
Lake

To
Sturgeon
Valley Rd

arrive at Tin Bridge, where there is parking east of the bridge for a pair of vehicles on a gravel pad.

The river is 35 to 45 feet wide here, more than wide enough for fly casting, and generally less than four feet deep, except at high flows. A few holes are more than four feet deep even at normal flows. Bottom is mostly gravel with some boulders, while upstream are some nice stretches of riffled water. The large boulders and downed logs offer plenty of cover for trout but also demand that you wade with caution. About half a mile below the bridge the river gets deeper and the bottom is mostly sand.

The trout at Tin Bridge are a mix of browns, rainbows, and an occasional brookie. There are some large, fat brown trout in this water, some migrating from Mullett Lake in late summer. In mid- and late season you often have this stretch to yourself.

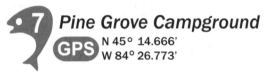

7 Pine Grove Campground
GPS N 45° 14.666'
     W 84° 26.773'

This small, scenic, and somewhat secluded campground is located in a stand of red pine on high ground above the Pigeon River. Nearby is a footbridge for the High Country Pathway, providing anglers even more access. From Tin Bridge Road, head north on Osmun Road for 3.5 miles and then west (left) on Webb Road for 0.6 mile. The intersection with Campsite Road is posted with a "Pine Grove State Forest Campground" sign. Turn south (left) on Campsite Road and follow it 2.5 miles until it ends at the six-site campground.

The access can also be easily reached from I-75 by departing at exit 301 and heading east on Afton Road for a mile until it turns north. Continue east on Webb Road to reach the Campsite Road in 7.8 miles.

From site No. 3 a log stairway leads down a steep clay bank to the Pigeon at a narrow stretch where there are large boulders and a deep hole. Use caution here. Otherwise the Pigeon is 35 to 45 feet wide and generally more than four feet deep at mid-channel upstream from the campground. Downstream, it is shallower at normal flows for about a half mile, then becomes deeper again. The river bottom is mostly sand. The banks are generally low with overhanging brush that hide trout but will also snag your fly. To fish here you have to wade and cast carefully and in some spots even turn to a roll cast.

From the campground a posted trail heads downstream to connect to the High Country Pathway. The pathway crosses the Pigeon on a footbridge that was built in 2008 after the original one was washed out by a flood. The bridge provides additional access away from the campground, but the pathway not so much as it tends to quickly swing away from the river on either side of it.

Large brooks, browns, and rainbows are in this water. This part of the river is not heavily fished, probably because wading is never easy. At high

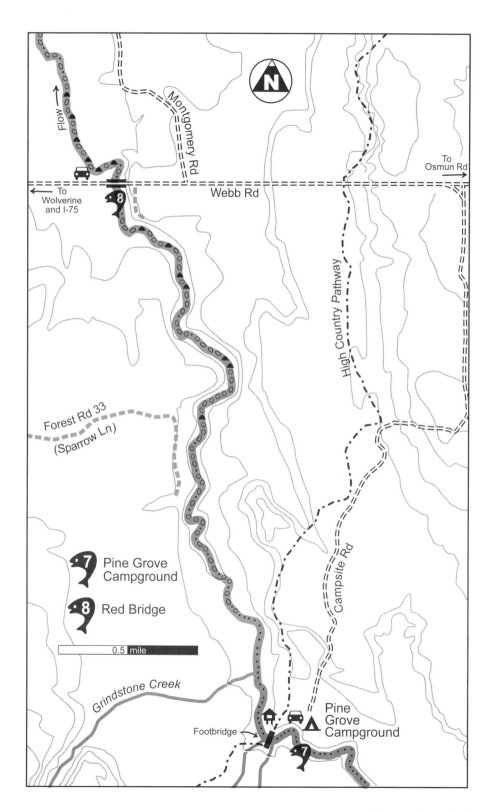

Flow ↑

Montgomery Rd

N

To
Osmun Rd

To
Wolverine
and I-75

Webb Rd

8

High Country Pathway

Forest Rd 33
(Sparrow Ln)

Campsite Rd

7 Pine Grove
Campground

8 Red Bridge

0.5 mile

Grindstone Creek

Footbridge

Pine
Grove
Campground

7

The Lure of Bamboo

Before there were graphite and fiberglass, there was bamboo. Bamboo fly rods were being built in England by the early 1800s and in the U.S. within 50 years. By 1874, H.L. Leonard Rod Company switched from ash and lancewood to bamboo, producing the first commercially-built, six-strip bamboo rods.

The best bamboo comes from China with Tonkin cane from the Guangdong Province being the most highly prized. Its high density of fibers gives Tonkin rods strength and flexibility unmatched by other species. The trade embargo imposed on China in 1950s devastated rod makers and the shortage of quality bamboo gave rise to the development of synthetic fibers for fishing rods. But bamboo survived and has made a steady comeback since the embargo ended in the 1970s.

Despite the advances in carbon fibers, few rods cast as well as those made from Tonkin cane. The bamboo for each rod is hand-split, hand planed and then pressure glued into a six-strip, hexagonal tube that is strong but wonderfully flexible. Bamboo enthusiasts claim that even the

flows, wading is impossible. This is all state land upstream and nearly a mile downstream.

8 *Red Bridge*

GPS N 45° 16.330'
W 84° 27.614'

Map: page 165

For most fly anglers, the final spot conducive for wading is where Webb Road crosses the Pigeon. Red Bridge is reached from the intersection of Osmun Road and Webb Road by heading west on Webb Road for 2.1 miles, passing Campsite Road to Pine Grove Campground along the way. From I-75, depart at exit 301 and head east on Afton Road for a mile to the intersection with Webb Road. Continue east on Webb Road for 6.3 miles to the bridge.

There is parking for three vehicles just west of the bridge, and then a second parking area overlooking the river a hundred yards further west. How deep are some of the holes here? At the second access site a rope swing dangles from a tree leaning over the Pigeon.

In general the river is about 50 feet wide here and two to four feet deep in most places and even less at low flows. The bottom is gravel and boulders. The banks are alternately high and low, forested with hardwoods. The river is wide enough and open enough for easy fly casting, but wading can be difficult because of the swift flow and slippery cobbles and boulders. At high flows, wading is dangerous to impossible. Trout cover is good with sweepers, sunken logs, and large boulders hiding browns, rainbows and even some brookies. By putting in at the parking area farthest to the west, you can fish the 300 yards upstream to the bridge and then the more open water beyond it before returning to your vehicle on Webb Road.

best graphite still rattles and vibrates when compared to bamboo. With a six-strip rod, you have opposing flats helping the tip get back and settle quickly and that produces fluid back and forward casts with a dampening effect at the end so your line lays out smoothly and precisely where you want it.

"A six-weight bamboo rod weighs twice as much as a six-weight graphite rod so graphite has a faster line speed and a faster stroke," said Bob Summers, who has been building bamboo rods for more than 30 years in Traverse City. "But I like to feel the weight of a rod coming forward. It's like comparing a light hammer with a heavy hammer. I want to feel a little weight in my hand when I hit that nail."

Raised on the west side of Detroit, Summers began fishing at an early age and was tying his own flies by the time he turned 12, purchasing his materials from a nearby fly shop operated by Paul Young. In 1956, Summers, then only 16, began working for Young after school in his rod-building workshop and learned the intricacies of bamboo from the master of cane rods. Summers followed the company north when it moved to Traverse City and in 1974 opened his own bamboo rod shop, R.W. Summers Company (231-946-7923; *www.rwsummers.com*).

Now 70, Summers still builds up to 30 rods a year that range in price from $2,100 to more than $2,300. Each one requires more than 50 hours of work and, like a Paul Young rod, many of Summers' models are sought after by collectors.

But Summers builds rods for anglers, who want to catch trout with them. The appeal of bamboo is not only a smooth cast and accuracy but also tradition and heritage, the same reason you cherish the shotgun your father used as a young hunter. Most of all, a hand-crafted rod seems more natural in a setting where trout thrive; a cold-water stream somewhere up north, lined by overhanging cedars and swirling around sweepers, submerged logs and other woody debris.

Bamboo, said Summers, is ageless, the reason you don't buy a bamboo rod, you invest in one.

"Buying graphite is like buying a car; something newer is going to eventually come along," Summers said. "Anglers who buy my rods fish with them but they also like to think of them as a decent investment. And once they buy a rod I think a lot of them convert totally to bamboo."

A fly angler and his dog hike into Green Timbers to fish the Sturgeon River and enjoy a bit of wilderness solitude in the Pigeon River Country State Forest.

Sturgeon River

Cold, fast, and filled with trout, the Sturgeon River north of Gaylord is renowned for large lake-run browns and rainbows in its lower reaches and resident browns and brookies in its upper reaches. But the Sturgeon is swift. Along with the equally swift Pine, the Sturgeon is the fastest river outside the Upper Peninsula, with an average descent of almost 14 feet per mile.

Most of the larger trout are caught in the lower river, where a swift flow and deep holes make wading difficult if not impossible. The upper river is easier to wade, but downed timber and overhanging brush can raise havoc with fly anglers. Between climbing over logjams and probing the currents and holes, you earn your trout in the Sturgeon River.

Like the Pigeon and the Black to the east, the Sturgeon begins on the northern flank of a moraine, which forms the divide between these streams and the Au Sable drainage to the south. The Sturgeon then flows 36 river miles northward before discharging into Burt Lake at Indian River.

From the headwaters to Sturgeon Bridge, ten river miles, the Sturgeon is a small stream, 15 to 25 feet wide and three feet deep, with a mostly sandy bottom. In these reaches it is shallow enough to wade, but logjams, snags, and drowned logs are hazards to the wading angler. The narrow channel and brushy banks make fly fishing extremely difficult if not impossible.

Sturgeon Bridge in the Pigeon River Country State Forest is often considered the first area suitable for a fly rod and the river's Blue Ribbon designation begins here, extending 21 miles to Burt Lake. Downstream to Trowbridge Road, ten river miles, the Sturgeon varies from 30 to 50 feet wide and the depth is generally less than four feet at normal flows.

Within the first half of this reach, the Sturgeon flows through the Green Timbers, a special, nonmotorized tract of the state forest. Access is far more difficult here, and anglers will find that the drowned logs and snags, while providing good cover from trout, can still make wading difficult at times. The river bottom is sandy near Sturgeon Bridge, but gravel becomes more abundant the further downstream you go. On the positive side, canoeists are non-existent here and other anglers rare. If you're willing to spend the effort—in other words hike or mountain bike in—to reach the heart of the Green Timbers, you'll enjoy a near-wilderness fishing experience that's hard to match elsewhere in the Lower Peninsula.

The best stretch of the Sturgeon for fly anglers is the Trowbridge Road area. Here the bottom is almost entirely gravel and boulders, the river more open, the trout cover still good and the casting considerably easier. In normal water levels, the river is wadable and can be quickly reached from several access points on both sides of I-75. Small resident browns dominate, but in late summer an occasional large lake-run brown enters the upper river to give fly fishers a shot at an eight- to ten-pound trophy.

From Trowbridge Road downstream to Haakwood Campground, a distance of six river miles, the bottom is mostly gravel and boulders, the flow is swift, and wading is more challenging even in normal levels. At high flows, almost all of this stretch is unwadable. The West Branch enters the Sturgeon at Wolverine, greatly increasing its flow. Most of the river above Wolverine is less than four feet deep at normal flows, but there are some deeper runs. The river varies in width from about 30 to 60 feet with the narrow reaches being the most difficult and thus the most dangerous for the wading fisherman.

Downstream from Haakwood Campground to the mouth at Burt Lake, ten river miles, the Sturgeon is usually too fast and too deep for safe wading. The river is 35 to 70 feet wide and three to six feet deep. Bottom is mostly gravel, with some hard, slippery clay below the campground and some sand near the mouth. Edge wading is possible in places, but most fishing is done from the banks. Three access downstream points are covered in this chapter—Rondo Road Bridge, Rondo Public Access and White Road Bridge—and extreme caution must be used when entering the river at any of them.

The Sturgeon is a cold stream, colder than the Pigeon or Black, and has a relatively large flow during dry periods. Fluctuations most years are less than two feet, but the high velocity of flow can make even a small rise dangerous to the wading angler. Midstream velocities at low flow in several parts of the river ranged from one to 4.5 feet per second. A velocity of three feet per second makes dangerous wading where the water is more than three feet deep.

Gravel beds are sparse in the upper river but abundant in most of the stream below the Green Timbers property. The river would appear to offer almost ideal spawning habitat for trout, but spawning successes are hampered by high levels of sand in the stream. Improvement is coming as the DNR and Trout Unlimited chapters are constantly stabilizing stream banks and maintaining sand traps—sedimentation basins where the sand can be trapped and removed—in the upper reaches of the river.

The healthy numbers of trout are the result of the Sturgeon being one of the few Michigan rivers that are home to an anadromous fish run from an inland lake—in this case Burt Lake—as opposed to a Great Lake. Once shallow Burt Lake warms up during the summer, browns, steelheads, and even walleyes head up the Sturgeon seeking cooler temperatures. Steelhead move upstream as far as White Road Bridge and large trophy browns are common in the deeper water beginning at Scott Road and at times even further upstream.

Boat fishing on the Sturgeon, except for the quiet water near the mouth, is not feasible. The flow is too fast to allow the anglers to cover the water adequately, whether with bait, spinner, or fly. Neither is the Sturgeon well

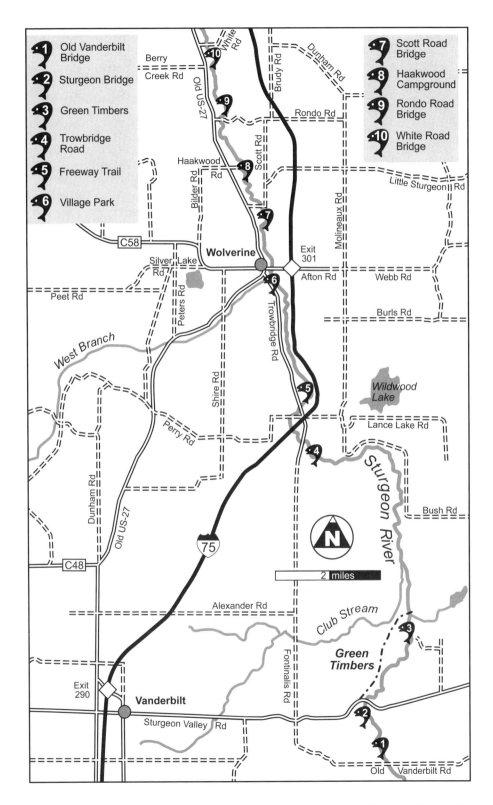

Legend:
1. Old Vanderbilt Bridge
2. Sturgeon Bridge
3. Green Timbers
4. Trowbridge Road
5. Freeway Trail
6. Village Park
7. Scott Road Bridge
8. Haakwood Campground
9. Rondo Road Bridge
10. White Road Bridge

suited for recreational canoeing. The upper river is hard going because of the narrow channel and many logjams, and the lower river is too swift for most inexperienced paddlers. There have been, however, a growing number of kayakers, rafters, and even tubers on the lower river.

Hatches on the Sturgeon are not as reliable or as prolific as the Black River or many other Michigan trout streams. Hendricksons, stoneflies, white-winged blacks, blue-winged olives and light and dark cahills occur on the river roughly two weeks later than they do on the Au Sable. Grassy meadows border much of the Sturgeon, making grasshopper, ant, and cricket patterns very effective from mid- to late summer.

Accommodations

Gaylord, a half-hour drive south of most of the Sturgeon, offers the largest range of accommodations in the area. See Accommodations in the Pigeon River chapter or contact the Gaylord Area Convention and Tourism Bureau (800-345-8621; *www.gaylordmichigan.net*). There are also considerable accommodations in Indian River, quickly reached from exit 310 of I-75. *Indian River Motel and Cottages* (231-238-7406; *www.mich-web.com/indianrivermotel*; 4148 Sturgeon St.) has 14 two-bedroom cottages with full kitchens overlooking the Sturgeon, along with an 11-room motel. Just north of Indian River on Old US-27 is the *Northwoods Lodge* (231-238-7729; 2390 S. Straits Hwy.), a log lodge with breakfast in the morning and fire in the lounge in the evening. For a complete list of area accommodations, contact the Indian River Tourist Bureau (231-238-9325; *www.irtourism.com*).

In Wolverine, the beautiful *Silent Sport Lodge* (231-525-6166; *www.silentsportlodge.com*; 14750 Old Sturgeon Rd.) overlooks the West Branch of the Sturgeon River. Calling itself a "wilderness bed and breakfast," this log lodge has four bedrooms and promotes silent sports in the area, from fly fishing and mushroom hunting to birding and snowshoeing.

Campgrounds: Right on the river and a major access site is Haakwood State Forest Campground, two miles north of Wolverine on Old US-27. The rustic campground has 18 sites, none of them directly on the water but all only a short walk from the river. There are also private campgrounds in Wolverine and Indian River. On the river near the Trowbridge Road access sites is *Sturgeon River Campground and RV Resort* (231-525-8300; *www.srivercampground.com*; 15247 Trowbridge Rd.) with 63 sites, full-hook-ups and two rental cabins. At the mouth of the Sturgeon is Burt Lake State Park (231-238-9392; 6635 State Park Dr.) with a 306-site, modern campground.

Fly Shops and Guides

If flies and fly fishing equipment are needed, it's best to stop in Gaylord at *Alphorn Shop* (989-732-5616; 137 W. Main St.) or *Jay's Sporting Goods* (989-705-1339; *www.jayssportinggoods.com*; 150 Dale Rd.). In Indian River limited supplies are available at *Northland Sports Company* (231-238-9382; 6074 River St.).

The Northland Sports Company

Northland Sports Company in Indian River is an old-fashioned outdoor shop. It's packed with a little bit of everything, whether you hunt for deer, turkeys or pheasants or fish through the ice in the winter, in small creeks for trout in the spring or troll lakes for pike at the height of the summer. But what catches your eye the first time you enter the shop is not what's on the shelves but what's hanging from the ceiling: lures, hundreds of them. More than 1,200 antique lures dangle from the rafters with some dating back to the early 1900s.

This is easily one of the largest collections of early tackle in Michigan. And the man behind the counter, Roger Jacobs, is not only the proprietor of the shop but the creator of this suspended display of fishing history.

"I've been in this business 48 years and I've been collecting them for most of that," Jacobs said. "Some are more than a hundred years old."

The majority of the tackle are plugs, spoons and topwater baits designed for species like bass, pike, and muskie. But not all. Jacobs's collection is so extensive there's probably a lure to catch every kind of fish swimming in Michigan. There is even a case of antique flies on the counter.

Jacobs purchased most of them but as the collection grew, other anglers began giving him their old lures. "If everybody brought me what they promised, well, I wouldn't have enough room on my ceiling to hang them all."

Jacobs is also an avid angler. When it comes time to fish, he passes up the antiques for the current spinners and spoons he stocks in his shop. But one thing has never changed, Jacobs said, whether the lure is 50 years old or the latest craze among anglers.

"New lures are like old lures; if it stays in your tackle box, you won't catch a thing with it," Jacobs said. "Put it on the end of your line, learn how to use it and you might just catch a fish."

Good advice no matter what's at the end of your line.

Maps of the Sturgeon

Access sites on the Sturgeon are far easier to find than those on the Pigeon or Black. Most of the secondary roads run along section lines, and there are few unmarked two-tracks that need to be followed.

Eleven access sites are covered in this chapter and are easily reached from Gaylord, Wolverine or Indian River. The first three, Old Vanderbilt Road Bridge, Sturgeon Bridge, and Green Timbers, are reached by departing I-75 at exit 290 and then heading east on Sturgeon Valley Road from Vanderbilt to the Pigeon River Country State Forest.

The next five—Trowbridge Road, Freeway Trail, Village Park, Scott Road, and Haakwood Campground—are accessible from Wolverine along Old US-27. The final three, Rondo Bridge, Rondo Road and White Bridge, are also reached from Old US-27 between Wolverine and Indian River.

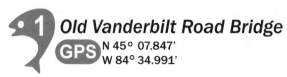

Old Vanderbilt Road Bridge

GPS N 45° 07.847'
W 84° 34.991'

Upstream from the Old Vanderbilt Road Bridge there is another access site, Doc Sehls Bridge along Whitmarsh Road, but there the Sturgeon is a small brook, less than 20 feet wide and crowded with overhanging brush, making it nearly impossible to use a fly rod. Even here you'll find fly casting very challenging.

To reach Old Vanderbilt Road Bridge, head east of Vanderbilt on Sturgeon Valley Road for 3.5 miles and then turn south (right) on Fontinalis Road. Within 0.5 mile Fontinalis Road curves east and becomes Old Vanderbilt Road and reaches the bridge within a mile from Sturgeon Valley Road. There is room to park two or three cars on the west of the bridge.

The Sturgeon is 30 to 35 feet wide, and mostly two to three feet deep, with some deeper holes. Velocity is moderate. The bottom is predominately sand. Wading is easy at normal flows, but downstream from the bridge is a sand trap that needs to be avoided. The banks are low and brushy, lined with swamp conifers that will easily grab a wayward fly. But there are some openings where a roll cast gets you into position to catch a brown or even a brookie. State land extends upstream about a quarter mile on both sides of the river. Downstream, there is state land on the east (right) bank, but the west (left) bank is private. This segment is not heavily fished.

Sturgeon Bridge

GPS N 45° 08.747'
W 84° 33.681'

Sturgeon Bridge is on the paved Sturgeon Valley Road 5.3 miles east of Vanderbilt. There is parking along the road east of the bridge, or you can leave a vehicle in the Green Timbers parking area, 50 yards west of the river and marked on the north side of the road by a pair of stone gates.

The Sturgeon is 35 to 45 feet wide here and two to three feet deep, with some deeper holes. The banks are low and forested with mixed hardwood and conifer. The bottom is mostly sand with some muck and velocity of flow is moderate. Wading is fairly easy at normal flows, but watch out for drowned logs, snags, and holes. There is also a pair of sand traps upstream from the bridge that need to be avoided. Both are posted with the first within sight of the bridge and the second a mile upstream.

The river is open enough in places to cast a fly. Cover along fallen logs and snags is adequate, and the trout here average substantially larger than in the upstream reaches. Browns and an occasional brookie will rise to your fly. Upstream, all property is private, but a foot trail on the east bank of the river will allow you to walk around the first sand trap before entering the river. Downstream from the bridge is state land all the way to the Cheboygan County Line.

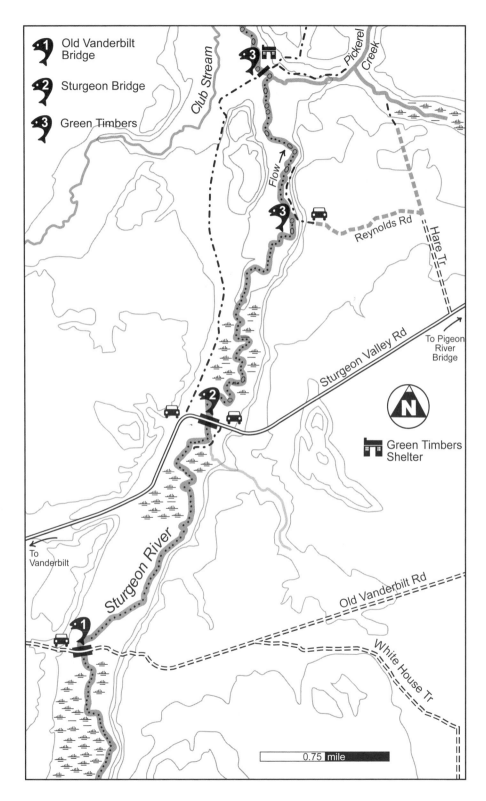

Old Vanderbilt
Bridge

Sturgeon Bridge

Green Timbers

Club Stream

Pickerel Creek

Flow

Reynolds Rd

Hare Tr

Sturgeon Valley Rd

To Pigeon
River
Bridge

N

Green Timbers
Shelter

Sturgeon River

To
Vanderbilt

Old Vanderbilt Rd

White House Tr

0.75 mile

An angler prepares his rod to fish the Sturgeon River near the Green Timbers Cabin in the Pigeon River Country State Forest.

 3 Green Timbers

GPS N 45° 09.507'
W 84° 32.499'

Map: page 175

Most of the Green Timbers is a hike- or bike-in adventure for fly anglers (see "Great Adventures and Cheap Lodging in Green Timbers"). This access, however, is the easiest to reach in the tract. From the Sturgeon Bridge, head east on Sturgeon Valley Road and within 1.6 miles turn north (left) on unposted Hare Trail, the first dirt road beyond the stream. Follow Hare Trail for half a mile and then turn west (left) on Reynolds Road, which is posted with a "Fisherman's Access Road" sign. Reynolds Road ends in 0.7 mile at a parking area capable of holding six to eight vehicles.

From the parking area, a distinct foot trail heads steeply down a bluff and in less than a quarter mile breaks out at a grassy opening overlooking a bend in the Sturgeon. At the bend the river is 40 to 50 feet wide, two to four feet deep, and holds a sand trap that needs to be avoided. Both upstream and downstream the Sturgeon narrows to 35 feet and features lots of sweepers, sunken logs, and overhanging cedars that need to be avoided when casting. But the structure provides excellent cover for trout, and both resident browns and at times even anadromous fish are present. Good numbers of lake-run browns enter this area in early fall; some fish have been known to travel all the way up to the Old Vanderbilt Bridge site to spawn.

The bottom is all sand, and wading is fairly easy if you watch out for snags and logs in the water. A faint foot trail can be followed downstream, but the easiest casting by far is upstream beyond the bend and sand trap.

Great Fishing and Cheap Lodging in Green Timbers

Downstream from the Sturgeon Bridge, the Sturgeon River flows near one of the oldest hunting and fishing clubs in the state and through one of Michigan's newest nonmotorized tracts. The Fontinalis Club, which surrounds most of Club Stream, was not incorporated until 1902 but was being used as a private hunting and fishing retreat by the 1880s when its wealthy members would arrive via a railroad car especially outfitted for camping.

Practically surrounding Fontinalis is Green Timbers. The successful reintroduction of elk to Michigan in 1918 took place just 1.5 miles north of the 6,300-acre tract and Green Timbers has remained an important area for the species. Eventually much of the area was logged, burned and then used for grazing before being purchased and named by Don McLouth in 1942. He turned Green Timbers into a hunting and fishing retreat for McLouth Steel employees that included a series of log cabins near the Sturgeon River.

In 1982, the state took over the property as part of the Pigeon River Country State forest and all but two of the cabins were removed. On the banks of the Sturgeon River stands the Green Timbers Cabin, while perched on the edge of a ridge, high above the Sturgeon River, is the Honeymoon Cabin. A wall in each structure was removed by the DNR to turn them into free-use, three-sided shelters.

Green Timbers Cabin in particular is a fine destination for fly anglers looking to escape into the woods for a night or two. From the Green Timbers parking area, it's a 2.3-mile hike along an old two-track before you arrive at a bridge across the Sturgeon River. On the other side is the confluence of Pickerel Creek and the trail to Honeymoon Cabin with Green Timbers Cabin tucked into the trees nearby. Many campers carry in a tent and use the classic, hand-hewn log cabin and its fieldstone fireplace to cook or to enjoy a fire in the evening.

The Sturgeon is just a few steps away from the Green Timbers Cabin. Above and below the foot bridge the river is 35 to 45 feet wide and two to four feet deep with a mix of sand and gravel patches on the bottom. There are plenty of sweepers, drowned stumps, and other cover for trout, but casting is relatively easy here. And most likely you'll have the river to yourself. The tract is closed to equestrians, and canoers are rarely seen this far upstream, if ever. Mountain bikers do frequent the area, and a knobby, fat-tire bicycle is an excellent way to reach the cabin quickly.

If you plan to spend the night, bring a water filter as there is no source of safe drinking water at the cabin. The Pigeon River Country State Forest headquarters (989-983-4101; Twin Lakes Rd.) has maps of Green Timbers but be aware that many of the trails on the map no longer exist or are extremely hard to find.

4 Trowbridge Road Access Site

GPS N 45° 13.230'
W 84° 35.043'

The Sturgeon River dips underneath I-75 at Trowbridge Road and then parallels the interstate on its way to Wolverine, providing anglers with a cluster of access sites where at times you hear the rumble of highway traffic.

The best for fly anglers is this public access site, near the south bridge on Trowbridge Road. From Wolverine head south on Trowbridge Road for 3.5 miles. After crossing the north bridge and passing underneath the interstate, turn east (left) on Cornwall Grade Road. The dirt road is marked on Trowbridge Road by a canoe access sign and in 0.3 mile ends at the launch, where there is parking for a half-dozen vehicles.

The fishing here is quite different from further upstream. The flow is swift, and the slippery cobbles and boulders make wading more difficult. At high flows, none of this water is wadable. The river is narrow, 30 to 40 feet wide, and two to four feet deep, with many deeper runs. There is a low-head rock dam about halfway between the access site and the south bridge and beyond the bridge rapids that you probably should avoid. It's a wade of 0.3 mile downstream to the south bridge and 1.5 miles to the north bridge.

The banks are low and brushy, with open meadows in many places and some hardwoods. Trout cover is good. Although narrow, the river is open enough for fly casting. Fishing pressure is usually light to moderate for resident browns, until mid-July when the lake-run browns begin appearing. Fishing activity increases then through the fall with anglers casting for an opportunity to land a brown from three to ten pounds and later steelhead. Night fishing can be very productive, but extreme caution must be used when stepping into water this swift after dark.

The north bridge is 0.6 mile north of the south bridge on Trowbridge Road and is actually a pair of bridges: one for vehicles and another for the Gaylord–Mackinaw City Rail-Trail, which parallels the Sturgeon River to Indian River. Parking is limited at the side of the road.

5 Freeway Trail

GPS N 45° 14.199'
W 84° 35.154'

Half a mile north from where Trowbridge Road dips under I-75, or 2.5 miles south of Wolverine, you will find Freeway Trail, a two-track that heads east a quarter mile to a bridge over the Sturgeon River. There is parking for two or three vehicles west of the bridge along the shoulder of the road.

The Sturgeon here is 25 to 30 feet wide and two to four feet deep. Velocity is moderate to fast, but the wading is easy in normal conditions. The west bank is grassy, making casting easier than it otherwise should be, and downstream from the bridge is a nice stretch of riffled water. Both upstream and downstream the river frontage is private.

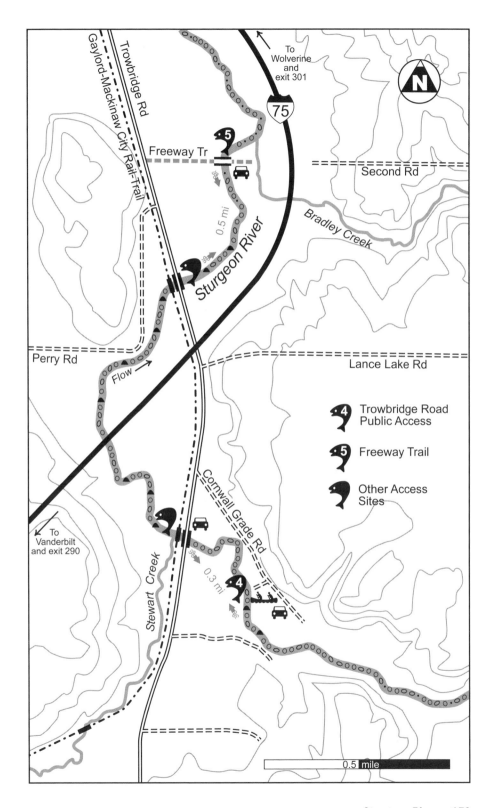

To
Wolverine
and
exit 301

75

Trowbridge Rd

Gaylord-Mackinaw City Rail-Trail

Freeway Tr

Second Rd

5

0.5 mi

Sturgeon River

Bradley Creek

Perry Rd

Lance Lake Rd

Flow

To
Vanderbilt
and exit 290

Cornwall Grade Rd

Stewart Creek

0.3 mi

4

Trowbridge Road
Public Access

Freeway Trail

Other Access
Sites

0.5 mile

6 Village Park
GPS N 45° 16.386'
W 84° 36.115'

Good river access is found in the heart of Wolverine at its charming Village Park. Unfortunately, this is also where many paddlers put in for a float down the Sturgeon River, something to keep in mind if you arrive on a summer weekend. The park is reached by departing I-75 at exit 301 and heading west along Afton Road for 0.7 mile. Village Park is on the south side of Afton Road, just after you cross the Sturgeon.

Within the park are a large parking area, picnic tables, and the historic Wolverine Railroad Depot which now houses Henley's Canoe & Kayak Rentals (231-525-9994). At the south end of the park is where the West Branch of the Sturgeon merges with the mainstream. Upstream from the confluence the Sturgeon is 35 feet wide and one to three feet deep over a gravel bottom. Here you'll find numerous submerged logs and sweepers for trout cover and easy wading and casting. Downstream the river is 40 feet wide, two to four feet deep and more difficult to wade due to the increased volume of water. This is particularly true on the north side of Afton Road, where the river winds past the Wolverine Festival Grounds. The grounds provide considerably more river to fish, but in places, particularly at the remains of an old bridge, the water can be too swift to wade through.

Passing through Village Park is the Gaylord–Mackinaw City Rail-Trail. Follow it south from the depot and you'll quickly come to a bridge over the West Branch. This tributary of the Sturgeon is 20 to 25 feet wide and one to three feet deep with a gravel bottom. Casting is tight but possible in this designated Blue Ribbon Stream. In the heat of the summer here and further upstream is an excellent area to fish for brookies and browns.

7 Scott Road Bridge
GPS N 45° 17.350'
W 84° 36.183'

Access at Scott Road is from the bridge over the Sturgeon and Meadows Access Site, a canoe launch just upstream. Scott Road is reached from Old US-27, 1.3 miles north of Wolverine. Turn east (right) and in a quarter mile you will reach the bridge, the first one on the Sturgeon downstream from Wolverine. Cross the bridge and turn south (right) on a dirt road for another quarter mile to reach Meadows Access Site on the east bank, where you'll find parking for a dozen vehicles and a vault toilet.

Downstream from Scott Road Bridge there is a large hole that needs to be avoided. Overall the Sturgeon in this area is deep and the wading difficult. But wading the 0.3 mile between the canoe launch and the bridge is considerably easier and so is casting a fly. Here the Sturgeon is 40 to 50 feet wide and two to four feet deep at normal levels. The bottom is gravel with

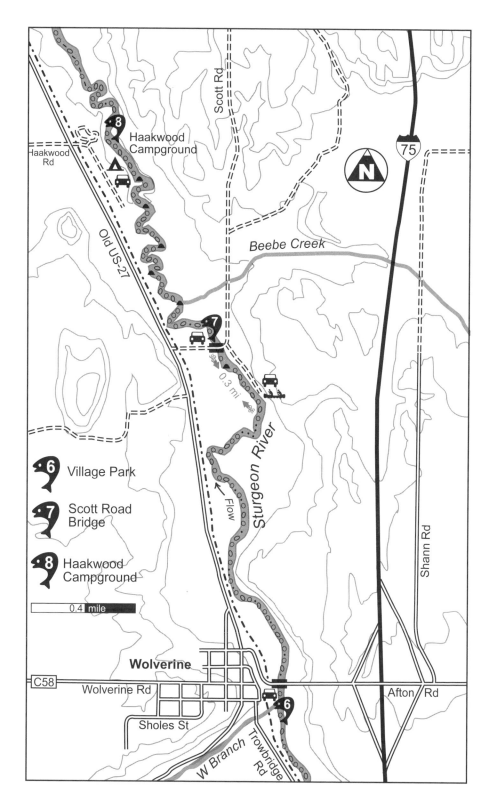

Scott Rd

75

Haakwood
Rd

Old US-27

Haakwood
Campground

8

7

Beebe Creek

N

0.3 mi

Flow

Sturgeon River

Shann Rd

6 Village Park

7 Scott Road
Bridge

8 Haakwood
Campground

0.4 mile

Wolverine

C58 Wolverine Rd

Sholes St

W Branch

Trowbridge Rd

6

Afton Rd

some slippery rocks and boulders and the flow swift, so felt-soled boots are helpful as is a wading stick. If you wade upstream from the access site you will come to some deeper water at bends that will cause problems even at normal levels.

The banks are low, sandy, and brushy, with some larger hardwoods and open grassland. Trout cover is somewhat sparse. Fishing pressure is usually moderate but can be heavy during the late summer run of browns and fall spawning runs.

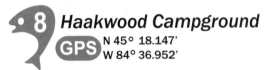

8 Haakwood Campground

GPS N 45° 18.147'
W 84° 36.952'

Map: page 181

What was once called "the old orchard" by early anglers eventually became Haakwood State Forest Campground due to the popularity of the area during the spring and fall spawning runs on the Sturgeon River. Posted along Old US-27, the campground is 0.8 mile downstream from Scott Bridge or 2.1 miles north of Wolverine on Old US-27. You cross the Gaylord–Mackinaw City Rail-Trail just before entering the campground.

None of the campground's 18 sites are directly on the river, but short trails from several of them provide quick access to the water. The Sturgeon runs 50 to 60 feet wide and two to five feet deep, with many deeper holes at the bends. Bottom is mostly gravel, with some boulders and patches of hard, slippery clay. The banks are sandy, alternately high and low, and forested with hardwood, including some old apple trees. This is fast water, and wading is difficult to impossible depending on the water levels. Most anglers stick to the quieter shallows or fish from the banks. There is room for fly casting, but most here use bait or spinning lures.

Near site No. 16 along the southern loop, there is parking for two or three vehicles and trails to the river both upstream and downstream. One footpath leads to the footings of an old bridge, where the Sturgeon is pouring too strong through the constriction to fish. But just upstream it is considerably wider and wadable during normal levels with room to cast. This is still a popular access site during the spring and fall spawning runs, when it often yields trophy browns and steelhead.

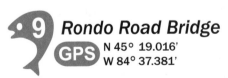

9 Rondo Road Bridge

GPS N 45° 19.016'
W 84° 37.381'

Map: page 185

Two access sites are referred to in conjunction with Rondo Road. The first is Rondo Road Bridge, reached 3.2 miles north of Wolverine by turning east (right) from Old US-27 onto Rondo Road and following it two hundred yards to the bridge. There is parking on the shoulders of the road on both sides of the bridge. The second is Rondo Road Access Site, reached 0.3 mile north of Rondo Road along Old US-27 where a dirt road is posted as a DNR launch

An angler casts on a reach of the Sturgeon River. The river is known for its fast current and trophy brown trout.

site. Turn right on this winding road and follow it down to the access site on the river.

At the bridge the Sturgeon is 50 feet wide and less than four feet deep upstream, but it is fast water and wading is difficult to impossible. Downstream from the bridge, most of the river is too deep and fast for wading. Bottom is mostly gravel with some sand. Banks are alternately high and low and are covered with hardwood trees, brush, and some open grassy areas. Most of the fishing here is done from the banks, usually with bait or spinning lures.

At the access site are a canoe launch and vault toilets along with a large parking area, indicative of its popularity among paddlers. There is also a former railroad trestle here where the Gaylord–Mackinaw City Rail-Trail crosses the Sturgeon. At the bridge the river is very fast and deep, making wading almost impossible. Upstream wading might be possible depending on the water level, but the bottom is a mix of gravel and large boulders and extreme caution must be exercised. Most wading is done only at areas that have been carefully scouted or from the edge of the river.

The only public land is the road right-of-way at the bridge and for a quarter mile to the north at the public access site. At either site fishing pressure is light, except during the spring and fall spawning runs when these are among the prime areas to catch a lake-run brown or steelhead.

10 *White Road Bridge*

GPS N 45° 20.322'
W 84° 37.687'

White Road loops off of Old US-27; its two bridges provide access to the lower Sturgeon River. The South White Bridge is 1.5 miles north of Rondo Road or 4.7 miles north of Wolverine and two hundred yards east of Old US-27. Parking is along the road on both sides of the bridge.

The Sturgeon is narrow, fast, and deep here. It is about 40 feet wide and too fast and deep most of the time for safe wading. Fishing is usually done from the banks with bait or spinning lures or from edge wading, usually upstream along a bottom of gravel and boulders. Fishing pressure can be extremely heavy during the spawning runs but is light the rest of the season. Except for the road right-of-way, this is all private land.

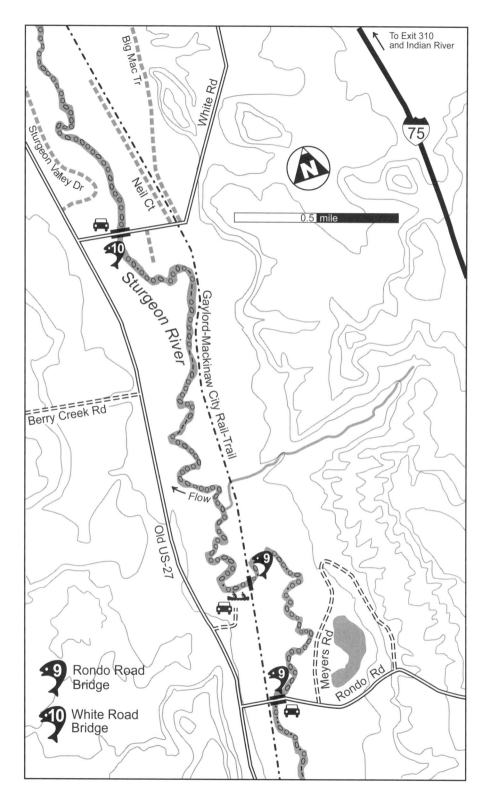

To Exit 310
and Indian River

75

0.5 mile

White Rd

Big Mac Tr

Neil Ct

Sturgeon Valley Dr

Sturgeon River

Gaylord-Mackinaw City Rail-Trail

Berry Creek Rd

Old US-27

Flow

9

9

Meyers Rd

Rondo Rd

9 Rondo Road
Bridge

10 White Road
Bridge

10

William Clay Ford Jr. was exactly where he wanted to be, sitting on the edge of a Zodiac boat in Southeast Alaska, dressed in waders and clutching a fly rod, heading up a river filled with salmon and rainbows. So eager was he to begin the fishing adventure that awaited him, barely able to contain his excitement, that when the inflatable boat was near the shoreline Ford jumped into the river. Big mistake: the icy Alaska river poured into his waders.

"I thought it was two feet deep and it turned out to be five feet deep," Ford said. "But even when you do stuff like that, it's still hard to have a bad day fly fishing."

His passions range from tennis and cars to the Detroit Lions and Tae Kwon Do. But Ford's first love in life is fly fishing. From stalking brookies in Michigan in his youngest days to chasing giant rainbows in Alaska while executive chairman of Ford Motor Company, Ford has always been intrigued with casting a fly in search of a trout.

William Clay Ford Jr. (Courtesy Ford Motor Company.)

Part of it is heritage. Ford comes from a family of anglers. His great grandfather, Henry Ford, fished as a member of the Huron Mountain Club in the Upper Peninsula and the North Branch Outing Club in Lovells. His grandfather, Edsel Ford, was a passionate fly angler.

But most of it was simply the appeal of Northern Michigan trout streams. Ford's father rarely picked up a rod but was a member of the Fontinalis Club, a private, three thousand-acre retreat in the Pigeon River Country State Forest, where the family would spend a week or two every summer. Right from the beginning Ford loved the wilderness-like setting of the club and would badger Walter Babcock, the property caretaker, with the inquisitive questions of a six-year-old. Babcock took the young Ford under his wing, led him into the woods, and put a fly rod in his hand.

"I would walk behind him, and I must have driven him crazy because I'd ask him a million questions about fishing and wildlife," Ford said. "We would walk through the woods and he'd point out a birch tree and say, 'you can see where a bear climbed it by those slash marks.' When he taught me how to fish, it was fly fishing right from the beginning."

Babcock taught Ford how to cast, identify hatches, and read water on Club Stream, which flows through Fontinalis and is loaded with brookies. But only a short hike east from the club is the Sturgeon River, where Ford quickly discovered the adrenalin rush of hooking a hard-charging brown. By the time Ford received his driver's license he was accomplished angler with a sense of adventure. He would drive up north for a week or more, stopping and fishing whatever river caught his eye, from the famed Au Sable to the most obscure brook trout stream in the Upper Peninsula. As a student at Princeton University in the late 1970s, he continued to fish every chance he could get away.

Ford was already entrenched in his automotive career in the 1990s when he read that the founder of Scott Rods, Harry Wilson, had died from a stroke. The company was an innovator in fly rods, pioneering the first nine-foot four-weight in 1975 and producing a five-piece graphite rod almost 15 years before another rod maker would come to market with one.

"I loved Scott rods. I fished with them all the time," Ford said. "So I wrote his wife a letter, asking her if she would ever consider selling the company." She wrote back and said yes. Ford purchased the rod maker and then enticed his best friend and fishing partner to move out to Colorado to manage the company. Today Scott Rods is second only to Sage in the high-end, high-performance fly rod market.

Despite his family name or the fact that he owns the company that makes his fly rods, in many ways Ford is like any other angler in Michigan. He occasionally ties flies but rarely puts one of his own at the end of his line. "It takes so much time for me to tie a good one, it's like a trophy," Ford said. "I don't want to use it and then lose it." He has floated his hat more than once, loves fishing with his sons, and is never out on a river as often as he would like to be.

And while he has caught his share of large trout in faraway places, in the end it is neither trophies nor exotic rivers that Ford finds most appealing. If he had his choice he would just as soon be standing in a Northern Michigan stream trying to entice a brookie on a small dry fly.

"If I had only one day left to fish, it would be in Northern Michigan and probably on Club Stream where I learned to fish," Ford said.

Technicians from the Michigan Department of Natural Resources use electric shockers to survey a stretch of the Black River. The procedure, used to determine the population and size of trout, does not harm the fish.

Black River

Rising from spring-fed creeks in the northeast corner of Otsego County, the Black River is a Blue Ribbon Trout Stream filled with brookies and bordered by some of the state's largest hunting and fishing clubs. It's long been considered the finest brook trout fishery in the Lower Peninsula and continues to be managed that way.

But getting to the river is not easy. Of the three streams—the Pigeon, Sturgeon, and the Black—that rise on the north slope of the moraine near Gaylord and flow north, the Black is the easternmost and thus the farthest from I-75, that great migration route for so many southern Michigan anglers. Once in the Pigeon River Country State Forest you have to navigate an unmarked maze of dirt roads, two-tracks and trails to reach many of the access sites. And just outside the state forest, much of the river runs through the Blue Lakes Ranch, the Black River Ranch and the Gaylord Fishing Club, large private tracts that restrict public access. Even a float-and-fish trip is not feasible as few paddlers are seen south of Crockett Rapids.

It shouldn't be surprising then that the upper Black is not as heavily fished as its more famous counterparts further south. Nor should it be surprising that many anglers consider it the premier stream in Michigan for wild brook trout, if not the Midwest, for the very same reasons.

The Black River is considered a coldwater fishery from its headwaters to Tower Pond, a distance of 50 river miles, and is designated a Blue Ribbon Trout Stream for 41 of those miles, from McKinnon's Bend to the Cheboygan/Presque County Line near Crockett Rapids. Upstream from McKinnon's Bend the river is narrow, often less than 15 feet wide, and so crowded with overhanging tag alders and brush it's hard to flick a fly much less cast one. This segment is best left to spin and bait anglers.

Between McKinnon's Bend and Tin Shanty Bridge, the Black widens to 20 feet or more as it flows through a lowland swamp. Access is limited and casting conditions are still challenging, demanding accurate roll casts. But the rewards are great for such difficult fishing. This four-mile stretch is home to the river's greatest concentration of brook trout as well as the largest ones, brookies that can exceed 15 or even 16 inches. This hard-to-reach stretch is one of the few along the Black River that contains silt areas suitable for hatches of Hexaginia limbata.

At Tin Shanty Bridge the Black widens even more, and the next 4.4 river miles to the Town Corner Lake access site is perhaps the most popular segment for fly fishing. Here the Black is 30 to 50 feet wide for easier casting and less than four feet deep in normal conditions with a predominately gravel bottom for easy wading. You have numerous access sites to explore and the only campground on the river to stay at.

It was along this reach of the river that in 2008 DNR biologists instituted special trout regulations as part of a research project. The new regulations reduce the daily possession limit to two trout and require anglers to use either artificial flies or lures. Minimum size limits were not changed; 10 inches for brook trout and 12 inches for brown trout.

After hearing from anglers who wanted more gear-restricted regulations on trout streams, fisheries managers set up the study to determine if such restrictions and reduced bag limits result in a lower trout mortality and an increase in large brookies. The study will last at least five years, and, if the new regulations work, they will become permanent and even be adopted for Michigan's other brook trout streams.

From Town Corner Lake downstream to Main River Bridge, six river miles, the Black often flows past state land to the west and private holdings to the east, primarily the Blue Lakes Ranch. There is public access, but it usually requires hiking in up to a half mile. For the price of a little walking, however, you're rewarded with a stretch of river that is 30 to 40 feet wide, easy to cast in, and yours for the afternoon.

Between Main River Bridge and Clark Bridge, a nine-mile stretch, the East Branch and Stewart Creek empty into the Black, doubling its size. There is little opportunity to fish as the Black River Ranch borders both sides of the river. Floating is also not feasible because of "the spreads" on the Black River property. At the spreads the Black divides into several narrow channels too small to float a canoe. Nor can you portage around them without trespassing on private property.

From Clark Bridge to Crockett Rapids, 8 river miles, the Black winds through large areas of state land, but road access to the river is limited to a pair of bridges. The river bottom is mostly sand at Clark Bridge, but gravel becomes more abundant downstream with gravel and boulders making up most of the river bottom at Crockett Rapids. The river is 60 to 80 feet wide and 3 to 6 feet deep, with plenty of deep holes and runs. This section of the river can be waded at normal levels, but caution must be used. Canoeists begin putting in at Clark Bridge, but the majority prefer the launch at Crockett Rapids.

The last access site described in this chapter is Milligan Bridge, located just 2.8 miles downstream from Crockett Rapids. The Black in the final ten miles from the bridge to Tower Pond is too deep to wade and usually fished from a canoe or driftboat. This is even true to some degree at Milligan Bridge, as it is often only wadable at low flows or by edge wading to avoid deeper areas.

Like many other streams in northern Michigan, the Black was known for its grayling fishing before it became famous as a trout stream. According to William B. Mershon, a Saginaw sportsman and early conservationist, the grayling held out longer on the Black than on the Au Sable. In his book,

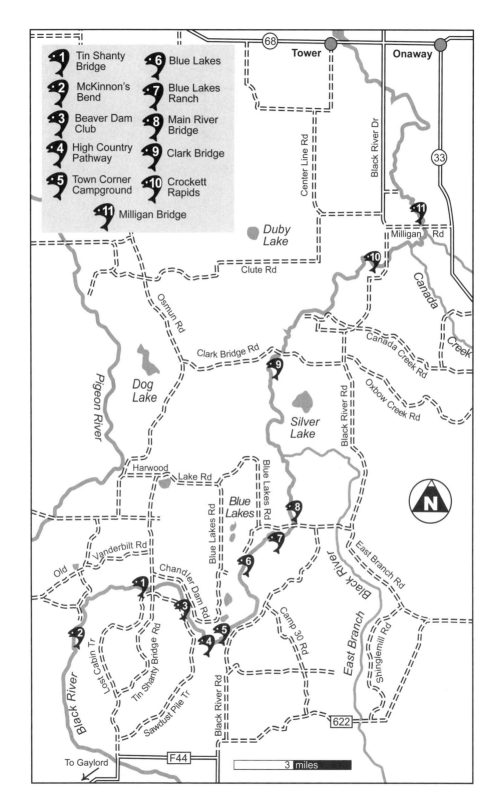

1	Tin Shanty Bridge	6	Blue Lakes
2	McKinnon's Bend	7	Blue Lakes Ranch
3	Beaver Dam Club	8	Main River Bridge
4	High Country Pathway	9	Clark Bridge
5	Town Corner Campground	10	Crockett Rapids
		11	Milligan Bridge

68 Tower   Onaway

Black River Dr

33

Center Line Rd

Duby Lake

Milligan Rd

Clute Rd

Canada Creek

10

Osmun Rd

Clark Bridge Rd

Canada Creek Rd

9

Oxbow Creek Rd

Dog Lake

Pigeon River

Silver Lake

Black River Rd

Harwood   Lake Rd

Blue Lakes Rd

Blue Lakes

Blue Lakes Rd

8

N

East Branch Rd

7

Old

Vanderbilt Rd

Chandler Dam Rd

6

Black River

East Branch

1

3

Camp 30 Rd

Lost Cabin Tr

Tin Shanty Bridge Rd

2

5

4

Shinglemill Rd

Sawdust Pile Tr

Black River Rd

622

To Gaylord

F44

3 miles

Recollections of My Fifty Years of Hunting and Fishing, he writes about a four-day fishing trip on the Black in 1903 when a party of seven caught 46 grayling and 346 brook trout; and later he comments that might have been the final year for the grayling. The species no doubt fell victim to the logging industry. In 1871 more than a hundred million board feet of logs were floated down the Black River, and by 1903 Onaway was a thriving lumber town with 12 mills and a plant that was the world's largest producer of wooden bicycle rims.

Brook trout replaced the grayling, and today that's where the Black River stands apart from most other Michigan trout streams; brookies dominate the fishery in the upper reaches, not browns. The growth rates for brook trout in the Black River watershed are among the best in the state so the river has long been managed for them. In 1981, the Black was electro-shocked from Clark Bridge Road upstream through the Black River Ranch, with up to 3,000 brown trout removed and planted in Town Corner Lake. The special regulations in 2008 are an effort to increase the number of brook trout ten inches or larger.

The healthy population of brookies in the upper Black is the best indication of good trout habitat. The discharge of the Black is relatively stable, with enough groundwater inflow to sustain the river during dry periods. There are some sandy areas, but most of the river has gravel bottom for spawning beds. The river is too warm in summer for ideal trout water, warmer than the Sturgeon, for example, but the trout seem to thrive nevertheless.

Like other streams in the area, the water in the Black is hard, slightly alkaline, with sufficient nutrients to support a good trout population, but not so much as to stimulate an undesirable growth of aquatic vegetation. Fluctuations on the Black, usually about two feet in a normal year, are enough to make drastic changes in wading conditions. Waters downstream from Clark Bridge that are easily waded at low flows can overtop your waders or sweep you off your feet when the river is high.

In general, hatches on the Black occur a week to two weeks later than the same ones on the Au Sable as shown in the hatch chart in this book. Most of the common hatches experienced elsewhere occur on the Black, including Hendricksons from mid-May to Memorial Day, blue-winged olives in July and August, sulphur duns, little black caddis, and tiny white wing black or tricos.

Accommodations

Gaylord offers the largest range of accommodations in the area, from resorts to budget motels. See Accommodations in the Pigeon River chapter (page 156), or contact the Gaylord Area Convention and Tourism Bureau (800-345-8621; *www.gaylordmichigan.net*). There are also accommodations in Onaway, though most tend to be north of town on the Black Lake. For a list contact the Onaway Area Chamber of Commerce (800-711-3685, 989-733-2874; *www.onawaychamber.com*).

An angler concentrates on the drift of his dry fly while fishing the Manistee River.

Ten Flies
for Michigan Trout Streams

Mastering a tight back cast is easy compared to learning what flies to use on Michigan trout streams and when to use them. Walk into a fly shop and you'll see such an array of dry flies, streamers, and nymphs that it boggles the mind and can quickly fill a fly box. But here are ten patterns that most experienced anglers carry and tend to be the most productive flies on classic streams ranging from the Au Sable to the Boardman.

The Adams

This is the dependable standby, created for the Boardman River and often called "the world's best dry fly." The beauty of the Adams is that its blend of gray, brown, and grizzly doesn't imitate any one insect in particular; rather it suggests a number of mayflies, caddisflies, stoneflies, even gnats, depending on the size you select. This is as close to a universal dry fly as you're going to find. Carry them in sizes 12 to 18 and, when nothing is hatching, tie one on as a prospector fly, casting it toward spots where a trout might be hiding.

Hendricksons

From early May to as late as Memorial Day, depending on how far north you are, the major hatches of *Ephemerella subvaria* and *Ephemerella invaria* or Hendrickson mayflies take place. For two to three weeks the daily hatches are a time when trout often refuse almost everything else on the river. Hendricksons will be sold in every fly shop and you should carry both dark and light patterns in sizes 12 to 14.

Blue-Winged Olives

The *Baetis cingulatus* or Blue-Winged Olive is a small mayfly with gray-olive body and smoky-blue wings appearing predominately from mid-May through July, often on overcast days. The fly, usually featuring olive-brown dubbing for a body, gray tail, and blue dun hen-hackle tips for wings, is readily available from most fly shops and should be included in your fly box in sizes anywhere from 16 to 20.

Golden Ribbed Hare's Ear

Nymphs represent insects in their underwater life stage before they emerge from a stream to mate and lay eggs as adults. For beginners, nymph fishing is one of the most difficult techniques to learn because you can't see when a fish takes it. Yet when mastered it's far more effective than dry flies because a majority of a trout's diet is nymphs. The Hare's Ear is one of the classic nymph patterns. It doesn't imitate any particular insect. Rather the fly's shaggy appearance resembles several species of nymphs when they are shedding their skins to emerge as adults. Carry in sizes 10 to 16. Other nymphs used on Michigan streams are the dark Hendrickson and the American Pheasant Tail.

Elk-Hair Caddis

Hatching at the same time as the Hendricksons are *Chimarra* or caddisflies, another abundant and important food source for trout. Most fly anglers will turn to an elk-hair caddis dry fly, which is little more than a body of Hare's Ear dubbing and a pinch of tan elk or deer hair for the wings. Simple but effective, the fly is durable, buoyant, and a good imitation of the many species of brown and mottled brown caddis. The flies are also available in other dyed colors, including black and olive, and should be carried in sizes 12 to 18 for Michigan streams. Many anglers will also use the Henryville, which was developed in the 1920s as a caddis imitation on the Henryville section of Brodhead's Creek in Pennsylvania.

Royal Coachman

One of the most popular all-around dry flies in Michigan, the Royal Coachman is an attractor, representing no particular insect at all. The fly is highly visible with its white duck-quill wings, golden pheasant tippet for the tail, and body of peacock herl with its trademark red floss center band. You can easily see the large white wings when the fly is riding in the current, and that visibility makes it as popular with anglers as it is with trout. Stock your fly box with sizes 12 to 16.

Borchers Special

Another Michigan original, this dry fly was perfected when Grayling guide Ernie Borcher modified an existing pattern. The fly is similar to the Adams—both have grizzly and brown hackle—but Borchers features a dark brown body, usually of turkey quill. When fished in sizes 10 to 12, the fly is an excellent match for brown drakes, which hatch in June through mid-July. It will also work well in early spring when Hendricksons, mahoganies, and Isonychias are on the water, while in smaller sizes it mimics mosquitoes.

Sulphurs

Sulphurs, or *Ephemerella dorothea*, are usually yellow but can range in color from cream to tangerine. The mayfly appears from May to September and in June its hatches can blanket the surface of a stream. Most anglers quickly recognize the "pale evening dun" hatch when on warm nights the duns are easy to see in the twilight. Carry sulphurs in sizes 12 to 18 as duns with wings positioned up and as spinners with a down-wing pattern, representing a returning, egg-laying mayfly.

Michigan Hopper

It is estimated that up to 40 percent of a trout's summer food supply consists of accidental, land-bred insects, usually the result of a breeze displacing them onto a stream. That makes terrestrials excellent flies to use from mid- to late summer. The Michigan Hopper, with its yellow wool body, brown mottled turkey wings, and red deer-hair tail, is easy to tie and very effective but often hard to find in shops. Most fly shops carry several other types of grasshoppers, including Dave's Hopper, in sizes 6 to 10. Another effective terrestrial is a size-12 black ant.

Muddler Minnow

Originally this fly was created to resemble a sculpin, a bottom-dwelling minnow that brookies love to feed on. Today the Muddler Minnow is considered an excellent all-around fly that can be fished wet or dry. Anglers use it to emulate bait fish, float it to simulate grasshoppers, or even tie it on during the Hex hatches. Its most distinctive characteristics are the spun-tapered head and clipped deer-hair body. Stock it in sizes 4 to 12.

Fishing Blue Lakes

In 1990, the state opened up three miles of prime trout stream to the public when it acquired the Blue Lakes Tract from the Blue Lakes Ranch. The 2,608-acre tract contains not only the west bank of the Black River from Hardwood Creek to almost the Main River Bridge, but the Blue Lakes themselves.

To protect their outstanding fisheries, special regulations were added when the small, private lakes turned public, including a reduced fishing season that coincides with trout season; the last Saturday in April to Sept. 30. Only artificial lures or flies are allowed and fishing is totally catch and release.

The pair of warm-water lakes offers fly anglers another opportunity in Pigeon River Country State Forest, if they come prepared with a float tube and flippers. The Blue Lakes are managed as a walk-in fishing experience, but the trek from Blue Lakes Road to the west side of either one is less than a quarter mile.

South Blue Lake features bass and some hefty bluegills; North Blue Lake has perch. Both are small enough that you can easily cover them in a belly boat. On a quiet summer evening you can troll the same nymphs and streamers you used all afternoon on the Black River and catch fish that fight almost as hard as the trout you were targeting.

Campgrounds: Two campgrounds in the Pigeon River Country State Forest are well positioned for anglers who want to explore the upper Black River. Round Lake Campground on Round Lake Road is located just off Old Vanderbilt Road between McKinnon's Bend and Tin Shanty Bridge access sites (see Site No. 2, McKinnon's Bend, later in this chapter, for directions). This pleasant campground features ten rustic sites in a stand of red pine overlooking the smallish lake.

Town Corner Lake Campground is off Blue Lakes Road (see Site No. 5, Town Corner Lake), 2.9 miles southeast of Tin Shanty Bridge, and is the only one adjacent to the Black River. The rustic campground has 13 sites with many of them on a lightly forested bluff overlooking the lake along with a boat launch. Site #1 is a charmer, off by itself right above the lake. From the sites it's a half-mile drive or walk to the Black River.

Fly Shops and Guides

In downtown Gaylord flies and fly fishing equipment are available at *Alphorn Shop* (989-732-5616; 137 W. Main St.) and south of town, just off exit 279, at *Jay's Sporting Goods* (989-705-1339; *www.jayssportinggoods.com*; 150 Dale Rd.). In Onaway you can pick up flies and equipment at *Parrott's Outpost* (989-733-2472; *www.parrottsoutpost.com*; 20628 State St.).

Area guides that offer catch-and-release fly fishing for brook and brown trout on secluded sections of the Black River include Mike Moreau of ***North-East Flyfishing*** (989-733-6050; *www.neflyfishing.com*) in Onaway.

Maps of the Black

For many anglers Gaylord is the departure point for the Upper Black River and Onaway for the lower portions from Clark Bridge to Milligan Bridge. This chapter covers 11 numbered access sites, and Tin Shanty Bridge can serve as a starting point for the first five.

To reach Tin Shanty Bridge from Gaylord, drive east on M-32 and within a mile turn left to continue east on County Road F44 (also labeled Wilkinson Road). Within 3.4 miles County Road F44 turns north (left) on Marquardt Road and in a mile it turns east (right) on Sparr Road in the hamlet of Sparr. County Road F44 continues east on Sparr Road for 7.3 miles and then swings sharply north. In 0.7 mile County Road F44 swings to the east at an intersection with Tin Shanty Bridge Road. Instead of continuing east on the paved county road, head north on Tin Shanty Bridge Road, a well-graded dirt road that is not signposted at this intersection. Within 5.9 miles of County Road F44 you'll reach Tin Shanty Bridge (see site No. 1, Tin Shanty Bridge, below).

The six sites on the lower portion of the Black River can easily be reached from M-68 by turning off on Black River Road, two miles west of Onway. The first, Milligan Bridge, is 5.2 miles south of M-68 but can also be easily reached via M-33. See the site descriptions below for detailed directions to the rest of them.

Tin Shanty Bridge

GPS N 45° 07.624'
W 84° 24.467'

Tin Shanty Bridge marks the start of special fishing regulations on the Black River and for many anglers the first acceptable stretch of water for fly fishing. Tin Shanty Bridge Road is reached from paved County Road F44 where it takes a sharp turn from north to east 13.4 miles east of Gaylord. Continuing north is Tin Shanty Bridge Road, a well graded dirt road that is not signposted at this intersection. Head north and bypass Sawdust Pile Trail, an unmarked dirt road that heads off to the east (right), and then Lost Cabin Trail that is signposted and veers off to the west (left). Within 5.9 miles of leaving F44 you'll arrive at Tin Shanty Bridge where there's parking for two or three vehicles on the north side.

Upstream from the bridge the Black River is open to all tackle with an eight-inch minimum size for trout and a daily possession of five fish. Downstream it's artificial lures and flies only, a 10-inch minimum for brookies, 12-inch for browns, and a daily possession of only two fish.

The river is 30 to 40 feet wide and generally less than four feet deep, with

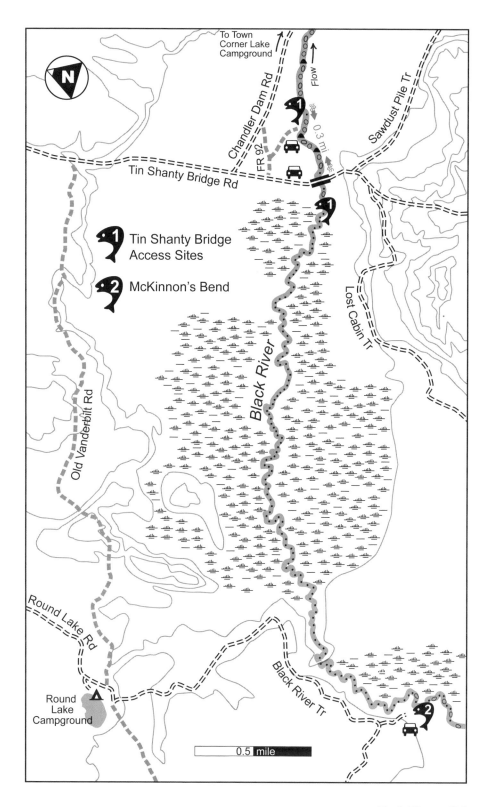

To Town
Corner Lake
Campground

Chandler Dam Rd

Flow

0.3 mi

Sawdust Pile Tr

FR 92

Tin Shanty Bridge Rd

Tin Shanty Bridge
Access Sites

McKinnon's Bend

Lost Cabin Tr

Black River

Old Vanderbilt Rd

Round Lake Rd

Round
Lake
Campground

Black River Tr

0.5 mile

some deeper holes. The bottom is mostly gravel and boulders at the bridge and downstream. Upstream, it is chiefly sand. The banks are a little higher than in the upstream reaches, not so swampy, and not so brushy. Fly casting is easier here than McKinnon's Bend, but you're still going to lose flies to the alder upstream or the overhanging cedars downstream. Wading is fairly easy at normal flows, but watch out for the holes, boulders, and snags.

Another access point is reached from Forest Road 92 just 0.2 mile north of Tin Shanty Bridge. The two-track is posted and heads east to quickly arrive at a split. Head right, and within 0.2 mile the two-track arrives at a low bluff overlooking a stretch of the Black River (N45 07.711' W84 24.231'). This is a scenic spot that is often used for dispersed camping. The river is 25 to 30 feet wide here with a bottom of sand and gravel. The streamside brush is heavy, but careful casts allow fly anglers to fish here. It is a 0.3-mile wade upstream to Tin Shanty Bridge and a half-mile walk back to your vehicle.

Overall the Tin Shanty Bridge area is good brook-trout water, with plenty of state land on both sides of the river upstream and downstream of the bridge. You'll find fishing pressure is usually light to moderate.

McKinnon's Band

GPS N 45° 07.048'
W 84° 27.051'

Map: page 195

From Tin Shanty Bridge head north on Tin Shanty Bridge Road for a mile and then turn right on Old Vanderbilt Road. It's the first two-track that heads west but is not signposted. Within 2.4 miles Old Vanderbilt Road reaches a graded dirt road and by heading north (right) you would be on Round Lake Road and quickly reach the posted entrance to Round Lake State Forest Campground.

Turn south (left) and you'll quickly arrive at a signposted intersection, a rarity in these woods. Continue in a southerly direction on Black River Trail, where you will pass a handful of log cabins on the banks of the river, and in 1.6 miles veer to the left into McKinnon's Bend Public Access Site. There is ample parking here, and no doubt the access site has served as an undeveloped campsite for many anglers. A set of steps leads down to the Black River where at first sight the abundance of overhanging brush scares off most fly anglers. Make no mistake, this is tight quarters where even a roll cast could be challenging.

The Black is 15 to 20 feet wide here and one to three feet deep with a bottom that is mostly sand with a few small patches of gravel. Wading is fairly easy at normal flows but casting can be frustrating in this water. Obviously bait or spin anglers have the upper hand. Still some fly anglers manage to flick their fly into the current sweeping past the brushy banks, where eager brookies are often waiting for a morsel under the overhanging alder. Just upstream from the steps the river widens a little, but either upstream or downstream the banks are generally low, swampy, and covered with brush. Make sure your fly box is well stocked.

The most impressive tributary of the Black River is its East Branch, which begins in the Green Swamp of Montmorency County and flows 22 miles north before merging with the main stream within the Black River Ranch. The final 13 miles of the East Branch is a designated Blue Ribbon Trout Stream and for good reason. A classic coldwater trout feeder to the Black River, the East Branch is filled with brookies yet receives little fishing pressure.

The East Branch features colder water than the Black River. When the river temperatures warm up, trout often retreat to the smaller tributaries like the East Branch, making it a far better choice in late July and August than such access sites as Main River Bridge and Clark Bridge. The final eight miles of the East Branch lies in Black River Ranch where there is no public access. Below Shingle Mill Bridge on County Road 622, the river is too narrow for fly anglers.

The best access sites to explore with a fly rod in hand are Barber Bridge and just upstream. At the east end of Blue Lakes Road, the dirt road to the north is signposted as Black River Road and to the south as East Branch Road. Barber Bridge (N45 09.147' W84 17.806') is 0.4 mile to the west from here on Blue Lakes Road or 1.4 miles east of Main River Bridge. Here the East Branch is 25 feet wide and one to four feet deep with numerous holes that need to be cautiously waded around. The bottom is a mix of sand and gravel, and the trout cover is excellent. Black River Ranch property begins a quarter mile upstream from the bridge.

East Branch Road heads south from its intersection with Blue Lakes Road and parallels the East Branch where it flows through state land. Another excellent access site (N45 08.897' W84 17.812') is reached by heading south from the intersection and within 0.6 mile turning west (right) on an unmarked two-track. Follow the two-track but drive cautiously and slowly as it is very rutted and sandy in places. Within a half mile it ends on a low bluff above the stream in a spot that anglers occasionally use as a dispersed campsite. The East Branch here is 30 feet wide and one to three feet deep with a gravelly bottom. There are also lots of downed timber and submerged logs for scrappy brook trout to hide while waiting for an insect to float by or for your well-placed fly.

Beaver Dam Club

GPS N 45° 07.521'
W 84° 23.383'

Map: page 199

Chandler Dam Road is signposted and located just 0.3 mile north of Tin Shanty Bridge. The graded dirt road heads east (right) briefly, then southeast from Tin Shanty Bridge Road where it parallels the Black River. Within a mile you pass the entrance to the Beaver Dam Club and just beyond it an unposted two-track that heads west (right). Follow it and within 150 yards you end in a parking area with a fire pit, indicating it's used occasionally for dispersed camping. A short trail leads to the Black River where the water is 40 to 50 feet wide but shallow over a gravel bottom. Wade in either direction and quickly the river narrows and depths increase to two to three feet. The 2008 special regulations also apply here.

Continuing south for another mile, Chandler Dam Road remains close to the Black River, and at one point the trout stream is clearly visible from the road. It would be easy to park and hike west 0.2 mile to the river at a number of spots. What isn't state land is clearly marked with No Trespassing signs.

4 High Country Pathway
GPS N 45° 06.693'
W 84° 22.964'

Within 2.2 miles from Tin Shanty Bridge Road, Chandler Dam Road swings sharply to the east. At the bend there is an access site just to the west, a large parking area in a pleasant grove of jack pine, maple, popple, and spruce overlooking a beautiful bend of the Black River. The river is 35 to 45 feet wide and not nearly as brushy as it is upstream, making for far easier casting. Depths are mostly two to three feet deep with the exception of a few deep holes that can cause problems if you're not careful.

Velocity is moderate, and wading is easy at normal flows. Drowned logs and snags make good trout cover. The bottom is mostly gravel upstream, sand and gravel downstream. The left bank (northeast side) is high and sandy and vulnerable to erosion if you are not careful when entering or leaving the river. The right bank is low and mucky.

Also at the access site, Forest Road 118 heads south as a rough two-track and within 300 yards arrives at the posted High Country Pathway (N45 06.630' W84 22.789'). This long-distance trail crosses FR 118 and to the east reaches a new foot bridge over the Black River within 200 yards. The river here is 25 to 30 feet wide and two to four feet deep. Its bottom is predominately sand with occasional patches of gravel and a few boulders. Trout cover is good.

A quarter mile from Chandler Dam Road, Forest Road 118 arrives at a dispersed camping spot on a low bluff above the river (N45 06.551' W84 22.721'). A short trail descends to the Black where it is still 25 to 30 feet wide and two to four feet deep. The 2008 special regulations apply for all three access sites.

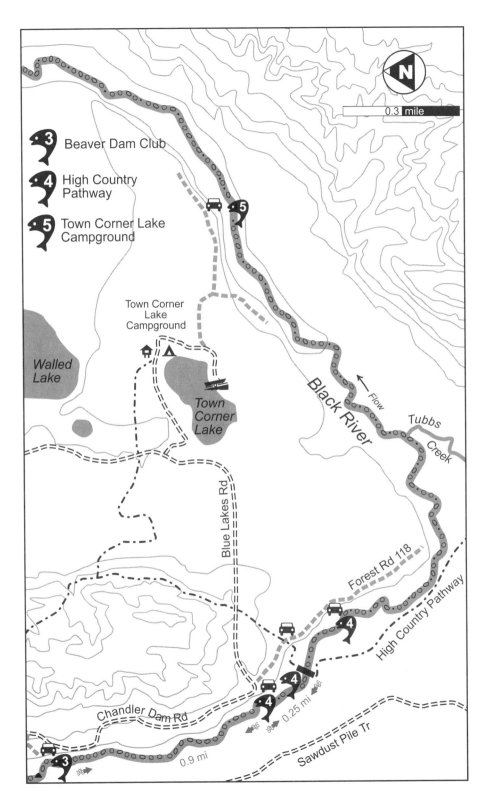

0.3 mile

3 Beaver Dam Club

4 High Country Pathway

5 Town Corner Lake Campground

Walled Lake

Town Corner Lake Campground

Town Corner Lake

Black River

Flow

Tubbs Creek

Blue Lakes Rd

Forest Rd 118

High Country Pathway

Chandler Dam Rd

0.25 mi

Sawdust Pile Tr

0.9 mi

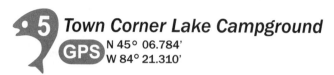

Town Corner Lake Campground

GPS N 45° 06.784'
W 84° 21.310'

Map: page 199

Chandler Dam Road becomes Blue Lakes Road when it swings to the east and within 0.7 mile or 2.9 miles from Tin Shanty Bridge Road swings sharply north and passes the entrance to Town Corner State Forest Campground, which is signposted. If you follow the entrance road around the lake, you pass 13 campsites, many of them on a low bluff overlooking the water, and end at a boat launch. Right across from site No. 11 is a two-track that heads south. Within a quarter mile veer to the left and within 200 yards you'll reach a large sandy parking area on a bluff above the Black River. Dispersed camping is allowed here.

A stairway of railroad ties leads down the bluff to the Black, where the river is 30 to 40 feet wide and one to three feet deep. The bottom is a mix of gravel and sand and the casting is easy, making this a choice spot for fly anglers. The special regulations for the Black River that were put in place in 2008 end here. Downstream from the stairway the Black River is open to all tackle with an eight-inch minimum size for trout and a daily possession of five fish. Upstream it's artificial lures and flies only, a ten-inch minimum for brookies, 12 inch for browns, and a daily possession of only two fish.

Blue Lakes

GPS N 45° 08.876'
W 84° 20.912'

From Town Corner Lake Campground, you can head north on Blue Lakes Ranch (also labeled Meridian Road on some maps) and within 1.3 miles cross an open wetland area that is Hardwood Creek, then pass a two-track that provides access to the Black River just north of its confluence with Hardwood Creek. In another mile you pass the two-track entrance to the Blue Lakes.

Continue north and in 4.8 miles from Town Corner Lake Campground you arrive at a well-posted intersection. To the left (west) is Hardwood Lake Road, which leads past Tin Shanty Bridge Road and eventually to Twin Lakes Road near Pigeon River Campground. Blue Lakes Road is to the right, and both are well marked. Blue Lakes Road first heads north, then northeast, east, and finally due south but is always the only graded road. Within 3.6 miles from the Hardwood Lake Road intersection, Blue Lakes Road swings sharply east and at the bend Forest Road 49 continues south.

The two-track is not posted but quickly passes a trail to the Blue Lakes, marked by a large gate posted with a "Help Keep It Wild—Walk In" sign. Within 0.4 mile from Blue Lakes Road, the two-track ends at a trail that continues south. It's a half mile hike south on the wide trail before you reach where the Black River swings close to the bluffs you're traversing. At times

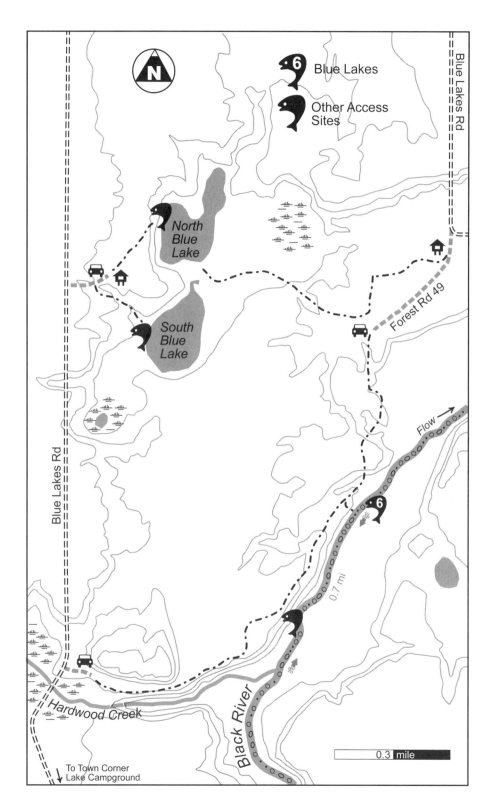

Blue Lakes

Other Access Sites

North
Blue
Lake

South
Blue
Lake

Forest Rd 49

Blue Lakes Rd

Blue Lakes Rd

Flow

·6

0.7 mi

Black River

Hardwood Creek

To Town Corner
Lake Campground

0.3 mile

you can catch a glimpse of the water while passing faint angler trails that descend the wooded blue to the river below.

It's a steep descent—be careful with that prized bamboo rod—before you reach the Black River, where it is 35 to 45 feet wide and two to three feet deep with a firm gravel bottom and lots of trout cover. The wading is easy under normal conditions and so is the casting. West of the river is state land, to the east the Blue Lakes Ranch, a private hunting and fishing club. This is a beautiful and lightly fished area, and the hike in and especially out after a long day of fishing is well worth the effort. To the south the trail eventually reaches an access site near Hardwood Creek, passing its confluence with the Black River along the way, a walk of almost two miles.

7 Blue Lakes Ranch

GPS N 45° 09.123'
W 84° 19.850'

The next access to the Black River is along Blue Lakes Road, 0.7 mile east from Forest Road 49. It is marked by a large parking area on the north side of Blue Lakes Road and a pair of blue-tipped posts on the south side. The posts mark a foot path that is faint at times but can still be easily followed as it descends a gentle ridge and within 300 yards reaches the river.

Where the path ends, the Black River is slow and shallow over sandy-and-silt bottom. But just downstream the river widens to 35 to 40 feet with depths of two to four feet over a predominately gravel bottom and remains this way all the way to Main River Bridge. The casting is easy here, and the overhanging brush and deep holes hold good populations of brook trout. It's a little more than a mile of wading from the path until you reach Main River Bridge. In the beginning the land on the south side of the river is Blue Lakes Ranch. Halfway to the bridge, both sides of the river are part of the private Gaylord Fishing Club. This stretch makes for a pleasant afternoon of fishing and once out at Main River Bridge you're faced with only a 0.3-mile uphill walk to return to your vehicle.

8 Main River Bridge

GPS N 45° 09.146'
W 84° 19.386'

The road right-of-way at this bridge is a popular access point to the river even though there is only limited parking on the narrow shoulders here. Downstream from the bridge is the Black River Ranch, a private hunting club. Upstream is Gaylord Fishing Club, whose gated entrance is just east of the bridge on the south side of the road.

From Hardwood Lake Road, Main River Bridge is 4.6 miles along Blue Lakes Road. From M-68, two miles west of Onaway, head south on Black River Road for 14.8 miles and then west (right) on Blue Lakes Road. You cross the East Branch of the Black River on Barber Bridge within 0.4 mile and in

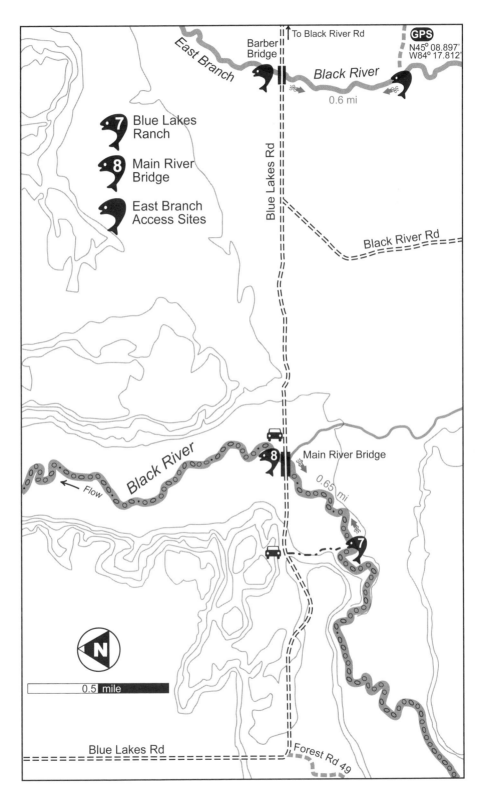

East Branch

To Black River Rd

Barber
Bridge

GPS
N45° 08.897'
W84° 17.812'

Black River

0.6 mi

7 Blue Lakes
Ranch

8 Main River
Bridge

East Branch
Access Sites

Blue Lakes Rd

Black River Rd

Black River

← Flow

8 Main River Bridge

0.65 mi

7

N

0.5 mile

Blue Lakes Rd

Forest Rd 49

another 1.4 miles you reach Main River Bridge.

The Black River is 30 to 35 feet wide here and two to four feet deep, with some deeper holes. The bottom is a mix of gravel, sand, and some muck, while the velocity is moderate to fast. Upstream from the bridge the banks are high and sandy, with hardwood forest. Downstream, the banks are low and brushy, with some open grassland. The river is open enough for fly casting, but in some spots the overhanging brush will snag a wayward fly. Other than at high flows, wading is fairly easy.

9 Clark Bridge

GPS N 45° 13.446'
W 84° 19.853'

Downstream from the Main River Bridge, the Black River passes through the Black River Ranch where it is joined by the East Branch and then splits into a web of narrow channels known as "the Spreads." By the time it reaches the next public access, Clark Bridge, it is considerably deeper and wider.

To reach Clark Bridge, head north on Black River Road from the east end of Blue Lakes Road, a T intersection that is signposted. Within 4.9 miles turn west (left) on Clark Bridge Road, and the bridge will be reached in 2.1 miles. From M-68, Clark Bridge Road is reached in ten miles.

Parking is available on the south side of the road east of the bridge, a spot that doubles as a canoe launch. Upstream from the bridge, the river is 60 to 80 feet wide and generally two to four feet deep, with some deeper holes. You can wade upstream at normal flows, but caution must be used. Downstream is too deep to wade with the exception of carefully scouted spots. Most anglers fish downstream by canoe. Velocity is moderate to fast. The bottom is sand and patches of gravel, and the banks are low and mucky, forested with hardwood and some brush.

Needless to say, there is plenty of room to cast. State land extends nearly a half-mile upstream to the Black River Ranch property and about a mile downstream. Fishing pressure at Clark Bridge is usually light to moderate, and the stretch is known for yielding good-size brookies and even an occasional brown. But by late summer the water often warms to the point that many trout seek cooler temperatures elsewhere.

10 Crockett Rapids

GPS N 45° 15.772'
W 84° 15.981'

Map: page 207

Crockett Rapids is a beautiful stretch of the Black River, and its public access is a busy one, shared by paddlers, anglers, and even backpackers as the High Country Pathway uses Crockett Bridge. The parking lot is along Black River Road, 6.3 miles south of M-68 or 3.6 miles north of Clark Bridge Road.

The rapids are downstream from the bridge where the Black River is 70 to 80 feet wide and less than four feet deep. There are some holes, like

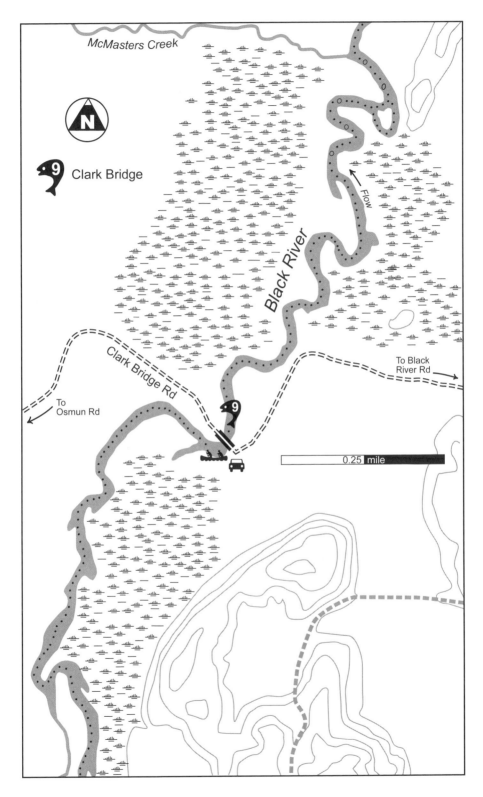

McMasters Creek

N

9 Clark Bridge

Black River

Flow

Clark Bridge Rd

To Osmun Rd

To Black River Rd

9

0.25 mile

the one just below the bridge, that will fill your waders, and the swift water and slippery boulders can be treacherous at times. But overall the river can be waded here during normal conditions. At high flows the river is simply too deep and too fast for safe wading.

The bottom is gravel and boulders while the banks are low and mucky, forested with hardwood. Trout cover is sparse in this part of the river, but upstream from the bridge is a stretch of riffled water too intriguing not to cast to. State frontage extends upstream 0.3 mile from this bridge. Downstream, the frontage is mostly private. This is the most common place to begin a Black River float trip, but still the number of paddlers is light compared to rivers such as the Au Sable and Manistee.

William Mershon, a Saginaw lumberman and conservationist, watches the camp cook fry grayling during a fishing trip to the Black River in 1903. (Courtesy Bentley Historical Library, University of Michigan.)

11 *Milligan Bridge*
GPS N 45° 16.673'
W 84° 14.588'

This access site can be reached by heading south from Onaway on M-33 for 5.4 miles and then west on Milligan Highway for a mile or north on Black River Road, one mile beyond Crockett Rapids. There is parking on both sides of the bridge.

In between Crockett Rapids and Milligan Bridge, Canada Creek empties into the Black River, increasing its size and depth considerably. The river is 70 to 80 feet wide and three to six feet deep in most places with a bottom of predominately sand. State land extends both upstream and downstream, providing access to some stretches of the river that can be waded during normal flows. But extreme caution has to be used here, and you should be ready to head elsewhere when the water levels are high.

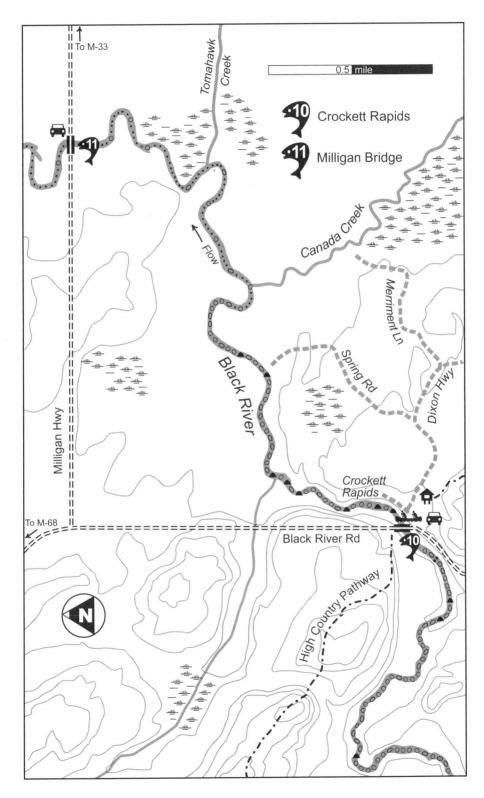

To M-33

Tomahawk Creek

0.5 mile

10 Crockett Rapids

11 Milligan Bridge

Flow

Canada Creek

Merriment Ln

Black River

Spring Rd

Dixon Hwy

Milligan Hwy

Crockett Rapids

To M-68

Black River Rd

10

High Country Pathway

N

Michigan Angler: Ernest Hemingway

Author Ernest Hemingway was born on July 21, 1899, in Illinois, but it was in the woods and rivers of northern Michigan where he adopted his father's outdoor passion for fishing, hunting, and camping. The family arrived in northern Michigan in the late 1890s when Hemingway's father, a successful doctor in the Chicago suburb of Oak Park, bought an acre of land on Walloon Lake and in 1900 built a large cottage called Windemere. As a child Hemingway spent entire summers there, learning to fish for trout on nearby Horton Creek and Schultz's Creek.

As he grew more confident in the woods and his skill with a fly rod improved, Hemingway began spending entire weekends away from the cottage, exploring rivers on his own. In 1916 he and a friend took a steamer from Chicago to Onekama and then commenced on a 10-day trek to Petoskey. Along the way they fished Bear Creek near Brethren in Manistee County, the Manistee River and the Boardman River, where he reportedly set up camp near Scheck's Place State Forest Campground.

But it is clear from his writing that Hemingway had a love for the Pigeon River Country State Forest, known back then as the Pine Barrens. In the early 1900s there were still logging trains crisscrossing the area, and it was easy for the author to take one to a hamlet close to where he wanted to fish. He would then hoist his backpack filled with only basic equipment and hike to a river to fish and camp for days at a time. Such a train dropped Hemingway off in Wolverine, where he wandered a short distance upstream of the Sturgeon River and made camp at its confluence with the West Branch, now the site of the town's Village Park.

Hemingway also fished the Pigeon, but the Black was his favorite. From either Vanderbilt or Gaylord, he would make his way to Tin Shanty Bridge or Chandler's Dam Road to camp along the river. The Black appealed to Hemingway because of his love for brook trout. He liked the aggressiveness of the fish and loved to cook them for dinner, rolling the trout in corn meal and frying them in bacon grease.

After serving with the Red Cross in Italy in 1918, Ernest returned home and spent the next two summers at Windemere. In 1921, he and his new wife were married in Horton Bay and honeymooned on Walloon Lake. It was the last time Ernest ever stayed at Windemere or visited Michigan for any amount of time.

The best portrait of how Hemingway fished for brook trout, camped, and cooked is found in *In Our Time*, his first book of stories which was published in 1925. Among the short stories is his classic "Big Two-Hearted River," about the effect of war on a young man who seeks solace with a fishing trip to the Upper Peninsula. The short story is based on a fishing trip Hemingway took with two fiends in 1919 to the Fox River near Seney. But the Fox is never mentioned in the story and other than the title, a

A young Ernest Hemingway fishing in Horton's Creek, near Michigan's Walloon Lake in 1904. (Photo from the Ernest Hemingway Photograph Collection, John F. Kennedy Presidential Library and Museum, Boston.)

river Hemingway never saw, much less fished, the only other trout stream Hemingway mentions is the Black.

Although critics often believe Hemingway's best writing was behind him in the years following World War II, he wrote his Pulitzer Prize–winner and his best-known fishing story, "The Old Man and the Sea," in 1951. The novella about a poor Cuban fisherman's struggle to land a great fish won the Pulitzer Prize the following year and the Nobel Prize for Literature in 1954.

A well-trained dog waits patiently while her owner steps into the Jordan River to fish for native brook trout.

Jordan River

Two years after the Michigan Natural River Act was passed and signed by Gov. William Milliken in 1970, the first river to receive that special designation was selected: the Jordan. Once you see the river or, better yet, stand in it with the water swirling around your waders, you'll understand why.

It's that clean, cold, and clear.

Located primarily in the northwest corner of Antrim County, the Jordan tumbles out of the morainal hills west of Elmira and into the Jordan Valley, where thousand-foot ridges form a fortress around this pristine trout stream and the lush forest it meanders through. The only man-made intrusions are a foot trail and a narrow, two-track road that is impassable by vehicles after the first snowfall. The lack of development here and the fact that 90 percent of its flow is derived from springs has led many to claim that the Jordan has the purest water of any stream in Michigan.

Almost the entire valley is state owned. The 23,000-acre Jordan Valley Management Area is part of the Mackinaw State Forest and includes 12 miles of the Jordan, from near its headwaters to its confluence with the Green River. So special, so wilderness-like, is this section of the river that when a natural gas exploration well was proposed for the area in the 1990s, the public outcry was deafening and the project was eventually denied. This stretch of the Jordan is brook trout country and always has been. Native brookies inhabited the Jordan long before any trout were planted in Michigan streams, and it was Jordan brook trout that were planted in the Au Sable River in 1885. The Jordan is still a good brook trout fishery in its upper reaches.

After the Green River gives the Jordan size and volume, the river swings north and brookies gradually give way to a good population of browns. The nine miles of river from the confluence of the Green River to the Charlevoix County Line, a mile south of Rogers Road, is a designated Blue Ribbon Trout Stream. There are also some resident rainbows, mostly small fish less than ten inches in length, that have not yet made their way back to Lake Charlevoix and Lake Michigan. The lower river hosts a good run of steelhead, whose numbers peak in mid-November, as well as lake-run brown trout and even Chinook salmon that were stocked until 1983.

In the South Arm of Lake Charlevoix, the Jordan comes to the end of its relatively short journey, only 24 miles. But along the way the river and its tributaries drain a watershed of 125 square miles and drop 600 feet in elevation from its headwaters above the Jordan River Valley to the shores of Lake Charlevoix, contributing to the Jordan's reputation of being not only clear and cold but fast flowing.

By the mid-1800s, homesteads were appearing around the mouth of the Jordan and within 40 years the logging era was in full swing in and around the Jordan Valley. Most of the valley was sequentially clear cut with the river being used as a log driving stream. Following immense wildfires in the early 1900s, the East Jordan Lumber Company and the White Lumber Company built small railroads in the valley in an effort to cut and haul out the remaining hardwoods.

By 1925 most of the timber, saw mills, and logging camps were gone from the watershed. Like other logged-out areas in northern Michigan, some attempted to farm the cleared lands but soon found the thin soils unproductive and moved on. Many of these barren lands reverted to state ownership when property taxes went unpaid during the Great Depression; today they make up the bulk of the Jordan Valley Management Area.

But while the state owned the land surface, it didn't acquire all the mineral rights. There are pockets of privately held mineral rights in the valley that in some instances have been leased to energy companies. That has led to battles pitting the companies that wanted to build service roads and distribution lines to the well sites against conservationists who were horrified by the thought of such industrial intrusions into this special valley.

The first threats of drilling occurred in the late 1980s and gave rise to the Friends of the Jordan River Watershed (231-536-9947; *www.friendsofthejordan. org*). Organized in 1990, the group adopted the then novel concept of being watershed based, whereas all their conservation efforts and concerns would be focused not on preserving land but a river system; the Jordan. As diligent watchdogs, Friends of the Jordan have led the fight that kept drilling interests out of the valley in 1997 and again in 2004.

Every angler should give thanks to this group for fighting what could be an endless battle.

Because of the incredibly high percentage of groundwater that flows into the Jordan, the river is probably one of the most stable rivers in the Lower Peninsula. Nevertheless, fly anglers will discover it's not the easiest one to wade in, either in its upper reaches or its lower sections.

The upper Jordan flows westward in a relatively straight channel from the Jordan River National Fish Hatchery to Pinney Bridge. Skirting the river much of the way on the south side is the Pinney Bridge Road. The river is braided here with individual channels from 10 to 30 feet wide and one to four feet deep. The bottom is mostly sand, with small patches of fine gravel. Wading is difficult in places, not because of a fast current or deep water, but due to the many drowned logs and tangled deadfalls that crisscross the stream. It is easy to get your foot jammed in all that timber. Trout cover is prolific, and the brook trout, though often small, are extremely aggressive. The key for fly anglers is to search for pockets of open water and old beaver floodings with enough room to drop a fly carefully into them.

Below Pinney Bridge the Jordan flows northwestward in braided channels to its junction with Green River. Here it turns north and flows more rapidly

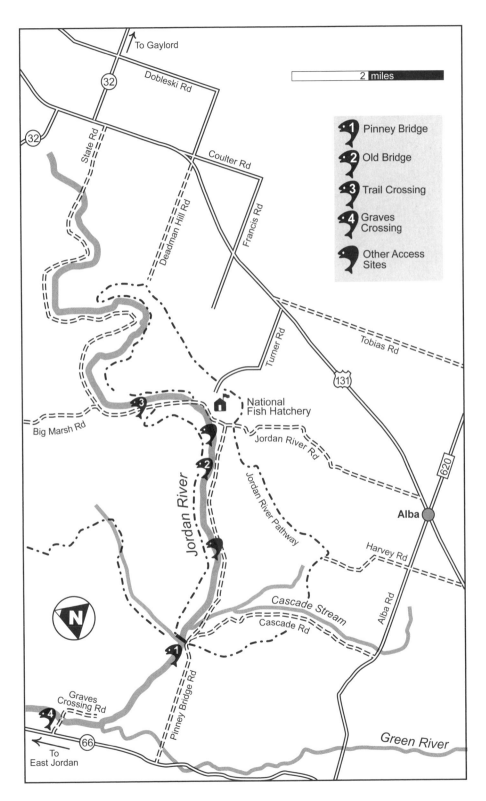

To Gaylord

Dobleski Rd

32

32

State Rd

Deadman Hill Rd

Coulter Rd

Francis Rd

2 miles

1 Pinney Bridge

2 Old Bridge

3 Trail Crossing

4 Graves Crossing

Other Access Sites

Turner Rd

Tobias Rd

131

National Fish Hatchery

Big Marsh Rd

3

Jordan River Rd

620

4

Jordan River

2

Jordan River Pathway

Alba

Harvey Rd

Alba Rd

Cascade Stream

N

Cascade Rd

1

Pinney Bridge Rd

Graves Crossing Rd

4

66

To East Jordan

Green River

in a single channel 30 to 50 feet wide and two to four feet deep, with some deeper runs and holes. The riverbed becomes less sandy downstream, and at Graves Crossing the bottom is mostly gravel, cobbles, and boulders in the faster reaches and sand in the slower areas.

Downstream from Green River there is more than enough room to cast toward logjams, undercut banks, overhanging brush, and deep holes along bends that hide numerous browns and good-size brookies. But the current can be strong, particularly from Graves Crossing where the Jordan drops more than 16 feet in less than a mile. Such deep and fast conditions demand careful wading at all times here and make it impossible at high water.

To Graves Crossing the Jordan is open during the trout season from the last Saturday in April to Sept. 30, with a daily possession of five fish of which only three can be larger than 15 inches. Minimum length is eight inches for brookies and browns. From Graves Crossing to Lake Charlevoix the Jordan has an extended season for steelhead, and fishing is open year round. You can only keep brookies and browns during the trout season, and they have to be at least eight and ten inches, respectively.

The Jordan does not receive nearly the amount of canoeing activity that the Au Sable and more popular rivers to the south do. From the headwaters to Graves Crossing the Jordan is too narrow and choked with logjams to make canoeing possible. From Graves Crossing to Lake Charlevoix the Jordan can be floated by paddlers of moderate competence, but it is not well suited to boat fishing until you are downstream from Rogers Road. Until then the river is too narrow for easy fly casting from a boat and too fast for effective fishing of any kind.

The hatches of mayflies, stoneflies, and caddisflies are better downstream from Graves Crossing than in the upper river. In general, hatches occur a week later than on the Au Sable due to the Jordan's northern latitude and cold summer water temperatures. That includes the Hexagenia hatch, which begins later on the Jordan than on most Michigan streams. The hatch of these big mayflies often doesn't begin until early July in the lower river and then travels upstream to reach Pinney Bridge in early August.

Accommodations

The town of East Jordan at the mouth of the river is the most convenient place to stage a fishing trip to the Jordan. There is a handful of motels and bed and breakfast inns in town, including *D.J's Westbrook Motel* (231-536-2674; *www.westbrookmotel.com*; 218 Elizabeth St.) off of M-66 and just north of M-32, offering seven rooms. In downtown East Jordan is the *Jordan Inn* (231-536-9906; *www.jordaninn.com*; 228 E. Main St.), a sprawling lumber baron's home that has 11 rooms with shared baths, a restaurant, and even a small bar where you can toast your good fortune on the river.

Campgrounds: There are two state forest campgrounds along the Jordan River: Graves Crossing and Pinney Bridge; both are described below as access sites with driving directions to them. Graves Crossing has ten drive-

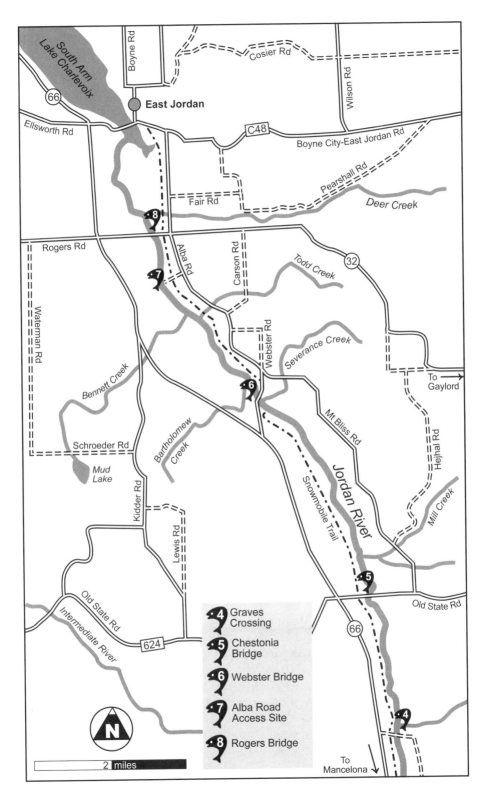

South Arm
Lake Charlevoix

Boyne Rd

Cosier Rd

Wilson Rd

66

East Jordan

Ellsworth Rd

C48

Boyne City-East Jordan Rd

Pearshall Rd

Fair Rd

Deer Creek

Rogers Rd

8

Alba Rd

Carson Rd

Todd Creek

32

7

Waterman Rd

Webster Rd

Severance Creek

To
Gaylord

Bennett Creek

6

Mt Bliss Rd

Hejhal Rd

Schroeder Rd

Bartholomew Creek

Mud
Lake

Kidder Rd

Snowmobile Trail

Jordan River

Mill Creek

Lewis Rd

5

Old State Rd

Old State Rd

Intermediate River

624

66

4 Graves
Crossing

5 Chestonia
Bridge

6 Webster Bridge

7 Alba Road
Access Site

8 Rogers Bridge

N

2 miles

4

To
Mancelona

The Jordan River Pathway

The Jordan River Pathway is the most popular weekend backpacking trip in the Lower Peninsula, one that attracts more than three thousand hikers a year. It's easy to understand why.

The 18.7-mile trek is a loop, eliminating complicated transportation arrangements, and features a walk-in campground near its halfway point. The fact that it is a two-day walk makes it an ideal weekend outing for backpackers from southern Michigan. Most of all, the Jordan River Pathway is a scenic walk where much of the first day is spent skirting the cedar banks of a Blue Ribbon Trout Stream and the second day climbing to overlooks for views of the valley below.

The Jordan River Pathway is not an easy trek. You must be prepared to haul a backpack almost ten miles each day and are constantly climbing in and out of the valley. Few of the backpackers that walk the entire trail are carrying a fly rod, but adventurous anglers will also find the pathway a useful route to some interesting small stream fishing for wild brook trout.

The main trailhead for the Jordan River Pathway is Deadman's Hill, a scenic overlook posted along US-131, 11.5 miles north of Mancelona or six miles north of Alba. From US-131, turn west on Deadman's Hill Road and drive two miles to the parking area and trailhead at the end. But for anglers, the best place to pick up the trail is where it uses a bridge on Old State Road to cross the Jordan River to the west bank (see access site No. 3, Trail Crossing, in this chapter).

A parking area and trail signs are on the south side of the bridge. From there you hike north on Old State Road for 300 yards to the point where the well-posted pathway dips back into the woods. The trail climbs a bit, swings south, and reaches the river in less than a mile from Old State Road. You then hug the banks of the Jordan for more than a mile for one of the most scenic stretches of the pathway. The clear and cold current of the Jordan swirls and weaves its way through a maze of grassy humps and islands, some supporting huge cedars, others little more than a bouquet of wildflowers in the spring. The Jordan is braided and cluttered with timber this far upstream but still offers opportunities to step in and fish.

in sites, while Pinney Bridge is a walk-in campground that is used primarily by backpackers hiking the Jordan River Pathway. The walk to Pinney Bridge is only a quarter mile, but the parking area where you would leave your car is capable of holding only eight to ten vehicles. Dispersed camping is not allowed along the river in the Jordan Valley.

Right on M-66 and overlooking the South Arm of Lake Charlevoix is the **East Jordan Tourist Park** (231-536-2561; *www.eastjordancity.org/touristpark.html*; 218 N. Lake Street). The city-operated campground has full hook-up sites that include electric, water, sewer, even cable for goodness sakes, along with partial hook-ups, tent sites, and restrooms with showers.

A hiker crosses a spring-fed stream along the Jordan River Pathway. The 18.7-mile loop includes stretches along the upper Jordan River that anglers can follow to some excellent brook trout fishing.

Once the trail climbs away from the river at post No. 10, you can backtrack two miles to your vehicle on Old State Road. Or have somebody drop you off at the bridge and hike the remaining 3.2 miles to Pinney Bridge Campground.

For a trail map to the Jordan River Pathway call the DNR regional head-quarters (989-732-3541) or stop at the office just west of Gaylord on M-32.

Fly Shops and Guides

East Jordan lacks a good fly shop, but tiny Ellsworth, six miles to the west via Ellsworth Road (County Road C48), has one. ***Chain-O-Lakes Outdoor Sports*** (231-588-6070; 6517 Center St.) stocks flies and fly-fishing equipment and has a handle on what's hatching during the season. A member of its staff, Bill Bellinger (231-675-2228), also guides on the Jordan.

For a float-and-fish outing, there are two canoe liveries in the area: ***Swiss Hideaway*** (231-536-2341; *www.jordanriverfun.com*; 1953 Graves Crossing Rd.) on the River at Graves Crossing and ***Jordan Valley Outfitters*** (231-

536-0006; *www.jvoutfitters.com*; 311 N. Lake St.) in East Jordan.

Maps of the Jordan

Pinney Bridge Road, a narrow, winding, but beautiful dirt road, provides the easiest access to the three sites described on the upper Jordan: Pinney Bridge, Old Bridge, and Trail Crossing, and many more that are not covered in detail in this chapter. The road is posted and picked up from M-66, 11.3 miles south of M-32 near East Jordan. From M-66, Pinney Bridge Road heads east, often skirting the river itself. This is a road that demands to be driven slowly, both to savor the beauty of the valley and to preserve your muffler.

You can also pick it up near the US-131 and M-32 intersection, 13 miles west of Gaylord or 14 miles north of Mancelona. Just south of the intersection, State Road heads west from US-131 as a graded dirt road before plunging into the Jordan Valley. Within nine miles or 0.6 mile past the fish hatchery, it arrives at an unmarked intersection with Pinney Bridge Road and Jordan River Road.

The next two sites, Graves Crossing and Chestonia Bridge, are reached from M-66, either heading south from East Jordan or north from where M-66 splits from US-131 near Mancelona. The final three sites, Webster Bridge, Alba Road, and Rogers Bridge, can be reached from East Jordan by heading south on either M-66 or M-32.

1 *Pinney Bridge*

GPS N 45° 00.799'
W 85° 01.803'

Everybody gathers at Pinney Bridge: backpackers, hikers, campers and anglers. The foot bridge provides access from Pinney Bridge Road across the Jordan to Pinney Bridge Campground, a walk-in facility used primarily by backpackers hiking the two-day, 18.7-mile Jordan River Pathway.

From M-66, head east on Pinney Bridge Road for 1.7 miles to a large parking area on the south side of the bridge capable of holding eight to ten vehicles. If coming from US-131, it's a 13-mile drive through the valley to Pinney Bridge beginning with State Road. The bridge is for foot traffic only; a gate prevents vehicles from using it. From the parking area you head north on the pathway to reach the bridge immediately, while the campground is a 400-yard walk. The state forest campground is a grassy meadow above the river and features vault toilets, a hand pump for water, and picnic tables.

Landslide Creek joins the Jordan 0.3 mile above Pinney Bridge, giving the river body, depth, and a stronger flow not seen further upstream. At the bridge the Jordan is 40 to 50 feet wide and two to four feet deep with many deeper holes. The bottom is mostly sand with small patches of gravel along with some muck and small patches of dark, almost black, bottom vegetation.

Upstream from the bridge the Jordan flows in channels around small

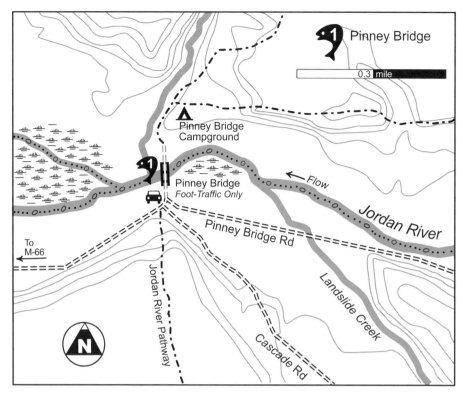

islets of fallen trees and clumps of grass; downstream it is heavily braided. The stream channels in many places are choked with a crisscross of drowned logs, like giant jackstraws. Trout cover, including drowned logs and deep holes, is abundant. Banks are low, only one to three feet high, and swampy, lined with cedar, spruce, hemlock, and brush.

Careful casting into pockets of water will produce strikes by eager brookies. But the jumble of drowned logs makes wading extremely difficult in some places and dangerous to impossible in others. Other hazards to the wading fisherman are deep holes, fast flow in some channels, and soft sand. This is not the kind of water you would want to wade alone at night.

 **2 *Old Bridge***

GPS N 45° 01.204'
W 85° 59.044'

Map: page 221

Pinney Bridge Road heads east from its namesake bridge and within a mile begins skirting the Jordan River. For the next 1.5 miles you are within sight of this beautiful trout stream and pass numerous stretches of it that look like places where you could cast a fly. However, a lack of parking or even a place to pull over along this extremely narrow road prevents most anglers from stopping.

Within 2.5 miles from Pinney Bridge or 4.2 miles from M-66, you arrive at this access site where there is a defined parking area capable of holding two to three vehicles on the north side of Pinney Bridge Road. From there a stairway leads down to the water.

The Jordan is a shallow, sandy stream here, one to two feet deep with some deeper holes but few that you have to worry about. The stream is very braided with individual channels as narrow as two feet and as wide as 30 feet with the total width ranging from 30 to 40 feet.

The stream divides into two main channels about a hundred yards above the stairway, forming a low island two hundred yards long. The streambed here is sand with some muck and patches of fine gravel. The velocity is moderate in the wider channels but can be fast in some of the narrower ones. Banks are mostly low, lined with cedar, brush, and some hardwood. The chief obstacles to the wading fisherman are drowned logs and snags, soft sand, deeper holes, and fast flow in some of the channels. But the drowned logs and deep holes provide very good trout cover, and the stream is wide and open enough for fly fishing.

3 Trail Crossing
GPS N 45° 02.333'
W 85° 58.276'

Continuing east on your Jordan Valley adventure, Pinney Bridge Road hugs the river for another half mile and then climbs a ridge to a "T" intersection, a mile from the Old Bridge Access Site or 5.2 miles from M-66. The fork to the south (right) is Jordan River Road, which climbs out of the valley to reach the village of Alba on US-131 in 3.5 miles. To continue following the river, turn north (left) on what is now Old State Road. Of course, nothing is posted.

Within 0.6 mile you'll pass the entrance to the Jordan River National Fish Hatchery and then resume skirting the river for 0.7 mile, passing several parking areas off the road where it would be possible to stop and fish. At 4.8 miles from Pinney Bridge or 6.5 miles from M-66, you cross the Jordan River from its east bank to its west bank. There are parking and benches near the bridge as the pathway also uses it to cross the river.

The pathway then follows the dirt road north and is well marked where it dips back into the woods to the west. In another hundred yards or a quarter mile from the bridge you arrive at a small parking area on the east side of the road with two large boulders blocking a footpath. The short trail leads to a beautiful meadow split in half by the Jordan.

The river is 30 feet wide and one to two feet deep with a sandy and silt bottom and a very gentle current. Though the brook trout tend to be small here, they readily take a fly and there is room to cast, especially upstream. It would also be easy to fish downstream, avoiding an occasional deep hole (one of which is posted), and then get out at the bridge and walk back along Old State Road.

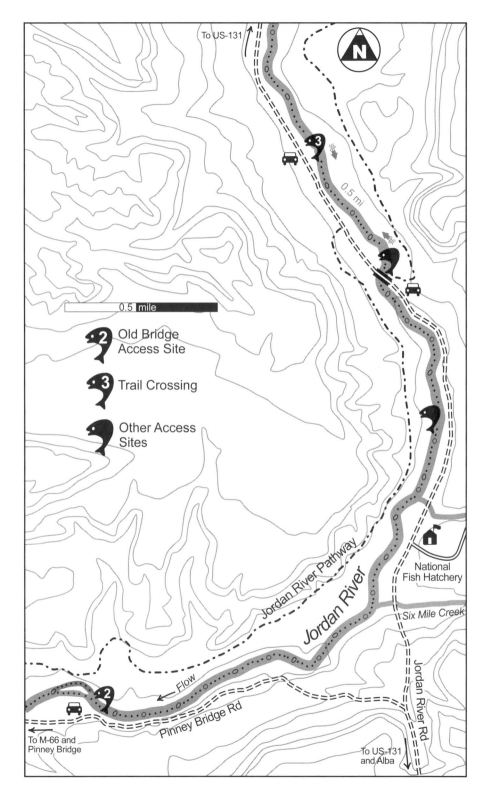

To US-131

N

0.5 mi

0.5 mile

2 Old Bridge
Access Site

3 Trail Crossing

Other Access
Sites

Jordan River Pathway

Jordan River

National
Fish Hatchery

Six Mile Creek

Jordan River Rd

Flow

2

Pinney Bridge Rd

To M-66 and
Pinney Bridge

To US-131
and Alba

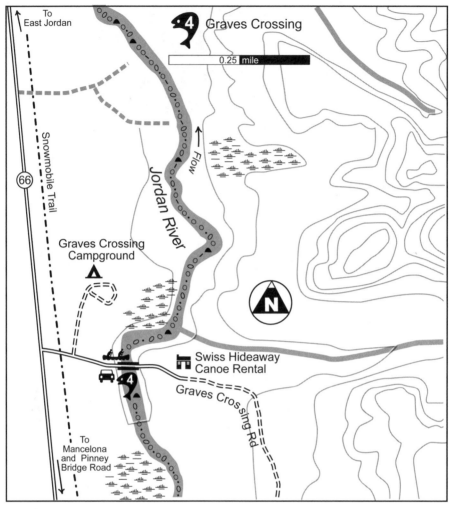

 **Graves Crossing**

GPS N 45° 01.992'
W 85° 03.866'

Graves Crossing is the site of a state forest campground and marks where paddlers can begin a float down the Jordan. From M-32 a mile west of downtown East Jordan, head south on M-66. Within 9.5 miles turn east (left) on Graves Crossing Road, a paved road that is also marked on M-66 with a DNR campground sign. Within a few hundred yards you pass the entrance to the campground, and in a quarter mile you come to the Graves Crossing Bridge. If coming from the south, pick up M-66 where it splits from US-131 just north of Mancelona and follow it nine miles.

Graves Crossing Campground has ten rustic sites on two loops along the west side of the Jordan. None of the sites are directly on the river, but all are just a short walk away. There is also parking for a dozen vehicles on both

An angler fishes the Jordan River at the Graves Crossing access site. Near the bridge is rustic Graves Crossing State Forest Campground.

sides of the bridge where you can access the river at the canoe launch. Angler trails extend from the bridge along both banks of the Jordan. Just east of the bridge is Swiss Hideaway Canoe Rental (231-536-2341).

Just 0.6 mile upstream the Green River merges with the Jordan to give it substantially more width, depth, and velocity than the mellow trout stream seen along Pinney Bridge Road. Wading upstream to the mouth of the Green River is challenging due to the abundance of submerged stumps, logjams, and cedar slash combined with a fast current. All that timber along with undercut banks and deep holes is trout cover hiding a growing number of browns, an occasional rainbow, and brookies up to 15 inches in length. Access is limited, nor can you float this stretch, so fishing pressure is light.

At the campground the Jordan flows fast and deep in a single channel and is 30 to 50 feet wide and two to four feet deep with deeper holes. The bottom is gravel, cobbles, and boulders, with some sand and muck. Patches of hard white clay, overlaid in places by gravel or boulders, begin to appear in the riverbed below Graves Crossing. The white clay is resistant to erosion and forms ledges in places that resemble limestone bedrock. This material appears intermittently in the streambed at least as far downstream as Chestonia Bridge.

The velocity is fast to very fast. The swift current and wader-topping holes require caution and an alert eye for deep water, especially at bends. Drowned logs, boulders, and some soft sand and muck are additional hazards. Banks are low, one to three feet, forested with spruce, popple, cedar, and pine, with some brushy areas. The river is wide and open enough for fly fishing, and trout cover is very good. By wading upstream you escape all canoeing activity, even on the weekends.

5 *Chestonia Bridge*

GPS N 45° 03.626'
W 85° 04.126'

The next access site north from Graves Crossing is Chestonia Bridge where Old State Road crosses the Jordan. From M-32 in East Jordan, Old State Road is 7.7 miles to the south on M-66 or 1.5 miles north of Graves Crossing Road. Turn east on Old State Road to reach the bridge in 0.4 mile. There is limited parking on the south side of the road, both east and west of the bridge.

The river is 40 to 80 feet wide and two to four feet deep. The Jordan flows beneath the road through a pair of culverts that funnel the water into a deep hole. The bottom is gravel, cobbles, and boulders, with sand in the slower areas. Patches of hard white clay or marl are exposed in the streambed above and below the bridge, in places forming ledges that resemble limestone bedrock. Banks are mostly low, but somewhat higher than at Graves Crossing. Bank vegetation is cedar, spruce, popple, and brush.

Overall trout cover is good and there is ample room for fly casting, but you have to be careful wading downstream from the bridge as this is deep

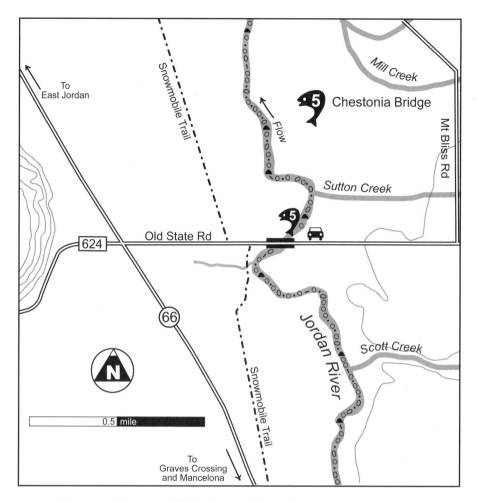

and swift water. Often you'll find yourself treading close to the banks where foliage and brush can snag a fly or two. Upstream the wading is a bit easier if you watch out for deep holes and ledges of hard clay. One such ledge, about 180 yards upstream from the bridge, extends across most of the channel.

A snowmobile trail, resembling a rough two-track, heads south into the woods a hundred feet west of Chestonia Bridge. This trail quickly reaches a snowmobile bridge crossing a feeder creek, and on the south side you can cut over to the Jordan, though it will require a bit of bush bashing. Watch that rod! This far upstream the river is wider and easier to wade without the velocity it has downstream from Old State Road.

The Upper Jordan River has a gentle flow and a healthy population of native brook trout. But the many submerged logs and sweepers force fly anglers to search for an opening with enough room to cast.

Webster Bridge

GPS N 45° 06.136'
W 85° 05.874'

Webster Bridge is the site of a U.S. Geological Survey gauging station as well as a popular canoe launch. From M-32 in East Jordan, Webster Bridge Road is 5.3 miles to the south on M-66. The paved road veers sharply to the northeast off M-66 and in 0.7 mile reaches the bridge. The canoe launch is on the east bank of the river and is reached from a gravel entrance road on the north side of Webster Bridge Road.

The launch site has parking for more than a dozen vehicles, along with vault toilets. Next to the small brick water station, an angler's trail heads downstream a bit where you can enter the river and wade upstream to Webster Bridge or further downstream. In either direction caution is needed. Drowned logs, snags, brush, and boulders add to the difficulty of wading while under the bridge. For a short distance upstream you need to watch out for broken concrete.

The river varies in width from 40 to 65 feet and is three to four feet deep in most places. Bottom is sand and gravel, with more sand than in upstream reaches. Banks are low, lined with cedar, brush, and some hardwood, but there are also some grassy areas by riverside homes. Trout cover is very good, and the river is wide and more than sufficiently open for fly fishing.

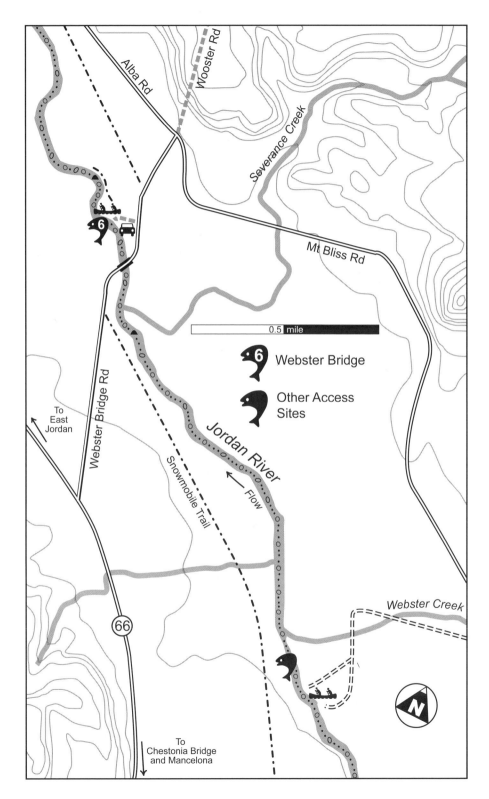

Alba Rd

Wooster Rd

Severance Creek

Mt Bliss Rd

0.5 mile

6 Webster Bridge

Other Access
Sites

Jordan River

Flow

Webster Bridge Rd

To
East
Jordan

Snowmobile Trail

66

Webster Creek

N

To
Chestonia Bridge
and Mancelona

Alba Road Access Site

GPS N 45° 07.362'
W 85° 07.310'

This site allows paddlers to launch their crafts or portage around a former electric weir located in the river here. The weir was put in place to prevent lamprey eels from spawning, but hasn't been operated since 2005 and the U.S. Fish and Wildlife Service has plans to remove it. When water levels are normal, this is another place where the wading angler can cast for trout.

The easiest way to reach the access site from East Jordan is to head south on M-32. Within 1.5 miles, when M-32 curves to the east (left), you continue south on Alba Road (also labeled Mt. Bliss Road here on some maps) at an intersection that includes Rogers Road heading west. The access site is posted along Alba Road half a mile to the south, where a gravel road heads west (right), reaching the east bank of the Jordan in 0.3 mile.

If coming from the south, pick up M-66 where it splits from US-131 on the edge of Mancelona and head north for 13.8 miles. Turn off on Webster Road and follow the paved road as it crosses the Jordan and then comes to an intersection with Mt. Bliss Road. Turn left on Mt. Bliss Road, which becomes Alba Road and in 1.7 miles passes the access site.

The site includes a large parking area, a vault toilet, and the landing dock upstream of the weir. A short path then leads downstream to a second landing that allows paddlers to portage around the fish barrier.

Overall the river is 50 to 60 feet wide and three to five feet deep. The bottom is sand with a little gravel, and the banks are low—two to five feet in height—and lined with hardwood and cedar. The flow is fast, and wading upstream is very difficult even at normal water levels. Downstream the wading conditions are better when the river levels are low to normal.

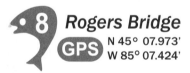

Rogers Bridge

GPS N 45° 07.973'
W 85° 07.424'

Being so close to East Jordan, only 1.5 miles upstream from where the Jordan empties into Lake Charlevoix, the river here is lined with homes, while traffic will be rumbling overhead on Rogers Road. A far cry from that tranquil trout stream you fished in the middle of the Jordan Valley.

From East Jordan, head south on M-32 and in 1.5 miles, where M-32 curves sharply east (left), turn west (right) on Rogers Road at an intersection that also includes Alba Road heading south. Within a quarter mile west you will reach the bridge and the large access site on the east bank of the river and the north side of the road.

The access site is a popular place for canoers to pull out of the river as evidenced by the split-level parking areas capable of holding 30 vehicles. Other than the access site, all frontage is private; riverside houses and well-

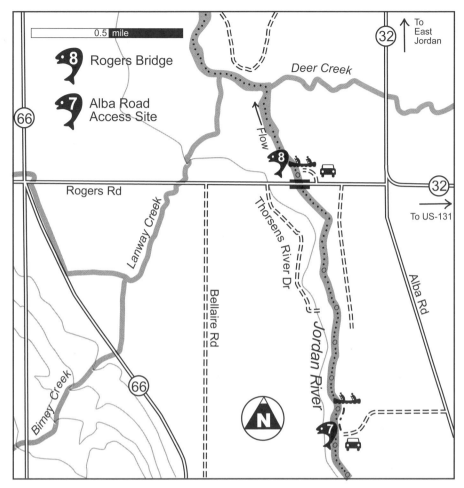

kept lawns line both sides of the river. The river is 50 to 75 feet wide and two to four feet deep with some deeper holes. Bottom is mostly sand, making this stretch a favorite during the Hex hatch. The flow is moderate in the wide areas, and you'll find the wading is generally easier than at the Alba Road access site.

Wading downstream a few hundred yards is fairly easy at normal summer flows, but there are still some deep holes that need to be avoided. Wading upstream from the bridge against the current is difficult and soon becomes impossible where the stream is narrow, fast, and deep. Trout cover is mostly undercut banks and deep runs.

A fly angler fishes in front of the Brown Pond Dam on the Boardman River. This classic trout stream is just south of Traverse City and is home to the Adams fly.

Boardman River

Emerging as springs on the outskirts of Kalkaska and ending in downtown Traverse City, the Boardman is one of the best streams in Michigan for resident brown trout. It also has a good population of brook trout in the upper reaches and tributaries, particularly the North and South Branches. Although trout are caught in the entire length of the river, for many fly anglers the best fishing is from the headwaters, known as "the Forks," downstream to Brown Bridge Pond. The favorable water quality and abundant gravel spawning beds here and particularly in the North and South Branches support natural reproduction sufficient to maintain the trout population. Below the pond a series of hydroelectric dams, most of them now inactive, prevent passage of steelhead and other anadromous fish into the upper river.

In the early 1800s, maps labeled the Boardman as the Ottawa or "Ootawas" River, for the local Native American tribes of that name. Later it was renamed after Captain Harry Boardman. The captain sailed into the Grand Traverse Bay in 1847 looking for timber, found plenty of it, and had his son build the first sawmill near the mouth of the Boardman River. Within a decade much of the Boardman River was being used to float timber to sawmills clustered around Traverse City. To allow for the easy passage of millions of logs, lumberjacks had to clear the Boardman of debris. The massive log drives then gorged the banks of the river and changed its course, hastening the extinction of the grayling.

Eventually the Boardman healed itself, and in 1976 the upper portions of the river, including segments of the North and South Branches, were designated a Natural Scenic River by the state, making it worthy of special protection and management. In 1986, the Boardman was added to the state's list of Blue Ribbon Trout Streams.

The Boardman River drains a 287-square-mile watershed split between Grand Traverse and Kalkaska Counties and is the largest tributary to the west arm of Grand Traverse Bay. Almost 54 percent of the river frontage is privately owned but the remaining 46 percent is public land as part of the Pere Marquette State Forest or other protected natural areas. More than half of the watershed is now forested. Flora along the river include tag alder, willow, ninebark, and dogwood with varying mixtures of cedar, balsam, hemlock, tamarack, aspen, and white birch.

The North Branch begins a few miles northeast of Kalkaska in the Mahan Swamp; at a length of 24 miles it is longer than the mainstream. It flows southwest to join the South Branch about seven miles south of the village of Williamsburg. The South Branch rises south of the village of South Boardman and flows ten miles northwest to its junction with the North

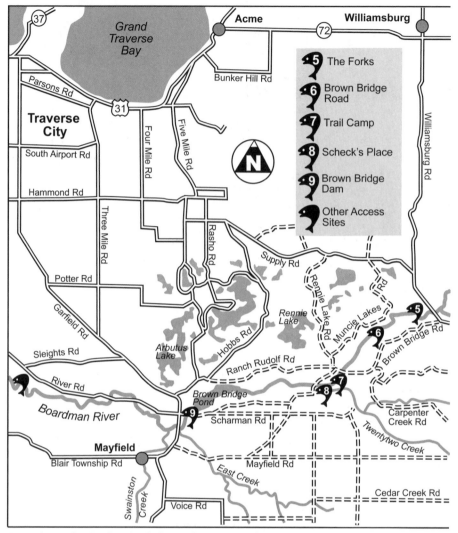

Branch at the Forks. Both branches are wide enough to fly fish, though you often find yourself casting in tight quarters, but the trout population of the South Branch is substantially greater than that of the North Branch.

From the Forks the river flows southwest to Brown Bridge Pond in a seven-mile stretch known as the Upper Boardman. This is ideal fly water with an excellent population of brown trout and a fair population of brookies. Most of it has a firm gravel bottom for easy wading. More than half of the river frontage in this section is state land, providing ample access for fishermen. Above Brown Bridge Pond the river is too narrow and fast for the beginner paddlers, so canoe traffic here is considerably lighter than what you experience below the dam. Anglers new to fly casting might find sections of the Upper Boardman tight, with the cedars along the banks readily grabbing flies on their backcast. But thanks to the foliage and the shade it provides, the river here provides everything trout need to thrive:

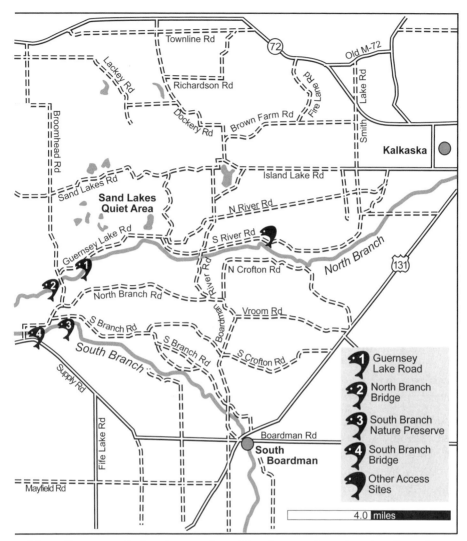

Map legend:

1 Guernsey Lake Road
2 North Branch Bridge
3 South Branch Nature Preserve
4 South Branch Bridge
Other Access Sites

4.0 miles

cold, well-oxygenated water, undercut banks, overhanging brush and tree roots for suitable cover, and a gravel bottom for healthy hatches.

The river continues northwest and north, reaching Grand Traverse Bay twenty miles from the Forks. From Brown Bridge Dam to Boardman Pond, the river is referred to as the Middle Boardman, a stretch where almost all the frontage is private and public access is sparse. This part of the river also provides good fishing and is considerably wider for casting, but it does not have the population of stream-bred trout that characterizes the Upper Boardman.

Although the Upper Boardman does not rise more than about two feet at high flows, this is enough to make most of the river unwadable because its flow is generally fast. The Boardman, which originates at an elevation of 1,090 feet above sea level and drops to 580 feet at the mouth, is much faster than what you'll experience on the upper Au Sable. Thus wading in hip-deep

The Adams Fly

The Boardman River is not only home to brook and brown trout but is also the birthplace of one of the best-known and most productive dry flies ever tied, the Adams. The famous fly was created by Leonard Halladay for his friend, Charles F. Adams, a Lorain, OH, attorney with a summer cottage on Arbutus Lake, but who could often be found fishing the Boardman River.

In 1922 Adams was casting on the Mayfield Millpond, an impoundment of Swainston Creek just a mile south of the Boardman River, when a hatch of insects caught his eye. He described the insect to Halladay, who quickly came up with a dry fly to match it, using two strands of Golden Pheasant tippet for the tail, gray muskrat fur for the body, grizzly tips for the wings, and brown and grizzly tips tied together for the hackle.

Adams tried the fly for the first time that evening on the Boardman. The next morning he excitedly told Halladay it was "a knock out" and asked what the fly was called. In a letter to historian Harold Smedley, Halladay wrote, "I said we would call it the Adams, since he had made the first good catch on it."

Originally the Adams was thought to represent caddisflies and stoneflies that are so common on Michigan trout streams. In reality, this venerable fly is an imitator. Now tied in countless variations, some pattern of the Adams can be used in nearly any dry fly situation in Michigan. Many anglers claim if their fly box contained only one pattern it would be the Adams.

water is usually not feasible. The river declines somewhat in dry periods, but not enough to seriously reduce trout cover.

Like all good trout streams in the Midwest, the discharge of the Boardman is chiefly from groundwater, so water temperatures in the summer remain low. The Boardman is colder than the Au Sable but not quite as cold as the Manistee. The colder water tends to delay hatches as compared to other area trout streams. Early in the season the Boardman supports strong hatches of Hendrickson followed by brown drakes and stoneflies from late May to early June, then little sulphur and black caddis hatches in July. The Boardman also experiences a strong Hex hatch anytime from late June through July.

Accommodations

Anglers fishing the Boardman River usually camp or book accommodations in the Traverse City area. For those who want to headquarter on the river itself, there is **Ranch Rudolf** (231-947-9529; *www.ranchrudolf.com*; 6841 Brown Rd.), 12 miles south of Traverse City or three miles downstream from the Forks. The river winds conveniently through the resort, which offers 25 full-service campsites, a 16-room motel, restaurant, lounge, and small general store. Near Brown Bridge Pond is **Shoe String Resort Motel** (231-946-9227; *www.shoestringresort.com*; 2960 Arbutus Hill Rd.) near the corner of Garfield and River Roads. Shoe String features 19 fully furnished cottages ranging from one to three bedrooms and equipped with washers, dryers, cable television and linen.

Within Traverse City there is a wide range of accommodations; a list can be obtained from the Traverse City Convention and Visitors Bureau (800-872-8377; *www.visittraversecity.com*). For anglers, one of the more interesting places to book a room is **Mitchell Creek Inn** (800-947-9330; *www.mitchellcreek.com*) adjacent to the Traverse City State Park and three miles from downtown on US-31. The inn has motel rooms, kitchenettes, and cottages, while flowing behind it is Mitchell Creek where anglers fish in the summer for trout and in the winter for steelhead. For a bed-and-breakfast experience there is **Cherry Knoll Farm** (231-947-9806; 2856 Hammond Road), a pleasant, five-room bed-and-breakfast south of town, making it a short drive to the Boardman River.

Campgrounds: The most popular campground on the Boardman for fly fishers is the Forks State Forest Campground, a small eight-site facility right on the banks of the Upper Boardman. Located on Brown Bridge Road just west of Supply Road, the campground was closed briefly in 2007 due to budget cuts but has since been reopened. Another public campground on the river is Scheck's Place, a state forest facility with thirty rustic sites on both sides of Brown Bridge Road, four miles west of Forks Bridge and Supply Road. None of the sites are directly on the river but there are access stairs and canoe ramps on the water.

Near the North Branch of the Boardman River is Guernsey Lake State Forest Campground with 36 rustic sites on Guernsey Lake Road south of Island Lake Road, while south of Traverse City is **Timber Ridge Recreation Resort** (800-909-2327; *www.timberridgeresort.net*), a commercial campground with full hook-ups, cabins, and all the amenities any camper could want.

Fly Shops and Guides

There are several quality fly shops in Traverse City including the **Northern Angler** (231-933-4730, 800-627-4080; *www.thenorthernangler.com*; 803 W. Front St.) and **Orvis Streamside** (231-933-9300; *www.streamsideorvis.com*; 223 E. Front St.). In Kalkaska, you'll find a selection of flies and good stream advice at **Jack's Sport Shop** (231-258-8892; *www.jackssport.net*; 212 Cedar St.).

Contact the Northern Angler or Orvis Streamside in regard to guided fly fishing outings. Also offering guided float service on area rivers and fly fishing schools is **Hawkins Fly Fishing Outfitters** (231-228-7135; *www.hawkinsflyfishing.com*).

Maps of the Boardman

Traverse City is a logical staging area for fishing the Boardman, but the river can also be reached from the smaller towns of Kalkaska on the east and Kingsley on the south, or the little villages of Williamsburg on the north and South Boardman and Fife Lake on the southeast. The location map shows the river channel and public roads leading to it.

Nine numbered access sites are covered in this chapter, two on the North Branch, two on the South Branch, four on the Upper Boardman, and one just below Brown Bridge Pond. You can use the Forks Bridge as the starting point for each of the sites. To reach the Forks Bridge, head south of Williamsburg on the paved Williamsburg Road. Within 5.7 miles south you arrive at an intersection with Supply Road. Continue south (left) on Supply Road and in 1.3 miles you'll reach the Forks Bridge on the Upper Boardman just below where the North and South Branches merge to form the main stream.

 Guernsey Lake Road

GPS N 44° 41.873'
W 85° 21.202'

In the upper reaches of Boardman's North Branch you'll find a clear, cold river, making it the perfect haven for native brook trout. The drawback is that in most places it is only 20 to 25 feet wide and hemmed in by heavily forested banks. It is best suited for a six-foot fly rod of three to four weight and equipped with light tippet. The most successful anglers will be able to roll cast effectively or, at the very least, be able to flip their flies a short distance with a sidearm motion. There are casting lanes on the North Branch that you can position yourself into, just not nearly as many as you'll find downstream from the Forks.

From the Forks Bridge head southeast on Supply Road for 0.4 mile and then turn north on Broomhead Road, a well-graded dirt road. You'll quickly cross the South Branch Bridge and then in a little over a mile the North Branch Bridge, two areas that are covered later in this chapter. Within 150 yards turn northeast (right) on Guernsey Lake Road, which forms the southern border of the Sand Lakes Quiet Area, a 2,500-acre tract that is popular with hikers and mountain bikers. Within a mile on Guernsey Lake Road look for a small parking area with a log fence protecting the edge of the bluff and a stairway to the river below.

This is a picturesque spot as the North Branch swings from east to south in a sweeping curve and is bordered by banks 10 to 25 feet high and forested in pines. The river is twenty feet wide here and one to three feet deep with a sandy bottom with intermittent gravel runs. There is room to cast through the bend, while heading west is an angler's trail to more runs upstream. Unlike the main stream, you'll find the fishing pressure relatively light.

An additional access point for the North Branch is reached by following Guernsey Lake east for 1.2 miles and then turning south (right) on unmarked South River Road. Follow this road two miles to reach a large parking area with another log fence. A pair of stairways will provide access to the North Branch below.

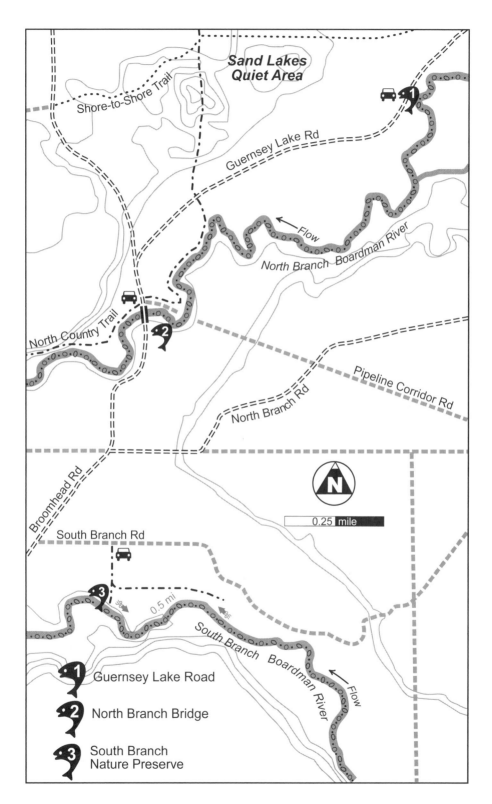

Sand Lakes
Quiet Area

Shore-to-Shore Trail

Guernsey Lake Rd

Flow

North Branch Boardman River

North Country Trail

Pipeline Corridor Rd

North Branch Rd

N

0.25 mile

Broomhead Rd

South Branch Rd

0.5 mi

South Branch Boardman River

Flow

1 Guernsey Lake Road

2 North Branch Bridge

3 South Branch
Nature Preserve

North Branch Bridge

GPS N 44° 41.421'
W 85° 22.049'

Map: page 237

The North Branch Bridge provides direct access to the river and to the North Country Trail (NCT). The NCT is a national trail that someday will extend from North Dakota to New York, including winding more than a thousand miles across Michigan. West of the bridge the NCT skirts the North Branch for almost two miles, to the east another half mile, providing anglers with a considerable amount of water to explore depending on how far they're willing to hike in their waders.

To reach the North Branch Bridge from the Forks, head east on paved Supply Road for 0.3 mile to the intersection with Broomhead Road and turn north (left) on the well-graded dirt road. Within a quarter mile you cross the South Branch and 1.8 miles from Supply Road cross North Branch Bridge.

There is good off-road parking for several cars on the west side of Broomhead Road just north of the bridge, a spot that is posted with a NCT trail marker. On the east side of Broomhead Road, a very rough pipeline corridor road skirts the North Branch for a hundred yards and then ends where the trout stream makes a sweeping bend to the north. From here you can easily spot the NCT as it continues to skirt the North Branch.

At this stretch the North Branch is thirty to forty feet wide and two to four feet deep with some deeper holes. One hole, in particular, is just below the bridge and is more than six feet deep. The bottom is sand and gravel with some muck. Banks are sandy, brushy, and forested with mixed hardwood and conifer. The river is wide enough for fly fishing. Velocity is only moderate, and wading is fairly easy at normal flows if you watch out for the deeper holes, snags, and soft sand. The river frontage is mostly state land, and fishing pressure is light, especially if you first walk a portion of the NCT. Population studies show that the North Branch of the Boardman has more brown trout per unit area than the mainstream, but fewer brookies.

South Branch Nature Preserve

GPS N 44° 40.916'
W 85° 22.224'

Map: page 237

In the 1920s Theron and Della Morgan of Traverse City purchased a small tract southeast of their Traverse City home that was split in the middle by the South Branch of the Boardman River. The area was a mix of second-growth forests, meadows, steep bluffs, and a beautiful trout stream, which the family enjoyed as their private retreat for almost eighty years. But in 2002 Theron's son, James Morgan, offered the tract to the Grand Traverse Regional Land Conservancy as the only way to ensure it remained undeveloped and wild forever.

Thanks to the Morgan family and the fund-raising ability of the conservancy, the South Branch Nature Preserve is now open to anybody

238 TWELVE CLASSIC TROUT STREAMS IN MICHIGAN

Enrolling at Ranch Rudolf

Within a fly cast of the trout-filled waters of the Boardman River is Ranch Rudolf, one of Traverse City's most unusual resorts. The lodge, dining room, and campground is spread over 195 acres and surrounded by the Pere Marquette State Forest. The resort is an ideal base for any angler wanting to spend a few days exploring the Boardman River—and has been since the early 1900s.

Ranch Rudolf picked up its name from Rudolf Pazanier, the long-time chef and general manager of the ranch. In the 1920s it was said that for $150 a week you could get "the use of a horse and buggy, lodging and gourmet meals prepared by Rudolf himself."

Anglers still gather at the ranch as it has been the home of the Michigan Council of Trout Unlimited's Fly Fishing School for more than 25 years. Held in early June during Michigan's Free Fishing Days, the weekend school offers three levels of instruction. They range from a beginners' class designed for people who have never picked up a fly rod to an advanced class in which students undergo a personal casting review and learn advanced casting theory and techniques. The school combines classroom lectures with outdoor instruction on the ponds at Ranch Rudolf and outings to nearby Boardman and Manistee Rivers.

For more information on the Michigan Council's Fly Fishing School, check its web site (*www.mctu.org*). For rates on rooms, campsites, and meals at other times of the year, contact Ranch Rudolf (231-947-9529; *www.ranchrudolf.com*).

and should be particularly appealing to adventurous fly anglers. The 47-acre preserve contains almost a half mile of frontage on the north bank of the South Branch and 1,200 feet on the south side. You reach it from Supply Road by heading north on Broomhead Road for 1.1 miles and then turning east (right) on South Branch Road, a rough dirt road. Within a quarter mile you will arrive at a gated two-track, a large display sign for the preserve, and parking for a handful of cars.

From the locked gate follow the two-track south for a hundred yards until it curves sharply east. Continue south on an even more overgrown two-track and in another hundred yards you will arrive at the South Branch, where a set of old bridge abutments still stand on each side of the stream. The South Branch is twenty feet wide here and two to three feet deep with a bottom of sand, silt, and patches of fine gravel. It's tight casting near the bridge abutments with plenty of trees and alder hanging over the banks ready to snatch a wayward fly. But by fishing in an upstream direction you'll soon arrive where the stream breaks out of the woods and is bordered to the north by a meadow. You can fish for almost a half mile without leaving the preserve in water that is home to a healthy population of native brook trout. Most likely you will have this stretch to yourself.

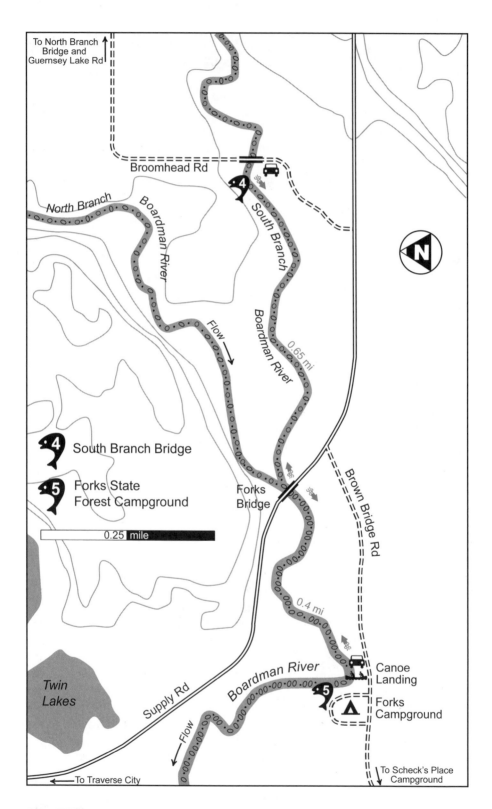

To North Branch
Bridge and
Guernsey Lake Rd

Broomhead Rd

4

North Branch

Boardman River

South Branch

Boardman River

0.65 mi

Flow

4 South Branch Bridge

5 Forks State
Forks Forest Campground

0.25 mile

Forks
Bridge

Brown Bridge Rd

0.4 mi

Twin
Lakes

Canoe
Landing

5 Forks
Campground

Supply Rd

Boardman River

Flow

To Traverse City

To Scheck's Place
Campground

South Branch Bridge

GPS N 44° 40.526'
W 85° 23.202'

A wider South Branch can be accessed further downstream from the South Branch Bridge. The bridge is reached from the Forks by continuing east on Supply Road for 0.3 mile and then turning north (left) on Broomhead Road. Within a quarter mile you reach the South Branch Bridge, where you'll find very limited parking on the narrow shoulders. One or two cars can park on the west side of the road just south of the bridge. Pull off as far as you can without going into the ditch so you are out of the traffic lane.

The South Branch of the Boardman is 25 to 30 feet wide here and averages about three feet deep. However, there are some holes that will flood your waders. The bottom is predominately gravel and sand with some muck. The banks are low, mucky, and brushy, with some open grassland at the riverside cabins. The velocity is moderate, and the river can be waded at normal flows if you keep an eye out for the deep holes. The brushy banks make fly casting somewhat difficult but not impossible, particularly if you have mastered the roll cast. Fishing pressure is usually light.

The water is cooler here in summer than in the North Branch or mainstream, and trout populations are greater. The fall standing crop of brown trout, in weight per unit area, is more than double that of the North Branch, and nearly three times that of the mainstream. There are few brookies in this water. Except for the road right-of-way, this is all private land.

Forks State Forest Campground

GPS N 44° 40.383'
W 85° 24.082'

Just south of the Forks Bridge turn west (right) on Brown Bridge Road and follow the graded road 0.3 mile to Forks State Forest Campground on the south bank of the Boardman River.

This small, rustic facility is extremely popular with fly anglers who use it as a base for fishing the entire Upper Boardman and both branches. The campground was closed and gated in 2007 due to budget cuts and it might be wise to double check its current status on the DNR web site (*www.michigan. gov/dnr*) or by calling the Traverse City DNR office (231-922-5280). If not staying at the campground, the best place to park and access the river is the adjacent canoe launch, which has steps leading down the bank to the river and parking for a handful of cars.

The river frontage at the former campground is still state land, which extends for a quarter mile on both banks upstream and down before you encounter private land. You can access most of that stretch via an angler's trail along the south bank and will find the Boardman to be 25 to 35 feet wide and averaging about two feet deep at mid-channel with a few deep holes. The velocity of the mainstream is faster than on the North and South Branches, but wading is relatively easy at normal flows because of the generally shallower depth. The riverbed is mostly gravel, with some sand and a little muck. The banks are sandy, average about four feet high, and are forested with mixed conifers and hardwoods with considerable brush near the water's edge.

Fishing pressure can be moderate to heavy on the weekends, due to the close proximity to Traverse City, but light the rest of the week. If you fish early and late you'll also avoid paddlers and have the river to yourself.

6 Brown Bridge Road

GPS N 44° 40.171'
W 85° 25.217'

From the Forks Bridge, Brown Bridge Road heads west and parallels the south side of the Boardman River before crossing it on a bridge near Ranch Rudolf. Within a mile of the campground the road swings very close to the river and passes a series of access sites to the water. The first is reached 1.1 miles from the former campground, the second 1.4 miles (N44 40.171' W85 25.467'), and both have "No Camping" signs and parking for three or four vehicles.

The river is 30 to 35 feet wide here and one to four feet deep, with some deeper holes that could cause you problems. The bottom is sand and gravel. The flow is fast, much faster than in the flies-only water of the Au Sable, but the river can be waded with care if you avoid the deeper runs. At high flows this segment of the Boardman is unwadable.

The banks on the south side are five feet high and mostly low and swampy on the north side. At the second access site a set of log steps leads down to the water, but tread softly on the sandy banks at the first site. There are considerable brush and overhanging cedars at the river's edge, backed by white and red pine and mixed hardwoods. It can make casting a challenge at times but provides the cover that large browns love. You'll find the fishing pressure in this area is moderate to heavy on the weekends, light the rest of the time.

A third access site is reached 1.9 miles from the Forks Campground and is an unmarked two-track (N44 29.846' W85 25.376') that winds north from Brown Bridge Road. It reaches the river in 0.4 mile, but you'll want to stop a couple hundred yards short of the river where there is room to park two cars or turn around. Near the river the two-track is extremely rutted and muddy. At this stretch the Boardman is wider than the first two access spots, thirty to forty feet across, and features a series of gravel runs and riffles. As you can imagine, the fishing pressure here is considerably lower than at other nearby sites.

7 Scheck's Place Trail Camp

GPS N 44° 39.120'
W 85° 26.790'

Three miles west of Supply Road, Brown Bridge Road crosses the Board-man River, passes Ranch Rudolf, and then heads for a pair of state forest

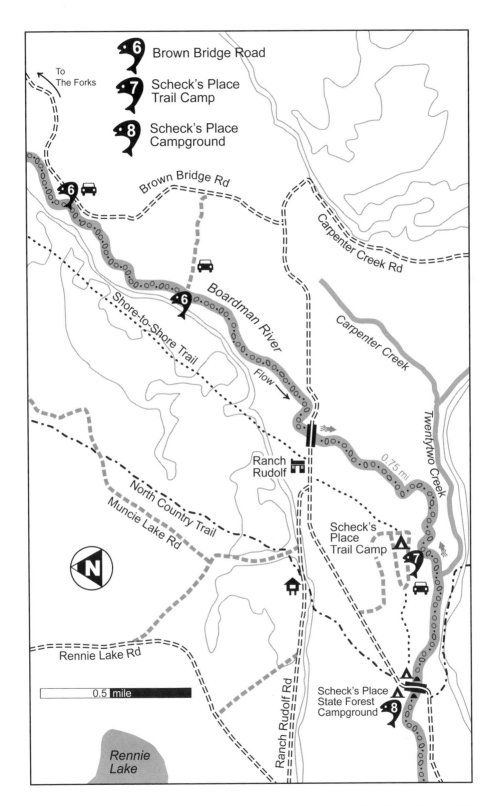

6 Brown Bridge Road

7 Scheck's Place Trail Camp

8 Scheck's Place Campground

To The Forks

Brown Bridge Rd

Carpenter Creek Rd

6

6

Boardman River

Shore-to-Shore Trail

Flow

Carpenter Creek

Twentytwo Creek

0.75 mi

Ranch Rudolf

North Country Trail

Muncie Lake Rd

N

Scheck's Place Trail Camp

7

Rennie Lake Rd

0.5 mile

Ranch Rudolf Rd

Scheck's Place State Forest Campground

8

Rennie Lake

campgrounds on the river that double as access sites for anglers. The first is Scheck's Place Trail Camp, an equestrian campground along the Shore to Shore Trail that stretches 220 miles from Empire on Lake Michigan to Oscoda on Lake Huron. To reach the campground after crossing the Boardman River, remain on Brown Bridge Road when Ranch Rudolf Road veers to the left in a quarter mile. Within a half mile turn south on a two-track signposted "Trail Camp" and follow the road as it veers east into the campground.

Scheck's Place Trail Camp is a sprawling, rustic campground with rows of hitching posts for equestrians riding the Shore-to-Shore Trail. But anglers and other non-equestrians are more than welcome to pitch a tent here. At the very back of the campground loop is a short trail posted as "Horse Watering" that leads to the Boardman River.

The watering trail ends at a fan of pea gravel that allows horses to drink from the Boardman without damage to the riverbed. Here the Boardman is 25 to 30 feet wide and generally two to three feet deep with a scattering of deeper holes. Angler's paths lead off in both directions from the watering hole, and both upstream and down there are some stretches of gravel with riffles along with good cover along the banks for trout.

8 *Scheck's Place Campground*

GPS N 44° 39.144'
W 85° 27.325'

Map: page 243

Another half-mile west on Brown Bridge Road from the Trail Camp, or four miles from Supply Road, is Scheck's Place State Forest Campground. This facility is actually a pair of campgrounds, one on each side of Brown Bridge Road where it crosses the Boardman River a second time. To the south the campground has ten sites and a canoe launch. To the north Scheck's Place features twenty sites, though none directly on the water, and an observation deck overlooking the river. Both provide parking and access to the Boardman for anglers.

The Boardman is forty to fifty feet wide here and averages two feet deep at mid-channel at normal flows. There are some shallow riffles and some deeper holes to watch out for. The streambed is mostly gravel and boulders, with some sand and muck. The velocity of flow is fast, but the stream can be waded with care at normal flows. The banks are mostly low, one foot to five feet high, and very brushy, with some large white pine, smaller red pine, and poplar. The overhanging brush and snags provide good cover for trout.

State land extends from the bridge upstream about a half mile and downstream about one-quarter mile. You can launch a canoe at the campground and fish on down to Brown Bridge Pond, a paddle of two river miles. Locals often come here when the Hex hatch is on.

A fly angler enters the Boardman River from an access site along Brown Bridge Road just downstream from the Forks State Forest Campground.

9 Brown Bridge Pond Dam

GPS N 44° 38.525'
W 85° 27.620'

West of Scheck's Place State Forest Campground, Brown Bridge Road skirts the Brown Bridge Quiet Area. The heart of this 1,300-acre natural area is Brown Bridge Pond, a 191-acre impoundment of the Boardman River. The dam at the west end of the pond is 4.5 miles from Scheck's Place or 11 miles southeast of Traverse City. This area features a boat launch, a large parking area, and vault toilets.

Just a quarter-mile further west on Brown Bridge Road is a public access that was built by Traverse City Light and Power on the Boardman River just below its dam. This stretch marks the beginning of what is commonly referred to as the Middle Boardman River. Here the river is wider and deeper as it swings to the northwest to begin a journey through three more impoundments before finally emptying into Grand Traverse Bay in downtown Traverse City.

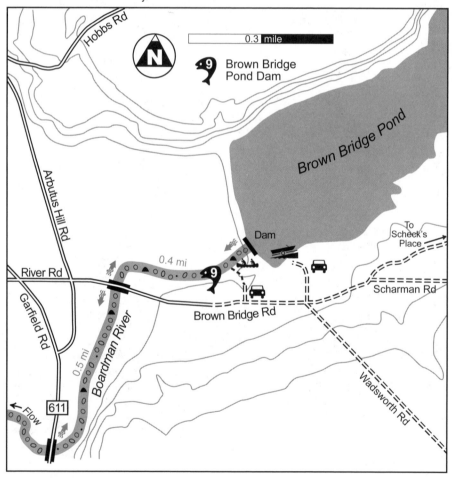

A fly angler casts into the crystal clear waters of the upper Boardman River, a designated Blue Ribbon Trout Stream.

From the parking area of the Traverse City Light and Power access site, a short trail with a series of log steps descends to the canoe landing on the river. The Boardman is 45 to 65 feet wide and one to three feet deep in most places, making it wadable under normal conditions. The bottom is mostly gravel with an occasional boulder splitting the current, while the banks are heavily forested. The width of the river makes casting a fly fairly easy, even for beginners, while the cascading discharge from the nearby dam leads to the feeling that you're fishing in front of a waterfall in the Upper Peninsula.

In the Middle Boardman, the brook trout are replaced by brown trout. The size of the river and the healthy population of crayfish just below the dam can result in good size browns, including trophies that exceed twenty inches. Most anglers fish a half-mile stretch of the river to where Brown Bridge Road crosses the river a third and final time. They'll either return by fishing upstream to the canoe landing or walking to Brown Bridge Road a quarter mile uphill to the access site.

There are other public entry points on the Lower Boardman, the best being the Shumsky Road Access Site on River Road four miles west of the dam at Brown Bridge Pond. But keep in mind that the further downstream you go, the heavier the recreational activity on the water will be, particularly canoers and kayakers.

Art Neumann, one of the original founders of Trout Unlimited and its first executive director, fishes the Rifle River.

Rifle River

Of the 12 classic trout streams covered in this book, the Rifle River stands alone. It's located furthest to the east, the only one not in the trout-rich northwest corner of the Lower Peninsula. It has no waters or tributaries designated as a Blue Ribbon Trout Stream. And it's arguably better known for its sucker runs, thanks to the Omer Sucker Festival that the tiny town stages in April, than it is for trout.

But there are resident browns in the Rifle River. And thanks to numerous habitat projects that have taken place over the years, the trout fishery is good and getting better. The best water for fly anglers is the upper Rifle, which flows through Ogemaw County. From its confluence with Houghton Creek downstream to the village of Selkirk, more than ten river miles, the Rifle is shallow enough for wading and wide enough to cast a fly. Even some of the larger tributaries found here, particularly Houghton Creek, can be explored with a fly rod. This is the section covered in this chapter.

The Rifle begins in the Rifle River Recreation Area, where the cold waters of Gamble, Oyster, and Vaughn Creeks merge to form the mainstream. It then heads south through the recreation area for six river miles, providing anglers easy access either by vehicle or on foot. From the south end of the park at Sage Lake Road (County Road F26) to half a mile north of Selkirk, 5.5 river miles, the Rifle passes through the Au Sable State Forest where two-thirds of the frontage is public land.

Beyond Selkirk, the river is bordered primarily by private land, and for the most part public access is confined to road bridges. At the Old M-70 Bridge on Melita Road north of Sterling, the Rifle swings east, and warm-water species, including northern pike, are encountered. At the hamlet of Omer, the Rifle resumes its southward flow and within six river miles empties into Saginaw Bay.

Overall the Rifle flows 60 river miles from the state recreation area to Lake Huron, drains a 385-square-mile watershed, and, amazingly, is not slowed or altered by a single dam. This explains the Rifle's reputation among anglers for lake-run steelhead, Chinook salmon, and even brown trout, which spawn from October to early November. But the focus of the upper river has always been resident trout and improving the river as a cold-water stream.

When surveyors arrived in the Upper Rifle in 1838 they reported that the uplands were forested in large red and white pine, two to three feet in diameter, alongside hardwoods. Lumbermen arrived in 1885, and within 30 years the area was a logged-out wasteland, burned over by slash fires, depleted of its wildlife by market hunters, and abandoned by farmers after their failed attempts to grow crops.

In the early 1920s most of what is now the recreation area was purchased by Harry M. Jewett, a Detroit-based auto manufacturing pioneer, who had visions of creating a wild game estate modeled after those he had seen in Europe. Jewett built a massive log lodge, which he called "Grousehaven Farms," overlooking Lodge and Grebe Lakes on a narrow ridge that divides the Au Sable and Rifle River valleys. The view, needless to say, was unsurpassed and still is to this day. The location might have been remote but the lodge featured steam heat, electric lights, a two-story living and dining room and a wine cellar. In an early attempt at land and forest management, Jewett released 15,000 ringneck and Mongolian pheasants onto his preserve and built trout-rearing ponds. In 1932 alone, he raised and stocked 100,000 trout fingerlings in Ogemaw County streams.

After Jewett's death in 1933, his family showed little interest in Grousehaven, and the property, some 4,300 acres, was purchased by the Michigan Department of Conservation in 1944. Originally the tract was administered by the Fish Division and used as an experimental fishing site. At that time the source of the Rifle River was Devoe Lake, whose warm water was hampering the trout fishery. In the early 1950s a diversion was dredged around the lake to allow the relatively cold water from Gamble Creek and its tributaries to flow directly into the Rifle.

The Parks Division acquired the area in 1963 and established the Rifle River Recreation Area, but trout restoration work continued. In 1988, a 2,500-foot-long canal was built to reroute Gamble Creek around Mallard Pond, whose temperatures average 75 to 80 degrees. Two years later Trout Unlimited chapters from Saginaw, Midland, and Bay City assisted the DNR in installing a 1,400-foot pipe at the outlet of Devoe Lake. The pipe was designed so that the lake discharge into the Rifle River was cold water from its bottom and no longer the warm surface water. In the early 1990s, the Rifle River Watershed Restoration Committee was formed from conservation groups that included TU chapters and has since raised and spent $1.5 million on streambank erosion control and road-stream crossing improvements.

The soil in the Rifle River basin is not nearly as sandy as the other rivers covered in this book. In the headwaters area there is extensive clay that prevents the snowmelt and rainfall from soaking into the ground. Consequently more of the precipitation runs directly into the river, making the Rifle one of the least stable trout streams in the Lower Peninsula. After heavy rains, even in mid-summer, the river rises quickly and becomes quite cloudy. Wading becomes more difficult then, due to the swifter flow and the murky water that hides the holes that can flood your waders.

The water in the Rifle is hard, moderately alkaline, and generally of suitable quality for trout. Gravel for spawning beds is somewhat sparse in the Rifle River Recreation Area but appears adequate downstream from the park to Selkirk. The population of resident trout in the Rifle, almost exclusively brown trout, is lower than most other streams considered here. Still, the Rifle yields good catches of browns from May through June and often again after

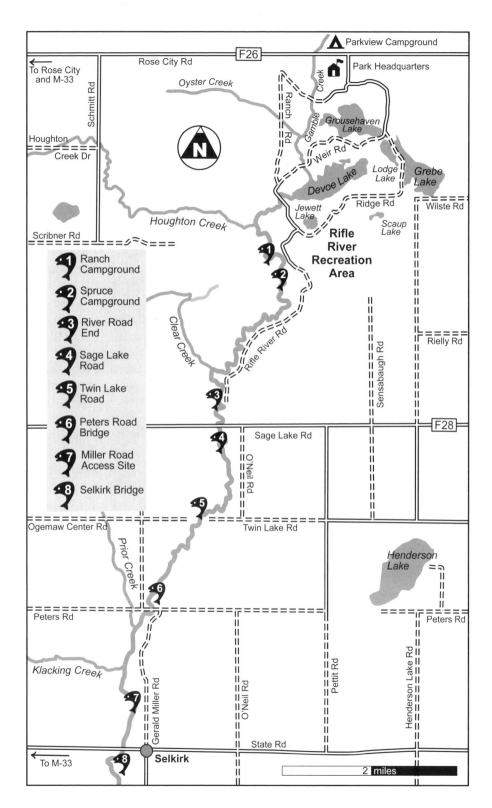

To Rose City
and M-33

F26

Parkview Campground

Park Headquarters

Rose City Rd

Oyster Creek

Schmitt Rd

Ranch Rd

Gamble Creek

Grousehaven Lake

Houghton
Creek Dr

Weir Rd

Lodge Lake

Grebe Lake

Devoe Lake

Jewett Lake

Ridge Rd

Wilste Rd

Houghton Creek

Scaup Lake

Scribner Rd

Rifle River Recreation Area

Clear Creek

Rifle River Rd

Sensabaugh Rd

Rielly Rd

1 Ranch Campground

2 Spruce Campground

3 River Road End

4 Sage Lake Road

5 Twin Lake Road

6 Peters Road Bridge

7 Miller Road Access Site

8 Selkirk Bridge

F28

Sage Lake Rd

O'Neil Rd

Ogemaw Center Rd

Twin Lake Rd

Prior Creek

Henderson Lake

Peters Rd

Peters Rd

Klacking Creek

Gerald Miller Rd

O'Neil Rd

Pettit Rd

Henderson Lake Rd

To M-33

Selkirk

State Rd

2 miles

Labor Day. In mid-summer warmer water temperatures tend to send most of the larger trout up into the feeder creeks.

Some of the tributaries to the upper Rifle also provide good fishing. Houghton, Gamble, and Klacking Creeks have trout populations substantially greater than the mainstream for comparable area. Houghton Creek, the largest of the tributaries, is more than 30 feet wide in places below the junction with Wilkins Creek. Both Houghton and Klacking can be fished beginning with their confluence on the Rifle. Gamble Creek is too narrow and brushy for most fly anglers.

The Rifle supports good hatches of mayflies and caddisflies and in general they occur three to four days earlier than on the Au Sable. In early May anglers will encounter blue-winged olives and Hendricksons followed by sulphurs in early June, brown drakes in late June, and mahogany duns from late June through July. There are sporadic hatches of Hexagenia limbata, but rarely are there enough to stimulate the feeding activity of large browns seen on rivers like the Manistee and the South Branch.

The entire Rifle River is open to all tackle. Within the recreation area, the river is open during the trout season from the last Saturday in April through September. Browns and brook trout must be eight inches to keep, and the daily limit is five fish with no more than three of them 15 inches or longer. From Sage Lake Road to the mouth, the river is open to fishing year-round with the same daily possession as the recreation area but with minimum size of 15 inches for both brook and brown.

You will encounter canoe traffic on the Rifle, particularly downstream from Sage Lake Road, but not nearly the numbers you do on the Au Sable or the Pere Marquette.

Accommodations

Rose City is ideally located to fish the upper Rifle River and has a handful of motels along M-33. Among them is **Scenic Motel** (989-685-2668; *www. scenicmotel.com*; 618 S. Bennett Rd.) with mini-refrigerators and cable TV. For a list of area accommodations call the Rose City–Lupton Area Chamber of Commerce (989-685-2936).

There is a much wider selection of motels, including national chains, in West Branch. **The Tri-Terrace Motel** (989-345-3121; *www.triterracemotel. com*; 2259 S. M-76) is just south of M-55 and has 45 rooms, some with coffeemakers, microwave ovens, and mini-refrigerators. For accommodations in the area contact the Ogemaw County Travel and Visitors Bureau (800-755-9091; *www.visitwestbranch.com*).

Campgrounds: Rifle River Recreation Area has four campgrounds scattered across the park, including two on the river that are described below as access sites: Ranch Campground and Spruce Campground. Both are rustic facilities with vault toilets, hand pumps for water, and fire rings. Grousehaven Lake Campground is a modern facility with 75 sites on the north shore of the lake with hook-ups for recreation vehicles, showers, and heated bathrooms.

A Cabin in the Woods

Within the Rifle River Recreation Area are five snug little cabins, set back in the woods well away from the campgrounds and busy day-use areas of the park. All are available for rent through DNR's central reservation system (800-447-2757; *www.midnrreservations.com/campgrounds*) and four of them are on lakes.

The lone exception is Birch Cabin, which is reached from Ranch Road a quarter mile after crossing the Rifle River near Devoe Lake. The one-room cabin sleeps six in three bunk beds and inside features table and chairs and a propane wall furnace. Outside are a fire ring, standing charcoal grill, picnic table, hand pump for water, and vault toilet.

From Birch Cabin it's a short walk to the Rifle River, where the trout stream is only 15 to 20 feet wide and one to two feet deep over a sand and gravel bottom. The narrow stream with its wooded banks makes for tight casting. But wade less than 0.4 mile downstream and the river opens up where Houghton Creek flows in. Here you can easily spend an afternoon fishing the mainstream or heading upstream into Houghton Creek to cast for browns. When the day is done, you head back upstream to your cabin in the woods, a bargain at $65 a night.

Birch Cabin on the Rifle River in the Rifle River Recreation Area.

Devoe Lake Campground offers 57 rustic sites on the south shore of the lake. A site in any of the campgrounds can be reserved in advance through the DNR's central reservation system (800-447-2757; *www.midnrreservations.com/campgrounds*). For more information on the campgrounds call the park office (989-473-2258).

Just outside of the entrance of Rifle River Recreation Area is Parkview Acres (989-473-3555; 2575 E. Rose City Rd.) with a modern campground, showers, and a convenience store.

Fly Shops and Guides

There is little available in Rose City, but in West Branch you'll find a limited selection of flies and fly fishing equipment at **_J&P Sporting Goods_** (989-345-3744; 3275 West M-76). If coming from the south on I-75, an excellent place to stop for flies is **_Frank's Great Outdoors_** (989-697-5341; _www. franksgreatoutdoors.com_; 1212 M-13), reached by departing at exit 173 and in Linwood heading north on M-13. Not many guides work the Rifle River but one exception is Au Sable Angler (989-826-8500; _www.ausableangler.com_; 479 S. M-33), a fly shop just north of Mio that arranges guided outings.

Several canoe operators service the Rifle River and can arrange fish-and-float trips. In the upper Rifle, located near the entrance to the recreation area, is Big Mike's Canoe Rental (989-473-3444; 2575 E. Rose City Rd.).

Maps of the Rifle

Rose City is the main staging area for fishing the Rifle River and the first three access sites, Ranch Campground, Spruce Campground and River Road, are in the Rifle River Recreation Area. To reach the state park from M-33 in Rose City head east on Rose City Road (County Road F28). In 4.5 miles you'll pass Lupton Road heading north and a quarter mile further is the entrance of the recreation area. A daily vehicle permit or an annual state park pass is required to enter the park.

The other five access sites can be reached by heading south of Rose City on M-33. You can also reach them from West Branch by departing I-75 at exit 215 and heading east on M-55 for five miles and then north on M-33.

1 Ranch Campground

GPS N 44° 23.597'
W 84° 02.277'

From its headwaters at Mallard Pond, the Rifle River flows six miles through the Rifle River Recreation Area, a 4,449-acre state park that offers good access to the trout stream and two nearby campgrounds where you can pitch your tent. Ranch Campground is the first and is reached from the park entrance by heading south for 0.3 mile to Ranch Road. Turn south (right) on Ranch Road and follow it as it swings east and then resumes its southerly direction. You cross the Rifle River near its outlet on Devoe Lake in 2.5 miles and reach the posted entrance to Ranch Campground in 3.2 miles.

Ranch is a rustic campground with a loop of 23 sites in a semi-open grassy area with many of the sites overlooking the river. A two-track leads northwest off the campground loop to arrive quickly at a foot bridge and a canoe launch. At the bridge the Rifle is 25 to 30 feet wide, two to three feet deep, and easily wadable. Bottom material is sand, gravel, and muck, with sand predominating. The banks on the east side are brushy, but the west side is a meadow of sorts, making casting considerably easier despite the narrow width of the stream.

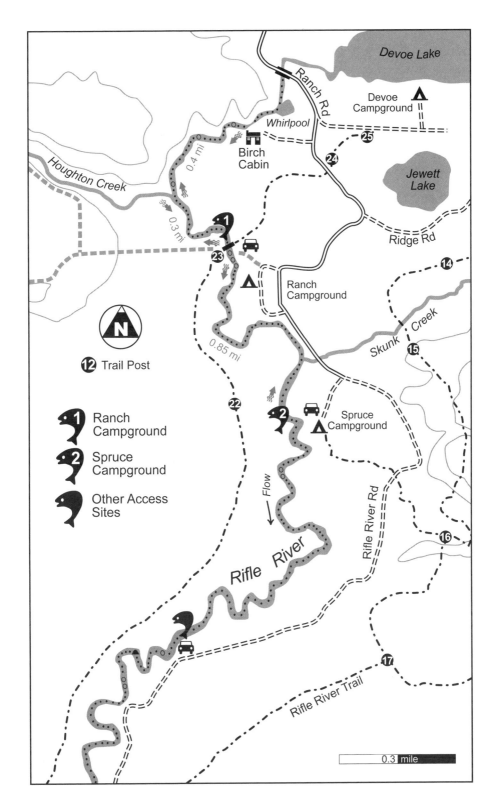

Devoe Lake

Ranch Rd

Whirlpool

Birch
Cabin

Houghton Creek

0.4 mi

0.3 mi

Devoe
Campground

㉕

㉔

Jewett
Lake

Ridge Rd

1

㉓

Ranch
Campground

0.85 mi

⑭

Skunk Creek

⑮

N

㉒

2

Spruce
Campground

Rifle River Rd

⑯

⑫ Trail Post

1 Ranch
Campground

2 Spruce
Campground

Other Access
Sites

Flow

Rifle River

⑰

Rifle River Trail

0.3 mile

Just 0.3 mile upstream is the confluence of Houghton Creek, a major tributary of the Rifle. The stream supports a healthy brown trout fishery and is wide enough for roll casts and at some bends even more. In 1952, a 36.6-inch, 17-pound, five-ounce brown was caught in Houghton Creek that at the time set the state record.

2 Spruce Campground

GPS N 44° 23.184'
     W 84° 02.051'

Map: page 255

The recreation area's second riverside campground is 0.3 mile farther south on Ranch Road. Spruce Campground has 17 rustic sites set back from the river in a much more wooded setting than Ranch. You can park at a log fence perched above the river or just before entering the campground and walk in.

The Rifle River maintains the width, depth, and velocity here as it does upstream at Ranch Campground. The bottom is predominately sand with patches of gravel. It's a mile wade to fish from this campground upstream to the foot bridge at Ranch Campground.

3 River Road End

GPS N 44° 22.020'
     W 84° 02.866'

At the entrance of Spruce Campground, River Road continues in a southerly direction as a narrow, dirt road that plunges into the forest. In 1.2 miles the road swings within sight of the Rifle River, where it is easy to park and enter the river. The Rifle here is still only 25 to 30 feet wide and lined by brushy bankside vegetation that can easily snatch a wayward fly.

Two miles south on River Road is a small pull-off to the west (right), capable of holding two vehicles. The Rifle is 25 to 35 feet wide and one to two feet deep, with a firm bottom of sand and fine gravel. A quarter mile downstream is the confluence of Clear Creek.

River Road ends at a turnaround 2.3 miles from Spruce Campground at the south end of the recreation area. Just before the turnaround, the Rifle River Trail crosses River Road and by heading west on the foot path you'll quickly arrive at post No. 20 and a footbridge. The bridge provides access to the west bank, where the trail heads upriver, reaching post No. 21 at the mouth of Clear Creek in less than half a mile. From the south end of the turnaround, a trail leads 0.4 mile to a gate on Sage Lake Road, providing additional access to the east bank of the river.

The Rifle here is a bit wider, 30 to 40 feet, and still easy to wade with a depth of one to three feet on a sand and gravel bottom. The grassy fields that surround the end of River Road provide excellent hopper fishing in late July and August. To fish from the foot bridge upstream to the pull-off above Clear Creek is a 0.7-mile wade.

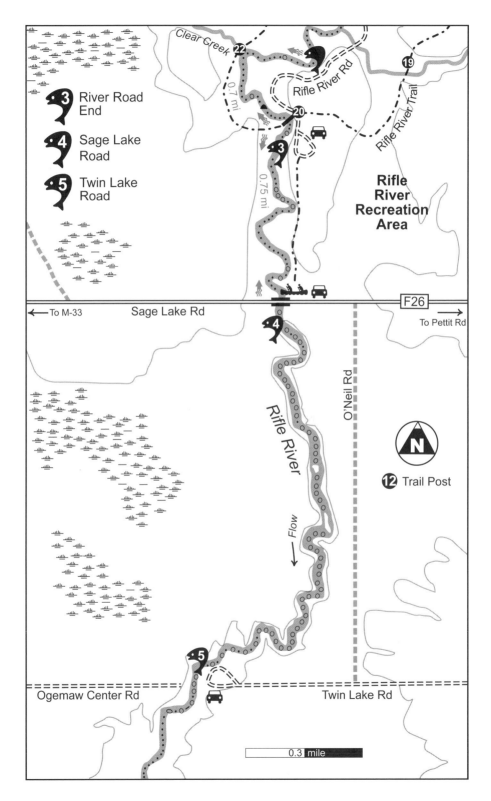

River Road End

Clear Creek

3 River Road
End

4 Sage Lake
Road

5 Twin Lake
Road

22

19

Rifle River Rd

Rifle River Trail

0.7 mi

20

3

0.75 mi

**Rifle
River
Recreation
Area**

F26

← To M-33   Sage Lake Rd   To Pettit Rd →

4

Rifle River

O'Neil Rd

N

12 Trail Post

Flow

5

Ogemaw Center Rd   Twin Lake Rd

0.3 mile

4 Sage Lake Road

GPS N 44° 21.816'
W 84° 02.909'

Map: page 257

Sage Lake Road is the boundary between the Rifle River Recreation Area to the north (upstream) and the Au Sable State Forest to the south and its bridge across the Rifle River is a popular site with both anglers and canoers. From Rose City head south on M-33 for 4.2 miles and then turn east (right) on Sage Lake Road (County Road F26). The bridge is reached in 3.4 miles. On the east side of the bridge is a large parking area with a vault toilet and a canoe launch.

The river here is 40 to 60 feet wide and one to three feet deep, with some deeper holes. The bottom is primarily sand upstream but downstream you'll find stretches of gravel and several gravel riffles. The banks are low and brushy for the most part, but there are some high banks and even open grassy areas that can be fished from. At normal levels the wading is easy and the water is clear. A heavy rain, however, can quickly turn the river cloudy and make wading hazardous.

From the back of the access site a gated trail heads north into the Rifle River Recreation Area. Fishing upstream to the footbridge across the river in the recreation area is a wade of 0.75 mile with half a mile walk back to your vehicle. Downstream from Sage Lake Road the Rifle is open year-round to fishing. Upstream it's open only during the trout season from the last Saturday in April through September. Fishing pressure is moderate here except during the steelhead runs.

5 Twin Lake Road

GPS N 44° 20.982'
W 84° 03.132'

Map: page 257

At one time this was the site of Rifle River State Forest Campground. The campground is long gone but the grassy fields remain and, as evident by old campfire pits, are still a favorite place to pitch a tent. Twin Lake Road is a mile south of the access site on Sage Lake Road. From the bridge continue east on Sage Lake Road for 1.2 miles, passing up rutted O'Neil Road along the way, and turn south (right) on Pettit Road. Follow the paved road for a mile and then turn west (right) on Twin Lake Road. Within 1.4 miles you reach a clearing at the end of Twin Lake Road with the Rifle River nearby.

The river is about 40 feet wide here and two to three feet deep, with some holes that will cause you problems. The river bottom is sand and gravel with patches of clay. Banks are low and brushy, which makes this stretch better suited for spin or bait anglers than fly fishers. But on both sides of the river there are grassy openings that allow for easier casting. Wading is fairly easy at low to normal flows. At high flows, wading may be impossible.

There are some large fish in the deeper holes in this part of the river.

Learning to Avoid a Pig's Tail

One of the most disheartening moments for a fly angler is to pull up his line and where the hook is supposed to be is a pig's tail: monofilament with a wiggly end. The trout was there, the cast good, but the knot gave out and resulted in a lost opportunity to catch a fish.

In fly fishing the importance of the right knot being tied properly can not be stressed enough. To tie the backing to a reel, fly anglers use an **arbor knot**. To attach the fly line to the backing they use what is often referred to as a **nail knot** or a version called a **nail-less nail knot**. The next step is to tie a leader to the fly line and for that anglers will use a nail knot or **double surgeon's knot**. To tie tippet to a leader they use a **blood knot** and, finally, to tie the tippet to the hook they turn to an **improved clinch knot**.

The easiest way to learn how to tie any of these knots is through the website Animated Knots By Grog (*www.animatedknots.com*). From the home page click on "Fishing" and you will be presented a choice of 14 knots that anglers often utilize. Click on a knot and an animated presentation will show you how to tie it with one step merging slowly into the next. You can also stop the presentation at any particular step until you've mastered it. There are also tying tips and notes on when to use a particular knot and the advantages of it.

At times other than the steelhead runs, you will usually find few other fishermen on the river here.

6 *Peters Road Bridge*

GPS N 44° 20.085'
W 84° 03.841'

Map: page 261

This site is a beautiful stretch of water wide enough for easy casting. From Rose City head south on M-33 for 6.3 miles and then east (left) on Peters Road to reach the bridge in three miles. The state land is located right at the bridge, while most of the frontage is private. There is room to park five or six cars west of the bridge.

At Peters Road Bridge the Rifle River is 40 to 50 feet wide and one to three feet deep with a bottom of mostly gravel and boulders. The flow is swift and the rocks can be slippery, but the river can be waded at normal levels. Upstream there are some deep holes to stay clear of; downstream, where there are gravel riffles, the wading is easier. The banks are low and mucky, lined with brush and hardwood.

In 2008 the Lake Superior State University Aquatic Research Laboratory shocked this stretch looking for Chinook fry. They found few. They did find an abundance of brown trout, some exceeding 20 inches in length.

Gerald Miller Road

GPS N 44° 19.275'
W 84° 03.995'

The canoe launch at the Gerald Miller Road Access Site can be a quiet place in the middle of the week while providing you with a fine stretch of water to explore. From Rose City head south on M-33 for 7.8 miles and then turn east (left) on State Road (County Road F24) to reach Selkirk Bridge in 2.7 miles. A quarter mile east of the bridge, in the village of Selkirk, turn north (left) on Gerald Miller Road. Within half a mile you arrive at a two-track, posted with a DNR canoe launch sign, that heads west (left). You can also pick up State Road in West Branch and follow it east for nine miles to reach Gerald Miller Road.

The launch has parking for a dozen or more vehicles along with a vault toilet and canoe ramp. A short trail leads to the river, where it is 40 to 60 feet wide and two to four feet deep with a bottom of gravel and boulders. Casting is easy, but use caution wading here. There are short angler trails extending upstream and downstream. By wading 0.6 mile upstream you reach the confluence of Klacking Creek, an extremely clear stream with a good population of brown trout, many exceeding 15 inches in length. The creek is narrow and brushy in most places but wide enough at its mouth to cast a fly or at the very least flick one into promising holes.

Selkirk Bridge

GPS N 44° 18.785'
W 84° 04.218'

This bridge near the village of Selkirk is generally considered the last bit of water for wading anglers. To reach the bridge from Rose City, head south on M-33 for 7.8 miles and then turn east (left) on State Road (County Road F24) for 2.7 miles. From West Branch the bridge is 8.7 miles east on State Road.

This is all private land along the river except for the road right-of-way, and parking is not permitted near the bridge. Just 50 yards east of the bridge is a small parking area on the south side of the road capable of holding two or three vehicles. A short distance to the west on State Road is Churchill Township Hall, with additional parking.

The Rifle is 60 feet wide here and generally less than four feet deep, with some deeper holes. The river bottom is gravel and boulders with a bit of sand. The river can be waded at normal flows, but wading is never easy. The flow is swift, and the cobbles and boulders do not provide a stable footing. Felt-soled boots would be helpful in this water as would a walking staff. Needless to say, at high flows the river here is unwadable. Banks are generally low and mucky. Trout cover is sparse. Fishing pressure may be heavy during steelhead runs, but it usually is light the rest of the season.

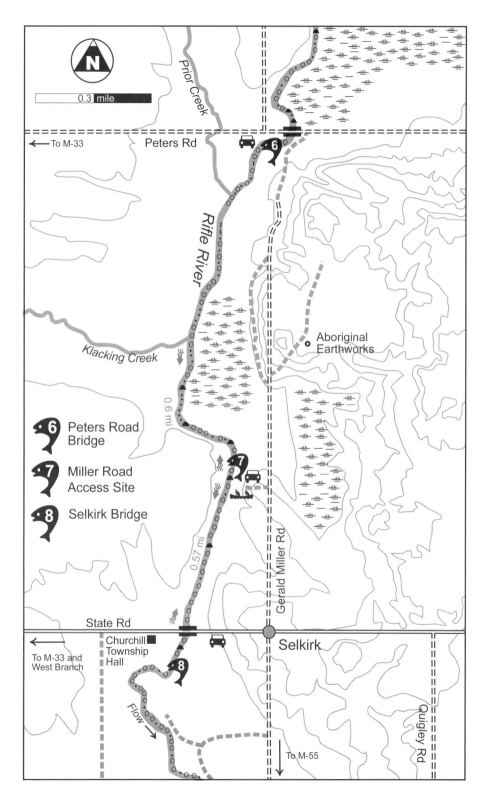

N

0.3 mile

Prior Creek

← To M-33

Peters Rd

6

Rifle River

Klacking Creek

0.6 mi

Aboriginal Earthworks

6 Peters Road
Bridge

7 Miller Road
Access Site

8 Selkirk Bridge

7

0.57 mi

Gerald Miller Rd

State Rd

Churchill
Township
Hall

8

Selkirk

←
To M-33 and
West Branch

Flow

To M-55

Quigley Rd

Michigan Angler: Art Neumann

Art Neumann, one of the original founders of Trout Unlimited, was rambling down the road near Selkirk when he suddenly applied the brakes and did a double take at the side of the road. "Good lord, look at that," Neumann said. I looked, but all I saw was an open gate.

But what is simply an open gate to one person is an invitation to Neumann. "That's my old access," he said. "I'm going in and play ambassador."

There are those who say nobody knows Michigan trout streams better than this Saginaw angler, and there is probably no stretch of water Neumann loves more dearly than the Rifle River. He may be able to catch more trout in the Holy Water of the Au Sable or bigger trout in its South Branch, but it's the Rifle where Neumann as a youth mastered the rudiments of fly fishing and eventually came to appreciate everything that a trout symbolizes.

Of all the holes and pools within this river, this is the one stretch Neumann liked to fish most. And he did until he lost his access to the water when the cottage owners he knew either died or moved away. But today the gate was open.

Neumann turned down the dusty dirt road and stopped at the first cottage. "There is a good pool just downstream from here," he said, but nobody was home. So he drove to the next one, and I watched him enter a beautiful log cabin where he played ambassador for at least ten minutes. I wasn't inside, but I could just hear Neumann tell the owners about the days when the Rifle was a top trout stream, or how Trout Unlimited was formed, or how he served as TU's first executive director. And when he finally stepped outside and had a little spring in his step, I knew this master fly angler had received what he so dearly possessed in the past.

Permission to fish.

"Were they fly anglers?" I asked.

"Nah, they just dangle a worm once in a while," said Neumann. "But when I get home I'll send them some flies and an instruction book. That'll get 'em started."

We drove down to a spot on the river, stepped out of the car, and walked past the trunk filled with our gear. Neumann, who had fished this river since the 1930s, first just wanted to see the Rifle flow through his favorite stretch. It was a thing of beauty, then and now. "It's pretty clear," said Neumann as we stood on the bank watching a few trout rise upstream. "I caught a 20-inch brown in a pool around that bend once."

When Neumann finally did open his trunk, I discovered I'd grabbed the wrong metal tube at home and now had my eight-weight rod when what I needed was a five-weight. It might have been a problem any other time, but not with Neumann.

Always somebody who was dabbling in rod refinishing, in 1948

Neumann converted his garage in Saginaw into the Wanigas Rod Company, where he built fiberglass fly rods and sold only the flies and equipment you truly needed to catch a trout in Michigan. For the next 42 years that shop, which had enough room inside for only three customers, two if they walked in wearing vests and waders, was the pulpit from which Neumann preached what was then a revolutionary concept: catch and release. You catch a trout, you put it back. The trout is then there to catch again. Neumann liked that concept, preserving the resource for what he really enjoyed: catching trout on a fly.

Art Neumann

What I discovered that night on the Rifle was when your fishing partner is a rod builder, you'll never lack a rod. Neumann unzipped a black case that held almost a dozen of them and selected one for me, a fiberglass rod he had built years ago. "I'm going to spoil you with this one," he said.

Next he gave me a leader, a Neumann 60-20-20, after he saw the knotless leader tied to my line and lectured me on the benefits of tying your own. And then just before we split, with him heading downstream to try and find that 20-inch brown again and me upstream, he gave me a few flies. "Not much is hatching right now," he said. "Try the pale blue dun."

I did, and the first fish I caught was so small I couldn't tell what it was. But half an hour later I floated that fly over a dissipating ring, and the fish returned to take it. It jumped three times before I gently lifted the seven-inch brown trout out of the water.

It wasn't another 20 minutes later when the current took that fly, swept it along the bank, and gave me my hardest strike of the evening, almost catching me off guard. I kept the tip up, working the fish away from the brush along the shore and into the middle of the river.

The trout never jumped, but there was little question it was large. When it finally tired and came to the surface I saw the largest brown I had ever caught on a fly in Michigan in the short time I had been fly fishing. It was 14 inches long with a band of reddish dots along the side. I marveled at the fact that I caught it in a river where I never expected to catch such fish.

Then again maybe I didn't catch it. I was using an Art Neumann rod with a leader he tied and flies he selected. And I was fishing in his river. Knowing all this, I gently took the hook out and watched the trout return to the depths from which it came.

It was, after all, Art's fish.

Two anglers pause to share advice while fishing the Pere Marquette River near Claybanks Access Site.

Pere Marquette River

Unencumbered by dams, wild and free, the Pere Marquette is a world-class steelhead and salmon river and one of the state's most storied trout streams. Only the Au Sable is more revered by fly anglers. Part of it is heritage: the river was the site of the first planting of brown trout in North America. Part of it is natural. The Pere Marquette is one of Michigan's few large rivers free of impoundments, from the headwaters of its tributaries all the way to its end at Lake Michigan. So beautiful and unspoiled, the Pere Marquette has been classified as a National Scenic River by the U.S. Forest Service and Wild Scenic by the state.

The Pere Marquette and its four main tributaries—the Baldwin River, the Middle Branch, the Little South Branch and the Big South Branch—drain a 755-square-mile watershed spread over four counties: Lake, Newaygo, Oceana, and Mason. They provide 138 miles of Michigan's finest trout water with 66.5 miles of it designated as Blue Ribbon Trout Streams.

From its headwaters southwest of the village of Chase, the Pere Marquette rises in the morainal hills that form the eastern boundary of the drainage basin. The river begins as the Middle Branch and flows westward for 17 miles across a broad plain of sand and gravel. The mainstream is formed when the Middle Branch merges with the Little South Branch a mile upstream of the M-37 Bridge. Three miles downstream from the bridge the Baldwin River enters to give the Pere Marquette size and depth. This stretch, from M-37 eight miles downstream to Gleason's Landing, is the river's cherished flies-only segment that in 2000 became a year-round, catch-and-release fishery.

Pere Marquette's main tributary, the Big South Branch, merges with the main stream 1.3 miles before Custer Road Bridge or 41 miles from M-37. The river crosses another belt of moraine between Custer and Scottville and then winds through a sandy lake plain until it reaches Lake Michigan at Ludington, 67 miles from where the Middle and Little South Branches converge. But it's further upstream, in the broad plain of sand and gravel between the headwaters and Custer, where groundwater constantly seeps into the Pere Marquette to maintain cool temperatures during even the hottest summer. This is what makes the "PM" such a great trout stream: a steady flow of cold water uninhibited by dams. If only we had more such rivers.

Above the hamlet of Nirvana, the Middle Branch is a small stream best suited for bait fishing. Five miles downstream at Broadway Road, just south of Idlewild, the Middle Branch is fishable with a fly rod, though casting can be challenging. Here the Pere Marquette begins its Blue Ribbon Trout Stream designation that extends for 39 miles until the main stream flows under Indian Bridge near Custer. This chapter focuses on the Pere Marquette from near the confluence of the Middle and Little South Branches to just west of Lower Branch Bridge, with the heart of the coverage devoted to the flies-only, catch-and-release section. Naturally. Downstream from Gleason's Landing the Pere Marquette gains considerably more volume, velocity, and depth, usually three to six feet, making wading more difficult and even treacherous at times. Although many anglers float fish this section of river, you can still wade certain sections if you are conscious of the water levels before entering the river and then keep a watchful eye out for holes and deep bends once you do.

The Pere Marquette is named after Father Jacques Marquette, a Jesuit missionary who established Sault Ste. Marie and St. Ignace and then accompanied French-Canadian explorer Louis Jolliet in discovering the upper Mississippi River watershed. During that exploratory trip Marquette fell ill in 1675 with a bout of dysentery and tried to return to St Ignace. He never made it; instead he died and was buried at the mouth of the river that now bears his name.

At that time only grayling flourished in the Pere Marquette, but intense logging in the mid-1800s took its toll. Not only was the entire watershed extensively logged but the river was dredged from Pere Marquette Lake upstream to Walhalla to permit the passage of massive log drives. By the turn of the century the grayling had disappeared from the Pere Marquette as in most other Michigan streams.

The Pere Marquette was first stocked in 1882 with rainbow trout from the state of Washington. But by then Fred Mather, superintendent of the Cold Springs Harbor Federal Fish Hatchery at Long Island, New York, had already met Baron Friedrich Von Behr, the president of the German Fishing Society, at the 1880 International Fisheries Exposition in Berlin. Von Behr introduced Mather to the brown trout and in 1883 Mather arranged for brown trout eggs to be shipped to the United States. The eggs were distributed to various hatcheries, including the U.S. Fish Commission Hatchery in Northville. On April 11, 1884, 4,900 fry raised from those eggs were planted in the Pere Marquette, making the river the first in the country to be stocked with brown trout.

The species thrived to help heal a watershed that loggers had left war-torn just a decade before, and by the 1920s the Pere Marquette had a reputation as a world-class brown trout fishery. Banking on that reputation was the Pere Marquette Railroad, which built a clubhouse on the river three miles south of Baldwin; soon other prestigious fishing clubs appeared in the flies-only segment. That includes a wealthy contingent of Flint-area anglers who in 1916 established the Flint Rainbow Club, a private fishing club that is still in existence today.

When the lamprey eel was brought under control in the 1960s and salmon were introduced in the Great Lakes to control the alewives, anadromous fish began to spawn in the Pere Marquette and have a major impact on the

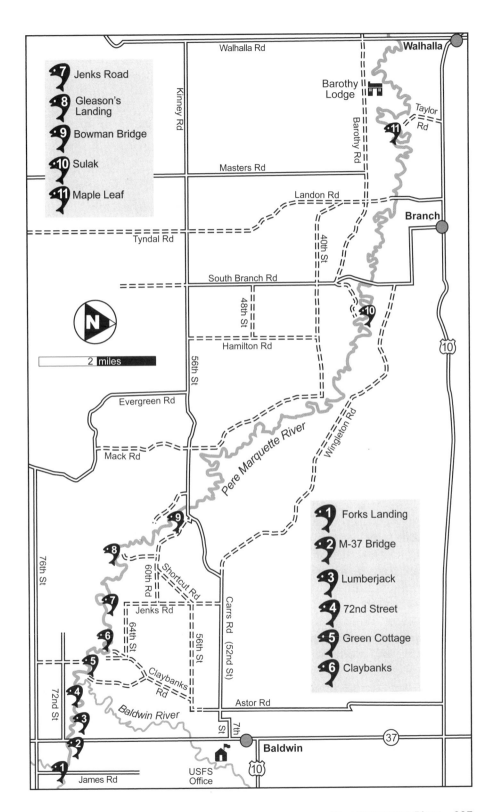

Jenks Road
Gleason's Landing
Bowman Bridge
Sulak
Maple Leaf

Walhalla Rd
Walhalla
Barothy Lodge
Taylor Rd
Kinney Rd
Barothy Rd
Masters Rd
Landon Rd
Branch
40th St
Tyndal Rd
South Branch Rd
48th St
Hamilton Rd
Wingleton Rd
Evergreen Rd
56th St
Mack Rd
Pere Marquette River

Forks Landing
M-37 Bridge
Lumberjack
72nd Street
Green Cottage
Claybanks

76th St
60th Rd
Shortcut Rd
Jenks Rd
Carrs Rd (52nd St)
64th St
56th St
Claybanks Rd
Astor Rd
72nd St
Baldwin River
St
7th St
Baldwin
James Rd
USFS Office
10
37

N
2 miles

river to this day. Chinook salmon enter the river in mid-August with the run peaking at the end of September and fishing remaining good through October. Fall-run steelhead follow the salmon into the river to feed on eggs and stage a spring spawning run of their own from the third week of March through April. During these periods the Pere Marquette attracts large numbers of anglers, and at times combat fishing—anglers lining up elbow to elbow in the river—takes place at popular access sites.

Since the 1980s, the Pere Marquette's brown trout fishery has been overshadowed by its steelhead and salmon runs, and not every angler is pleased with that. Many believe the competition of the salmon for spawning beds caused a decline in the brown trout fishery. Others contend that steelhead have an even greater effect on the browns. Immature steelhead live in the river year round until they grow large enough to migrate to Lake Michigan as seven-inch smolts, and the Pere Marquette can support only so many trout, whether they are browns or rainbows. In recent years conservation groups, most notably the Pere Marquette Watershed Council (*www.peremarquette.org*), have worked tirelessly to improve river habitat prompted in part by a desire to see the brown trout fishery restored to its former glory. It's debatable if that will ever happen.

Regardless, the Pere Marquette River is still a fine stream for resident browns, even if the majority of angler interest is focused on the anadromous species of steelhead and salmon. This is particularly true for the flies-only section that offers a diversity of hatches, classic riffle-pool-run waters, easy wading, and more than enough room to cast. From May to September the number of anglers on the river here also pales compared to what takes place in April and October. There are canoers in July and August, but their numbers are restricted by the U.S. Forest Service through a permit system. Nor are they allowed to put in before 9 a.m., and they must be off the river by 6 p.m.

Although the Pere Marquette is a relatively stable stream, it rises and falls three to four feet in a normal year. Because much of the river is only marginally wadable at low flows, high water on the Pere Marquette makes most of the river unwadable. The velocity of flow on the Pere Marquette ranges from less than one foot per second in the pools to more than five feet per second at Rainbow Rapids. It is the velocity as well as the depth that makes much of the river unwadable.

The quality of water in the Pere Marquette is excellent for trout. The water is hard, and moderately alkaline, and its temperature rarely goes much above 70 degrees F, even on the hottest summer days. The extensive gravel spawning beds in the upper river also contribute to the Pere Marquette's status as ideal trout habitat.

Second only to the Au Sable River's Holy Water, the aquatic and terrestrial insect life of the Pere Marquette is astonishingly rich and diverse. The pools, riffles, and silt-ridden eddies provide the necessary habitat for free-swimming and clinging mayflies and stoneflies as well as caddis and the

Floating the Pere Marquette

The Pere Marquette lends itself well to a float-and-fish trip in the summer. The river can be paddled from the Forks Landing just a mile upstream from the M-37 Bridge to Pere Marquette Lake south of Ludington. Most anglers, however, concentrate on the stretch to Indian Bridge and in particular the flies-only section between M-37 and Gleason's Landing.

Gently floating along the Pere Marquette River.

From May 15 to September 10, a watercraft permit from the U.S. Forest Service is required to paddle the river from Forks Landing to Custer Road Bridge. Permits are $2 per canoe per day, and you can reserve them beginning Jan. 1 of that year by calling the Baldwin Ranger Station (231-745-4631). You also need a vehicle pass if you leave a car at an access site. If you rent a canoe from a local livery, the watercraft permit is included in the rental fee.

Liveries that service the Pere Marquette include Baldwin Canoe (231-745-4669, 800-272-3642; *www.baldwincanoe.com*; 9117 S. M-37) and Ivan's Campground and Canoe Rental (231-745-3361, 231-745-9345; *www.ivanscanoe.com*; 7332 S. M-37) in Baldwin and River Run Canoe Livery (231-757-2266, 231-757-2429; *www.riverruncanoerental.com*; 600 S. Main St.) in Scottville.

The following are Pere Marquette float times. Keep in mind they don't include breaks to fish a run:

From – To	Hours/Minutes	Miles
Forks – M-37	0:15	0.7
M-37 – Green Cottage	1:30	3.7
Green Cottage – Gleason's	1:30	4.7
Gleason's – Bowman	1:00	2.6
Bowman – Rainbow Rapids	2:00	7.3
Rainbow Rapids – Sulak	1:15	3.1
Sulak – Upper Branch	0:45	2.7
Upper Branch – Elk	0:10	0.5
Elk – Lower Branch	1:05	2.6
Lower Branch – Log Mark	1:10	2.7
Log Mark – Walhalla	1:50	4.8
Walhalla – Indian Bridge	3:00	5.5
Indian Bridge – Custer	2:00	2.4

large, burrowing drakes. The first mayfly of prominence is the Hendrickson, both dark and light, first appearing in late April and hatching through May, usually from noon to 4 p.m. Also appearing simultaneously are the slate-winged mahogany and the blue-winged olive, the river's longest hatch, beginning in early May and lasting well into August.

Even more spectacular is the emergence of the gray drake from the third week of May to the third week of June and to a lesser degree the brown drake from mid- to late June. Gray drakes will hatch sporadically throughout the day, and then at dusk the spinner fall occurs. It's a phenomenal sight when black clouds of gray drake spinners appear above the riffles and then fall to blanket the river. At such times trout rise to the surface and feed with reckless abandon on the drakes.

By mid-June, the Pere Marquette offers the opportunity at times to combine an evening of fishing gray drake spinners and then staying out on the river in hopes of a Hex hatch. The strongest hatches of the Hexagenia limbata are found in the lower Pere Marquette, with the giant mayfly first appearing in the second week of June with hatching lasting well into July. Late summer fishing with dry flies is usually a mix of casting minute Tricos in the morning and tossing grasshoppers at clay banks in the afternoon.

Accommodations

Baldwin is ideally located in the heart of Pere Marquette country and features numerous motels, lodges, and private campgrounds. Many if not most offer guide service or vehicle drop-offs for river floats. An extensive list of area lodging can be obtained from the Lake County Chamber of Commerce (231-745-4331, 800-245-3240; *www.lakecountymichigan.com*), which has a visitor's center on M-37 in Baldwin.

On the banks of the Pere Marquette, adjacent to the M-37 Bridge Access Site, is *Red Moose Lodge* (231-745-6667, 888-939-6667; *www.redmooselodge. com*; 8982 S. M-37), with seven motel rooms and a cabin available a mile away on the Little South Branch. Rooms include coffeemaker, continental breakfast, and wader hangers. Practically across the street is *Pere Marquette River Lodge* (231-745-3972; *www.pmlodge.com*; 8841 S. M-37) with ten rooms in the lodge and five cabins, all within walking distance of the flies-only section of the river, as well as dining facilities and a fully stocked fly shop.

Other accommodations include *Baldwin Creek Lodge* (231-745-4401; *baldwincreeklodge.com*; 7038 S. M-37) overlooking the Baldwin River with very affordable motel rooms and cabins as well as a rental cabin on the Pere Marquette. Three miles north of Baldwin is *Cloud 9* (231-745-3070; 3360 S. M-37) with modern cabins, guiding service, and fly-fishing classes. Finally, one of the great fishing lodges in Michigan is on the Pere Marquette, southwest of Walhalla: *Barothy Lodge* (231-898-2340; *www.barothylodge. com*; 7478 Barothy Rd.) with nine elegant log cabins.

Campgrounds: Within our coverage of the Pere Marquette are four

A pair of anglers begin their day in the flies-only section of the Pere Marquette, one of the few large rivers in Michigan free of impoundments and dams.

campgrounds near the river, all maintained by the U.S. Forest Service and described fully as access sites below. The first two are along the flies-only segment of the Pere Marquette. At Claybanks there are nine numbered sites split between Forest Road 6222 and Claybanks Road (Jigger Trail). Amenities include vault toilets but not drinking water, and it's a 10-minute walk to the river. The flies-only stretch ends at Gleason's Landing, a walk-in campground with eight sites overlooking the Pere Marquette, vault toilets, and drinking water.

The largest campground is Bowman Bridge four miles west of Baldwin. The campground features 16 paved sites, four walk-in sites for tent campers, and four group sites as well as vault toilets and drinking water. Bowman Bridge is an extremely popular campground during the summer for both families and paddlers. At the Sulak Access Site are 11 sites within walking distance of the river and vault toilets but no drinking water.

Other rustic campgrounds located nearby include Leverentz Lakes State Forest Campground with 18 sites two miles east of Baldwin and just north of US-10 on Mud Trail. Two miles west of Branch on US-10 is Timber Creek National Forest Campground with nine sites overlooking its namesake stream. Private campgrounds in Baldwin can provide modern sites with hook-ups for RVs. *Pere Marquette Campground* (231-898-3511; *www.pmcampground.com*; 11713 W. 40th St.) also has full-service sites and is three miles south of Branch via South Branch Road and only 1.5 miles from the Sulak Access Site.

Fly Shops and Guides

Baldwin is blessed with several quality fly shops that can set you up with a guided trip or sell you the patterns that will make trout rise. *Pere Marquette River Lodge* (231-745-3972; *www.pmlodge.com*; 8841 S. M-37) is an Orvis dealer offering guided fishing trips, car spotting service, wader rental, and accurate daily river reports. The *Baldwin Bait & Trackle* (BBT) (231-745-3529, 877-422-5394; *www.fishbaldwin.com*; 9331 S. M-37) also arranges guide service both half days and full days. Also offering flies and equipment in Baldwin is *Ed's Sport Shop* (231-745-4974, 231-745-2696; *www.edsports.com*; 712 Michigan Ave.), a venerable outdoor store that has been selling flies from the same location since 1945.

As well as the above shops, *Baldwin Creek Lodge* (231-745-4401; *baldwincreeklodge.com*; 7038 S. M-37) and *Red Moose Lodge* (231-745-6667, 888-939-6667; *www.redmooselodge.com*; 8982 S. M-37) arrange guide service on the Pere Marquette. Other guides that work the PM include *Marsh Ridge River Guide Service* (231-920-7527; *www.marshguide.com*), *West Michigan Fly Fishing Ventures* (616-656-4172, 616-560-3195; *www.westmichiganflyfishing.com*) and *Sprey Rod Flyfishing Outfitter* (231-757-3411; *www.spreyrodoutfitters.com*). Most guides utilize a driftboat and charge $325 to $350 for an eight- to ten-hour trip.

Maps of the Pere Marquette

Since most of the roads in the area run north–south or east–west along section lines, it is easy to find your way to access sites or one of the five bridges that cross the Pere Marquette between Baldwin and Walhalla.

Baldwin is the main staging area for the upper Pere Marquette. The first five access points, Forks Landing, M-37 Bridge, Lumberjack, 72nd Street, and Green Cottage, are reached by heading three miles south of Baldwin on M-37. The next four, Claybanks, Jenks Road, Gleason's Landing, and Bowman Bridge, are reached from M-37 by heading west in Baldwin on 7th Street for five blocks, then south (left) on Cherry Street briefly, and finally west (right) on 52nd Street (also known as Carrs Road).

The final two, Sulak and Maple Leaf, are easily reached from the village of Branch, located on US-10 almost ten miles west of M-37.

Forks Landing

GPS N 43° 51.188'
W 85° 50.486'

Map: page 275

The Forks, where the Middle Branch and the South Branch converge to form the main stream, is upstream from the flies-only section of the Pere Marquette but still offers the width and depths that make it inviting to wading anglers. To reach Forks Landing, a state boat launch near the confluence, head south of Baldwin on M-37 for 3.2 miles. Half a mile after crossing the Pere Marquette turn east (left) on 76th Street, and within half a mile turn north (left) on James Road. Within a quarter mile you reach Forks Landing that is well posted.

Forks Landing is designed primarily for canoes and kayaks, and its large parking lot, boat racks, and vault toilets are indicative of its popularity among area liveries as a staging area for a Pere Marquette float. The river is about 35 feet wide here and two to three feet deep, with some deeper holes. It is shallow enough for wading at normal flows and open enough for fly fishing. The bottom is mostly gravel, with some sand. The banks are low and sandy, brushy in places, and partly forested with hardwoods and conifers.

The canoe launch is on the South Branch, 0.4 mile upstream from the actual confluence. You can wade to where the mainstream begins and then depart at James Road Bridge over the Middle Branch and walk the quarter mile back to Forks Landing. James Road also skirts the banks of the South Branch in several places on the way to the bridge for additional access. Upstream from the canoe launch it is a 0.6-mile wade before you reach 76th Street Bridge, where there is space for a vehicle or two. The South Branch here is 30 feet wide with a nice combination of runs and riffled water. During the summer fishing pressure on the stream is light to moderate but on the weekends canoe activity can be intense.

2 M-37 Bridge
GPS N 43° 51.432'
W 85° 51.016'

M-37 Bridge marks the beginning of the flies-only water on the Pere Marquette, which extends eight river miles downstream to Gleason's Landing. This stretch is no kill, catch and release, and open to artificial flies only. A boat launch is located on the south bank, 2.7 miles south of Baldwin. It is tucked behind the Red Moose Lodge, but the access road is signposted along M-37.

The state boat launch is a large public access site just upstream from the M-37 Bridge with a ramp, paved parking area for 25 vehicles, and vault toilets. This site is popular not only with canoers but also guides and anglers launching driftboats for a float through the flies-only stretch of the river. The river is 60 feet wide and two to four feet deep, with some deeper holes. The bottom material is gravel and sand with a few boulders. Downstream from the bridge the north bank is high and sandy. Upstream from the bridge standard regulations apply and the banks are low and lined with brush and hardwoods.

In either direction are classic riffles and pools with deep holes at the bends and log structures hiding impressive browns. In early spring spawning steelhead are scattered across the gravel or hiding in pools at the end of the riffles. This segment of the Pere Marquette can be waded with care at normal flows and is wide enough for easy fly casting. Needless to say, fishing pressure is heavy during the spring and fall spawning runs. Except for the public access site, this is all private land.

3 Lumberjack
GPS N 43° 51.445'
W 85° 51.684'

Three access sites on the flies-only stretch of the Pere Marquette are reached from 72nd Street and all are excellent destinations for the wading angler. The first is this somewhat obscure walk-in site known as Lumberjack. From M-37 head west on 72nd Street for a half mile and look for the dirt road that heads north just past Flint Rainbow Club. It's unposted with the exception of a "Dead End" sign. Park on the shoulder of 72nd Street where there is room for two or three vehicles on the north side.

It's a 50-yard walk to a trail and a "Pere Marquette Quality Fishing" sign at the end of the dirt road. The trail is a former railroad bed that gently descends a hundred yards to the mainstream at a spot where a fallen tree lies across the river with most of it under the current. The width is 60 feet and the depth two to four feet, making it ideal for wading under normal conditions. The bottom is a mix of sand and gravel.

As evident by the proliferation of "No Trespassing" signs, all the land around the access site is privately owned. Wade upstream and you'll reach

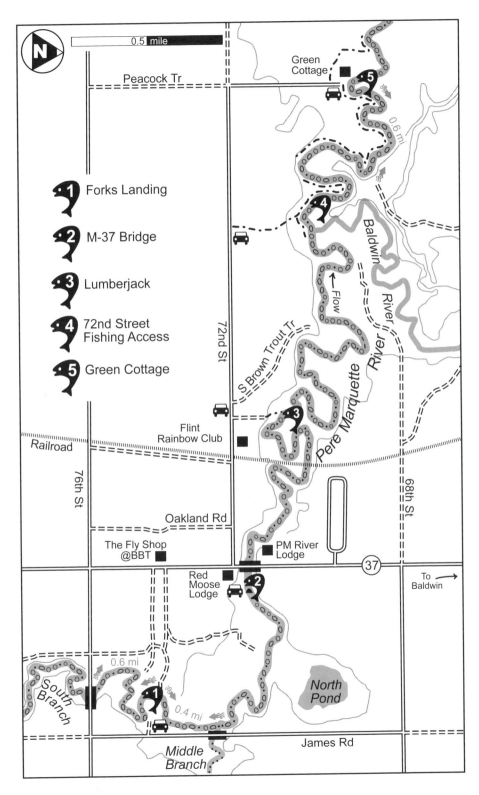

0.5 mile

Peacock Tr

Green
Cottage

5 0.6 mi

1 Forks Landing

2 M-37 Bridge

3 Lumberjack

4 72nd Street
Fishing Access

5 Green Cottage

72nd St

4

Baldwin River

Flow

S Brown Trout Tr

Pere Marquette River

3

Flint
Rainbow Club

68th St

Railroad

76th St

Oakland Rd

37

The Fly Shop
@BBT

PM River
Lodge

Red
Moose
Lodge

2

To
Baldwin

North
Pond

0.6 mi

South Branch

1

0.4 mi

James Rd

Middle
Branch

the iron footbridge of the Flint Rainbow Club within 300 yards. Along the way are log-jammed pools, overhanging cover, and dark undercuts that hide large browns. Under the bridge itself is a deep pool with a gravel tail-out. Continue upstream and you'll wade through a pair of tight loops and reach a railroad trestle in 0.6 mile. You'll find deep holes at the stone embankments of the trestle and on the outside bends of the loops. In between are beautiful stretches of riffles.

4 72nd Street

GPS N 43° 51.451'
W 85° 52.462'

Map: page 275

This is a walk-in access for fly anglers that puts you near the confluence of the Baldwin River and the mainstream. From M-37, across the road from the Red Moose Lodge, turn west on 72nd Street and follow the paved road for 1.2 miles. A small parking area and well-defined path are marked with a national forest fee area sign and fee pipe ($5 daily vehicle, $15 weekly, $30 annual). The path leads 200 yards through the woods and down a bank to the river where angler's trails lead both upstream and downstream.

The Pere Marquette is 50 to 60 feet wide at this point and one to three feet deep over a bottom of predominately gravel, which holds a lot of spawning steelhead in the spring. Within a hundred yards upstream, the smaller Baldwin River merges into the mainstream and forms a deep hole at the confluence that can be extremely productive.

5 Green Cottage

GPS N 43° 51.685'
W 85° 52.877'

Map: page 275

This boat launch is indeed next to the "Green Cottage" and is perhaps the most popular access site in the flies-only stretch of the Pere Marquette. The site is reached from M-37 by turning west on 72nd Street across the road from the Red Moose Lodge and following the paved road for 1.5 miles to Peacock Trail. Turn north (right) on Peacock Trail, which ends in 0.3 mile at the launch site.

The launch and parking area is a Forest Service fee area ($5 daily vehicle, $15 weekly, $30 annual) with envelopes and a fee pipe located near the entrance. The facility is large and includes a ramp that descends the steep bank as a series of steps, requiring most boats to be hand carried or dragged across it. Still, Green Cottage is a popular take-out site for anglers beginning their float at the M-37 Bridge launch.

Green Cottage is also an excellent stretch of river for the wading angler. The river is 60 to 80 feet wide and two to six feet deep with a predominately gravel bottom. The Pere Marquette here is a wonderful mix of pools, riffled water, and deep runs with longstanding names. Heading upstream you'll come to Island Hole, Basswood Run, and the Whirlpool. Downstream is

Spruce Hole. When water is at normal levels, the wading is not difficult as the various holes, and swift runs are easy to identify and avoid.

There are angler's trails in both directions of the river. Upstream the trail follows the river for almost 0.75 mile. Downstream the path skirts around Green Cottage and across private property. It's imperative that you stick to the angler's path downstream and not wander off on unmarked trails. Stay off the banks and private property downstream, or, as the sign in the launch site warns, this important access will be closed to anglers in the future.

Anglers will find fishing very productive for browns, immature steelhead and salmon pooling up during their spawning season here. There are very reliable hatches in this stretch, and it is crucial during emergence periods and spinner falls to match them as accurately as possible as the trout can be very selective. Among the best hatches are gray drakes, blue-winged olives, and to a lesser degree sulphurs.

6 *Claybanks*

GPS N 43° 52.182'
W 85° 53.049'

Map: page 279

This Forest Service site includes rustic campsites, two parking areas, and a variety of places to enter the flies-only section of the river. From M-37 in Baldwin, turn west on 7th Street for five blocks and then south (left) on Cherry Street to quickly reach 52nd Street. Turn west (right) on 52nd Street (also labeled Carrs Rd. on some maps); just past the railroad tracks turn south (left) on Astor Road, which quickly becomes a dirt road. Within a quarter mile turn west (right) on 56th Street, and then in a half mile turn south (left) on Claybanks Road, which is signposted—but is also labeled Jigger Trail on some maps.

In less than a mile you'll come to the intersection of Forest Road 6686 to the west and then pass four rustic Forest Service campsites ($5 a night). Just beyond is a well-posted junction where 64th Street heads west to quickly cross Forest Road 6222. Turn south (left) on FR 6222, and within a quarter mile, or 2.5 miles from 52nd Street, the dirt road ends at a parking area capable of holding a dozen vehicles. This is the main access point to the Claybanks stretch. While the above directions may make for a confusing read, all the dirt roads are surprisingly well posted.

From the parking area ($5 daily vehicle, $15 weekly, $30 annual) a foot trail heads to the west and in 250 yards arrives at a massive stairway that uses more than a hundred steps to descend the 200-foot-high banks to the river. You'll find the Pere Marquette 60 to 80 feet wide and two to six feet deep with a moderately strong velocity across a gravel bottom. You can wade here but need to keep a cautious eye out for the deep holes and runs. Just downstream from the stairway is a brushy islet that splits the river in two. Upstream a path hugs the banks for almost a mile, ending across the river from the angler's trail from Green Cottage.

The Claybanks is a popular area for wading anglers, particularly during the fall and spring spawning runs, and a second parking and camping area has been set up by the Forest Service. At the junction with 64th Street, if you continue straight on Claybanks Road, you will pass five numbered rustic campsites ($5 per night) and then in a quarter mile end at a parking area (N 43 52.097 W85 52.901') large enough to hold a dozen vehicles ($5 daily vehicle, $15 weekly, $30 annual) and featuring a vault toilet. A path here heads west and skirts a wooden log fence marking private property before reaching the aforementioned stairway to the river in a quarter mile.

7 Jenks Road

GPS N 43° 52.332'
W 85° 54.095'

For the price of a little boot leather you can often escape other anglers on the river with a half-mile walk in from Jenks Road. The access site can be reached from 52nd Street by turning south on Jenks Road 2.4 miles west of M-37 in Baldwin. Follow Jenks Road for 1.5 miles and then look for a pair of posts marking a footpath on the west side of the road. The posts are 0.4 mile north of where Jenks Road curves sharply east to become 64th Street.

The trail winds along private property for 0.6 mile and is easy to follow thanks to an occasional red blaze on trees and an abundance of no trespassing signs. At the end it descends sharply down a bank and arrives at the river, which is bordered by a small section of Forest Service land extending downstream.

The Pere Marquette is 60 feet wide here and two to five feet deep along a gravel bottom. Wading is possible, but caution must be used: at high water it's best to look elsewhere to fish. A portion of the banks downstream is grassy meadow making for extremely easy fly casting even if you're not in the water. Sunken logs, submerged roots, and overhanging brush provide ample cover for the large browns found in this stretch.

8 Gleason's Landing

GPS N 43° 52.287'
W 85° 55.192'

This popular Manistee National Forest campground marks the end of the quality fishing waters of the Pere Marquette. Upstream the river is no kill, catch and release, with flies only. Downstream the fishing is open to all tackle, and the limit is five fish daily with no more than three fish 15 inches or larger.

To reach the campground from M-37 in Baldwin, head west on 7th Street for five blocks, turn south (left) on Cherry Street briefly and then west (right) on 52nd Street (also known as Carrs Road). Drive west two miles and turn south (left) on Jenks Road for half a mile, where you will veer to the southwest on Shortcut Road. Within a mile is 60th Street. Turn west (right) for a half mile and then south (left) on Brooks Road, which ends within a

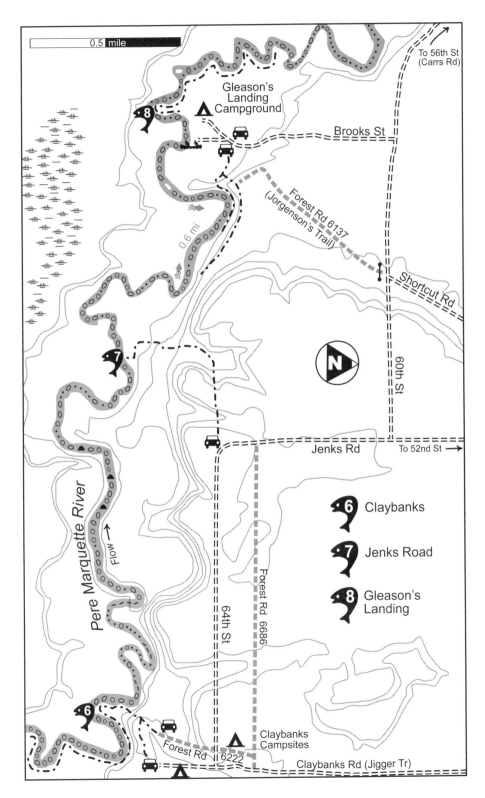

0.5 mile

Gleason's Landing Campground

To 56th St (Carrs Rd)

Brooks St

Forest Rd 6137 (Jorgenson's Trail)

Shortcut Rd

0.6 mi

Pere Marquette River

Flow →

N

60th St

Jenks Rd

To 52nd St →

6 Claybanks

7 Jenks Road

8 Gleason's Landing

64th St

Forest Rd 6686

Claybanks Campsites

Forest Rd 6222

Claybanks Rd (Jigger Tr)

mile at the campground.

Gleason's Landing has four walk-in sites and four walk-in group sites that are popular with canoers, anglers, and families who don't mind carrying their equipment 50 yards before pitching their tent. There are also two parking areas for anglers, one on each side of Brooks Road, that require a vehicle entry permit ($5 daily vehicle, $15 weekly, $30 annual), and a boat launch for hand-carried boats.

From the angler's parking area on the east side of Brooks Road, a foot trail heads into the woods and within 100 yards breaks out at the Pere Marquette, upstream from the campground and thus in the flies-only waters. Here one trail scales the high banks along the river for more than half a mile, while another threads its way along the water's edge at the base of the bluff. Upstream the Pere Marquette is three to six feet deep and 60 to 70 feet wide. Much of it can be waded with care at normal flows, but you will overtop your waders at mid-channel in places. The velocity is moderate to fast, so wading is never easy. The bottom is sand and gravel, making this a favorite area during the spawning runs.

Downstream a trail winds 0.7 mile along the river past the campground. In general the river is wider here, with more numerous holes that need to be avoided. Still anglers—whether they are using flies, bait or tackle—wade stretches of it carefully. The banks downstream are lower and forested with hardwoods. Fishing pressure is heavy during the fall and spring spawning runs, and on weekends it is difficult to find a space to park your car. In the rest of the season pressure is moderate but never combat fishing–crowded. Most of the river frontage downstream is federal land, but there are some private holdings. Upstream, most of the land is private.

 9 Bowman Bridge

GPS N 43° 53.383'
W 85° 56.434'

Downstream from Gleason's Landing the Pere Marquette is wider, 70 to 85 feet in most places, and considerably more swift. This is big water, and the best way to fish it is from the front of a driftboat with a knowledgeable guide manning the oars in the back. But there are a few access sites where, if the water levels are normal or low, you can fish with careful wading.

Bowman Bridge is one of them. The bridge is the site of a large Forest Service campground and a busy canoe launch that is reached by following 52nd Street (also known as Carrs Road) four miles west of Baldwin. The boat launch is a Forest Service fee area ($5 daily vehicle, $15 weekly, $30 annual) and its parking area is large enough to hold 48 vehicles. There is limited parking on the east side of the bridge, which has a path leading to the water.

The river is about 70 to 85 feet wide here with a bottom that is chiefly sand broken up by patches of gravel. Upstream from the bridge, the river is three to six feet deep. Downstream, it is generally less than four feet deep,

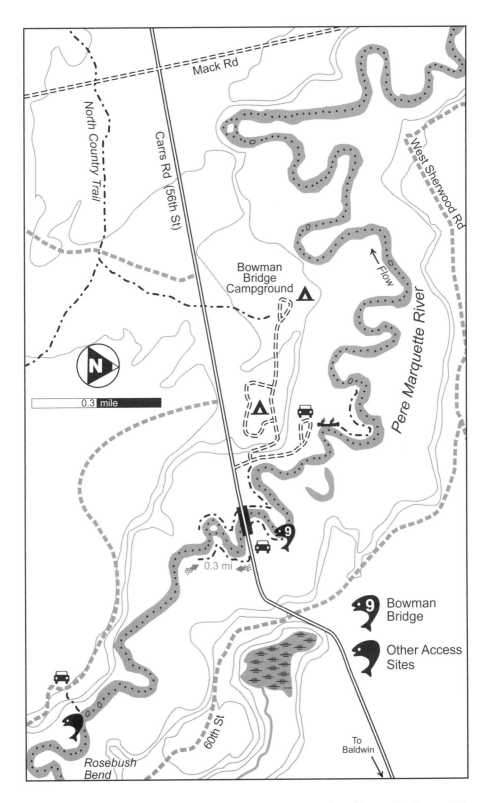

Mack Rd

North Country Trail

Carrs Rd (56th St)

West Sherwood Rd

Bowman
Bridge
Campground

Flow

Pere Marquette River

N

0.3 mile

0.3 mi

9

Bowman
Bridge

Other Access
Sites

60th St

To
Baldwin

Rosebush
Bend

with some deeper holes. Wading downstream from the bridge is possible at normal flows if you avoid the deeper parts. Upstream, wading is difficult to impossible even in normal water levels. Banks are low downstream, a little higher upstream, and are forested with hardwoods. The banks are Forest Service land, and from the bridge angler trails extend 0.3 mile downstream and upstream. Paths also follow the river along the west side from the launch area. Fishing pressure here is moderate except during the spring and fall spawning runs, but the canoeing activity can be intense during the height of the summer.

Another access site nearby is Rosebush Bend, which is reached from a two-track 0.2 mile west of Bowman Bridge. Follow the two-track south 0.7 mile to an angler's trail that is posted and leads 200 yards to the river. The Pere Marquette is generally deeper at Rosebush Bend than at Bowman Bridge, and the wading much more challenging but possible in low water conditions. Trout cover is thick here.

10 Sulak

GPS N 43° 55.473'
W 85° 00.774'

This public site is jointly managed by the Forest Service, which oversees the campground, and the Michigan DNR, which maintains the launch and access sites on the river. To reach Sulak from US-10, head south on Tyndal Road in the village of Branch. In half a mile, Tyndal Road swings east and becomes Stevenson Road and then in a mile resumes a southerly direction as South Branch Road. You reach Upper Branch Bridge in 2.1 miles from US-10. Continue south another 0.6 mile beyond the bridge to a gravel road marked by a DNR launch site sign, which leads off to the northeast (left). You can also reach this site from Bowman Bridge by heading west on 56th Street (also known as Carrs Road) for 4.2 miles and then north (right) 2.3 miles on South Branch Road.

The access road heads north and then swings east where you pass 11 Forest Service rustic campsites on the south side. On the north side, half a mile from South Branch Road, is a posted angler's trail with a parking area for six to eight vehicles and a vault toilet. From here a foot trail leads a quarter mile north to the river, descending a hundred feet, steeply at times, before reaching the water. At this point the trail swings downstream. The Pere Marquette is 60 to 70 feet wide and three to six feet deep here, flowing across a bottom of sand, gravel and clay. It is generally too deep and fast for safe wading at mid-channel, but some parts can be waded with care along the banks and certainly at low water levels. In places the banks are grassy, making it possible to cast close to shore. Overall the trout cover is good.

The access road ends in 0.8 mile at a DNR boat launch, where there are parking for a dozen vehicles, a launch site for boats and canoes, and a vault toilet. Water conditions are the same here, but the wading tends to be more

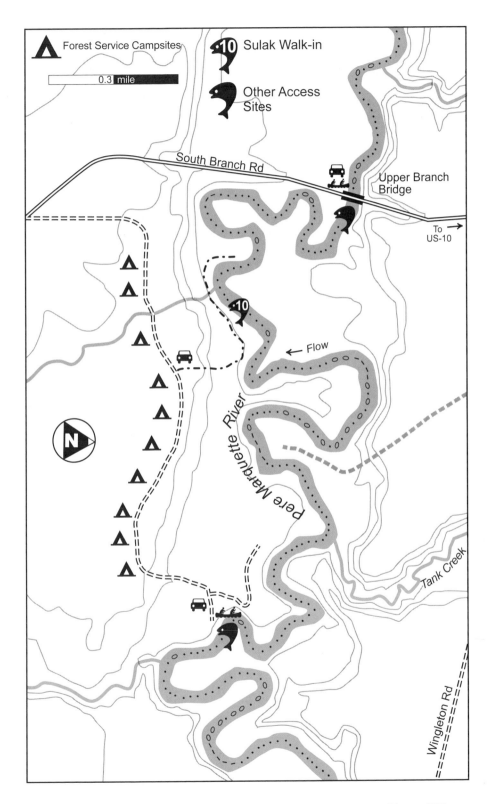

Forest Service Campsites

0.3 mile

10 Sulak Walk-in

Other Access Sites

South Branch Rd

Upper Branch Bridge

To US-10

10

← Flow

Pere Marquette River

N

Tank Creek

Wingleton Rd

An angler uses an inflatable pontoon boat to float the Pere Marquette River and reach his favorite holes.

treacherous during normal water levels. At both of these sites the river is heavily fished in the spring and fall spawning runs but is moderate to light the rest of the season.

11 Maple Leaf

GPS N 43° 56.243'
W 85° 04.748'

This is the last site that can be waded safely. Any further downstream from Maple Leaf and the Pere Marquette is generally too deep and swift for anglers in waders. From Branch head west on US-10 for 1.8 miles and then south on Taylor Road. Within a quarter mile, Taylor Road crosses railroad tracks and then becomes a two-track until it ends 0.6 mile from US-10 at a large parking area capable of holding 15 to 20 vehicles.

From the parking area a foot path leads almost a quarter mile to the river where just downstream is a beautiful stretch of riffled water. Overall in this area, the Pere Marquette is 60 to 70 feet wide and three to six feet deep. The bottom is mostly sand with some gravel patches. Angler paths extend both upstream and downstream, and if water levels are low to normal you can wade a considerable distance if you are careful.

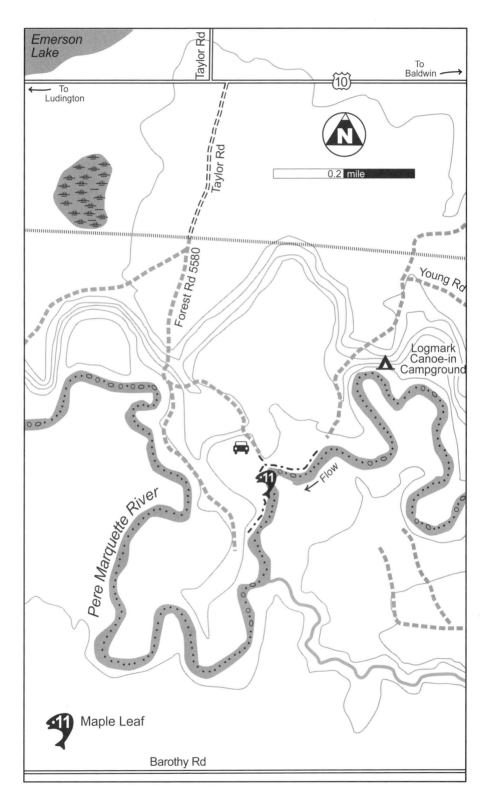

Emerson Lake

Taylor Rd

To Baldwin →

← To Ludington

10

N

0.2 mile

Taylor Rd

Forest Rd 5580

Young Rd

Logmark Canoe-in Campground

Pere Marquette River

Flow

11

Maple Leaf

Barothy Rd

Fly Fishing for Steelhead on the Pere Marquette

What many fly anglers find so endearing about the Pere Marquette is the variety of its fishery. Hooking a 15- or 16-inch brown trout is one thing. Enduring a 20-minute battle with a 12-pound steelhead cart-wheeling down the river is something else altogether. It's an adrenaline rush, even when the fish breaks off, that can never be explained, only experienced.

Although there are summer steelhead called Skamania and immatures in the river year round, steelhead begin showing up in numbers in late September for a fall run that peaks in late October. Some fish stay in the river all winter. At the end of February a spring run of spawning steelhead begins, peaking in late March with fish in the river through April.

Nymphing for steelhead, or what is often referred to as the chuck-n-duck method, is an effective and probably the most popular way to fish for the large rainbows. Begin with a seven- or eight-weight rod, nine to ten feet in length, and equipped with a disc-drag fly reel. Load the reel with lots of backing and a shooting line, which will move more easily through the guides than a standard, double taper fly line when a steelhead is running.

Tie a ten-foot long, 12- to 16-pound monofilament to the fly line and slide a No. 10 black snap swivel onto it. Tie the monofilament off to a No. 10 black barrel swivel. From the barrel swivel, tie on a three-foot piece of six-pound tippet and then a nymph fly. Some anglers prefer to fish two flies at once if they are targeting steelhead in pools and will tie a second piece of tippet, 18 inches to three feet in length, from the hook bend of the first fly to a second fly. Keep in mind that two flies make casting and managing your line much more challenging.

From the snap swivel tie a four-inch piece of monofilament and squeeze a split shot or two on it. How much weight depends on the river conditions. The faster the current, the deeper the pool, the more weight you'll need to get the fly down to where the steelhead are. In theory, if the split shot snags along the river bed, it will simply slide off and save the rest of your rig.

Gravel beds where steelhead are spotted spawning are called redds, and you should position yourself upstream from them at a 45-degree angle. Use as little weight as possible, just enough so you can feel the split shot lightly ticking along the gravel on the bottom. Casting a fly line with split shot and making sure it doesn't hit you on the back cast is where this method picks up its nickname "chuck-n-duck." Anglers who are used to dry flies on a five-weight rod will find this awkward at first but should get the hang of it quickly.

Cast straight across the stream or slightly quartered downstream so the current pulls your fly without creating a belly in the line. Ideally you want your fly to swing in front of the fish, not through the redd. Once the weight hits the water, lift the slack line from the river surface and follow the drift with the rod slightly elevated. Concentrate on the ticking of the split shot along the bottom: if it ever pauses, set the hook.

Other than egg flies during the fall spawning run of salmon, nymphs are the most productive fly you can tie on. You could stop at one of the many fly shops in Baldwin for advice, but you will find that popular patterns for steelhead usually include Hare's Ears, black stonefly nymphs, Hex nymphs, and green caddis larvae.

Anglers line the Pere Marquette River in the flies-only stretch during the fall steelhead run. At this time of year fly anglers can easily hook a 10-pound steelhead and then spend 15 to 20 minutes battling the fish.

The Pine River, one of the fastest rivers in the Lower Peninsula, attracts large numbers of canoers throughout the summer.

Pine River

Wild and fast, the Pine is a top-quality trout stream and unique among rivers in the Lower Peninsula. Only the Sturgeon comes close to matching the gradient speed of the Pine, where in the spring thrill-seeking paddlers arrive to enjoy legitimate Class II rapids.

Equally impressive to many, however, is the wild appearance of the Pine. Unlike the Sturgeon, which at times parallels I-75 and ends among the resorts of Indian River, the Pine flows past no towns and features few riverfront cabins or other development. Portions of the Pine will always remain that way because 35 percent of the river corridor lies in public ownership either as Pere Marquette State Forest or the Manistee National Forest.

Wild, fast, and ours.

In this wild setting you find wild trout: brookies, browns, and rainbows. The Pine flows through mostly hardwood forest south and west of Cadillac and ends in the backwaters of Tippy Dam, which prevents steelhead and salmon from entering the river. Nor is the Pine stocked. All its trout are self-sustaining populations, with the Pine being home to the largest nonmigratory rainbow population in Michigan.

That's the main reason 57 miles of the river, from the mouth of the East Branch to Tippy Dam Pond, is designated as a Blue Ribbon Trout Stream. Only the mainstream of the Au Sable with 79 miles has more water classified as Blue Ribbon in Michigan. In 1992, the Pine was also designated as a National Wild and Scenic River, giving it further protection.

The Pine begins at an elevation of 1,102 feet where the North Branch and East Branch merge to form the mainstream 3.5 miles west of Tustin in Osceola County. It then flows in a southerly direction to the Osceola County Line, where it turns northwest, cutting across Lake County and on into Wexford County. From Peterson Bridge it flows into Manistee County, where it again turns northwest to end its 57-mile journey. By the time the Pine discharges into the south arm of Tippy Dam Pond, it has drained a watershed of 265 square miles and descended 417 feet from its headwaters to its mouth. That leads to a gradient that averages 10 to 15 feet per mile and is as high as 25 feet per mile in stretches below Low Bridge. This is fast water.

The only thing more impressive than the speed of the current was, in the late 1800s, the towering white pine that lined the river's banks. The trees led loggers to name the river the Pine. They then used the river to float the timber down to sawmills in Manistee. In 1912, the Stonach Dam was built across the Pine, the first hydroelectric dam on the Manistee River system.

To anglers the most significant moment in the history of the Pine was when Gideon Gerhardt, intent on catching a trout, stepped into the river in 1925 near Skookum Bridge. That led to *Collins v. Gerhardt,* some would argue the most important public waters case in the history of the country. Gerhardt was charged with trespass because a private club owned both sides of the river. A local court ruled in favor of the Ne-Bo-Shone Club, but in 1926 the Michigan Supreme Court reversed the decision. Speaking for the majority, Justice John S. McDonald wrote, "so long as water flows and fish swim in the Pine River, the people may fish at their pleasure in any part of the stream subject only to the restraints and regulations imposed by the state."

Federal appeals kept the issue alive until 1936. But the legal principle established by the Michigan Supreme Court remained unshaken; that case alone ensured future generations the right to fish, paddle, and float Michigan's rivers and streams no matter who owns the land along them.

Another significant date was 2003, when the final pieces of the Stronach Dam were removed. In a process called a staged drawdown, eight inches of the dam were removed every three months for six years to minimize the amount of silt washing down the river. At every stage of the dismantling, a little more of the impoundment disappeared, while farther upstream a fast river became a little bit faster.

That swift current makes the Pine a challenging river to fish with a fly and is the main reason fishing pressure is light. A small, brush-lined stream in the headwaters, the Pine is 30 to 40 feet wide, two to four feet deep, and fly fishable where it flows into Lake County and toward Edgetts Bridge, the first access point covered in this chapter. As it flows across the northeast comer of Lake County the Pine increases to 40 to 70 feet in width and three to four feet in depth and often features riverbanks that are alternately high and low, some more than 70 feet high.

Up to this point, the minimum length in the Pine is ten inches for rainbows and eight inches for brook trout and browns, with a daily possession of five fish. The river is open to all tackle during the regular trout season from the last Saturday in April to Sept. 30. At Elm Flats to Tippy Dam Pond the minimum length is ten inches for brookies and 12 inches for rainbows and browns.

From the southern border of Wexford County the Pine grows to 50 to 80 feet in width and two to five feet in depth as it flows past the final two access sites covered, Dobson Bridge and Peterson Bridge on M-37. There are few places in this stretch where you can wade more than a few hundred feet without taking to the banks on one side or the other.

Overall the Pine is never easy to wade, and at high flows it's impossible. The average depth at normal summer flows is less than three feet, but this figure can be misleading. At mid-channel, the stream usually exceeds three feet and in many places tops your waders. Then there is the hard, consolidated clay found in the riverbed, especially near Peterson Bridge. This material is resistant to erosion and underlies shallow areas in the stream. Where the resistant layer ends, an abrupt drop-off to deep water generally occurs.

Fishing the Pine is not like fishing the Holy Water on the Au Sable, where you can wade for miles at mid-channel, fishing the good cover on both sides, easily avoiding the few deep holes and snags. On the Pine, wading anglers will constantly have to take to the bank to get around deep holes and runs. Overhanging brush and steeply cut banks can make such maneuvers difficult at times. But often there is a path of some sort along one or both banks of the river. These vary from well-marked trails to those indicated only by a faint trace of bent or broken vegetation. Rest assured you're not the first to fish the Pine.

The Pine has a large component of groundwater flow and consequently is a cold-water river with summer water temperatures below 70 degrees. But the river also has a large overland flow from the clay soils in the morainal hills of the watershed. This makes the Pine unusual among area rivers in that it may rise one to four feet above its average level during heavy rains or spring melt, the highest by far of any trout stream covered in this book. After heavy rains the Pine not only rises quickly but becomes so cloudy that it can be difficult to see the bottom even in shallow areas. At such times wading, even along the banks, may be hazardous, and fly fishing is nearly impossible.

Population surveys indicate that the Pine River has a third of the trout of similar rivers in northern Michigan. The main culprit to trout reproduction is sand deposition in the river. Early studies predicted that a streambed stabilization program would reduce the sediment load by about half and result in great trout populations. That led to conservation groups, including Trout Unlimited chapters, forming the Pine River Watershed Restoration Partnership in 1990 to address eroding streambanks and road–stream crossings within the watershed. Since then more than a hundred sites have been stabilized.

Many fisheries biologists also believe the abrading action of the large amounts of sand that move down the Pine has resulted in the river's less-than-stellar hatches. Hendrickson hatches do occur in late April and early May, but the high water levels in spring often prevent fly anglers from taking advantage of them. Perhaps the best hatch on the Pine is little yellow stoneflies that occur in the first two weeks of June followed by hatches of little sulphurs.

Finally, it is important to remember that the Pine River from Lincoln Bridge to Low Bridge is one of the most heavily canoed waterways in Michigan, if not the country. To control the number of paddlers, the Forest Service has established a permit system that reserves 44,000 launch permits annually for the six canoe liveries that work the river and 11,000 permits for private canoes.

That's a lot of canoes. But the vast majority arrive during the weekends, from July through August. Nor are paddlers allowed on the river before 9 a.m., and must be off by 6 p.m., leaving early morning and late evening hours for anglers. To avoid canoers, anglers should fish before noon below

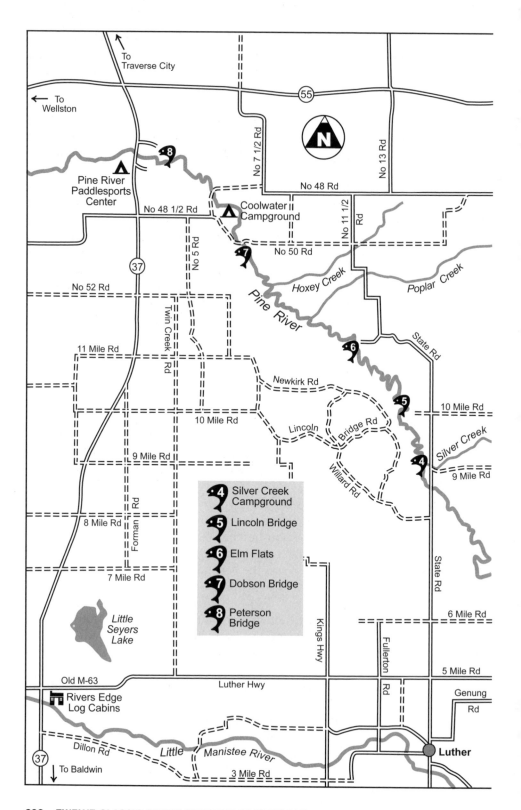

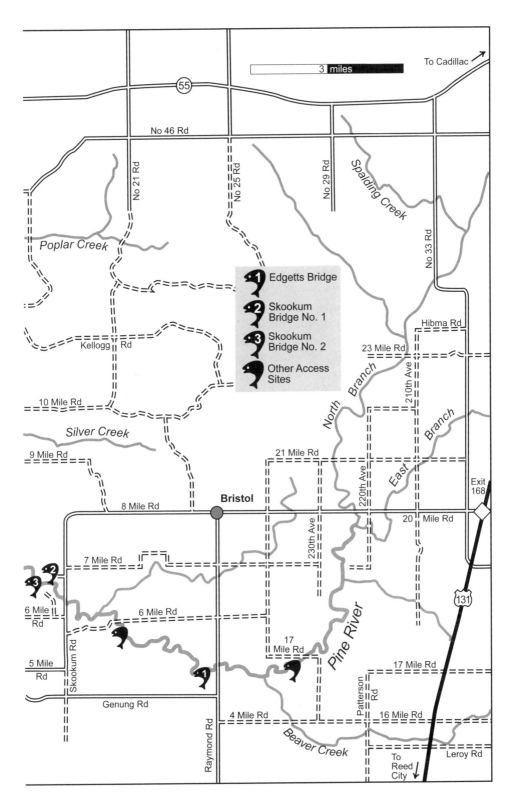

To Cadillac

3 miles

55

No 46 Rd

No 21 Rd

No 25 Rd

No 29 Rd

Spalding Creek

No 33 Rd

Poplar Creek

Kellogg Rd

Hibma Rd

23 Mile Rd

210th Ave

1 Edgetts Bridge

2 Skookum Bridge No. 1

3 Skookum Bridge No. 2

Other Access Sites

North Branch

East Branch

10 Mile Rd

Silver Creek

9 Mile Rd

21 Mile Rd

220th Ave

Exit 168

8 Mile Rd

Bristol

20 Mile Rd

7 Mile Rd

230th Ave

131

2

3

6 Mile Rd

6 Mile Rd

Skookum Rd

Pine River

17 Mile Rd

5 Mile Rd

1

17 Mile Rd

Patterson Rd

Genung Rd

Raymond Rd

4 Mile Rd

16 Mile Rd

To Reed City

Beaver Creek

Leroy Rd

Peterson Bridge or after 3 p.m. above Elm Flats.

Or come at other times of the year. If it is a mid-summer weekend when you arrive with fly rod in hand, explore the tributaries that feed the Pine, many of which are high quality brook trout streams. Either way, you'll discover it's still possible in this fast and wild river to catch a wild and lively trout. Or maybe two.

Accommodations

Cadillac is a 30- to 40-minute drive from most of these access sites but offers a much wider range of accommodations, including chain motels, than the small villages closer to the river. For a complete list of accommodations contact the Cadillac Area Visitors Bureau (231-775-0657, 800-225-2537; *www.cadillacmichigan.com*; 222 North Lake St.).

On the corner of M-63 and M-37, nine miles west of Luther, is **Rivers Edge Log Cabins** (231-266-6014; *www.riversedgelogcabins.com*; 1853 W. Old M-63). Dating back to 1947, Rivers Edge features five classic cabins overlooking the Little Manistee River. The cabins range from single rooms to five-bedroom lodges and are equipped with full kitchens. In Wellston, **Schmidt Outfitters** (231-848-4191, 888-221-9056; *www.schmidtoutfitters. com*; 918 Seaman Rd.) has a seven-room lodge just off M-55, 7.5 miles west of M-37. Every room has a kitchenette with a microwave, coffeemaker, refrigerator, and dining table. Outside on every deck is a gas grill.

Two miles east of M-37, **Coolwater Campground** (231-862-3481; *www.coolwatercampground.com*; 9424 W. 48 ½ Rd.) offers a pair of camping cabins as well as sites with full hook-ups on the Pine River near the Dobson Bridge Access Site. The one-room cabins sleep four and are equipped with microwave and refrigerator.

Campgrounds: The Pine flows past a pair of state forest campgrounds and a Forest Service campground; all are described as access sites below with directions to them. Upriver are Silver Creek State Forest Campground and Lincoln Bridge State Forest Campground, which are connected not only by the Pine but also by the Silver Creek Pathway. Lincoln Bridge has only walk-in sites; Silver Creek has 19 drive-in sites as well as seven walk-in sites. Located where the Pine flows under M-37 is the large Peterson Bridge National Forest Campground with 20 drive-in sites and 10 walk-in sites designed primarily for canoers. All three campgrounds are heavily used by paddlers during the summer, and Peterson Bridge in particular can be filled on any weekend from late June through August.

The closest state park, offering 215 modern sites, is **William Mitchell State Park** (231-775-7911; reservations 800-447-2757; *www.michigan.gov/ dnr*; 6093 E. M-115) in Cadillac. Across from the entrance to the Peterson Bridge Campground is **Pine River Paddlesports Center** (800-717-4837, 231-862-3471; *www.thepineriver.com*; 9590 S. M-37). The canoe livery doubles as a campground with rustic sites, a camping cabin, and a heated restroom with flush toilets and coin-op showers.

Paddling the Pine

The Pine was attracting 6,000 to 7,000 paddlers on a summer weekend when in 1978 the Forest Service instituted a watercraft permit system, the first of its kind in Michigan. The system to prevent overcrowding is still in effect. A permit for each canoe is required for paddling the Pine from Elm Flats to Low Bridge between May 15 and Sept. 10, for both private and rental canoes. Reservations are almost mandatory for any weekend from mid-June through August, and normally by mid-March most of the weekend permits have been reserved. When you rent a canoe, the livery will handle the permit for you.

The solution for anybody contemplating a fish-and-float trip is to arrive in the middle of the week when the water is uncrowded and plan on paddling for two days as the Pine is an excellent overnight float.

The Pine is generally too fast and too narrow in most places above Peterson Bridge for easy fishing from a canoe. Overhanging brush, low sweepers, and recent blowdowns add to the difficulty. Some river guides use driftboats to fish the Pine with the oarsman/guide slowing the boat by rowing upstream but gradually allowing the boat to drift slowly downstream. This gives the fisherman more time to search and cover the favorable water. The easiest way to fish the Pine from a canoe is to float down to a shallow spot, beach the canoe, and fish by wading.

Canoe liveries providing boats and drop-off service are *Pine River Paddlesports Center* (800-717-4837, 231-862-3471; *www.thepineriver. com*; 9590 S. M-37), *Bosmans Canoe Rental* (877-622-6637; 8027 S. M-37), and *Horina's Canoe and Kayak* (231-862-34-70; 9889 S. M-37).

Forest Service lists the river miles and approximate time to float between some of the access points on the river:

From – To	Hours	Miles
Skookum Bridge – Walker Bridge	2	6.5
Walker Bridge – Lincoln Bridge	1:15	3.0
Lincoln Bridge – Elm Flats	1	3.0
Elm Flats – Dobson Bridge	2	6.0
Dobson Bridge – Peterson Bridge	2	6.0
Peterson Bridge – Low Bridge	6	6.0

Fly Shops and Guides

If coming from the south, you can stop for flies in any of the shops in Baldwin (page 272). The area's best fly shop is *Schmidt Outfitters* (231-848-4191, 888-221-9056; *www.schmidtoutfitters.com*; 918 Seaman Rd.) which has good hatch advice and selection of flies and equipment. In Luther, the *Luther Hardware & Sports* (231-797-0000; 209 State St.) sells a limited selection of local flies.

Any Baldwin-based guide will also work the Pine River if requested. Also offering guided fly-fishing trips on the Pine are Schmidt Outfitters and

Hawkins Outfitters (231-228-7135; *www.hawkinsflyfishing.com*) based in Lake Ann.

Maps of the Pine

The directions to the eight access sites described in this chapter take you through parts of three counties: Osceola, Lake, and Wexford. That leads to confusing road names as many of the roads change names where they cross county lines; sometimes the numbering system in one county is not continued in the next. East–west roads in Wexford County are labeled as No. 46 Road, No. 48 Road, and so on. As soon as you cross into Lake County east–west roads become 11 Mile Road descending to 5 Mile Road near Luther. Adding to the confusion are the numbered roads of the U.S. Forest Service, which are totally unrelated to those of the counties.

The easiest way to reach the first site, Edgetts Bridge, is from US-131 departing at either exit 168, 12 miles south of Cadillac, or exit 162, 11 miles north of Reed City. The two access sites at Skookum Bridge can also be reached from exit 168 of US-131 or from State Road, the main street in the village of Luther, reached from M-37 by heading west on Luther Highway (also labeled Old M-63) for nine miles. Luther Highway is eight miles north of US-10 on M-37 or 12 miles south of M-55.

Luther is a convenient starting point for the next three sites. Silver Creek Campground, Lincoln Bridge Campground, and Elm Flats are all north of Luther and posted along State Road. The final two access sites, Peterson Bridge and Dobson Bridge, are either on M-37 or reached from the state highway on No. 48 1/2 Road.

Edgetts Bridge
GPS N 44° 03.841'
W 85° 35.411'

Eleven miles downstream from where the North and East branch from the mainstream, the Pine flows under Edgetts Bridge and past this access site. If coming from the south, the easiest way to reach the site is from US-131, departing at exit 162, 11 miles north of Reed City. At the exit, head west on Luther Road (also labeled 14 Mile Road) and in four miles turn north (right) on Raymond Road. Edgetts Bridge is crossed in 3.2 miles. A quarter mile north of it, turn west (left) on an unposted two-track. Within a quarter mile veer to the left on the two-track. The two-track ends at the access site 0.4 mile from Raymond Road.

If coming from the north, you can depart US-131 at exit 168 and head west on 20 Mile Road (also labeled Marion Road) for 5.4 miles to reach the intersection with Raymond Road in the hamlet of Bristol. Head south on Raymond Road to reach the two-track in 2.6 miles and the bridge a quarter mile beyond it.

The access site is a large, grassy clearing surrounded by hardwoods and

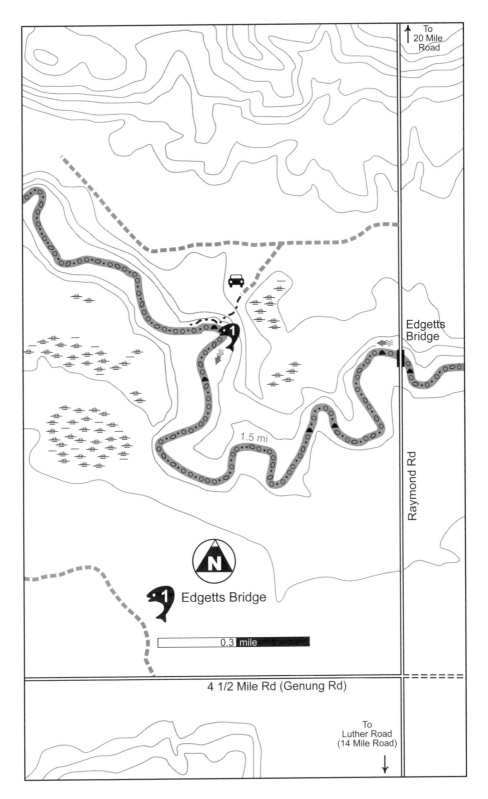

To
20 Mile
Road

Edgetts
Bridge

Raymond Rd

1.5 mi

N

🐟**1** Edgetts Bridge

0.3 mile

4 1/2 Mile Rd (Genung Rd)

To
Luther Road
(14 Mile Road)

perched on the high bluffs above the Pine. It makes for a pleasant, dispersed camping area and, being on state forest land, is often used that way. From the parking area a wide path descends into the woods and in 50 yards reaches a log stairway. The stairway will lead you down the steep bluff to the north bank of the Pine.

Thanks in part to Beaver Creek 1.8 miles upstream, the Pine is 20 to 40 feet wide here, and two to four feet deep, with deeper runs and holes. One of those deep runs is at the base of the steps, but angler trails lead you around it either upstream or downstream. The bottom is mostly gravel, cobbles, and boulders with some sand and clay, while just downstream is a stretch of riffled water. Flow is fast to very fast, and wading is difficult, even at low flows. At high flows, wading is impossible. The banks are alternately high and low and lined with much brush.

The abundant trout cover includes overhanging brush, submerged logs, boulders, and deep holes. All three species, brookies, browns, and rainbows, can be caught here. Downstream the river flows through a series of seven bends before reaching Edgetts Bridge. If the water conditions are conducive, you can fish from the stairs upstream to Bridge, a wade of 1.5 miles with only a half mile walk back to your vehicle.

Skookum Bridge Access Site No. 1

GPS N 44° 04.940'
W 85° 38.881'

This is the first of two canoe launches on opposite sides of the Pine just downstream from Skookum Bridge. To reach the bridge from Luther, head north on State Road for 1.5 miles and then turn east (right) on 5 Mile Road. In two miles turn north (left) on Skookum Road and you will cross the bridge in 1.3 miles. A quarter mile farther north turn west (left) on a dirt road posted with a DNR canoe launch sign. Within 0.3 mile the road ends at the access site.

If coming from US-131, the most direct route to the bridge is to depart at exit 168 and head west on 20 Mile Road (also labeled Marion Road). As you enter Lake County, 20 Mile Road becomes 8 Mile Road, and 7.4 miles from US-131 you turn south (left) on Skookum Road. Follow paved Skookum Road 1.3 miles to the dirt road posted with the DNR access sign, 300 yards north of the bridge.

The Pine ranges from 40 to 60 feet in width and is less than four feet deep with some deeper holes. Bottom is gravel, cobbles, and boulders in the fast runs and sand in the slower waters. Banks are low and soft with mud in places and high and sandy in others. Some banks at the outsides of bends are more than 50 feet high. Banks are lined with brush, hardwood, and conifer.

The stream velocity is moderate to fast at low flows, fast at high water. Parts of the river here can be waded with care at normal low flows but are unwadable at high water. Boulders, soft sand, drowned logs, snags, and deep holes are hazards to the wading angler no matter what the water level is.

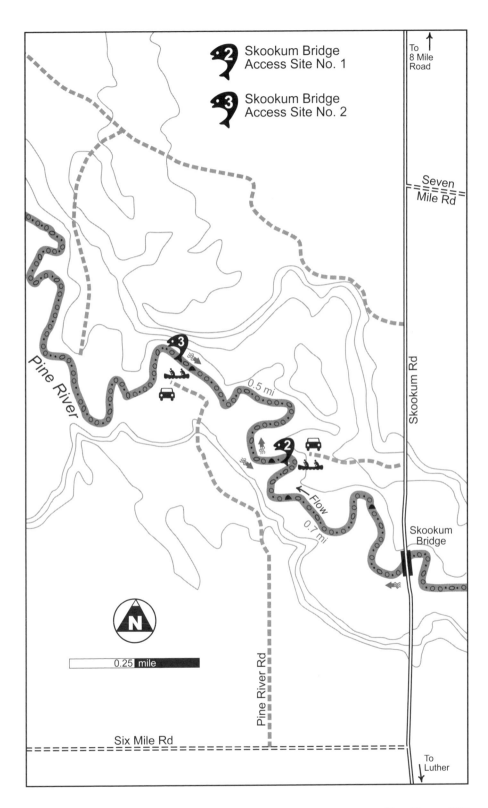

2 Skookum Bridge
Access Site No. 1

3 Skookum Bridge
Access Site No. 2

To
8 Mile
Road

Seven
Mile Rd

Skookum Rd

Pine River

0.5 mi

Flow

0.7 mi

Skookum
Bridge

N

0.25 mile

Pine River Rd

Six Mile Rd

To
Luther

3 Skookum Bridge Access Site No. 2

GPS N 44° 05.055'
W 85° 39.071'

Map: page 299

Downstream on the south bank is the second canoe launch at Skookum Bridge. To reach the bridge, see the directions for Skookum Bridge Access Site No. 1 above. From the bridge, head south 0.3 mile and turn west (right) on 6 Mile Road. Follow the gravel road for a quarter mile and then turn north (right) on Pine River Road. Within a mile this dirt road ends at the canoe launch.

In addition to the canoe launch, this access site also has a vault toilet and parking for six to eight vehicles. Like the access site across the river, camping is not permitted here. The river width and bottom are similar to upstream. Other than holes and deep runs, most of the depth is three feet or less, making it slightly easier to wade here. Trout cover is abundant both upstream and downstream.

Skookum Bridge Access Site No. 1 is a half-mile wade upstream, and Skookum Bridge is a 1.2-mile wade from this site. In either direction, the Pine flows through a series of sharp bends, forming many trout-holding pools on the outside that range up to nine feet in depth. They are good places to cast while carefully wading around them.

4 Silver Creek Campground

GPS N 44° 06.955'
W 85° 41.057'

This wonderful state forest campground is a popular one for anglers to pitch a tent at as it offers 12 sites right on the Pine and, as one end of the Silver Creek Pathway, provides access that can be reached on foot. From Luther, head north on State Road and, within 5.2 miles you cross Walker Bridge. A quarter of a mile beyond the bridge is the posted entrance to the campground, on the west (left) side of the road.

Within the campground is a parking area capable of holding ten vehicles, and from there a crushed stone path leads a short way to seven walk-in sites, all overlooking the Pine where it flows through a horseshoe bend. Although designed for canoers, this is a beautiful spot for anybody to set up camp. Five more of the 26 sites in the campground are also on the river. Across from Site #14 is a footbridge to the Silver Creek Pathway on the west side of the Pine.

At the campground the Pine is 40 to 60 feet wide and two to four feet deep at midstream, with deeper holes. Bottom is gravel and boulders in the fast water and sand in places along the banks and in slower runs. The banks are low in places but mostly high and sandy, more than 50 feet in some places downstream. Bank cover is brush and hardwood with some conifer. Trout cover is abundant. Stream velocity is fast at all times and very fast at high water. The river can be waded at normal low flows, but you must watch

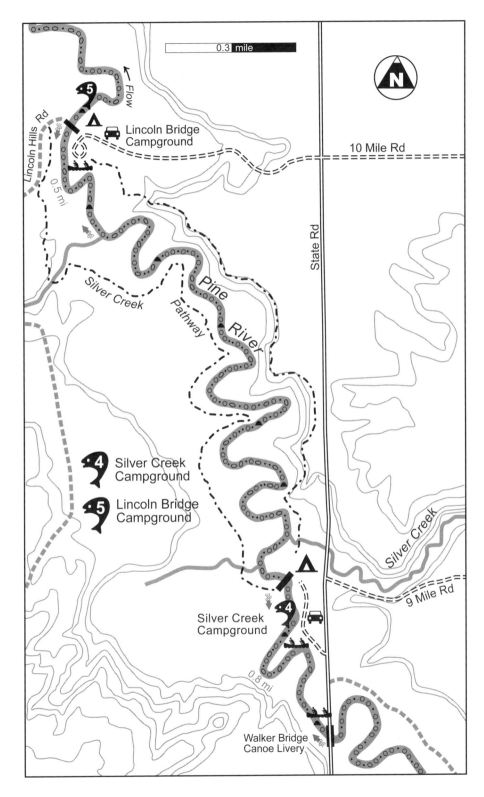

0.3 mile

Flow

Lincoln Hills Rd

0.5 mi

5

△ Lincoln Bridge Campground

10 Mile Rd

State Rd

Silver Creek

Pine River

Pathway

4 Silver Creek Campground

5 Lincoln Bridge Campground

Silver Creek

9 Mile Rd

△

4

Silver Creek Campground

0.8 mi

Walker Bridge Canoe Livery

out for boulders, snags, deep holes, and soft sand in places like the mouth of Silver Creek. You will have to take to the banks to get around some of the deep areas.

Upstream it is a wade of 0.8 mile from the footbridge to Walker Bridge, including the horseshoe bend where the walk-in sites are located. You can depart the river at Walker Bridge Canoe Livery and then walk up State Road to return to your vehicle. You can also cross the footbridge to reach more of the Pine from its west bank. The pathway hugs the river in the beginning, passing some nice stretches of riffled water just a short walk downstream.

5 Lincoln Bridge Campground

GPS N 44° 07.975'
W 85° 41.515'

Map: page 301

In 1985 the DNR purchased the Baxter Bridge across the Manistee River, which was being replaced with a newer structure for vehicles. The DNR shortened the old trestle bridge by removing its middle section and then transported the structure south to a state forest campground on the Pine River and renamed it the Lincoln Bridge. The bridge, now 80 feet long, was originally intended for snowmobilers, but it's well used in the summer by hikers, campers, and anglers looking for new spots to fish on the Pine River.

To reach Lincoln Bridge State Forest Campground, head north from Luther on State Road. Within 6.6 miles, or 1.2 miles past Silver Creek Campground, turn west (left) on 10 Mile Road, which is posted. The gravel road ends in 0.3 mile at the Pine River, where there are a large canoe launch, vault toilets, and a large turnaround where parking isn't permitted. From here a trail leads to Lincoln Bridge.

The only place to park is at the campground, set on higher ground and reached just before the canoe launch. The state forest campground features seven walk-in sites that are only 50 yards from your vehicle and well spread out in a stand of pines and hardwoods. None are directly on the river, but a set of steps leads from the last site to the canoe launch and bridge.

At the bridge, the Pine is 40 to 60 feet wide and two to four feet deep with some deeper runs and holes. Bottom is mostly gravel, cobbles, and boulders in the fast reaches and sand in the slower areas. Banks are alternately high and low, but mostly high. Bank vegetation is predominately brush and conifer, with hardwood in the uplands. The flow is fast at normal flows and very fast at high water. The river can be waded in places, but some parts are too fast and deep even at low flows. Boulders, snags, and a fast current require caution at all times, and at high flows the river cannot be safely waded.

The Silver Creek Pathway is a four-mile loop that follows both banks of the river between the two state forest campgrounds. The west bank, easily reached via the Lincoln Bridge, provides the best access for anglers as it dips to the river several times at the north end. For much of the east bank, the pathway skirts a series of bluffs that must be descended before reaching the Pine. Both sides of the pathway feature angler trails that lead to the water.

Michigan Angler: Clarence Roberts

The first flies may have originated across the pond in England but Michigan fly tiers have contributed more than their share of original patterns throughout the years. Two of the state's most prolific fly tiers were Len Halladay, who created the Adams (see page 234), and Clarence Roberts.

Born and raised in Onaway, Roberts went on to become a conservation officer who was assigned to Grayling in the 1940s. By the very nature of his job and where he lived, Roberts quickly became an avid fly angler and eventually a renowned fly tier. Roberts was exceptionally fast and is often credited with being one of Michigan's first "production tiers." It's said that he tied and sold enough flies to put his two children through college.

"I have been in his fly tying room in his basement many times when he and the boys, meaning sportsmen like Fred Bear, would gather to tie flies and talk about trout," said his nephew Ray Schmidt. "He was a very fast tier but precise."

Roberts' best-known pattern is the Roberts Yellow Drake, designed to imitate sulphurs, little yellow stones, light Hendrickson, and other mayflies that are often found hatching in Northern Michigan streams. The Roberts Brown Drake is another venerable pattern used in larger sizes as an emerging hex and in smaller sizes to imitate brown drakes, March browns and golden stones. Other patterns still occasionally tied today include Roberts Black Drake, Roberts Deer Hair Hopper, and the Bradley, a brown dry fly attractor.

Roberts died at the age of 70 in 1970, but his family legacy as fly tiers continues with Schmidt. A fly fisherman and tier most of his life, Schmidt began guiding full-time in the mid-1980s, specializing in fly fishing for steelhead. He gained national acclaim when in 1989 *Fly Rod and Reel* magazine named him one of the top ten guides in the country.

In 1995 Schmidt opened Schmidt Outfitters, a full-service fly shop and lodge just minutes from the Pine River in Wellston. Among the flies the shop sells are Schmidt's own creation—a parachute hex pattern—and the Roberts Yellow Drake.

To see a collection of 74 flies that Roberts tied, ranging from a huge night bug to a light Hendrickson, stop at the Foote Room at the Ralph A. MacMullen Conference Center (989-821-6200) next door to North Higgins Lake State Park. To purchase Roberts flies head to Schmidt Outfitters (888-221-9056, 231-848-4191; *www.schmidtoutfitters.com*).

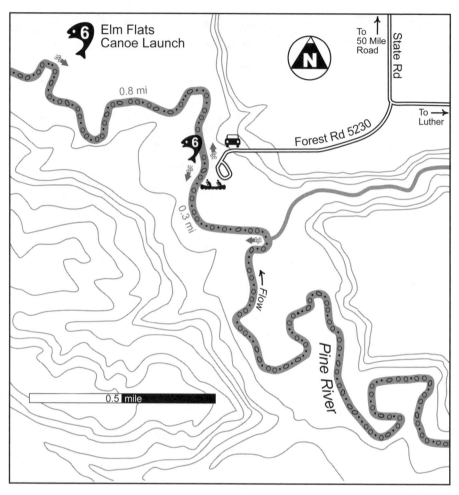

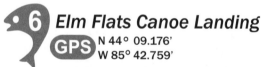

Elm Flats Canoe Landing

GPS N 44° 09.176'
W 85° 42.759'

A mile downstream from Lincoln Bridge, the Pine enters the Manistee National Forest and in another 2.8 miles swirls past this large and, in summer, busy Forest Service canoe landing. To reach Elm Flats, head north of Luther on State Road. Within 7.6 miles, or a mile past Lincoln Bridge Campground, State Road swings northwest for 0.7 mile, then due west for a half mile. When State Road resumes its northerly direction, continue west at the curve onto the paved entrance drive to Elms Flats, reached in 0.4 mile.

The site features a large canoe landing, turnaround area, and vault toilets but no parking. Nearby on a hill is a large parking lot capable of holding 20 to 30 vehicles with a stairway for quick access to the river. There is drinking water at the site and a picnic area but camping is not permitted. Elm Flats is a national forest fee area and has a fee pipe ($5 daily vehicle, $15 weekly).

All trout in the Pine River, including browns, are self-sustaining populations.

The Pine is 40 to 80 feet wide here and two to four feet deep with deeper holes. The riverbed is mostly gravel in the fast water, sand in the slower areas. The riverbanks are generally low, three to five feet, with some higher banks at the outsides of bends. Bank vegetation is mostly hardwood and brush with some cedar. There is some bottom vegetation here. Stream velocity is moderate at low flows, fast at high. The river can be waded with care at normal low flows, avoiding the deep holes, snags, boulders, and soft sand—but not at high flows. The Pine is more than wide and open enough here for fly fishing.

7 *Dobson Bridge*

GPS N 44° 10.795'
W 85° 45.519'

Map: page 307

Dobson Bridge is another large Forest Service canoe launch located seven river miles downstream from Elm Flats. By road the site is two miles north of Elm Flats on State Road and two miles west on 50 Mile Road.

To reach the site from M-55, head south on M-37, and in 2.5 miles, or 1.3 miles south of Peterson Bridge, turn east (left) on No. 48 1/2 Road. Follow the paved road for 1.5 miles, and, when No. 48 1/2 Road turns north at Coolwater Campground, continue east and then southeast on No. 50 Road. From this direction the dirt road reaches Dobson Bridge within a mile.

The parking area is located above the launch area on the west side of Dobson Bridge and the north side of No. 50 Road. It is connected to the river by a steep stairway. There are a vault toilet and drinking water at the launch site. Like Elm Flats, there is a fee pipe where you can purchase your vehicle permit. Camping is not permitted. Coolwater Campground, a private facility, is only a mile away (see Accommodations above).

The river is 50 to 70 feet wide at Dobson Bridge and three to four feet deep with deeper holes. Bottom is mostly gravel, cobbles, and boulders, with sand in the slower areas. Banks are alternately high and low, with brush, cedar, and hardwood cover. The velocity is moderate at low flows in the wider areas, fast in the narrow chutes. Upstream from the bridge there is a bit of riffled water at normal levels, and downstream you will find fair wading if you avoid the deep holes and narrow chutes. Do not try to wade under the bridge; the river moves through extremely fast.

8 *Peterson Bridge*

GPS N 44° 12.234'
W 85° 47.797'

This large Forest Service campground and access site borders both sides of the Pine and is the epicenter for canoeing activity on the river. It also provides anglers with a place to fish and camp. But keep in mind the large number of paddlers who will be passing through at certain times of the summer, and that they can be on the water from 9 a.m. to 6 p.m.

Peterson Bridge is also a popular campground partly because of its easy to reach location just south of the major intersection of M-55 and M-37. From the intersection, head south on M-37 and within 1.3 miles you reach Peterson Bridge. Just north of the bridge is Forest Road 5186, the entrance to the day-use area and the canoe launch (vehicle permit required). On the south side of the bridge is the campground entrance. Just across from the campground entrance is Pine River Paddlesports Center (800-717-4837, 231-862-3471; *www.thepineriver.com*), a canoe livery and campground.

Renovated in 2008, Peterson Bridge Campground has 20 paved sites, ideal for trailers and recreational vehicles, and ten walk-in sites designed for paddlers, as well as vault toilets, drinking water, picnic tables and fire grills. The day-use area also has a picnic area, vault toilets, drinking water, and canoe racks for the paddlers who end their trip here. It's easier to access the river here than from the campground. There's no question this spot is a busy place on weekends; at times it can be a canoe zoo, but on weekdays or early and late in the season it's not too crowded to fish.

The Pine is 50 to 75 feet wide here and two to five feet deep, with holes and runs that are over your head. Bottom materials are gravel, boulders, and hard clay in the fast areas, sand in the slow. Where the bottom material is hard clay, one step can take you from ankle-deep water to a hole over your head. Velocity is fast at low water and very fast at high. There is some wadable water at low normal flows at the canoe landing and a short distance downstream toward the bridge. Upstream from the canoe landing are a series of boulder riffles and hard clay with some sand in the intervening areas. Wading in the boulder riffles is difficult to impossible. The hard clay resembling bedrock restricts the river in places to a narrow channel of very fast water that should not be attempted by wading anglers.

The stream banks above the landing are mostly high to very high, some more than 50 feet high. Some of the paths along the river skirt the top of steep sand banks. The paths run very close to the edge in places and may be undercut. Forest cover is mostly hardwood with some conifer and not as brushy as in some upstream reaches.

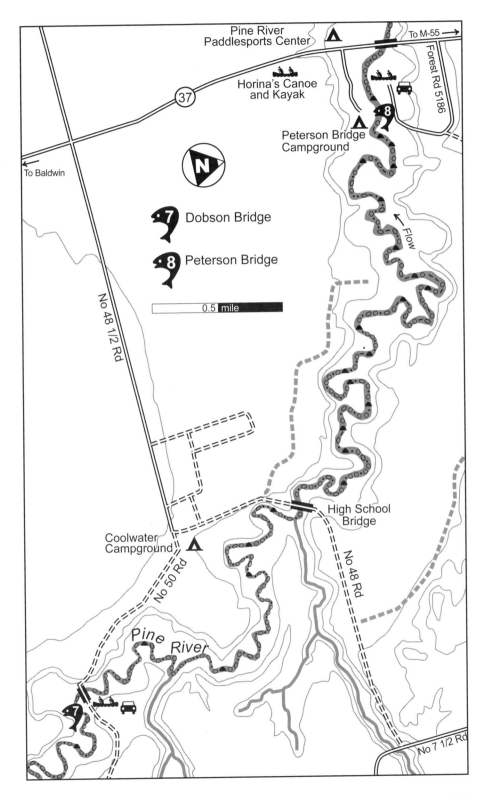

Pine River Paddlesports Center

To M-55 →

Horina's Canoe and Kayak

Forest Rd 5186

37

Peterson Bridge Campground

To Baldwin

N

Flow

7 Dobson Bridge

8 Peterson Bridge

0.5 mile

No 48 1/2 Rd

High School Bridge

Coolwater Campground

No 50 Rd

No 48 Rd

Pine River

7

No 7 1/2 Rd

Michigan Flies and Emergence Dates

Hatch	Group	Apr	May	Jun	Jul	Aug	Sept	Oct
Blue-Winged Olive *Baetis vegans*	Mayfly	mid-April to mid-August						
Slate-Winged Mahogany *Paraleptophlebia adoptiva*	Mayfly	mid-April to July						
Dark Hendrickson *Ephemerella subvaria*	Mayfly	April 20 to May 20						
Little Black Caddis *Chimarra aterrima*	Caddisfly	late April through August						
Grannom Caddis *Brachycentrus americanus*	Caddisfly	late April to late July						
Borcher's Drake *Leptophlebia cupida*	Mayfly		May 1 to August 15					
Green Rock Worm *Rhyacophilidae fenestra*	Caddisfly		May to July 1					
Light Hendrickson *Ephemerella rotunda*	Mayfly		May 3 to June 20					
Cinammon Caddis *Hydropsyche sparna*	Caddisfly		May 7 to September 15					
Sulphur Dun *Ephemera dorothea*	Mayfly		May 12 to July 15					
Yellow & Green Stonefly *Alloperla caudata & imbecilla*	Stonefly		mid-May through October					
True Hendrickson *Ephemerella invaria*	Mayfly		May 15 to July 20					
March Brown *Stenonema vicarium*	Mayfly		mid-May to mid-July					
Early Gray Drake *Siphlonurus rapidus*	Mayfly			May 26 to June 19				
Brown Drake *Ephemera simulans*	Mayfly			June 2 to July 14				
Light Cahill *Stenonema canadense*	Mayfly			June 5 to August 14				
Giant Michigan Mayfly *Hexagenia limbata*	Mayfly			June 10 to July 10				
Late Gray Drake *Siphlonurus alternatus*	Mayfly			June 17 to July 26				
Mahogany Dun *Isonychia sadleri*	Mayfly			mid-June to August				
Yellow Drake *Ephemera varia*	Mayfly			mid-June to August				
White-Gloved Howdy *Isonychia bicolor*	Mayfly			June 15 to Aug 15				
Slate-Winged Olive *Ephemerella lata*	Mayfly			June 25 to Aug 13				
Tiny Blue-Winged Olive *Pseudcloen anoka*	Mayfly			June 21 through September				
Terrestrials								
Ants				mid-June through September				
Crickets & Beetles					July to mid-October			
Grasshoppers					July 15 to Sept 15			
Tiny White-Winged Black *Tricorythodes stygiatus*	Mayfly				July through September			
Small Slate Mahogany Dun *Paraleptophlebia debilis*	Mayfly				July 20 to October 30			
Black Dancer Caddis *Mystocides sepulchralis*	Caddisfly					Aug 1 to Sept 30		
White Fly *Ephoron album*	Mayfly					late Aug through Sept		
Slate-Winged Brown *Baetis heimalis*	Mayfly						Sept 1 to Oct 30	

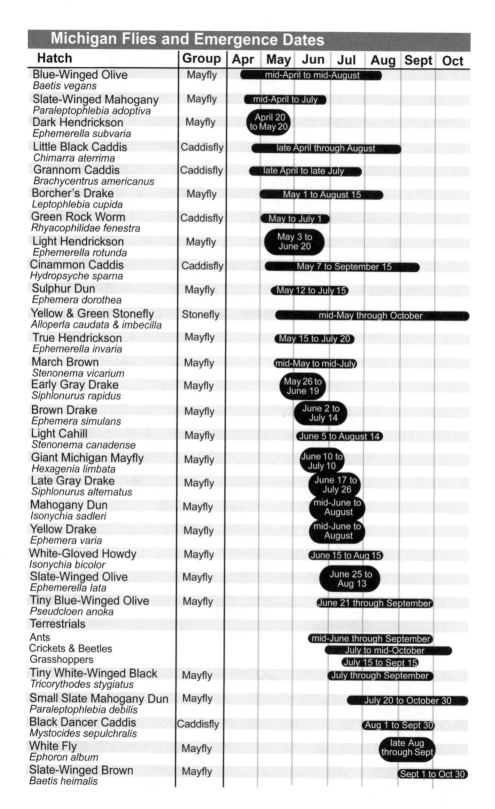

Peak	Hatch Time	Fly Imitations	Size
May 1-7 & June 14-21	early afternoon	Blue-Winged Olive, Sparkle Dun	18-20
May 1-14	10 am to 4 pm	Mahogany, Little Red Quill, Rusty's Spinner	16-18
May 1-14	10 am to 4 pm	Dark Hendrickson, Red Quill, Rusty's Spinner	12-14
May 7-14	noon to 10 pm	Black Elk Hair Caddis, Little Black Caddis	16-20
	late afternoon	Grannom, Black Elk Hair Caddis	14-16
	daytime	Borcher's Special, Black Quill	12-14
	2 pm to dusk	Green Caddis, Olive Elk Hair Caddis	10-18
	afternoon	Light Hendrickson, Hendrickson, Red Quill	14-16
	4 pm to dark	Cinnamon Elk Hair Caddis	14-20
June 14-30	afternoon	Sulphur Parachute, Sulphur Spinner, Sparkle Dun	16-18
	afternoon	Yellow Stonefly, Green Stonefly, Cream Sedge	14-18
May 21 to June 7	afternoon	Robert's Drake, Borcher's Special	14-16
	afternoon	March Brown	10-12
June 1-7	evenings	Gray Drake, Spent Wing Adams, Dark Cahill	12-14
June 1-14	evenings	Robert's Brown Drake, March Brown	10-12
	2 pm to 10 pm	Light Cahill, Robert's Drake	12-14
June 21 to July 7	10 pm to 4 am	Hex Wulff, Michigan Caddis, Madsen's Hex Spinner	4-6
July 1-14	evenings	Gray Drake, Spent Wing Adams, Dark Cahill	10-12
June 21 to July 14	evenings	Borcher's Special, Isonychia Spinner	10-12
	dusk to midnight	Robert's Yellow Drake, Wet Light Cahill	10-12
	evenings	Leadwing Coachman	10-12
		Slate-Winged Olive, Blue-Winged Olive	14-18
		Blue-Winged Olive, Blue-Winged Olive Thorax	22-24
		Terrestrials	
	day & evening	Foam Ant, Hi-Vis Ant	12-20
	day & evening	Beetle, Michigan Dry Skunk	12-14
	daytime	Michigan Hopper, Muddler Minnow, Michigan Dry Skunk	6-12
	6 am to 10 am	Black Midge, Tricos, Griffiths Gnat	20-26
		Mahogany, Little Red Quill,	16-18
		Black Elk Hair Caddis, Tiny Black Caddis	18-20
		White Fly, Gray's Ghost	12-14
		Slate Winged Brown, Little Brown Quill	14-16

An angler casts a hopper pattern in August on the Manistee River at Upper Manistee River State Forest Campground.

Michigan Fly Shops

The following outdoor stores sell flies and fly fishing equipment. Many are fly shops, which only stock equipment for fly anglers. Others are general outdoor stores, but have a corner or aisle dedicated to fly fishing. For fly shops near the rivers look in the Fly Shops and Guides section of each chapter that covers a trout stream.

Alpena

Buck's Bait & Tackle
8501 US-23 N.
989-595-2121
www.bucksbait.com

Ann Arbor

Colton Bay Outfitters
4844 Jackson Rd., Ste. 202
734-222-9776
www.coltonbay.com

Auburn Hills

Bass Pro Shops
Great Lakes Crossing
248-209-4200
www.basspro.com
Pere Marquette River Lodge
8841 S. M-37
231-745-3972
www.pmlodge.com

Baldwin

Baldwin Bait & Trackle
9331 S. M-37
231-745-3529, 877-422-5394
www.fishbaldwin.com
Ed's Sport Shop
712 Michigan Ave.
231-745-4974, 231-745-2696
www.edsports.com

Benzonia

Backcast Fly Shop
1675 US-31
231-882-5222

Brighton

Midwest Sport Shop
10049 E. Grand River Ave.
810-227-3141

Clare

Jay's Sporting Goods
8800 S. Clare Ave.
989-386-3475
www.jayssportinggoods.com

Coldwater

Gander Mountain
373 North Willowbrook Rd.
517-279-2900
www.gandermountain.com

Dundee

Cabela's
110 Cabela Blvd.
734-529-4700
www.cabelas.com

East Tawas

Nordic Sports
218 Bay Street
989-362-2001
www.n-sport.com

Ellsworth

Chain-O-Lakes Outdoor Sports
6517 Center St.
231-588-6070

Fairview

Streamside Custom Rods
2085 N. Abbe
989-848-5983
www.michiganstreamside.com

Flint

Gander Mountain
5038-A Miller Rd.
810-230-1212
www.gandermountain.com

Gaylord

Alphorn Shop
137 W. Main St.
989-732-5616
Jay's Sporting Goods
150 Dale Rd.
989-705-1339
www.jayssportinggoods.com

Grand Rapids

Al & Bob's Sports
3100 S. Division Ave.
616-245-9156, 888-256-2627
www.alnbobs.com
Gander Mountain
2890 Acquest Ave. SE (Kentwood)
616-975-1000
www.gandermountain.com

Gander Mountain
4655 Canal Ave. (Grandville)
616-249-0400
www.gandermountain.com

Grayling

The Fly Factory
205 Ingham St.
989-348-5844
www.troutbums.com
Old Au Sable Fly Shop
200 Ingham St.
989-348-3330
www.oldausable.com
Skip's Sport Shop
5765 W. M-72
989-348-7111
Gates Au Sable Lodge
471 Stephan Bridge Rd.
989-348-8462
www.gateslodge.com

Hastings

Al & Pete's Sport Shop
111. S. Jefferson Rd.
269-945-4417
Bob's Guns and Tackle
2208 W. M-43 Hwy.
269-945-4106
www.bobsgt.com

Hesperia

Hesperia Sport Shop
65 W. Alpha St.
231-854-3965
www.hesperiasportshop.com

Kalamazoo

D & R Sports Center
8178 W. Main St.
269-372-2277
www.dandrsports.com

Gander Mountain
5348 South Westnedge Ave. (Portage)
269-388-9770
www.gandermountain.com

Kalkaska
Jack's Sport Shop
212 Cedar St.
231-258-8892
www.jackssport.net

Lake Orion
Hank's Fly Fishing Unlimited
1015 S. Baldwin Rd.
248-393-1500
www.hanksflyfishing.com

Lansing
Gander Mountain
430 N. Marketplace Blvd.
517-622-5700
www.gandermountain.com
Grand River Fly Shop
536 E. Grand River
517-267-1573

Linwood
Frank's Great Outdoors
1212 M-13
989-697-5341
www.franksgreatoutdoors.com

Lovells
Hartman's Fly Shop
6794 E. County Rd. 612
989-348-9679, 877-363-4702
Fuller's North Branch Outing Club
6122 E. County Rd. 612
989-348-7951
www.fullersnboc.com

Ludington
Pere Marquette Sports Center
214 W. Ludington Ave.
231-843-8676
www.pmsports.net

Manton
Ron's Sporting Goods
1729 N. US-131
231-824-9093

Midland
Little Forks Outfitters
143 E. Main St.
989-832-4100, 877-550-4668
www.littleforks.com

Mio
Au Sable Angler
479 S. M-33
989-826-8500
www.ausableangler.com
Trophy Waters Fly Shop
701 N. Morenci Ave. (Gotts Landing)
989-826-3411
www.trophywatersflyshop.com

Newaygo
Parsley's Sport Shop
70 State St.
231-652-6986

Novi
Gander Mountain
43825 West Oaks Dr.
248-380-4000
www.gandermountain.com

Okemos

Nomad Anglers
5100 Marsh Rd.
517-349-6696
www.mchanceflyfishing.com

Onaway

Parrott's Outpost
20628 State St.
989-733-2472
www.parrottsoutpost.com

Pinckney

Golden Drake Outdoors
9280 Mcgregor Rd.
734-426-2256
www.goldendrake.com

Port Huron

Gander Mountain
4055 24th Ave.
810-385-6700
www.gandermountain.com

Rockford

Great Lakes Fly Fishing Co.
8460 Algoma Ave. NE
616-866-6060, 800-303-0567
www.troutmoor.net

Royal Oak

Orvis
29500 Woodward Ave.
248-542-5700
www.orvis.com

Saginaw

Gander Mountain
2270 Tittabawassee Rd.
989-791-3500
www.gandermountain.com

Taylor

Gander Mountain
14100 Pardee Rd.
734-287-7420
www.gandermountain.com

Traverse City

Gander Mountain
3500 Market Place Cr.
231-929-5590
www.gandermountain.com
Northern Angler
803 W. Front St.
231-933-4730, 800-627-4080
www.thenorthernangler.com
Orvis Streamside
223 E. Front St.
231-933-9300
www.streamsideorvis.com

West Branch

J&P Sporting Goods
3275 W. M-76
989-345-3744

Utica

Gander Mountain
13975 Hall Rd.
586-247-9900
www.gandermountain.com

Wellston

Schmidt Outfitters
918 Seaman Rd.
231-848-4191
www.schmidtoutfitters.com

About the Authors

Born in Wisconsin and a 1940 graduate of the University of Wisconsin, Gerth E. Hendrickson was an avid fly angler and a member of Trout Unlimited and the Federation of Fly Fishers. In the early 1970s he surveyed many of Michigan's top trout streams, including the 12 in this book, as a hydrologist for the U.S. Geological Survey (USGS). He carefully recorded bottom characteristics, stream flow and bank vegetation for each river and the resulting hydrologic maps are still used by fisheries biologists today. His USGS work and love of trout resulted in *The Angler's Guide to Ten Classic Trout Streams in Michigan* that was published in 1985 by the University

Jim DuFresne

of Michigan Press. In 1994, Hendrickson produced an enlarged second edition, *The Angler's Guide to Twelve Classic Trout Streams in Michigan.*

Jim DuFresne is an outdoor writer based in Clarkston, Michigan, and author of more than a dozen wilderness/travel guidebooks. His books cover areas from Alaska and New Zealand to Michigan's own Isle Royale National Park.

DuFresne is a journalism graduate from Michigan State University and the former outdoors and sports editor of the *Juneau Empire,* where in 1980 he became the first Alaskan sportswriter to ever win a national award from the Associated Press. Shortly after that, DuFresne spent a winter in New Zealand to backpack and write his first book, *Tramping in New Zealand* (Lonely Planet Publications). Six editions and 25 years later *Tramping in New Zealand* is the world's best-selling guidebook to backpacking in that country.

In 1986, DuFresne enrolled in a one-day fly fishing clinic staged by the Mershon Chapter of Trout Unlimited in Saginaw and fell in love with casting a fly. When he was confident enough that not every one of his back casts would result in his fly dangling from a tree, he purchased the first edition of Hendrickson's guide and began exploring Michigan's classic trout streams. DuFresne has since written extensively on fly fishing for the *Saginaw News* as well as chapters on wilderness fly fishing in his guidebooks on New Zealand and Alaska.

The link between the two authors was completed in 2007 when the University of Michigan Press asked DuFresne to update and revamp the classic fishing guide by Hendrickson, who had passed away several years earlier.